REPRODUCTIVE
CITIZENS

REPRODUCTIVE CITIZENS

GENDER, IMMIGRATION, AND THE STATE IN MODERN FRANCE, 1880–1945

NIMISHA BARTON

CORNELL UNIVERSITY PRESS
Ithaca and London

Copyright © 2020 by Cornell University

All rights reserved. Except for brief quotations in a review, this book, or parts thereof, must not be reproduced in any form without permission in writing from the publisher. For information, address Cornell University Press, Sage House, 512 East State Street, Ithaca, New York 14850. Visit our website at cornellpress.cornell.edu.

First published 2020 by Cornell University Press

Library of Congress Cataloging-in-Publication Data

Names: Barton, Nimisha, author.
Title: Reproductive citizens : gender, immigration, and the state in modern France, 1880–1945 / Nimisha Barton.
Description: Ithaca [New York] : Cornell University Press, 2020. | Includes bibliographical references and index.
Identifiers: LCCN 2019050551 (print) | LCCN 2019050552 (ebook) | ISBN 9781501749636 (hardcover) | ISBN 9781501749698 (pdf) | ISBN 9781501749681 (ebook)
Subjects: LCSH: Immigrants—Government policy—France—History—20th century. | Immigrants—France—Social conditions—20th century. | Family policy—France—History—20th century. | Women—France—Social conditions—20th century. | Sex role—Political aspects—France—History—20th century. | Sex role—Political aspects—France—History—19th century. | Citizenship—France—History—20th century. | France—Emigration and immigration—History—20th century. | France—Population policy—History—20th century. | France—Politics and government—1870–1940.
Classification: LCC JV7933.B37 2020 (print) | LCC JV7933 (ebook) | DDC 325/.4409041—dc23
LC record available at https://lccn.loc.gov/2019050551
LC ebook record available at https://lccn.loc.gov/2019050552

Contents

List of Figures and Tables vii
Acknowledgments ix
Abbreviations xv

	Introduction	1
1.	The Forces that Push and Pull	13
2.	Bachelors, Bureaucrats, and Marrying into the Nation	39
3.	Wives, Wages, and Regulating Breadwinners	71
4.	Mothers, Welfare Organizations, and Reproducing for the Nation	96
5.	Neighborhood, Street Culture, and Melting-Pot Mixité	127
6.	Motherhood, Neighborhood, and Nationhood	154
7.	Neighborly Networks and Welfare Work under Vichy	181
	Conclusion	209

Notes 217
Bibliography 261
Index 275

Figures and Tables

Figures

I.1.	The Goata family in Paris, ca. 1932	2
1.1.	"The Great Transportation Networks Used by Immigrants in France," 1932	16
1.2.	Foreign labor recruitment, Société générale d'immigration (SGI) pamphlet, 1929	28
1.3.	Foreign laborers signing labor contracts, SGI pamphlet, 1929	29
1.4.	Foreign laborers marrying in France, SGI pamphlet, 1929	29
3.1.	Polish Jew Gendel Mass née Scher, ca. 1922	75
4.1.	League for the Protection of Abandoned Mothers (LPAM) brochure, 1926	107
4.2.	Photograph of officials visiting LPAM offices, 1931	108
4.3.	The office of the League for the Protection of Abandoned Mothers, 1928	111
5.1.	The 11th arrondissement, 1926	129
5.2.	Romanian Jew Riva Hena Marcu née Matas, ca. 1921	132
6.1.	The marketplace at rue Richard Lenoir, 1922	163
6.2.	Turkish Jew Djoya Abouaf née Baralia and her three children, ca. 1923	165
7.1.	The personnel of the Groupe Amelot, ca. 1940–42	188
7.2.	Serbian Jew Sol Camhi née Colonomos, ca. 1923	200
7.3.	Polish Jew Elsa Handkan née Manachem, ca. 1926	201

Tables

1.1.	Spanish and Portuguese agricultural workers in France, 1915–18	17
1.2.	Italian agricultural workers in France, 1916–18	17
1.3.	Spanish and Portuguese agricultural workers in France, 1919–22	18
1.4.	Polish agricultural workers in France, 1920–22	18

2.1.	Marital status of the population of France, 1921	42
2.2.	Marital status of the population of France, 1926	43
2.3.	Marital status of the population of France, 1931	43
2.4.	Marital status of the population of France, 1936	43
2.5.	Naturalized men by marital status in France, 1889–1940	44
5.1.	French and foreign population of Paris residing *en garni*, 1926 and 1931	143

Acknowledgments

It is an impossible task to thank the many friends, colleagues, and mentors who made this project possible. And yet I will endeavor to do so anyway.

My first thanks go to Philip Nord, whose intelligence and insight were indispensable to the development of this project. Phil's guidance contributed immeasurably to my personal and professional development as a scholar. I am grateful that he was willing to share his wisdom with a novice to the discipline of history and to the academy, more generally. Margot Canaday offered perceptive feedback on this project as well as support, encouragement, and mentorship throughout. It was she who first introduced me to the (substantial) American literature concerning immigration as well as the study of gender and sexuality more generally. As a result, she has deeply influenced the way I think about history and, of course, the way I "do" history as well. Bonnie Smith asked searching and creative questions about this project from the start, which encouraged me to keep the human narrative central to the story. She is a model of brilliance, and ferocity, and I am lucky to have her as a mentor.

I had the great fortune to benefit from the advice of David Bell, who pushed me to clarify the stakes of my work. Gracious with his time and thorough in his feedback, David also offered more practical guidance on negotiating the strategic challenges of academic life. I also wish to extend a heartfelt thanks to Claire Zalc for a great many things that are too numerous to recount: it was Claire who provided key insight in the formative stages of this work, Claire who pointed me toward archival sources, Claire who vouched for me with archivists, introduced me to fellow scholars and colleagues, and helped integrate me into the intellectual life of Paris. Without Claire, I would truly have been lost during my time abroad.

Many of us find our way into the academy via an inspirational mentor. I am no different. As an undergraduate at UC Berkeley, Susanna Barrows first inspired in me a curiosity about all things French, encouraging me to pursue a graduate degree in French history and urging me to think about immigrant women in France and multiculturalism in Europe. Halfway through my graduate career, I was fortunate enough to find another historian of France who very much reminded me of Susanna: Rachel Fuchs. Both women were exceptional scholars, teachers, and mentors. Brilliant, enthusiastic, and compassionate, they modeled what it meant to be a scholar, both in the archives and in the classroom. They taught me that no woman is an island, no scholar cut off from a wider community. They also impressed on me, and all of us, the need to be compassionate with one another in order to make those relationships possible. I thank both Susanna and Rachel for these lessons as well as welcoming me—and so very many others—into their homes and hearts.

In Paris, I owe a number of debts of gratitude. From the start, Nancy Green met with me and offered helpful tips on untapped archival sources. She also suggested many references and offered kindly to look over drafts and outlines. Delphine Serre agreed to meet with an American graduate student unfamiliar with the ways of *quanti*. Undaunted in the face of my innumeracy, she helped me devise a sampling system to examine social worker files that made this precious source usable in the project. Evelyne Diebolt first alerted me to the existence of the Olga Spitzer Association, and without her, this project would not have come to fruition. In addition to her extensive knowledge of female-led philanthropic organizations in Paris, she was warm and inviting, and I thank her for the many kindnesses she showed me and my family while abroad.

The archives of Paris often proved formidable—even forbidding—places, but the help of archivists made them less so. From the *équipe de naturalisations* at the Archives Nationales of Paris, I thank Pascal Riviale, Brigitte Lozza, and Delphine Peschard for their tireless service each week from September 2010 to January 2012. A huge thanks goes of course to their fearless *chef d'équipe*, Annie Poinsot, who graciously bent the rules for me from time to time so that I could make more rapid progress on my research. For their companionship and good cheer, thanks also to *les jumeaux*, Charles and Chantal, as well as Cedric. At the Archives Nationales in Fontainebleau, I thank Pascal Philippides for helping me to process naturalization files *en gros*. A special note of appreciation also goes to archivists at the Archives de la Préfecture de Police, especially Françoise Gicquel, whose benevolent intervention on behalf of this immigrant woman in Paris ensured that I could remain there, OFII notwithstanding.

At the Archives de Paris, I thank the entire staff for making the archive a convivial place in which to spend months poring over sometimes gruesome court cases. Thanks especially to Jocelyne Ha who remained undaunted by the large number of *affaires judiciaires* I ruthlessly asked her to examine.

Without Jean-Charles Virmaux, I would never have gained access to the precious Olga Spitzer files. And without Vincent Tuchais, I never would have had anyone "on the inside" to vouch for me and advocate on my behalf for access to these *fonds* and others. Thank you all for allowing me to tell the stories that I so wanted to tell in this book.

Others along the way provided help at critical junctures in the development of this project. Thanks especially to Eliza Ferguson, Jennifer Heuer, Amelia Lyons, Paul-André Rosenthal, and Judith Surkis who offered useful feedback on papers and/or chapters. Thanks also to Linda Clark, Martha Howell, Mary Dewhurst Lewis, Linda Guerry, Kelsey McNiff, Clifford Rosenberg, Emmanuelle Saada, Tyler Stovall, Rosemary Wakeman, and Susan Whitney for offering pointers, suggesting sources, even sharing your archival materials with me. This work has also benefited from discussions generated at several conferences and workshops sponsored by the Institut d'Histoire Moderne et Contemporaine at the Ecole Normale Supérieure; the Sciences Sociales et Immigration seminar hosted by Claire Zalc, Alexis Spire, and Choukri Hmed in Paris; the Princeton-EUI-CEU Graduate Conference on Europe and the World; the Program in Gender and Sexuality Studies Graduate Works-in-Progress Series at Princeton University; the Modern Europe Workshop at Princeton University; the Society for French Historical Studies; the Western Society for French History; and the Gender, Family, and the State Conference at Tel Aviv University.

As research for the book took me back and forth across the Atlantic, I was fortunate to tap into a community of French scholars that included Anaïs Albert, Claire Cage, Hannah Callaway, Muriel Cohen, Katie Jarvis, Mehemmed Mack, Katie McDonough, Carolyn Purnell, Kelly Summers, and Emmanuel Szurek, among many others. I am so fortunate to be able to call many of you not just colleagues, but friends. To Gen Creedon, Christopher Kurpiewski, Beth Lew-Williams, Dov Grohsgal, and Shannon Winston—you may not be French historians, but your friendship has been *très magnifique*. For their mentorship since my Berkeley days, I thank especially Robin Mitchell and Sarah Horowitz who readily dispensed advice and did so with the sort of generosity of spirit that would have made Susanna proud. Given my professional trajectory out of academia, the "friend-torship" of Danna Agmon, Richard Hopkins, Minayo Nasiali, and Christy Pichichero has been most welcome.

Over the course of a decade at Princeton, I also benefited from the professional and personal support of many, especially as I transitioned into and out of administrative work at the university. My warm thanks to them for cheering me on: Alexis Andres, LaTanya Buck, Rochelle Calhoun, Anne

Caswell-Klein, Rebecca Graves-Bayazitoglu, Amy Ham Johnson, Kerstin Larsen, Diane McKay, Michele Minter, Amy Pszczolkowski, Keith Shaw, and Amanda Irwin Wilkins.

Some material from chapters 2 and 4 appear in articles from *French Politics, Culture, and Society* and the *Journal of Women's History*, respectively. I thank the editors for their feedback as well as for allowing me to reproduce portions of the articles here. Parts of chapter 3 appeared in the edited volume, *Practiced Citizenship*, and I thank the University of Nebraska Press for the permission to reproduce parts of it here. Moreover, though this project relies on a considerable amount of statistical data culled from census reports, naturalization dossiers, police files, court cases, and social worker dossiers, for the sake of readability, the majority of supporting graphs and tables have been removed from these pages. That said, the sampling methods used for these sources, and the resulting data, have been critical to shaping the contours of this project. For a full discussion of these sources, a description of methodologies, and supporting quantitative data, please see https://drnimishabarton.com.

I am grateful for the funding and support I have received from departments, centers, and institutes at Princeton University, including the History Department, the Graduate School, the Center for Migration and Development, and the Princeton Institute for International and Regional Studies. Of note, Princeton's Program in Gender and Sexuality Studies provided generous grant support throughout my graduate career as well as a subvention in the final publication stages, a testament to their commitment to supporting scholars with nontraditional career paths that, to date, remains exceedingly rare in academia. Research and writing for this book were completed thanks to financial support from the Society for French Historical Studies, the Georges Lurcy Education Foundation, and a Andrew W. Mellon–CES Fellowship from Columbia University. Two last institutional debts of gratitude: the Western Society for French History supported final-stage research for this project, and the University of California furnished the library resources necessary to complete this book.

A few people merit very special mention. To my Berkeley squad—Alamira Reem Al-Ayadrous, Efthymia Drolapas, Jacqueline Soohoo, and Tricia Sung—you are all precious and I appreciate the support you have given me over the years. To the Princeton posse—Ronny Regev, Franziska Exeler, Catherine Abou-Nemeh, Nikolce Gjorevski—it's honestly too painful to even imagine what on earth I would have done without all of you. Thank you for keeping me company and keeping me laughing all those years. Randi Garcia, Emmy Ganos, and Alexis Caldero—your friendship gave me strength and courage when I needed it most. To all of you: this book is a testament to what friendship makes possible.

To the incomparable Matthew Trujillo: this book has borne witness to more than a decade of our own migrations and wanderings, the rise and fall and rise again of our various fortunes. Thank you for learning far too much about French history than was strictly necessary, and for believing in me, always.

Finally, my family. I wish to thank my sister, who shows me every day how to be brave and live well. I thank my dad, who taught me the importance of a sense of humor, especially if you're as stubborn as we are about fighting the good fight. And of course, I thank my mother, whose life experiences first trickled down to me through stories when I was growing up, providing the inspiration for this book, even before I knew it to be so. Her intuitive joy for this world and relentless search for silver linings in it have long been a mystery to me. And so it must be to her and her mysteries that this book is dedicated.

Abbreviations

AdP	Archives de Paris
AN	Archives Nationales
AP-HP	Archives de l'assistance publique-hôpitaux de Paris
APP	Archives de la préfecture de police de Paris
ASVP	*Annuaire statistique de la ville de Paris*
BMD	Bibliothèque Marguerite-Durand
BnF	Bibliothèque nationale de France
BSA	*Bulletin de la Société amicable et d'études des administrateurs et commissaires des bureaux de bienfaisance à Paris*
CDJC	Centre de documentation juive contemporaine
CGQJ	Commissaire général aux questions juives
CRN	Commission de revisions de naturalisation
FF	Foyer français
HBM	Habitations à bon marché
LPAM	Ligue pour la protection des mères abandonnées
ONMA	Office national de la main d'oeuvre agricole
OSE	Oeuvre de secours aux enfants
PCBS	*Paris charitable, bienfaisant et social*
SAINA	Service des affaires indigènes nord-africaines
SGI	Société générale d'immigration
SSAE	Service social d'aide aux émigrants
SSCMD	Service social d'enfants en danger moral
SOTC	Service d'organisation des travailleurs coloniaux
UGIF	Union générale des israelites français

REPRODUCTIVE CITIZENS

Introduction

After years of haggling with naturalization officers regarding her Romanian husband, Emilienne Goata, a French national, had grown impatient. Dispensing with the niceties typical of official petitions, Madame Goata stated bluntly in her 1933 letter, "I have come to appeal to you to ask how it is possible that my husband still does not have his naturalization papers given that it has been two years since he made his request." She was "unhappy" and suggested that, if the state continued to deny her a sizable family allowance and her husband his unemployment benefits, all on account of his foreign nationality, disaster would surely ensue. Specifically, she suggested, her husband—who first arrived during the Great War—would most likely return to Romania and "leave me here with five children." "If I am alone," she threatened, "I will send my children to Public Assistance. They will not live in poverty." To drive home the point, Goata included a picture of the family standing in front of a working-class apartment building in interwar Paris where she undoubtedly spent most of her time caring for the large household (figure I.1).[1] By World War II, officials had relented to Goata's persistent appeals, and the family would swell to eleven, all French.

Emilienne Goata demonstrated an uncanny awareness of how to negotiate with bureaucrats and maneuver around a legal system in which, officially, neither she (a woman) nor her husband (an immigrant) registered formally as "citizens." She deftly exploited official anxieties about struggling wives

Figure I.1. The Goata family in Paris, ca. 1932. Nicolas Goata and Emilienne née Authemet, 8008x32 in Archives Nationales, Pierrefitte.

and mothers, uprooted and untrustworthy foreign men, and the specter of abandoned French-born children. She secured state benefits that served as a lifeline for rapidly multiplying mixed and immigrant households throughout France from 1880 onward. For their part, bureaucrats showed a surprising degree of responsiveness to her appeals and those of other French and immigrant women presenting themselves as wives and mothers in need of the state's benevolent, muscular protection. Emilienne Goata was thus able to bend the system to suit her ends by laying claim to social rights reserved for the reproductive. Thousands of immigrant women who flooded into France in the first half of the twentieth century—some acting on the advice of French friends, neighbors, and acquaintances, and others of their own volition—would learn to successfully petition the system as well.

The Goatas were one of many families in interwar Paris made—and unmade—by the turbulent political events that transpired across continental Europe throughout the fin-de-siècle period and into the first four decades of the twentieth century. During those fateful years, an old world order still partially comprised of large multinational empires came crashing down and a new world order organized stiffly along nationhood and ethnic belonging was summoned into being. A decade before Armenians fled genocide, Greeks and Turkish Jews steadily streamed out of the Ottoman Empire.

By the dawn of the First World War, France was home to these "Levantine Israelites," as French bureaucrats referred to them, as well as some thirty thousand Eastern European Jews who had escaped the murderous pogroms erupting in the hinterlands of late imperial Russia.[2] The Great War fueled additional migration throughout Europe, rippling to the outer reaches of its empires. Although colonial labor migration from North Africa, especially Algeria, was common in metropolitan France in the decades before the war, France—much like its imperial counterparts—mobilized men from the colonies as soldiers and as laborers for the war effort. Over half a million *troupes indigènes* served in the French Army during the war. Another 200,000 colonial workers from North Africa, Indochina, and Madagascar were brought to the metropole, accompanied by more than 36,000 Chinese workers.[3]

For some foreign-born soldiers and laborers, wartime sojourns in the metropole slowly morphed into something more permanent at war's end, even despite their own best intentions and, in the case of colonial and Chinese migrants, those of the French government. With the signing of the Treaty of Versailles, which remapped borders across Europe, and as a new age of national self-determination dawned, demobilized soldiers and workers cast adrift in France could hardly return home to countries that had vanished overnight with the stroke of a pen. A young Romanian soldier named Nicholas Goata, the future husband of then Emilienne Authemet, was among them. Like other soldiers who hoped to wait out world-altering regime change and revolution and eventually return home, he instead bided his time in France for what became a lifetime. For Goata, as well as other men, women, and children, the crumbling of the great European empires foreclosed any possibility of return. Thousands of Czechs, Hungarians, Poles, Yugoslavs, and Romanians poured out of the disintegrating Austro-Hungarian Empire. Eastern Europeans, too, fled their homes to avoid getting swept up in the maelstrom of the Bolshevik Revolution as the Russian Empire toppled over. Indeed, the rise and fall of political fortunes in the various European states after 1918 rendered the interwar period the great age of political exiles: alongside dispossessed "White Russians" came Italian Communists and anti-fascists, later German Jews and Spanish republicans. They were the outcasts and losers of civil war, and France beckoned.

The primary overseas recipients of European refugees in the early twentieth century had been North and South America, but as the United States and Canada introduced immigration quotas in the early 1920s that effectively closed their doors, the European continent was increasingly left awash with its own poor, homeless, and stateless exiles and refugees—in short, the "unwanted" from every corner of Europe and beyond.[4] From 1914 to

1922, refugees flooded into eastern Germany, and nearly a quarter of a million migrants managed to make their way to Great Britain throughout the 1920s.[5] But it was France that emerged as the immigrant nation of Europe par excellence by the mid-twentieth century, remaining one of the few European havens accessible to continental and colonial migrants even during the notoriously inhospitable 1930s.[6] Of course, France had its own reasons for welcoming these weary migrants: a terrible crisis of depopulation made immigrants indispensable to repopulation and national regeneration.

Though French contemporaries had observed the thinning of their ranks since the 1870s, the losses of the Great War cut deep and merciless. It was four years of gruesome reaping that would continue to haunt the French through the interwar decades. Robbed not only of 1.5 million countrymen but of the promise of the children they might have fathered, the French began to look anew at the foreign-born men and women of child-bearing age streaming in after the war. Though social policies and welfare assistance had, since the dawn of the Third Republic, incentivized reproduction and large families among the French, fertility rates remained stubbornly stagnant. In 1890, mortality rates in France exceeded birthrates for the first time; that would happen six more times before the start of the Great War.[7] Yet, statisticians, who documented the reproductive habits and behaviors of the French obsessively, noted something curious about immigrant newcomers: foreign families were substantially larger than French families.[8] As early as 1911, French demographers discovered that foreign families with three or more children were disproportionately more common than French families of comparable size.[9] In the wake of post–World War I migrations, that trend persisted.[10] It is no surprise, then, that wave after wave of immigrants washed ashore in the decade and a half between 1911 and 1926, a period of continentwide tumult and cresting populationist angst in France. If, in 1911, foreigners represented just 3 percent of the population in France, by 1926, they represented more than 6 percent of the nation's inhabitants.[11] By 1931, France's foreign population peaked at nearly 7 percent, or about 3 million, a growth rate that outstripped even that of the United States.[12]

Though the historical phenomenon of mass migration to France from 1880 onward is, by now, a familiar tale, less familiar is the fact that hundreds of thousands of immigrant women formed a critical part of those migration waves.[13] Asylum seekers and refugees, laboring wives and fiancées, impoverished mothers and daughters, foreign women streamed into France from the start of the twentieth century onward, accounting for nearly 47 percent of all immigrants in France by 1911 and throughout the interwar decades.[14] Their relative occlusion in the historical record to date hints at a larger and more problematic oversight in the existing scholarship: the role of sex and gender in shaping the experiences of both immigrant women and men who migrated to France in significant numbers prior to the Second World War.[15] Against the background of what contemporaries viewed as a dire depopulation crisis, ideas about gender, family, and reproduction embedded in social policy, official practice, and everyday encounters played a decisive role in defining the terms on which working-class immigrant women and men engaged with members of the French state and society. Significantly, the strength of populationist sentiment as well as the vast semipublic, semiprivate, and supremely local welfare apparatus it gave rise to in interwar France reveal a history of immigrant inclusion that lies in stark contrast to the exclusivist narratives that currently hold sway.

This book investigates how prevailing ideas about gender, family, and reproduction during the Third Republic shaped middle-class French officials' attitudes toward and interactions with immigrants as workers and citizens, husbands and wives, mothers and fathers of a depopulating French nation. It also is the first to center the voices and experiences of immigrants themselves, and of immigrant women, in particular, in those encounters. To date, the scholarship on immigration has served largely as a window into hierarchies of exclusion embedded within modern states: from restrictive labor, nationality, and citizenship laws to disciplinary systems of surveillance, bureaucratic logics of closure, and racist and xenophobic rhetorics of exclusion.[16] But countless French contemporaries saw immigrant men and women as an ideal solution to the population crisis, and they expected them, and immigrant men especially, to adopt "proper" moral, sexual, and familial comportments necessary to stem the tide of depopulation. For their own part, immigrants leveraged what little they had in these interactions, invoking marriage, family, and their reproductive service to France in their dealings with French employers, statesmen, bureaucrats, and social workers. Their claims, conflicts, and contestations with officials reveal a form of what I term "reproductive citizenship" in interwar France centered on marriage, child bearing, and the care and provision of families and households according to traditional gender norms and expectations.

Though formal citizenship has frequently been understood as the right to vote and the right to work, reproductive citizenship, this book contends, refers instead to a variety of social rights, privileges, and protections that accrued to procreative men and women in France before 1945, regardless of nationality. Immigrants who adopted profamily attitudes and procreative behaviors, and who presented themselves in the acceptable accents of heterosexual masculinity and femininity, amassed ample social rights in Third

Republican France. They benefited from a stream of citizenship entitlements that was not at all tied to formal citizenship status but rather depended on the fulfillment of gendered social obligations to the nation. For immigrant women, these obligations centered primarily on republican motherhood; for immigrant men, on marriage, breadwinning, and fatherhood.[17] It was a variety of heterosexual citizenship, premised as it was on marriage between one man and one woman and incentivizing procreative sex between them.[18] And it was an inclusive type of citizenship, opening pathways into the national community for the vast majority of immigrant men and women arriving in France from 1880 to 1940. In important ways, it proved a more lasting kind of citizenship than even formal citizenship, as the Second World War and the Vichy years would show.

Scholars have demonstrated how Third Republican state and social actors prevented the full incorporation of women, immigrants, and colonial subjects into the national polity as French citizens through restrictive laws, policies, and discourses.[19] Yet, they often measure citizenship according to narrow criteria: the attainment of political and economic rights as well as formal citizenship status. Recent works have helpfully refocused scholarly inquiries around the successful demands for social rights formulated by nineteenth-century Frenchmen and poor white, immigrant, and colonial workingmen in postwar France.[20] These interpretations invite us to conceptualize citizenship more capaciously and have the virtue of highlighting the voices of ordinary people in their claims. In this, they are emblematic of the larger field of citizenship studies that has steadily moved away from all-or-nothing threshold questions in favor of inquiries centered on gradations of practice, participation, and experience for so-called noncitizens.[21] Despite striking out in important new directions, however, these works continue to place men at the center of scholarly conversation, ignoring the abundant sex- and gender-based social policies that emerged in Third Republican France making both men and women essential to the project of population-building and nation-state development. Addressing that oversight, this book demonstrates that access to and deployment of gendered social rights drove the outward expansion of citizenship in twentieth-century France.

While officials resolved to harness immigrant men and women's reproductive capacities for the demographic future of France, they treated men and women differently, wielding social policy regulating marriage, divorce, breadwinning, and fatherhood as a weapon, with the hope of making foreign-born men hew ever closer to the French nation. By contrast, immigrant women often received generous social assistance in part because they were viewed as, and presented themselves as, vulnerable wives and mothers and, by extension, less problematic agents in the project to repopulate France. To a variety of state and social actors, foreign men would have to be convinced and compelled to adopt familial roles, whereas foreign women needed only moral and material assistance to support their already large families. Consequently, "disciplinary paternalism" and "supportive maternalism," the twin regulatory impulses that shaped official interactions with state subjects, undergirded reproductive citizenship in France during the Third Republic. Though applicable in theory to all men and women, regardless of formal citizenship status, disciplinary paternalism and supportive maternalism were accentuated in the case of immigrants: for immigrant men, due to their civil and legal vulnerabilities in a culture that viewed bachelors as potential sexual deviants to be domesticated through the edifying institutions of marriage, family, and fatherhood; for immigrant women, as a result of their perceived vulnerability in the eyes of paternalist and predominantly male French officials who happily equipped struggling widows, mothers, and heads of large families with the requisite legal tools and financial assistance they needed to survive.

In all this, "the state" was no faceless juggernaut. Rather, it was a nebulous thing knitting together a variety of national and local officials as well as powerful social actors embedded in specific institutional settings and dedicated to a singular cause: the repopulation of the French nation.[22] A vast movement that had gained adherents from the late nineteenth century onward, populationism served as a consensual terrain in the otherwise divisive political landscape of the Third Republic. Though an alliance of at times competing agendas and political opinions, the interwar decades offered a rare moment of widespread agreement from the Communist left to the Catholic right about the importance of boosting the French population with recourse to foreign migration.[23] During these decades, populationist bureaucrats held sway, especially in the Bureau de Sceau, the government office that processed naturalization requests. They found their aims complemented and amplified by tradition-minded familialists inspired by the doctrine of social Catholicism. These latter predominated among the industrial and agricultural *patronat* and among the "nonconformist technocrats" whom the Republic increasingly invited into the corridors of power as the thirties wore on.[24] Of course, the coalition had its more exclusionary fringes, notably French pronatalists and a small handful of eugenicists who held that the "Latin races" were more easily assimilable to the French than others.[25] These factions would gain influence over the movement's direction in the increasingly xenophobic 1930s, rising to power under Vichy, surviving the *épuration*, and shaping immigration, welfare, and population policy into the Liberation and the early years of the Fourth Republic.²⁶ But between the wars, the imperative to replenish France's depleted reservoirs of labor and soldiers with reproductive citizens won the day, and state officials in national, municipal, and neighborhood settings mobilized their bureaucratic power to bring family-minded foreigners into the national fold.

Nowhere was the force of populationism felt more strongly than in the "parastate" realm of welfare in interwar France.²⁷ In recent decades, scholars have shown that, from the fin-de-siècle period through the Vichy years, the many proponents of populationism profoundly influenced the development of the French welfare state, making it among the most advanced in Europe.²⁸ Moreover, throughout the nineteenth century, wealthy "ladies of the leisure class" and middle-class maternalists played a significant role in the elaboration of private charitable initiatives, contributing to the decidedly mixed character of the interwar French welfare state.²⁹ And while scholars originally focused on social work as a means of exercising and extending social control over the working classes, historian Rachel Fuchs and others have instead pointed to the ways that social worker intervention on behalf of women, children, and families could, instead, be understood quite differently, not least of all by working-class clients themselves.³⁰ Consequently, scholars have observed not only how public and private welfarist initiatives combined to spur the early appearance of an extensive French welfare state apparatus, but also how surprisingly inclusive it was, especially as compared to its American and European counterparts, for instance, in the provisioning of aid to unwed women and non-nuclear families.³¹

This book builds on that tradition of scholarship, showing how, against the background of depopulation, the politics of post–World War I populationism played a decisive role in shaping social workers' interactions with their foreign clients. Unlike other developing welfare states, the strength of populationism in France overrode ethnic, racial, and religious distinctions between social workers and immigrant clients, emerging as a sphere where cross-class, cross-national alliances among middle-class welfare agents and their foreign working-class clients were forged. Through a study of gendered interactions between French *assistantes sociales* and immigrant women, this book argues that the partially state-funded, largely privately run world of welfare underwrote the economic and social integration of immigrant families between the wars. Most significantly, in those welfare interactions, immigrant women, who stood at the crossroads of immigrant families and communities, on the one hand, and state and neighborhood resources, on the other, emerged as crucial figures through whom aid was channeled into foreign households, anticipating, in many ways, the postwar development of specialized social services for colonial women and children on metropolitan soil.[32]

In addition to the strength of populationism after the Great War, supportive interactions between French welfare agents and immigrant clients were possible because the interwar world of social work itself was in a state of great flux. After World War I, middle-class women who animated the private charitable world were transitioning away from nineteenth-century notions of Catholic charity and noblesse oblige to more secular ideas about the field of modern social work. Influenced by their American peers, French social workers increasingly reframed their activities as a uniquely feminine professional contribution to the public good, and to a nation-state in the throes of crisis.[33] Typically educated, middle-class, and unmarried, French assistantes sociales came largely from Catholic, conservative-leaning milieus.[34] Yet, given their maternalist mission and their very embeddedness in working-class communities, they were, more than any other state officials, on the front lines with immigrant women and their families, supporting their working-class foreign clients in the larger interest of promoting the welfare of children and families in France, regardless of ethnicity, race, and religion. A dynamic mix of public support and private charitable organizations, the French welfare state increasingly announced itself through the wide scope of daily activities undertaken by French social workers in neighborhoods across the country in the decades before 1940. It is, then, at the local level that these interactions and the lives of immigrant men and women unfold throughout the book.

This book begins in rural France. Chapter 1 retraces the trajectories of foreign-born men, women, and children driven out of their homelands and directed into French factories and fields by employers and labor recruitment organizations before, during, and after the Great War. It then follows immigrants to and through the capital, to the two lively melting-pot neighborhoods in Paris where they settled in greatest numbers between the wars and into the Occupation. The approach allows us to hew closely to the lived experience of immigrants, observing how gender, marriage, and family shaped the ways migrants moved through provincial France in search of work before setting their sights on the capital, as so many did. Of course, Paris was by no means the only city to attract foreigners during this period. As early as the 1850s, France's northern, eastern, and southern departments had drawn large numbers of seasonal border migrants from Belgium, Italy, and Spain, respectively. And after the war, migrant laborers increasingly concentrated in mining areas of the Pas-de-Calais region as well as large city centers like Marseille or Lyon and its industrial peripheries.[35] But there was one city alone where the proportion of immigrant residents remained nearly double the national average throughout the interwar decades, and that city was Paris.[36]

While securing housing in the capital did grow increasingly unpredictable for both French and foreign between the wars, foreshadowing immigrants' postwar relegation to urban peripheries, Paris nevertheless accommodated newcomers in significant numbers before the Second World War.[37] The following three chapters, then, reveal their dealings with officials in local settings throughout the capital: haggling with naturalization bureaucrats at their Parisian headquarters in the Ministry of Justice (chapter 2), pleading with officers in neighborhood police stations (chapter 3), requesting help from French social workers in local welfare offices and at charitable organizations throughout Paris (chapter 4).

Considering the massive concentration of foreigners in the capital, it is little wonder that Paris has long fascinated social historians of migration. Over the last few decades, numerous studies have uncovered vibrant communities of Russians, Italians, Poles, Spaniards, Armenians, Eastern European Jews, and colonial migrants who settled in and around the capital.[38] Yet, the scholarly focus on monoethnic communities belies the multicultural reality of the urban experience that was increasingly common in twentieth-century France and Europe, more broadly.[39] While residential segregation and ethnic ghettoization was indeed the rule in American urban environments, employment, housing, and settlement patterns in French cities, as in English cities, instead encouraged *mixité*.[40] As a result, melting-pot neighborhoods comprised of European and colonial migrants sprouted up throughout working-class districts of Paris between the wars. The last three chapters explore this variety of multicultural neighborhood life as it unfolded in the 11th *arrondissement*, and the adjoining neighborhoods of Sainte Marguerite and La Roquette, more specifically, which became home to the largest number of immigrant men, women, and children in Paris between 1881 and 1931.[41]

Unlike the more proletarian 18th, 19th, and 20th arrondissements where immigrant laborers toiled away in factories, the *onzième* housed a lively crafts economy in which woodworking, furniture making, and metalworking were especially popular trades drawing skilled immigrant craftsmen with high wages who could support large families. Mirroring Paris and France, more widely, these families hailed predominantly from Spain, Poland, Belgium, and Luxemburg as well as the defunct Austro-Hungarian, Ottoman, and Russian empires. These neighborhoods were also home to a significant number of Italians who clustered around artisanal faubourg Saint Antoine, Eastern European Jews spilling out of the old Jewish quarters in the Marais, as well as Ottoman Greek and Turkish Jews who had escaped communal violence enveloping the new Turkish nation-state.[42] Many men from North Africa and Indochina also put down roots in these neighborhoods, sometimes marrying French women and fathering *métis* children.[43]

Though scholars have examined the ways that urban environments encouraged cross-cultural solidarities, they have yet to interrogate how, apart from intermarriage, sex and gender influenced the formation of those solidarities.[44] Through a local study of neighborhood life in Sainte Marguerite and La Roquette, chapters 5 and 6 shed light on the gendered dynamics of multicultural sociability, including street life, apartment house life, and cultures of work and leisure that brought together French and foreign residents and itinerants. Frequently, neighborhood cultures mirrored official logics of disciplinary paternalism and supportive maternalism, holding immigrant itinerants and passers-through at arm's length while accommodating newly arrived French and foreign families, especially wives and mothers. Importantly, for inhabitants of melting-pot communities, these were commonsense *social* logics built on centuries of daily interactions between neighbors, the accrued social sediment of everyday life on which local urban communities were founded. In other words, as social logics embedded in the everyday life of the *quartier,* disciplinary paternalism and supportive maternalism simply reflected standard working-class norms about gender, family, and community in which distinctions of race, religion, and nationality came secondary. These gendered solidarities shaped the lived experience of reproductive citizenship for French and foreign-born, alike. As the last chapter shows, the relationships they established with one another during peacetime endured under tremendous strain during the Second World War, making the difference between life and death.

After the fall of France, the Vichy period ushered in a rare historical moment when formal citizenship status, far from protecting nationals, marked some out for deportation, persecution, and extinction. In fact, as chapter 7 shows, many foreign-born Jews living in Sainte Marguerite and La Roquette, whether French-naturalized or not, survived thanks to the relationships they had built in previous decades with friends, neighbors, and social workers of Jewish and non-Jewish charitable organizations. This book, then, contributes to a growing scholarship on that peculiar "French enigma"—that is, the puzzle of how and why 40 percent of Belgian Jews and 80 percent of Dutch Jews perished during the war and German Occupation while only 25 percent of Jews in France suffered a similar fate.[45] In fact, ongoing populationist state sentiment, wartime welfarism, and local gendered solidarities combined in surprising, and heretofore unexamined, ways to spare many foreign-born Jews residing in Sainte Marguerite and La Roquette during the Second World War. Unlike formal citizenship that could—and would—be stripped away from thousands of foreign-born Jews by Vichy officials, reproductive citizenship proved more lasting for the two classes of citizens the French state and society were most committed to protecting by 1940: women and children, even immigrant Jewish women and children.

To tell this story, however, we must begin with the panoply of forces that pushed and pulled immigrants like Romanian Nicholas Goata to France in the first place, shaping their gendered mobilities to and through the metropole as the first of two ruinous world wars convulsed the continent.

CHAPTER 1

The Forces that Push and Pull

Viewed from our vantage point, the first half of the twentieth century appears as a vast panorama of catastrophe all along the "Dark Continent."[1] The storyline is a familiar one: war, revolution, and general strife accompanied by the disintegration of empires, the radical remapping of Europe, and the rise of new nation-states, followed a mere twenty years later by yet another round of calamitous, more murderous warfare. This was supposedly the great age of "the unmixing of peoples," as Lord Curzon famously put it, but it could very well be understood as precisely the opposite.[2] Violence and poverty forcibly propelled men and women from their homelands, stimulating waves of migration that pulsated across the continent throughout the last decades of the nineteenth century and into the first half of the twentieth. They left in search of peace and bread and many found both in France.

In addition to the promise of safe haven, European men and women were drawn to France by the everyday allure of employment and a decent wage. As industrialization accelerated in the late nineteenth century, French employers came to rely increasingly on free, unregulated border migration from Belgium, Switzerland, Italy, and Spain to supplement the native labor force. And, by the early twentieth century, colonial labor migration from North Africa, especially Algeria, was also quite common. During the Great War, the large-scale mobilization of Frenchmen coupled with the demographic deficit that had long afflicted France created additional labor opportunities for colonial and European migrant workers. From Polish farming families at the turn of the century to seasonal female migrants from Italy on the eve of war, from colonial factory workers at the start of the Great War to the legions of demobilized soldiers that war left behind, French industry increasingly partnered with state officials to direct foreign labor into those sectors most affected by labor shortages.

Though scholars have long been attentive to the growing governmental impulse to control, regulate, and channel immigrant and colonial workingmen in France during and immediately following the First World War, they have been less attentive to how Catholic employers' ideas about gender and sexuality shaped the organized introduction of foreign labor into specific sectors of the French economy, and the agricultural sector in particular where foreign families and immigrant workingwomen clustered.[3] Meanwhile, although historians have successfully demonstrated how French employers inscribed gender inequality between the sexes, most notably in the textile industry and on the factory floor, they have yet to consider how a post–World War I atmosphere characterized by mass mobility and gender crisis influenced employer practices toward immigrant working*men* and working*women*, specifically.[4] In fact, interwar employers in agriculture and industry as well as their labor recruitment organizations experimented with marriage- and family-making policies in the hopes of persuading rootless, foreign-born wanderers to remain, at least long enough to bear the generations of French-born children the French themselves had lost. In this, the social Catholic conservatism that had long shaped the patronat's worldviews became outfitted to a modern industrial age. In other words, interwar employer paternalism adjusted to the realities of an increasingly foreign-born workforce who, in their view, would require sexual management.

This chapter reconstructs the laboring lives and winding trajectories of immigrant men and women, agricultural laborers and factory workers who lived in and moved frequently between the countryside and urban centers throughout France, often against employers' wishes and in rupture with their work contracts. It explores the gendered mobilities of foreign men and women in France during and after the Great War, the cultural anxieties their wanderings elicited from middle-class Frenchmen and -women, and how those moral fears shaped Catholic employers' evolving policies toward them. Above all, it points to some of the ways that French employers and officials hoped to control and contain their movements in the 1920s, in order to encourage them to put down roots and dissolve at last into the great French nation of families. As European and colonial migrants drifted through

Europe and alighted in France, barons of French industry and agriculture sought to make of them families, or remake them as such, if necessary.

The Forces that Push and Pull

Though a handful of French employer syndicates had dabbled in organized labor migration before 1914, the war inaugurated a new age of state- and employer-directed foreign labor recruitment to meet the growing demands of the French economy. Although the native labor shortage resulting from the removal of most able-bodied Frenchmen to the front precipitated these measures, the closing of national borders accompanying the onset of war also stifled spontaneous border migration particularly from Italy, which had long served as a crucial labor reservoir for France. French employers thus took great pains to draw European and colonial workers to France and then direct them toward specific industries. In the face of the mass internationalization of the workforce in France, a newly minted category of "work scientists" took advantage of the opportunity to measure, hierarchize, and racialize immigrant labor, and their conclusions in part determined how foreign-born labor was allocated.[5] Consequently, colonial and Chinese laborers were sent to docks and into military construction; Spanish, Portuguese, and Italian workers to agriculture; and Greeks, Armenians, and Italians toward industry, and more specifically, wartime munitions factories.[6] To ensure the regular entry of foreign workers into France, foreign labor recruiters pieced together transportation networks crisscrossing the continent. As the map below renders visible, all immigrant roads—railroads, as well as steamships, in this case—led to France after the war (figure 1.1).

Throughout the nineteenth and twentieth centuries, immigrant women had also heeded the invisible call of the market. Since the late nineteenth century, single young Italian women migrated seasonally to France to find work as domestic servants and wet nurses, often striking out on their own to work abroad.[7] In fin-de-siècle Paris, Italian and Eastern European Jewish women engaged primarily in the confection trades, participating in family-owned and -operated workshops that were often run directly out of their homes.[8] By the interwar years, the most successful immigrants, including immigrant women, operated small shops, restaurants, bars, and *débits* throughout the Seine Department.[9] On the whole, however, it was more likely for immigrant women to cluster in confection trades, textile industries, and domestic service—in short, those jobs that were low skill, low status, and low paying.[10]

While so-called free labor market forces confined immigrant women to jobs in confection and domestic service, the war inaugurated for them, too, a

FIGURE 1.1. "The Great Transportation Networks Used by Immigrants in France." Georges Mauco, *Les Étrangers en France: leur rôle dans l'activité économique. Avec. 100 cartes ou graphiques dans le texte et 16 planches de photographies hors texte.* Paris: Armand Colin, 1932, 124.

new era of state- and employer-controlled labor migration. Unlike immigrant men, however, foreign women were more often channeled directly into the agricultural sector by French employers, a funneling that must be set against the background of shifting rural and urban demographics in France throughout the nineteenth century and into the twentieth. Early twentieth-century contemporaries bemoaned "l'exode rural," or the migration of French peasants from the provinces to large urban cities and some found the loss of *paysannes* from the rural workforce particularly lamentable. Like many Third Republican Frenchmen, Michel Augé-Laribé (secretary-general of the Confédération Nationale des Associations Agricoles in 1925) admired the hardy *paysanne*, praising her "energy," "stoicism," and "professional aptitude" in executing "the punishing tasks" required by rural life.[11] Sadly, according to Laribé, her centuries of accumulated wisdom was now in danger of being lost forever as she left the rural hearth for factory work in the cities during the war. "Removing from the countryside women who were accustomed to living there," Augé-Laribé chided no one in particular, "was to compromise for many years the resumption of agricultural activity in France."[12] From the war years onward, French employers sought to fill the labor void left behind by French peasant women with foreign women.

The French state, employers, and foreign labor recruitment services worked in concert to replenish the rural workforce with immigrant women and their families. Since the early 1900s, Polish families had been imported to agricultural and coal-mining areas throughout France to replace native French families, and in the early twentieth century Polish communities sprouted up in the northern, eastern, and central regions of the country.[13] During the war, employers ramped up these efforts to introduce foreign families into agricultural and mining sectors, and in 1916 the Office National de la Main d'Oeuvre Agricole (ONMA) instituted schemes to organize the large-scale migration of Spanish and Portuguese men, women, and children (see tables 1.1 and 1.2).[14] ONMA directors even resorted to poaching refugees from Poland, Czechoslovakia, and Alsace Lorraine convalescing in internment camps in northern France during the war.[15]

Despite official efforts, French agriculture continued to experience labor shortages long after the war. Of the 3.7 million French rural workingmen mobilized during the war, 673,700 were killed and another 500,000 returned wounded and unable to undertake hard manual labor. Moreover, both

Table 1.1 Spanish and Portuguese agricultural workers in France, 1915–18

YEAR	MEN	WOMEN	CHILDREN	TOTAL
1915	9,814	2,755	1,892	14,461
1916	36,141	6,849	5,596	48,586
1917	36,883	6,897	3,630	47,310
1918	27,034	5,310	1,745	36,089
Total	111,872	21,811	12,863	146,446

Source: Michel Augé-Laribé, *L'agriculture pendant la guerre* (Paris: Les Presses universitaires de France, 1925), 73, 188.

Table 1.2 Italian agricultural workers in France, 1916–18

YEAR	MEN	WOMEN	CHILDREN	TOTAL
1916	223	66	54	343
1917	300	96	12	408
1918	1,044	369	61	1,474
Total	1,577	531	127	2,225

Source: Michel Augé-Laribé, *L'agriculture pendant la guerre* (Paris: Les Presses universitaires de France, 1925), 73, 188.

Frenchmen and -women continued to migrate to large urban centers that promised more lucrative and less arduous employment.[16] Consequently, employer-initiated and state-supported organizational efforts to recruit foreign workers continued throughout the 1920s. As tables 1.3 and 1.4 demonstrate, foreign women numbered prominently among those agricultural workers brought to France, representing about one-third of all Spanish, Portuguese, and Polish rural laborers. Between 1921 and 1926, 37 percent of Polish farm workers brought to France were women (29,549) as were 31 percent of Spanish, 18 percent of Italian, and 4 percent of Belgian agricultural workers.[17]

While the introduction of foreign women into the agricultural sector certainly met the gendered labor needs of the French economy, employers had yet another objective in mind. Employers sought not just immigrant women, but immigrant *wives*, to stabilize, settle, and even assimilate their unruly menfolk. Moreover, employers' efforts to re-create foreign families on French soil were also meant to protect foreign women from the perils of an alien environment that left them socially, culturally, and even sexually vulnerable without the protection—and supervision—of family members and husbands, especially. The introduction of foreign workingwomen into French agriculture solved three problems: it nestled immigrant women securely within families, and it put an end to what was perceived as the mobile ways of immigrant bachelors, all while meeting the persistent labor

Table 1.3   Spanish and Portuguese agricultural workers in France, 1919–22

YEAR	MEN	WOMEN	CHILDREN	TOTAL
1919	42,435	7,890	4,759	55,084
1920	28,884	7,059	5,499	41,442
1921	17,150	9,623	1,489	28,262
1922	26,117	12,523	3,211	41,851
Total	114,586	37,095	14,958	166,639

Source: Michel Augé-Laribé, *L'agriculture pendant la guerre* (Paris: Les Presses universitaires de France, 1925), 73, 188.

Table 1.4   Polish agricultural workers in France, 1920–22

YEAR	MEN	WOMEN	CHILDREN	TOTAL
1920	1,392	320	191	3,693
1921	1,535	433	273	2,241
1922	6,326	2,136	615	9,077
Total	9,253	2,889	1,079	15,011

Source: Michel Augé-Laribé, *L'agriculture pendant la guerre* (Paris: Les Presses universitaires de France, 1925), 73, 188.

demands of France's hardest hit sector—agriculture. But before continuing, we must first get a sense of what male continental mobility was truly like during this period and, thus, from whence these fears came.

The War and Wanderers

The Great War drew soldiering men from every corner of Europe and beyond, distributing them indiscriminately throughout—the purest manifestation of the greater continentwide "mixing" of populations described here. And when the war came to an end, some found themselves quite a long way from home with little desire to return. Nicolas Goata was twenty-five years old when he first took up arms to fight for his native Romania. The year was 1913 and the war was unraveling in the Balkans. One year later, he was sent to fight "the Second European War," as he called it. During that First World War (as we call it), Goata was taken prisoner by the Germans whom he eventually evaded, escaping to France in 1917. Fifteen years later, well after his marriage to Emilienne Authemet, he described his situation to a French official very plainly and with just a hint of frustration: "I did not come to Paris for pleasure, Monsieur. It was the war."[18]

For a great many like Nicolas Goata, war and its penumbral events set them on their crooked paths to Paris. It was a meandering fate shared by a generation of men, a fate encapsulated in literary form by novelist Joseph Roth, a former Austrian soldier himself. In his 1924 novel *Hotel Savoy*, Roth described how the Great War had made of the average man "a soldier, a murderer, a man almost murdered, a man resurrected, a prisoner, a wanderer."[19] Through the central character of Gabriel Dan, a POW who had fought in the Austro-Hungarian Army before returning after years of imprisonment in Siberia, Roth conveyed the enormity of the task facing soldiers as they demobilized. After years of warfare and imprisonment, many men were engulfed by a sense of aimlessness and some found themselves only by accident in or near France where they would commence their wandering anew. After all, so many years of deracination spawned habits of uprootedness that were not quickly forgotten.

For some, remaining in France was hardly a choice at all or, rather, it was a choice conditioned by larger geopolitical realities. Born in Turkey in 1888, Jean Kofler was an Austro-Hungarian subject until 1914. He was indeed considered an Austrian citizen by French authorities until 1919, when the erstwhile empire disintegrated and he suddenly found himself a Czech national, a designation as new as the nation-state itself.[20] His homeland, like his citizenship, was in a state of extreme flux during these years. Finding himself in

France in 1919, Kofler preferred to stay put rather than return to an uncertain future. This experience was common enough that Roth, too, commented on the strange impact of diplomatic relations on men's fates in the immediate postwar period. When hassled by police in Lodz for being a rowdy foreigner, Dan's Russian friend Zwonimir hurled back at officials: "I'm a soldier coming home and I'm forced, my friend, to stay here, because for some reason or another my government has signed a pact with yours."[21] Indeed, great power politics shaped the circumstances under which European soldiers made their choices to stay, to return, or to move on. While some may have had the option to return home after World War I, others, like Kofler, faced a murkier situation.

Many soldiers chose to remain in France due to the wealth of job opportunities created by labor shortages and the immediate prospect of a decent wage. For those with family already in France, the choice to remain was that much more obvious. Adrien Rossi, a Swiss national, was exactly eighteen years old when the Great War began. In 1916, Rossi was mobilized in the Italian army and, after the war, rather than return home, he instead made his way from northern France to an uncle living in the heart of Paris—the 1st arrondissement on posh rue Saint Honoré—where he worked at a neighborhood fruit shop.[22] Dimitri Wandiak also profited from kinship networks, though in a more roundabout manner. After four and a half months in the Polish Army, Wandiak was demobilized and, returning home, remained unemployed for several years. In 1925, he came to France to join two Polish cousins, both agricultural workers at a large farm in the Sarthe department of northwestern France where he stayed for six months. Restless for "a more lucrative job that was also more appropriate to his tastes and his aptitudes," he later called on additional cousins in Paris to help him find a job in the capital, which they did, at an electric company in the 9th arrondissement.[23]

Straightforward trajectories on the part of former foreign-born soldiers in France were a rare occurrence, indeed. On the whole, it was more common for years of soldiering to, rather than end abruptly, wind down slowly. This was the case for Jean Schwiderski, a Pole who, like Rossi above, was a teenager when war broke out. He was mobilized into the Russian Army but taken hostage by Germans during the war and sent to an internment camp in Aix-la-Chapelle in western Germany. Rather than return to Poland after the war, Schwiderski opted instead to stay and work in France in 1918. For nearly a decade thereafter he worked at various factories in Reims, Metz, and Strasbourg before finally settling in Paris in 1927.[24]

There was an intimate relationship between wandering and soldiering, as the story of a young Russian, Etienne Babenko, also illustrates. At the age of seventeen, Babenko left home in Nobocherskask without telling his parents to join a foot-soldier regiment and fight along the Austrian front. There, he was twice wounded and twice returned to the Eastern Front. With the start of the Bolshevik Revolution, Babenko then joined anti-Bolshevik forces in Dou. After his liberation in 1919, he opted for a quieter life as a telephone operator on Russian military ships drifting along the Black Sea and even worked briefly as a chauffeur. In 1920, he traveled to Constantinople where he continued his work on Russian ships. It was only four years later, in 1924, that Babenko finally made his way to France to find work. Once in France, however, his meandering recommenced anew. First, he found easy pay as an agricultural worker in the south near Arles. A few years later he headed to Lyon where he found employment (and probably higher wages) as a skilled worker. Several years afterward, Babenko was on the move again, this time to find work in the northeastern mining region of Meurthe-et-Moselle. Eventually, he would find his way to Paris in 1931.[25] Drawn by the allure of paid work, soldiers from the East like Schwiderski and Babenko flooded westward after the war, but their trajectories were winding and haphazard.

From 1917 onward, as Roth put it, "Russia, mighty Russia, [was] shaking them out."[26] For those coming from Eastern Europe during these years, war and migration were deeply entwined and fleeing was a recurring image in many of the narratives that Eastern Europeans formulated about their manner of arrival in France. Like Babenko, Russian Michel Smaguine, too, fled the Bolshevik Revolution. He had served in the Russian Army along the Austrian front during World War I, then in Wrangel's Army from 1920 to 1921. After a sojourn in Constantinople, he fled to Marseille in 1924 and eventually made his way to Paris two years later.[27] Similarly, Ukrainian Max Bloch attempted to shirk military service in Ukraine during World War I by seeking refuge in Poland in 1917 to, as he put it, "escape the Russian Revolution." Bloch then traveled to Germany in 1922 only to be forced to flee again, this time from the Nazis in 1937. He would find his final refuge in France.[28]

If the war heralded the presence of foreign soldiers in France, so too did the Great War inaugurate the mass arrival of colonial men on hexagonal soil. Like European men, they came both as soldiers and workers.[29] Over 500,000 troupes indigènes served during the war and another 200,000 colonial workers from West and North Africa, Indochina, and Madagascar were brought to the metropole. For some, wartime presence on the continent would lead to permanent residence in France. Ramdane Kacide, for instance, was twenty-two years old in 1915 when the French state removed him from his home in Beni-Bouchaïb, Algeria, and channeled him into the government-directed colonial workforce, the Service d'organisation des travailleurs coloniaux

(SOTC).³⁰ In fact, his service in war factories was considered a privilege: he had been exempted from military service on account of his Kabyle heritage.³¹ In contrast to tales of forcible colonial recruitment, Moroccan subject Mohammed Ben Driss voluntarily joined the colonial regiment after losing all his savings gambling in Casablanca. Of course, the extent to which Ben Driss "voluntarily" chose this path given his destitution is arguable. He was subsequently sent to Lyon to work in a munitions factory.³² Though the temporary exigencies of running the wartime economy had brought them to France, both Kacide and Ben Driss would remain long after.

Although many colonial soldiers first set foot on French soil during the war, others were drawn into the state war machine as a consequence of already being in the metropole. This was common for North Africans, and especially Algerians, who had evolved long-standing patterns of seasonal migration between France and Algeria since the dawn of the twentieth century.³³ Mohamed Aïchour, for instance, was an Algerian subject from Fort National who arrived in France in 1906 at the young age of fourteen. At first, he found work in the coal mines of the Pas-de-Calais region, then he left in 1914 to fight alongside colonial troops in the war. At some point, he was taken prisoner by German forces. When he was released at the end of the war, he remained in the North to aid in the reconstruction of war-devastated regions. Aïchour remained in the North where work was plentiful until 1922 when he returned to Paris. It was only after he married the French maid at his hotel in the 19th arrondissement that his peregrinations ground to a halt. Aïchour never returned home again.³⁴ What began as a short-term work migration transformed into long-term settlement upon marriage to a Frenchwoman, an occurrence that constituted something of a pattern among foreign-born men.

If war forcibly pulled men out of their homelands and placed them on French soil for the first time, marriages formed *in France* often constituted an effective means of keeping them put. Luigi Pellati, a twenty-three-year-old Italian from Gropparello, came to France in 1920 to find work and decided to stay when he met and later married the Paris-born daughter of his Italian lodgers, Victorine Bracchi.³⁵ The story was similar for Ferdinand Oe, a twenty-four-year-old Luxemburger who migrated to Lorraine to find work in 1923; later, in Dombasle, he met his future wife, Eugénie Thomassin, a French factory worker from Meurthe-et-Moselle, and together they migrated to Paris where they married and settled in 1924.³⁶ Le Van Hue was a seventeen-year-old Indochinese law student from Hanoi who arrived in France in 1924. Four years later, he went to Paris to study law at the Faculté de Droit, but, unlike most Indochinese students during this period, he never returned home. Why? By 1932, Hue had married a Frenchwoman, Marguerite Simon, and, with the birth of their daughter later that year, he had every intention of staying on in France.[37]

As the wayward trajectories of European and colonial male migrants wound through France, employers observed the strange efficacy of the marriage contract, a force more powerful than the myriad machinations that French industrial and agricultural magnates could conjure up. "Foreign agricultural labor introduced [in France] has not remained on the Land [sic]," complained agricultural *ingénieur* Paul Ballot to fellow French employers in 1929. Ballot went on to convey "the brutal fact" that "of the more than 30,000 foreign workers brought to France in the last ten years to make up the deficit in agricultural labor in the Paris Region, hardly 4,000 remain there."[38] Echoing Ballot, interwar demographer and ethnographic specialist Georges Mauco remarked that foreigners "flooded" into Paris, "coming from the countryside, the mines, the provincial factories, often in rupture with their work contracts and in an irregular situation."[39] Even in the 1930s, as the state apparatus increasingly punished immigrant laborers for breach of work contracts, foreign migrants continued to risk arrest, imprisonment, and deportation to strike out on their own in search of greener pastures.[40] Marriage, family, and children, did, however, succeed where work contracts failed, and French employers had begun to take note.

French Employers, Immigrant Workers, and the Marriage Contract

Employers' aversion to unmarried foreign workingmen who broke free of work contracts willy-nilly was, in part, shaped by the traditional values characteristic of the predominantly Catholic patronat. Large industrialists and agricultural employers, these men featured prominently among the Third Republic's ruling classes. Theirs was an essentially conservative alliance during the fin-de-siècle period, united as much by a shared aversion to laissez-faire capitalism as a begrudging tolerance of parliamentary politics.[41] Whether espousing progressive, traditionalist, or decidedly right-leaning social Catholic views, however, all strains of interwar employer paternalism placed family at the forefront of their mission to quell working-class radicalism and heal class divisions in French society.[42] Moreover, if, during the nineteenth century, anxieties over women's sexuality had informed the thinking of nineteenth-century employers and political economists, after the First World War, working-class male sexuality drew as much if not more attention from Catholic employers.[43] It was a preoccupation that brought them into the republican fold: that is, devotion to marriage and family was a hallmark of traditionalist Catholic values and dovetailed neatly with an emerging strain of republican thought that vilified bachelors in post–World War I French society.[44]

While French bachelors were looked down on, immigrant bachelors without any attachments to France were particularly maligned. In a special issue of the *Revue d'Hygiène* dedicated to the "problem" of immigration in 1926, a gaggle of doctors expressed this sentiment, among them René Martial—doctor, eugenicist, and future "racial expert" who found prominence under Vichy.[45] "The married foreign man," Martial reasoned, "even when he comes alone, thinks about his family and dreams of settling for as long as possible, forever perhaps, and the man who came with his entire family does not wish to wander from place to place in the country where he has arrived."[46] By comparison, the unmarried foreign man's lack of stability made him difficult to fix, to settle, and to tame. Consequently, single foreign men were a highly unstable population, Martial claimed. "They love to move from one place to the next," he explained, "and many of them do not remain fixed in one place more than six months out of the year." As Martial put it, it was "the spirit of travel or adventure that moves them."[47] He concluded that this wandering quality particular to unmarried foreign men was inimical to both economic and social relations in France, and many employers were inclined to agree with him.

The Société Générale d'Immigration (SGI) was the single largest conglomerate of French employers, and it was on account of SGI efforts during the 1920s that a large number of European migrant workers both arrived and reassembled in France as families. A commercial immigration company, the SGI was controlled by coal and farm interests that responded to employers' labor needs in the post–World War I years. In 1924, the Comité des houillères (Coal Committee) and a consortium of farm groups organized as the Confédération d'associations agricoles des régions devastées (CARD) coalesced as the SGI, essentially an instrument of organized capitalism operating largely without state oversight.[48] Poland, Austria, Czechoslovakia, and Yugoslavia constituted the four "principal countries of emigration"—the very heartlands of the former Austro-Hungarian Empire and overwhelmingly Catholic countries whose populations many employers would have deemed "assimilable."[49] Undoubtedly, recruiters inserted themselves into the chaos that ensued after the defeat, collapse, and disintegration of this empire, providing an attractive outlet to thousands of those uprooted by larger geopolitical events. In addition to the prospect of waged employment, the SGI furnished foreign migrants with train fare, work contracts with French employers, and diplomatic visas for legal entry into France. Upon arrival approximately four months later, immigrant workers were promptly conducted to their new workplaces.[50]

As the largest foreign labor recruitment organization, the SGI's course of action was representative of the policies implemented by most Catholic employers to resolve the issue of foreign male mobility. Theirs was a program that all but leaps from the pages of the *Revue de l'Immigration*, the official organ of the SGI read by a host of employers and state ministers. Published between 1928 and 1940, the *Revue de l'Immigration* was a monthly journal whose readership consisted of industrial and agricultural employers. Written contributions informed French employers on all matters concerning their foreign employees. The three main themes broached in the review concerned legislation and regulation, international accords, and recent updates in parliamentary and juridical statutes, which often reprinted questions posed by politicians and answered by the minister of justice in the *Journal Officiel*. On the whole, the journal touched on aspects related to foreign workers that might prove of concern to employers, from laws on nationality and military obligations to the regulation of identity cards and medical examinations. Importantly, family matters constituted a recurring theme.

In 1929, an unidentified author penned an article on the benefits of the introduction of foreign families, emphasizing that it was "an excellent factor in the stabilization and assimilation of foreign men." Indeed, he claimed, a family rendered the foreign worker a happy man and happy men made for productive workers. Moreover, he argued that married foreign men with children to care for made for more responsible men. "The employer, himself," the author began, "has an interest in employing a married man rather than a bachelor." He continued, "In general, the former is more well-behaved, more conscientious, more precise; his economic yield is better, because he is more stable, and because he is a better worker."[51] Thusly did he make an economic and social argument in favor of married immigrant men, articulating, too, the kind of "high-handed paternalism" that was so characteristic of the interwar Catholic patronat.[52]

Emmanuel Chaptal, a Paris-based priest and brother to well-known French philanthropist Léonie Chaptal, weighed in on the subject as well, and his contribution is noteworthy for at least two reasons. First, his own career was characterized by a dedication to the "francisation" of foreign-born workers in Paris through the church, a mission that earned him the nickname "l'evêque des étrangers," or "the foreigners' bishop." Second, he, too, was a proponent of marriage as a source of stability among the working classes, so much so that when, in 1920, fellow priest Jean Viollet founded the Association du mariage chrétien, he chose Chaptal as his first president.[53] Perhaps unsurprisingly, then, Chaptal expounded on the virtues of hiring married foreign men over single foreign men in the pages of the *Revue*, evoking the familiar images of stability versus mobility: "It is very evident that the bachelor, in comparison to the married man, is mobile and unstable. It matters little to him whether he works here or there. It matters little to him whether he leaves one industrial business or another agricultural enterprise. If he finds another job that pays better, he will take it." On the contrary, he continued, "The married man will think twice before exposing his family to leaving the country that they are accustomed to, where their children have been educated, where all the advantages and esteem that the families enjoy grows day by day."[54] In other words, the day-to-day concerns occasioned by family management rendered the married foreign man more cautious, responsible, and stable of character. He was not one to uproot his family on a whim, but one who could be relied on to stay true to his commitments—to his family, but also to his employer. This made him not only a stand-up *père de famille* but a valuable worker and, potentially, a worthy member of the French nation.

Of course, the inducement to marry rested on a similar assumption about the assimilatory potential of wives. As one 1925 industry brochure put it, "Women are the conservative and stabilizing element who will fix the displaced races to the soil." Without a wife and family, "the isolated man does not possess the moral guarantee and the incentive to work as a head of household."[55] Perhaps most significantly, wives and families prevented men from giving in to their baser instincts—that is, varieties of heterosexual and homosexual deviance with which employers and local officials grew increasingly exasperated. Even before the war, French employers had become aware of the kind of hanky-panky that majority-male, increasingly foreign workforces, could get up to—from "orgies" and all manner of "saturnalia" to more run-of-the-mill prostitution.[56]

The cultural embrace of family-minded foreigners and married male migrants was more than rhetoric. It galvanized Catholic employers to action. In 1929, SGI representatives boasted, "The Society is willing . . . if the employer so desires, to either furnish male workers accompanied by their families, or to undertake at a later date the introduction of the worker's wife and children once he is employed in France."[57] And this was no empty offer. Between 1924, when the SGI was founded, and 1929, the organization claimed to have furnished employers with not just 250,000 male workers, but "400,000 other persons," as well.[58] Of course, there was a clear economic gain to be had on the part of employers who took the SGI up on this offer: the introduction of foreign families expanded the available reservoir of foreign labor, allowing labor recruiters to supply employers with more workers, and cheaper female workers at that. But SGI efforts to introduce families were also part of a wider effort to neutralize the threat of single, foreign workingmen rapidly concentrating in the metropole, an effort that responded to wider cultural anxieties over unattached men in France, more generally.

In the pamphlets they printed for distribution to magnates of French industry and agriculture, the SGI gave potential employers a rough idea of the foreign men and women they would soon hire. In one such pamphlet, they even provided a photodocumentary consisting of a series of photographs following potential foreign workers from life in their unnamed European homelands to arrival in France. The first image pictured a group of foreign families picnicking in the distance, with the caption, "Before leaving their country, they lunch beneath the willow trees along the riverbanks" (figure 1.2). In the following image, SGI operatives diligently recorded the ritual of the contract signing. This photograph depicted a room crowded mostly with men, one with a toddler in his arms, and a few women. All stood in a long, disorderly line snaking through the room, up the stairs, around the second story, and ending at a small kiosk window where, presumably, an SGI agent waited to assist them with their work contracts (figure 1.3).[59] The stress on familial imagery was undoubtedly meant to reassure employers about the quality of the workforce they were about to import.

Besides the introduction of foreign families, the *Revue* frequently featured articles with the express intent of educating employers on the ins and outs of marriage laws as they concerned their various immigrant employees. One such article explained the conditions of entry for the foreign fiancées of workingmen in 1929.[60] Another issue published later that year included a feature on "the civil and religious effects of the celebration in France of marriages of Romanian, Yugoslavian, and Bulgarian subjects, either amongst themselves or with a French spouse."[61] Indeed, a great many articles were dedicated to the subject of intermarriage between French and foreign, and most all concerning foreign men and Frenchwomen.[62]

In fact, the final photograph in the 1929 SGI pamphlet depicted a wedding procession, with a brief but revealing caption beneath it: "Once in France, they marry" (figure 1.4). Was this merely a happy ending to an immigrant's story? Or was it, rather, a conscious tactic employed by the SGI to assure employers that they would not eventually have a roving horde of uncontrollable, highly mobile, unattached foreign men on their hands? Indeed, this image seemed intent to reassure employers that unmarried foreign men who ruptured work contracts with impunity and left their employers in the lurch would soon be grounded and stabilized through the sedentary,

FIGURE 1.2. SGI photodocumentary pamphlet advertising foreign labor to employers. SGI, "La Société Générale d'Immigration vous fournira de la main-d'oeuvre étrangère," 4 in 8/R pièce 17842 (BnF).

civilizing influence of women, whether French or foreign. Essentially, the SGI responded to wider cultural anxieties about unattached foreign men in the metropole by encouraging marriage and introducing foreign families to serve as stabilizing forces to fix foreign men.

The SGI was not alone in facilitating the introduction of foreign wives and children to, at once, contain the sexual threat and harness the economic potential of single foreign male laborers in France. The French state also supported such measures. In 1928, for instance, a Franco-Polish Protocol

FIGURE 1.3. "They take turns signing their contracts." SGI, "La Société Générale d'Immigration vous fournira de la main-d'oeuvre étrangère," 5 in 8/R pièce 17842 (BnF).

FIGURE 1.4. "Once in France, they marry." SGI, "La Société Générale d'Immigration vous fournira de la main-d'oeuvre étrangère," 14 in 8/R pièce 17842, Bibliothèque nationale de France.

required employers to pay 60 percent of the costs associated with bringing Polish workers' families to France.[63] The notion that marriage was the best way to stabilize and assimilate immigrants was a logic endorsed from the republican left to the Catholic right and inscribed into state practices to an ever-greater degree throughout the interwar years, as we will see in the next chapter. Families, then, provided a means by which the state and employers sought to stabilize, settle, and assimilate foreign men into the French nation—defined increasingly during the interwar years as a nation of families.

State, Society, and Single Immigrant Women

If immigrant wives and families were to contain the ambulatory threat posed by single foreign men in the metropole, attempts to inscribe immigrant women within families and marriages also responded to concerns of French state officials, Catholic employers, and middle-class moralists over the sexual vulnerability of single foreign women far from home, removed from their families. They drew in part from well-articulated fears over *femmes isolées* that became common in nineteenth-century writings on the French political economy, and which, with the increase in female migration, returned in late nineteenth- and early twentieth-century public discourses.[64] Against the background of postwar gender hysteria and mass international migration, these anxieties resurfaced once more and this time took immigrant women as their primary object of concern. As one anxious official wrote, "The female element among immigrants—above all when it concerns young isolated girls—most requires attention and protection against the multiple dangers that menace them in a new country." He listed with evident satisfaction the "multiplicity" of measures implemented by the French government to protect these migrating women: for instance, the formation of commissions to investigate the "morality" of employers and the establishment of a "service spécial d'assistance" equipped with female interpreters whose task it was to follow foreign workingwomen and visit them from time to time.[65]

A network of private charities seeking to provide refuge to migrant women supported early state efforts. Since the late nineteenth century, several private initiatives had developed to protect rural French girls migrating from the countryside. From the start of the twentieth century, however, their clientele grew increasingly foreign.[66] Confession-based charities for migrant women multiplied during this period and included the Protestant Service Social d'Aide aux Émigrants (SSAE), the Association Catholique des Oeuvres de Protection de la Jeune Fille, the Association Israélite pour la Protection de la Jeune Fille, and the Union Nationale Française des Amies de la Jeune Fille. Echoing the sentiments of state officials, the SSAE's *directrice* similarly invoked "the dangers that these young women traveling alone are exposed to" in order to justify the proliferation of various charitable organizations for their benefit.[67]

Indeed, many middle-class moralists believed that unattached foreign female migrants posed an essential problem, exposed as they were to a variety of moral and sexual threats. In 1929, Magny, director of the ONMA, claimed that "the presence of young foreign women [in France] is essentially the consequence of the waves of immigration that have taken place since the war," adding, "the great majority belong to the working classes." There were, he enumerated, "Italian and Spanish women in the Midi, Armenian and Russian women in the Rhône Valley, Belgian women in the North, Polish and Czechoslovakian women disseminated throughout the country." According to Magny, they found jobs as "maidservants in large hotels, workers in textile mills and food processing, [and as] milkmaids and farm girls."[68] In these various activities, Magny referred to shifting labor dynamics in France that we have already been attentive to—namely the process by which foreign women supplanted Frenchwomen from the provinces as the premier female migrant workforce engaged in either permanent or seasonal rural labor, as the market required.[69] Like concerns voiced by French middle-class men and women over migrant workingwomen arriving fresh from the countryside, there was bound to be similar consternation over foreign women traveling even further distances.

According to Magny, certain work conditions and, in particular, the heterosocial space of the workplace presented palpable danger to single foreign women, being as they were far from home and, consequently, bereft of a family's protection. The removal of foreign women from their families created a problematic situation in which "young foreign working women are too often left to themselves." Without "familial supervision," her morality could not be adequately safeguarded. Magny declared, "Foreign female personnel working in large hotels live and work in conditions of promiscuity with the masculine element . . . which can hardly guarantee her morality." In the absence of familial supervision, so Magny reasoned, foreign women could easily fall prey to all sorts of urban vices. "Upon leaving the workplace," he claimed, "they come up against all the temptations of the city and are too often obligated to find lodging in furnished rooms [*chambres meublées*]." The reference to chambres meublées is telling: rather than spending the night lodged with her family or, at the very least, in a respectable, all-female boarding house, the single foreign woman, wages in hand, could afford a cheap hotel room of her own. The subtext was clear: not only could she spend the night wherever, but she could spend it with *whom*ever. With control over her own wages (and sexuality), a single foreign woman could afford to purchase the cheap urban amusements, or "all the temptations of the city" as Magny put it, that were increasingly available to the working classes, men and women alike.

To counter this frightening image of foreign female economic and sexual emancipation, Magny believed that employers had to assume a dual role, providing her with both family and community. Magny praised factory owners for being "well-regulated" in this regard. The benign intervention of solicitous *surveillantes* surely provided some reassurance that foreign women were protected, or at least closely watched, in factories. Ignoring the potential for social and sexual experimentation borne of the factory floor, Magny believed instead that factories provided a social space for foreign women to congregate among themselves so as to find comfort with their countrywomen. "They often have the possibility of finding compatriots," he reasoned, "of conversing with one another in their mother tongue, which allows them not to suffer too much from the distance with their country and their family." In other words, foreign women could form surrogate families with their countrywomen in the workplace. French factories designed with these concerns in mind could perhaps provide immigrant women a kind of home away from home, with all the perks and protections therein.

Contrary to single foreign women in the cities, Magny believed that foreign female migrants employed in the provinces experienced a heightened degree of anomie. In particular, he noted that foreign women employed in the agricultural sector suffered from a lack of an "elementary knowledge of French," an "ignorance of our language" exacerbated by their isolation in the provinces (or, "the wide dispersion of foreign personnel in the farms spread out throughout the whole of our territory"). Consequently, it was up to French employers to take the welfare of their foreign female employees to heart, accommodating their ethnic particularity within the greater work structure to ensure both happiness and morality. Magny exhorted French employers to recognize "what an eminent role they must assume vis-à-vis these foreign women who form their personnel," taking it on themselves to regulate the material circumstances of their everyday life so as to uphold "the order of their moral protection." Naturally, he offered up religion as one key way to bind foreign women to the sexual norms of the French Third Republic.

If these were the primary drawbacks of agricultural work, however, there was at least one real advantage to rural life for single foreign women:

the strong logic of interwar employer paternalism rendered single foreign women the surrogate daughters of their French employer-family. "The female agricultural worker shares, undoubtedly, in the majority of cases, the life of the employer and his family," explained Magny. As a result, the situation of the single foreign female rural worker was "comparable to that of other women in his household."[70] Better than the mere horizontal bonds that formed between foreign women on the factory floor, the foreign female agricultural worker benefited from a vertical bond with her employer and his family, the very hallmark of employer paternalism between the wars. Again, then, Magny forwarded a singular platform to protect unattached foreign workingwomen—namely, to provide them with surrogate families—in this case, a rural French employer-family.

Magny's assertions aside, however, not all middle-class Frenchmen and -women believed the state and employers were doing enough to shelter foreign workingwomen from the harsh realities of working-class life in France. Reporting on the exploitation of foreign workingwomen in 1932, Maria Vérone, president of the Ligue Française pour le Droit des Femmes, wrote that industrialists, who "called on workingmen and workingwomen of every country" to fill French factories, were falling grievously short of their duty to "lodge them, feed them and pay them." She went on to relate how employers of a factory in the Moselle paid a group of Polish workingwomen just a little over one franc per hour, withholding eleven francs per day to cover the costs of their food and lodging. With only two francs of their own per month, "these unfortunate women are obliged to give themselves over to prostitution," Vérone asserted. "Is it not truly shameful," she asked rhetorically, "that these great industrialists exploit in such a fashion these poor women whom they have made come to France, and that they treat them little better than slaves?" Preying on middle-class fears that female poverty led inexorably to sexual depravity, she then warned that if employers persisted in this manner, "there will soon be in our country a great quantity of poor, prostituted women, miserable, deprived and revolted, prison or hospital fodder, who will be at once a charge and a danger to the nation." Only state and employer "protection of *travail féminin*" would prevent poor, foreign workingwomen from becoming a public charge—and, perhaps, a sexual menace.[71]

Strong paternalist and maternalist undercurrents characterized official and unofficial rhetoric surrounding single foreign female migrants, often manifesting in the urge to ensconce them firmly within families. Middle-class philanthropists, employers, social workers, and state actors sought to supply a surrogate presence to foreign women by exercising and encouraging a paternal, familial influence. Thus, single foreign workingmen and workingwomen elicited a similar response from French employers, though for manifestly different reasons: if single foreign men were perceived as dangerous, mobile, unruly, and unstable, single foreign women were perceived as vulnerable, morally corruptible in the absence of family and community, and easy prey to the dangers of urban vice and temptation. Yet, for both sets of singles, the "solution" was the same—tuck them away in families. Families, it would seem, served to contain foreign men and to protect foreign women.

Migrating Marriages and Foreign Families on the Move

Of course, the wholesome idea of reproductive marriage and the nuclear family endorsed by employers, statesmen, and philanthropists came up against the harsh realities of migrating marriages and foreign families on the move. After all, it was instability rather than stability that characterized men and women's patterns of mobility in the late nineteenth and early twentieth centuries. The very instability that prompted their flight from places once called home would continue to haunt many of them. In other words, while labor and refugee migration initially brought married men and women and their families to France from the 1880s onward, those husbands and wives endured, and at times even sought out, their own forms of rupture and dissolution, for reasons great and small.

The vast majority of immigrant women who came to France followed their men. Indeed, the archives abound with classic scenarios of "pioneering" immigrant men whose wives and children rejoined them in France.[72] Manuela Talavera epitomizes the archetypal foreign woman come to reunite with her husband with child in tow. Born in 1908 in Albaceta, Spain, she came to France at the age of twenty with her toddler son because her husband, Vicente Martinez, who had gone to Paris before her, found a job as a porter at Les Halles as well as an apartment for his family in the 1st arrondissement.[73] Salvatore Musso, an Italian soldier who demobilized in France after the Great War, similarly sent word to his wife in 1926 to rejoin him in Paris where he had found stable employment for a Spanish cobbler in Saint Philippe du Roule. Once he had found an apartment in the 17th arrondissement, his wife, Mariana, migrated from Italy with their four children later that year, in October 1928.[74] This pattern of migration initiated by foreign men who later sent for foreign wives and children to rejoin them in the metropole was exceedingly common. It was a form of migration that kept families intact during this tumultuous span of years that likewise spanned a tumultuous continent. In these instances, marriage and family were, indeed, the ties that bound men, women, and children together through uncertain times.

Still, the larger-than-life events of the period could separate men and women, husbands and wives, just as easily. In 1914, Catherine Girardo's husband, Lorenzo, was called away to serve in the Italian army. For more than a decade, Catherine had worked as a domestic servant in the 8th arrondissement of Paris, for a Monsieur Dressche on rue Tronchet. During the war years, she remained in Paris working with her two young daughters, Anna and Madeleine, until Lorenzo returned in 1919, now a decorated soldier.[75] Although Catherine Girardo's husband returned, not all foreign women in a similar predicament could expect a similar outcome. Jeanne Alcail was a Spanish woman who had lived and worked in Paris since 1913 with her husband and son, Charles. In 1915, her husband left to fight in the war—and he never came back.[76] Indeed, war divided families, sometimes temporarily as in Catherine Girardo's case, but other times permanently as Jeanne Alcail's story indicates. War, soldiering, and the atmosphere of male mobility it engendered allowed some men to "renegotiate" domestic arrangements.

To some extent, the very act of migration allowed men to revise domestic and familial arrangements. Italian Pascal Fenile was twenty-four years old when he married in his native Sarno in 1922. Although the exact details are murky, it would seem that, after a difficult pregnancy, his wife was no longer physically able to engage in intercourse. Fenile narrated, with brutal honesty, "I found myself completely disgusted with her. I had spent 60,000 francs on this illness and I could no longer have intercourse with my wife. So I left everything there and I went to France."[77] Though this example is admittedly extreme, Fenile's decision to migrate was motivated explicitly by a desire to reshape his sexual opportunities through marital rupture and, perhaps one day, renewal. Belgian Arthur Warinier presents us with a more typical scenario. A native of Bruges, Warinier came to France during the war and decided to remain after he met a certain Madame Delanay, a Frenchwoman, with whom he established a new household and consequently never returned home again.[78] As we will see in chapter 3, these ruptured and refashioned domestic situations among immigrant husbands and wives were common during and after the war years. For now, though, they demonstrate how, in spite of what French employers hoped, foreigners could use migration not to shore up marital and family bonds but to extricate themselves from them.

In fact, it was a common enough phenomenon that a certain amount of suspicion hung about immigrant men looking to wed French brides. French relatives of brides-to-be regarded foreign men with a degree of suspicion lest they already were married back home and were seeking to enter into an illicit union with unsuspecting Frenchwomen. This was particularly the case for Italian men once Mussolini banned divorce in February 1929. The French mistress of Fenile, mentioned above, even followed up with the Italian consulate to determine the exact marital status of her lover, suspecting something in his behavior that was not quite right. Indeed, she discovered that he was still legally married to the wife he had abandoned in Italy.[79] Without the possibility of a legal divorce, so the logic went, Italian men like Fenile could "revise" their marriage contracts through more informal means, namely, through migration and self-reinvention.

Immigrant women may also have migrated as a means to informally renegotiate undesirable domestic arrangements. Veronika Dererova is a case in point. In Czechoslovakia, Veronika's husband made some poor investments and, to repay his growing debts, he set off alone for America. Although he sent remittances back to his wife and daughter, Dererova considered herself "abandoned" for all intents and purposes. She set off for France in 1932, leaving behind her fifteen-year-old daughter, Maria, and her seventeen-year-old son. Upon arrival, she found employment as a domestic servant in L'Haÿ-les-Roses, a suburb of Paris.[80] During her frequent forays into the capital, she met Dimitrov Stefanow, a Polish day laborer living in the 4th arrondissement and the two soon began living together in the "Pletzl," an area of central Paris where Eastern European Jews settled in large numbers.[81] In fact, Dimitrov Stefanow had left his own wife and children behind him in Poland because, according to him, "he was in a disagreement with her."[82] In this case, both Dererova and Stefanow had migrated in order to extricate themselves from domestic situations they no longer desired. In these instances, migration to France provided foreigners with an opportunity to re-create and renegotiate domestic and familial configurations on French soil.

If migration allowed men and women to revise the proverbial marriage contract, mobility could also dissolve marriages entirely. Indeed, just because a couple set off for France together was no guarantee they would remain together throughout. Take Antonia Plotnikoff, a seventeen-year-old who fled from the Russian Revolution with her husband in 1919 upon learning that all their relatives had either "perished or disappeared." En route to France, the couple alighted temporarily in Bulgaria where Antonia fell ill with encephalitis. Shortly after, her husband left her. Once recovered, Antonia promptly sued for and won divorce, but fearing that her husband sought custody of their six-month-old daughter, she left Bulgaria for France under the guise of being the wife of another man. In France, she sought help from the League for the Protection of Abandoned Mothers, a maternalist organization founded in the capital in 1925, that helped mothers, whether French or foreign. Parisian social workers recorded with amazement, "She finds herself here absolutely without any resources, with her child, unable to speak a word of French, unwell . . . and in a state of visible physical poverty." And yet despite her multiple misfortunes, French social workers who greeted Antonia in 1927 were nearly beside themselves in the face of her abiding fortitude. "Having had nothing but tea all day," one *assistante sociale* jotted down hastily, "it is 3 o'clock, and she is looking for work!"[83]

The tumultuous life of Antonia Plotnikoff reminds us that while marriage could be used by French employers during and after the Great War to facilitate the migration of fiancées and wives and thereby encourage the permanent settlement of immigrant laborers, in the end, families were fragile things. Marriage could disintegrate as a result of occurrences both extraordinary (war, revolution, genocide) and ordinary (the death of a family member, the flight from poverty, the search for something—and someone—new) in scope. Moreover, far from alighting in France as fully intact migrant families, for some foreigners, migration itself was a tool to renegotiate domestic and familial arrangements, to remake and unmake their attachments. Contrary to the intended goal of official policies forwarded by French employers and the pervasive rhetoric of middle-class contemporaries, the realities of migration made marriage, settlement, and family formation among foreigners a fraught enterprise.

In concert with state officials, Catholic employers sought to direct foreign labor to those sectors of the economy experiencing the most acute labor shortages during and after the Great War. They followed market dictates, to be sure, but they also operated in accordance with larger cultural anxieties surrounding the real and imagined mobilities of foreigners in France, and especially foreign bachelors. Those anxieties, which they shared, led them to believe that men who did not tarry long might not marry ever, and it was married men who made good workers, fine fathers, and eventually, true citizens. To that end, employers and foreign labor recruitment organizations like the SGI implemented policies to settle immigrants within families, whether by helping them to reunite with family members left behind or by helping them to create and re-create families in France. While these measures were intended primarily to settle and stabilize immigrant bachelors through marriage and family life, they sought to protect and safeguard immigrant workingwomen, providing them husbands or, at the very least, a surrogate family of watchful employers in the absence of their own kin. Of course, immigrants' own stories reveal that migration offered just as many opportunities to hold on fast to loved ones as to elude them entirely. In fact, many foreigners migrated in order to refashion their domestic situations, taking advantage of the imperative to flee their homelands to desert wives and husbands. Though both foreign-born men *and* women engaged in behaviors of marital abandonment, it was roving immigrant bachelors that aroused French suspicion and drew particular ire. What would prevent them from leaving their women and children in the lurch once more? If French officials wanted to integrate and settle immigrants through marriage and family life, they would have to do more than merely facilitate the migration of foreign fiancées, wives, and children. As bureaucrats and police officials decided, they would have to compel immigrant men to marry and provide for children in France.

CHAPTER 2

Bachelors, Bureaucrats, and Marrying into the Nation

In 1917, French Odette Dulac sounded the alarm. "The war has poured on our soil millions of men from friendly nations," she wrote. "English, Russians, Serbians, Portuguese, Italians, Belgians, Americans go, come, heal, fight and fall in love." In response to their magnified presence, Frenchwomen had, Dulac insisted, "offered ourselves to these foreign heroes like ripe fruits to taste." She concluded, "For the last three years, our gallantry has constructed a non-biblical Tower of Babel because the confusion of languages allows us to understand one another only too well." More specifically, she pointed to the "disquieting proportions of legal marriages between Frenchwomen and foreign men," arguing, "Thousands of young girls marry Allies: [and] they bring them their dowry, their youth and the fruit of their womb." "Love will wreak havoc," Dulac warned, if France did not reform its marriage and nationality laws according to which Frenchwomen who married foreign men immediately lost their French nationality. She thus joined a chorus of population-minded, middle-class contemporaries during and after the war who sought to prevent those "thousands of young women" and the children they would bear from being stolen away from the French nation "by little more than the charm of a gray, beige, or kaki uniform."[1]

The specter of "love's ravages" certainly loomed large during and immediately after the war. From the declaration of war in August 1914 through 1932, nearly 285,000 mixed marriages were concluded in France; from 1915 until 1940, more than 64,000 alone took place in Paris.² Because of the absence of Frenchmen and the glut of foreign-born men, we are told, intermarriages surged, and French statesmen sought to capitalize on it. With the passage of the 1927 Law of Independent Nationality, French women who married immigrant men could for the first time retain their French nationality after marriage. The law also permitted their foreign-born husbands to obtain French citizenship with fewer delays and decreed that the children born of those unions on French soil would automatically become French. In other words, in the face of a significant uptick in intermarriages that threatened to siphon off women and children, the state moved to facilitate intermarriage between Frenchwomen and foreign-born men on a vast scale, using marriage as a means to repopulate France. In both official and semiofficial circles, these actions were premised on the notion of republican motherhood, which held that Frenchwomen could and would use their influence within the domestic sphere to "assimilate" their foreign husbands and their half-foreign children into the French nation.³ For many Third Republican contemporaries including Dulac, intermarriages between Frenchwomen and immigrant men were not merely favorable but indispensable in order to combat the demographic crisis that beset France.⁴

Yet, the overriding focus on arguments mobilized in favor of the law obscures the great lengths to which naturalization bureaucrats went in order to actually make immigrant men marry, offering instead a seductive narrative about how heterosexual desire "naturally" led to love and marriage. Certainly, the country and its capital were awash with immigrant men, but their sheer presence alone did not make them the straightforward solution to France's postwar dearth of men and its surfeit of "spinsters," as contemporaries viewed them.⁵ As officials came to learn, working together, living together, even having children together offered no "guarantee of stability" where unmarried immigrant men were concerned. How could French wives, or any wives for that matter, work their sedenterizing, and thus assimilatory, influence on foreign-born men if they could not be persuaded to stay?

It was not merely that marriage, as a social institution, offered a respectable middle-class means to express individual desire and naturalize bonds between men, women, and their children. For officials, it also fastened errant immigrant men to their wives and families, made them legally responsible for the financial well-being of their household and its members, and as a naturalization tool, linked them to the nation as reliable husbands and pères de famille. Correspondence between European immigrant bachelors and local officials in naturalization files reveals just how much haggling and bargaining, threatening and cajoling went into the formation of these marriages, unions that increasingly served as a precious demographic lifeline for France after the war. In contrast, officials' correspondence with Frenchwomen suggests how women themselves used naturalization processes to secure marriages with foreign *amis* and French nationality for their entire families. In other words, Frenchwomen engaged with the state on categorically different terms than their immigrant husbands, and often in ways that were to their singular advantage. While bureaucrats' dealings with immigrant men evidence a disciplinary form of both producing and enforcing heterosexual masculinity, their interactions with French women instead reveal the latitude accorded to women who expressed themselves in the familiar tones of patriotic wife and republican mother—that is, in categories that shored up heterosexual femininity in Third Republic France.

Of course, the war had brought a great many colonial and nonwhite men to France and, despite the best efforts of colonial administrators, they, too, often became involved—sexually, romantically, intimately—with Frenchwomen. What was to be done about these interracial unions and the *métis* children their nonwhite fathers sired? How far would officials go to create husband-citizens, for Frenchwomen and for the French nation, by way of marriage? Certainly, officials, like their middle-class contemporaries, were convinced that what the nation needed after the war was more fathers to French children and husbands to French wives, not selfish, parasitic, pleasure-seeking bachelors, and especially not ones that could pick up and move as they pleased. But could that logic extend to include nonwhite men? As they shuttled between conflicting imperatives—enforcing marriage to create families and preventing interracial unions that might produce undesirable families—naturalization bureaucrats, police officials, and colonial administrators enforced their notions of gender, sex, and marriage to define the terms on which foreign-born men joined the French national family. In the process, they had to decide how much foreign birth and racial otherness would matter in the larger project to repopulate France and whether it made sense to irrevocably bind these unknown and perhaps unknowable men to the French nation via wives as, indeed, some did not wish to be bound.

"No Guarantees of Stability": Bureaucrats Weigh in on Marital Matters

During the 1920s, mere consensual unions between French and foreign did not always assuage naturalization officers' concerns over the prevailing social, sexual, and moral (dis)order of the post–World War I period. Unless concluded by civil contract, these unions looked dangerously like informal domestic arrangements or what the French termed *concubinage*. While such relationships between men and women were quite plentiful in working-class neighborhoods throughout France and certainly throughout Paris from the nineteenth century onward, bureaucrats showed great disdain for foreigners, and especially foreign men, who lived in this manner.[6] Although the practice denoted sexual promiscuity and moral laxity for both French and foreign, concubinage, or living *maritalement*, reflected more poorly on immigrants, and immigrant men at that. "Concubinage" denoted a tendency for male flight, inconstancy, and mobility. *Vivre maritalement* also conflicted with proper notions of morality, respectability, and dignity demanded of honorable French citizens, both in the metropole and beyond.[7] Perhaps most significantly, however, bachelorhood called into question men's heterosexual credentials at a time when the Paris police force sought to expand its capacity to surveil homosexual male subcultures. Indeed, Parisian enclaves of "sexual vice" drew French and foreign workingmen in large numbers.[8] At the very least, perpetual bachelorhood suggested a foreign man's refusal to marry and, given the republican faith in the assimilative powers of French wives within mixed households, bachelorhood denoted, by extension, a disinclination to assimilate into the French nation via the heterosexual conjugal family.[9] As a result, naturalization bureaucrats, including members of the Bureau de Sceau and local police officers charged with investigating individual applicants, coerced foreign men into marrying their French partners as a means of policing heterosexual deviance, eliminating the sexual threat of mobile foreign men, and forcing their marital assimilation into the French nation via French wives.

Census data on marriage and nationality among French, foreign, and naturalized men and women lay bare with piercing clarity the conjugal politics at work in bureaucratic calculations during the period. As tables 2.1, 2.2, 2.3, and 2.4 show, naturalized men and women were married at rates that

Table 2.1 Marital status of the population of France (percentage), 1921

NATIONALITY	MARRIED	SINGLE	WIDOWED	DIVORCED	UNKNOWN
French	43	45.8	9.9	0.5	0.8
Naturalized	61.7	23.9	13.2	0.7	0.5
Foreign	43.3	47.7	5.9	0.5	3.6

Sources: SGF, Tome II, *Résultats statistiques du recensement général de la population effectué le 6 mars 1921* (Paris Imprimerie nationale, 1925), http://www.insee.fr/fr/insee-statistique-publique/bibliotheque/tableaux_sgf/tableaux.asp?domaine=rec; SGF, Tome I, *Résultats statistiques du recensement général de la population effectué le 8 mars 1931* (Paris: Imprimerie nationale, 1933), 76; SGF, Tome I, *Résultats statistiques du recensement général de la population effectué le 8 mars 1936* (Paris: Imprimerie nationale, 1938), 76.

Table 2.2 Marital status of the population of France (percentage), 1926

NATIONALITY	MARRIED	SINGLE	WIDOWED	DIVORCED	UNKNOWN
French	45	44.3	9.3	0.6	0.8
Naturalized	69.2	15.5	13.9	0.9	0.5
Foreign	44	48.7	4.5	0.5	2.3

Sources: SGF, Tome II, *Résultats statistiques du recensement général de la population effectué le 6 mars 1921* (Paris Imprimerie nationale, 1925), http://www.insee.fr/fr/insee-statistique-publique/bibliotheque/tableaux_sgf/tableaux.asp?domaine=rec; SGF, Tome I, *Résultats statistiques du recensement général de la population effectué le 8 mars 1931* (Paris: Imprimerie nationale, 1933), 76; SGF, Tome I, *Résultats statistiques du recensement général de la population effectué le 8 mars 1936* (Paris: Imprimerie nationale, 1938), 76.

Table 2.3 Marital status of the population of France (percentage), 1931

NATIONALITY	MARRIED	SINGLE	WIDOWED	DIVORCED	UNKNOWN
French	44.1	41.1	13.4	0.8	0.6
Naturalized	68.7	14.9	14.7	1.1	0.6
Foreign	45.9	44.9	7.3	0.6	1.3

Sources: SGF, Tome II, *Résultats statistiques du recensement général de la population effectué le 6 mars 1921* (Paris Imprimerie nationale, 1925), http://www.insee.fr/fr/insee-statistique-publique/bibliotheque/tableaux_sgf/tableaux.asp?domaine=rec; SGF, Tome I, *Résultats statistiques du recensement général de la population effectué le 8 mars 1931* (Paris: Imprimerie nationale, 1933), 76; SGF, Tome I, *Résultats statistiques du recensement général de la population effectué le 8 mars 1936* (Paris: Imprimerie nationale, 1938), 76.

Table 2.4 Marital status of the population of France (percentage), 1936

NATIONALITY	MARRIED	SINGLE	WIDOWED	DIVORCED	UNKNOWN
French	46	43.4	9.2	0.8	0.6
Naturalized	64.3	25.3	9	0.9	0.5
Foreign	48.1	44.6	5.3	0.6	1.4

Sources: SGF, Tome II, *Résultats statistiques du recensement général de la population effectué le 6 mars 1921* (Paris Imprimerie nationale, 1925), http://www.insee.fr/fr/insee-statistique-publique/bibliotheque/tableaux_sgf/tableaux.asp?domaine=rec; SGF, Tome I, *Résultats statistiques du recensement général de la population effectué le 8 mars 1931* (Paris: Imprimerie nationale, 1933), 76; SGF, Tome I, *Résultats statistiques du recensement général de la population effectué le 8 mars 1936* (Paris: Imprimerie nationale, 1938), 76.

far exceeded either French or foreign populations in France between 1921 and 1936. A glance at these figures even suggest that the unmarried were "punished" given the low rates of bachelorhood among those naturalized (between 15 and 25 percent) as compared to what constituted the norm among French and foreign populations (between 40 and 50 percent).

While Third Republican naturalization bureaucrats showed a pronounced preference for married foreigners throughout the period, that inclination accentuated after the First World War. As table 2.5 indicates, marital rates among naturalized men were consistently quite high, hovering around

Table 2.5 Naturalized men by marital status, 1889–1940

YEAR	PERCENTAGE OF: BACHELORS	MARRIED MEN	WIDOWERS AND DIVORCÉS	YEAR	PERCENTAGE OF: BACHELORS	MARRIED MEN	WIDOWERS AND DIVORCÉS
1889	26.7	70.5	2.8	1915	NA	NA	NA
1890	23.8	72.8	3.4	1916	NA	NA	NA
1891	26.8	70.4	2.8	1917	NA	NA	NA
1892	24.8	72.2	3.0	1918	NA	NA	NA
1893	25.2	71.7	3.0	*1919	5.6	86.1	8.3
1894	23.8	73.3	3.0	*1920	4.8	84.3	10.9
1895	24.5	73.3	2.2	*1921	5.2	88.3	6.5
1896	22.7	74.9	2.4	*1922	8.0	86.3	5.7
1897	25.1	72.1	2.8	1923	16.2	79.0	4.8
1898	23.9	72.9	3.2	1924	18.8	76.7	4.6
1899	24.2	72.5	3.3	1925	19.3	75.7	5.0
1900	23.4	73.7	2.9	1926	19.2	76.2	4.6
1901	23.1	73.5	3.5	1927	14.3	81.3	4.4
1902	23.2	73.9	2.9	1928	18.5	77.4	4.1
1903	21.0	76.0	2.9	1929	19.1	77.3	3.7
1904	22.2	73.1	4.7	1930	21.3	75.3	3.4
1905	19.0	76.4	4.5	1931	20.8	76.5	2.7
1906	22.2	74.6	3.2	1932	18.9	78.9	2.1
1907	19.3	75.3	5.5	1933	22.5	75.5	2.1
1908	15.6	79.7	4.6	1934	24.0	74.1	1.9
1909	16.1	80.0	3.9	1935	28.6	70.0	1.4
1910	16.5	79.7	3.9	1936	41.1	58.0	0.9
1911	18.4	78.4	3.2	1937	37.8	60.9	1.3
1912	18.6	77.1	4.3	1938	31.2	67.2	1.6
1913	15.3	80.5	4.2	1939	21.4	76.9	1.7
1914	NA	NA	NA	1940	27.6	70.5	1.9

Source: Pierre Depoid, *Les Naturalisations en France (1870–1940)* (Paris: Imprimerie nationale, 1942), 27, 47.

* Asterisks indicate that foreign men naturalized according to the Law of August 5, 1914, for military conscripts, have not been counted.

75 percent from 1889 onward, and spiking in 1908–9 to nearly 80 percent. The immediate post–World War I years (1919–22), however, marked a peak in conjugality among naturalizing foreign men, as nearly 90 percent of those naturalized each year were married. In other words, the demographic dips brought on by the war encouraged state officials to reward and enforce conjugality among immigrant men through the process of naturalization. In short, while the French state was notoriously accepting of nonmarriage among its own, the naturalization process gave bureaucrats a great deal of

influence in family formation among the foreign-born. Married, naturalized men would continue to remain proportionately more significant than unmarried, naturalized men, accounting for well over half of all men obtaining naturalization until the fall of France in 1940.

So what was the naturalization process like and who were the bureaucrats in charge? While naturalization was much easier to come by after the passage of the Law of 1927, the process nevertheless entailed significant hassles. From start to finish, naturalization could take either a few months or a few years, depending, as we will see, on bureaucratic whimsy and the efficacy of foreigners' rhetorical strategies when presenting their case.[10] Immigrants only opened a naturalization dossier if they met the proper conditions of age, residency, health, and "morality." They also had to amass twenty or more required documents for the successful completion of their file, including a testament of residency and morality from the mayor of each municipality in which they had resided since their initial arrival in France. The dossier then passed through three separate administrations spanning local, municipal, and national levels.

Immigrants seeking French citizenship filed the initial request at the local commissariat where they lived, at which point they became the subject of an official inquest. Next, the dossier was sent to the local Police Prefecture where it was assigned to another officer. Although this investigative brigade was housed in various departments within the Paris police department between the wars, naturalization dossiers show clearly that police officials all possessed a single modus operandi vis-à-vis immigrants: "To verify that the foreigner does not constitute a threat to the maintenance of social and political order."[11] To that end, police officers interviewed neighbors and acquaintances of the applicant at his or her apartment house and around the neighborhood to assess "morality" and "reputation in the *quartier*." Occasional descriptions of foreigners' dwellings and references to room size in their apartment buildings confirm that many police officers entered the homes of certain immigrant applicants in order to complete a thorough "enquête à domicile."[12] These four- or five-page police reports summarized the findings of earlier reports, but dwelled more particularly on "fréquentations" and French language fluency, both of which indicated degree of "assimilation" to French culture. The prefect of Police then pored over these investigative reports and issued an official *avis*, or opinion: "favorable," "very favorable," or categorically "unfavorable." At last, the file was sent to the Bureau de Sceau, the arm of the Ministry of Justice responsible for overseeing the naturalization process.[13]

The Bureau de Sceau, or Office of the Seal, was the national office dedicated to processing naturalization requests, and it operated outside parliamentary oversight from the nineteenth century onward. While the Bureau de Sceau had originated under the ancien régime, its "omnipotence" over the naturalization process was only established in the mid-nineteenth century, when the law of December 3, 1849, gave it sole power to decide the outcome of naturalization requests and to run background investigations on foreigners of its own accord. By 1889, the Bureau de Sceau had emerged as a fully autonomous office whose civil servants could develop their own policies, logics, and administrative practices unchecked by outside forces. Consequently, during the Third Republic, every naturalization request that arrived at the Bureau de Sceau was reviewed by at least three in-house officials: an attaché or rédacteur, the head or second-in-command of the office, and finally the director of Affaires civiles et du Sceau. In exceptional cases, the Minister of Justice himself reviewed the file. While these administrators took into consideration all notes, inquests, and formal opinions proffered by local and police officials, ultimate authority rested with them to decide whether to naturalize or not.[14]

In spite of the office's modernization in the 1920s, and even despite the sharp uptick in naturalization requests after the passage of the 1927 law, the Bureau de Sceau never attracted the cream of the crop. It became home instead to middling magistrates and mediocre functionaries who had a reputation for "not having given satisfaction" in their previous posts. Young middle-class men on the make sought expressly to avoid being consigned there throughout the interwar decades.[15] And they were all men: women were not permitted to work in the Ministry of Justice until 1945.[16] Those men who did find themselves in the employ of the Bureau de Sceau were necessarily populationist, adopting a solution to the population crisis that quite literally effected demographic growth through the naturalization of the foreign-born. Of course, they did not naturalize at random. When extending outward the boundaries of the French national community, naturalization officers adhered to populationist criteria, opting overwhelmingly for large foreign families, young immigrant women of reproductive age, and young foreign-born men liable to provide military service. In other words, bureaucratic adherence to populationist doctrine led invariably to the gendered application of naturalization law during the interwar decades.[17]

Significantly, the interwar years also marked a particularly acute moment of heteronormative gender conformity in a population-starved France. As such, marriage served as a tool wielded by naturalization bureaucrats to shape the demographic features of a prospective male citizenry. Unmarried couples, or couples who failed to conform to the conjugal model, invited bureaucratic distrust. For instance, when Russian caster Meyer Rotbourg sought naturalization in 1921, the Paris prefect of police noted, "Apart from his irregular liaison with a Frenchwoman whom he proposes to marry, his conduct does not occasion any particular remark."[18] Even Romanian Haschel Goldenberg's twenty-three-year-long relationship with his "concubine" invited official notice. In the section of his naturalization request where officials recorded "observations on the conduct and morality" of applicants, one bureaucrat, identified only as "L." noted, "lives maritalement."[19] Of note, traditional "red flags" in this section of the naturalization request indicated the immoral behavior of applicants, typically consisting of previous arrests and criminal activity related to one or the other spouse.[20] A failure to marry on the part of foreign men denoted, it would seem, not just immoral behavior, but vaguely criminal comportment.

Consensual unions that produced children had a better chance of escaping bureaucratic opprobrium and, fortunately for Goldenberg, that was the case. Though he lived "maritalement" with a Romanian woman, the couple had a twenty-year-old, French-born son who was away completing military service in the French Army at the time Goldenberg applied for naturalization, a fact he made sure to point out to officials on several occasions. Paris police and Bureau de Sceau officials looked kindly on the service of Goldenberg's son and thus overlooked the father's "irregular situation."[21] But reproductive service to the nation alone was not always a winning strategy. Mordko Wainer, a Polish watchmaker, for instance, had a seven-year-old daughter with his "concubine," but he did not succeed in leveraging the child in his dealings with officials. In this particular instance, it may well be significant that the child was a girl, not a boy, and young immigrant sons were more desirable to a population-starved, war-minded state in perpetual need of soldiers. Even if the populationist context allowed some unmarried couples with children to escape officials' judgment, on the whole, bureaucrats looked down on unmarried couples involving foreign men, whether mixed or foreign couples. When an opportunity arose to bring state power to bear by forcing these couples to marry, state officials took full advantage.

In some instances, state officials used access to French citizenship as the proverbial "carrot" to force foreign couples to marry. In 1929, for example, Italian metalworker Carlo Sappino hit a bureaucratic snag in his naturalization when officials from the Bureau de Sceau noted in his file, "This postulant could, it seems, regularize his union." They were referring to his cohabitation with a Frenchwoman with whom he had fathered no children. The combination of these damning facts reinforced the bureaucratic impression that Sappino's request represented "no interest for the future." The first Bureau de Sceau official, identified only as "D.," thus recommended deferral.[22] A few days later, the head officer of the Bureau de Sceau concurred, writing, "Same opinion, deferral so the postulant regularizes his situation." Officials at the Bureau de Sceau were, in other words, agreed: withhold naturalization until marriage.[23]

The "carrot and stick" approach reared its head often and with greater tenacity on other occasions. Wainer, mentioned above, experienced a fair amount of difficulty obtaining French citizenship on account of what more than one naturalization official between 1926 and 1930 termed his "irregular" liaisons with numerous women both French and foreign. In January 1928, officials postponed his naturalization expressly because of his "irregular situation," in this case with the widow Roubine. That they lived "maritalement" or "in concubinage," in other words, that the law had not conferred on their union the sanction and sanctity of marriage, caused bureaucrats to await "his more complete assimilation and his marriage to his mistress."[24] It is telling that assimilation is mentioned here, since his naturalization file made no mention of any lack of French fluency or "foreign frequentations" on his part, the traditional markers denoting a bureaucratic impression of foreigners' foreignness. Rather, the remark indicated a lack of *marital* assimilation to the French nation.

Over the next two weeks, Wainer was summoned to the Bureau de Sceau where he was "invited to discuss his matrimonial situation."[25] There, officials took stock of the entirety of his personal history. As it turned out, he was a former prisoner of war, interned in Moselle where he remained until German troops left. "He did not return to Russia," they remarked with approval, "fearing the excess of the revolution." They next turned to his dubious domestic situation: "He then established himself with the borrowed fortune of his concubine the lady Roubine of Russian origin, naturalized French with her husband." The "lady Roubine" had previously been married and acquired a small sum through both her successful shoe shop and the military pension she received after her husband's death, a tidy sum of a thousand francs per month. "Living since 1920 with this woman, with whom he has a seven-year-old daughter, the postulant affirms [that he] has the intention to regularize his situation as soon as he is naturalized."[26] But officials required more than good "intentions." Despite Wainer's pious promises to wed his betrothed, officials in the Bureau de Sceau issued a vote of no confidence. In the words of one exasperated bureaucrat, "The petitioner lives in an irregular situation and could not present guarantees of stability."[27] In other words, irresponsible domestic conduct afforded no "guarantees" that Wainer would ever make a responsible French citizen. On repeated occasions between 1928 and 1930, then, naturalization officers declared *their* intention to wait until Wainer married "his concubine" before bestowing the favor of French citizenship.

A year later, in 1929, Mordko Wainer and the widow Roubine tied the knot. In a long-winded and plaintive letter, Wainer wrote to the minister of justice, trying to decipher the cause of his repeated deferrals, concluding, "The sole reason that could have motivated the [previous] deferment decision was to my mind the de facto union with Madame Widow Roubine née Toke, a union that has already lasted many years and from which a daughter, Anna, issued in 1920." Indeed, it was the "de facto" not "de jure" character of their union that gave officials pause. Wainer immediately followed this observation by reassuring bureaucrats, "This situation has recently been regularized and our two children have also been legitimized by the marriage of their father and mother." Now safely married, Wainer ended his letter by turning bureaucratic logic against his official adversaries: "If . . . today, residing in France for ten years, speaking the French language fluently, [being a] former combatant in the Russian Army, being of Russian origin [but] without a precise nationality, married legitimately to a war widow, a mother of a French child aged 15 years and already French herself by naturalization, a father myself of two young girls of French nationality, I am today the only foreigner in a household that counts five persons."[28] Moved as much by his logic as the legitimacy of his union, bureaucrats finally conceded in March 1930.

The same bureaucratic logic was at work in the case of Mario De Faveri, an Italian cementer living with a Frenchwoman in Paris. De Faveri and Emilienne Henriette Loeuillet lived together on 133 rue de Montreuil and had a daughter together in 1924. De Faveri, bureaucrats recorded, "wishes to become French in order to marry a Frenchwoman and recognize the French child he had by her." But police officials questioned De Faveri's true motives, determining, "There is reason to examine De Faveri's request seriously." The officer decided further, "De Faveri's request is of no interest unless he marries the Frenchwoman and recognizes the child." In other words, months before the 1927 law would go into effect, bureaucrats were more concerned to procure a marriage between this foreign man and his French "concubine" than preserving a Frenchwoman for the French nation. They required, as they had of Wainer, more "guarantees" of his stability—that is, marriage. They held off on the decision pending a "serious investigation" into his marital motives, familial sentiment, and paternal sensibilities. This was in April 1927; Mario De Faveri and Emilienne Henriette Loeuillet married in July of that year. Officials did not even bother to draw up a new request. They simply scribbled out "bachelor" on the old form and wrote in his recent marriage date before granting him citizenship.[29]

Religious unions in France also drew attention from French naturalization officials, though Orthodox Jewish couples raised more suspicion than either Catholic or Protestant immigrant couples seeking French citizenship. The revolutionary law of September 20, 1792, first transformed the institution of marriage in France from a time-honored religious rite ordained by the Catholic Church to a civil contract concluded in the presence of the new high priests of the modern secular state—bureaucrats.[30] Typically, *officiers d'état civils* in town halls across France presided over civil unions, but police officials and naturalization bureaucrats expanded their role into this marital terrain in the twentieth century. Although many Catholic, Protestant, and Orthodox Jewish immigrants that married did so in religious ceremonies, it would appear that bureaucrats only required foreign Jews married "selon le rite israélite" to remarry in civil ceremonies. Naturalization dossiers provide numerous examples of Jewish couples who had married in religious ceremonies in their country of origin prior to migration and arrival in France: Russian Samuel Chelicevitch and Jachet Steinitz; Greek Samuel Covo and Sara Asseal; Polish Abraham Tycheboff and Léa Niantanha.[31] Remarriage in French civil ceremonies was also required of Jewish immigrants who married according to Orthodox custom in France. For instance, Schoel Guerchonovitch and Sarah Schwartz married in a Jewish ceremony in 1906 and again in Paris on November 10, 1925. The French marriage ceremony took place just one week before they submitted their naturalization request, indicating that they formalized their unions in preparation for naturalization, perhaps even at the behest of bureaucrats.[32] Fifteen years later, under Vichy rule, the stakes of civil marriage became higher for immigrant Jews, especially immigrant Jewish women, who were accorded certain rights and privileges as wives and widows, but only if they were seen as such in the eyes of French law.

In most instances, bureaucrats imposed their will with relative ease. At times, however, interactions between applicants and officials could be more labored, especially when immigrants mounted resistance to official power. Take the case of Joseph Korenblum whose marital situation sparked a small flurry of bureaucratic activity between 1926 and 1930. A forty-seven-year-old Polish furniture-maker, Korenblum was a remarried widower who had recently separated from his second wife, Fanny Pickman. Because he was in the middle of a divorce when he first applied for naturalization in 1926, his naturalization request initially fell on deaf ears. Although the police commissar of Sainte Marguerite, the prefect of police in Paris, and naturalization officials in the Bureau de Sceau all noted that he had failed to "render services to France" during the First World War, the absence of service alone was rarely enough to condemn an applicant outright. It is rather more likely that his pending divorce contributed to bureaucrats' conviction that he presented "insufficient" motives for naturalization.[33] Indeed, an anonymous letter sent to the minister of justice in 1927 (and probably written by Korenblum himself) attributed the denial of his request directly to his pending divorce a year earlier. The author of the letter also sought to reassure authorities that the applicant was now eager to remarry.[34]

In his second request lodged in 1927, bureaucrats still evinced alarm that Korenblum was "divorced from a Russian woman" but were gratified that he had used the preceding year gainfully by cultivating a new romance. They were pleased to note that, as of his second naturalization request, "he has the intention to marry a Frenchwoman." Yet, while admitting that Korenblum "continues to be the object of satisfactory information," and even noting approvingly that the "marriage plan appears serious," officials decided in the end to refrain from naturalizing Korenblum until the imminent "celebration of his marriage with a Frenchwoman."[35] In other words, while plans to marry certainly constituted a step in the right direction, bureaucrats wanted to see that the nuptials came off before they allowed foreign bachelors unmitigated entry to the French nation.

For his own part, however, Joseph Korenblum believed that his plans with Madame Gouetta, a French war widow, were sufficiently serious to warrant premarital naturalization. He wrote to the minister of justice several times over the course of 1927 to that effect. At each turn, however, bureaucrats held their ground. In fact, the archive preserves a letter from one bureaucrat to the postulant himself, a very rare find. In it, Georges de Berly, a legal representative from the Bureau de Sceau, registered near audible exasperation in his communication with Korenblum, writing sternly: "There is nothing to say on the matter so long as you will not marry; just as the letter that was written to you by Monsieur Charles Lambert, and just as I repeat now to you, as soon as you will have married, you will certainly be naturalized." He further explained bureaucratic reasoning as follows: "We want for you to be married before being naturalized because we want to be sure that you marry a Frenchwoman," adding as a reassurance, "This Frenchwoman will not suffer from any prejudice from this fact, since according to the law of 10 August 1927, she can conserve French nationality by making a declaration at the moment of the marriage."[36] In other words, although his betrothed would easily be able to keep her French nationality, bureaucrats nevertheless demanded Korenblum's marriage as a sign of his true attachment—to French Madame Gouetta, but also to the French nation. Mere promises would not suffice. Marriage alone signified a proof of worthiness for the obligations of husband and the privilege of citizen.

Despite the straightforward advice from de Berly, Korenblum did not marry Madame Gouetta. Consequently, his third naturalization request was once more denied in June 1928.[37] Perhaps realizing at last that officials would not budge on the issue, Korenblum lodged a fourth naturalization request. In it, he confirmed immediately that he had finally married, this time to a Russian-born, French-naturalized woman named Jeanne Feldmann. He further specified that his new bride had dutifully conserved her French nationality upon marriage. By 1930, then, Korenblum had finally earned French citizenship "by reason of his recent marriage," as the prefect of police put it.[38] A bureaucrat at the Bureau de Sceau summarized Korenblum's four-year odyssey more pithily: "Request deferred until marriage with a Frenchwoman (condition met)."[39]

Class may have been a factor in these bureaucratic back-and-forths centered on the marriage of foreign bachelors. The relatively unproblematic naturalization of Michael Hamilton, a successful Russian interpreter at the Compagnie Internationale de Wagons-Lits and self-proclaimed count, is a case in point. His engagement with a Frenchwoman occasioned no bureaucratic concern, no inducements to marry as quickly as possible. Moreover, his naturalization process lasted a mere nine months—record time, all things considered. At the moment of his naturalization, Hamilton lived in the 15th arrondissement, on rue Laos, just a handful of streets from the bourgeois 16th and 7th arrondissements.[40] Inhabitants of these neighborhoods were a class apart from the working-class residents of Sainte Marguerite and La Roquette, among whom he would live on boulevard Voltaire (with his French-born wife Jeanne) by 1931.[41] Thus, the fear of specifically working-class immigrant men and their dubious marital scruples may well have factored into the marital meddling of bureaucrats.

Of course, men had their own reasons to marry, and welfare benefits could sweeten the deal. In 1937, social workers at the Paris-based welfare organization, the Social Service for Children in Moral Danger, had suspicions about the marital scruples of one Frenchman, Monsieur Halary. After several documented instances of his stormy relationship with the Polish mother of his child, Dina Rubinsztain, they decided that Halary was "not very sincere, not very honest and of doubtful morality." Despite their stormy past, the couple presented a united front at their court appearance when a *décheance de puissance paternelle* was lodged against the mother. Social workers were stunned to learn that the couple was newly married. Doubting the purity of that rascal Halary's motives, they suggested instead, "We believe that the real reason for the union with [Dina Rubinsztain] was the lure of higher unemployment benefits that he could not get as a bachelor."[42] If, as we will see in the next chapter, marriage offered women inducement to marry, no less did it offer certain men similar advantages through the "lure" of state benefits. During the depressed 1930s, however, unemployment benefits may have been a more obvious advantage restricted to *French* rather than *foreign* husbands, as this example illustrates.

Officials may also have shown bias in favor of the French versus foreign family attachments of immigrant bachelors. Bureau de Sceau officials used their discretionary power to shore up families that were more French than foreign, or could become so. In so doing, they overlooked and disregarded evidence of foreign men's previous familial attachments that could prevent their easy marital assimilation into the French nation. In 1932, for instance, Nicolas Goata, the Romanian soldier discussed in the previous chapter, submitted his naturalization request. A year later, the minister of justice somehow caught wind of a rumor indicating a previous marriage. According to his unnamed sources, Goata had already been married with a Romanian woman in his home country. Although it is unclear exactly how the minister of justice chanced on this information, the news certainly caused Goata plenty of worry, imperiling as it did his acquisition of French nationality and, by extension, the family allocations that he, his French wife, and their five Paris-born children depended on for survival.

Adamantly denying the accusation, Goata wrote to the minister of justice frantically, "me, if I had been married I would not have sought to marry again in France." He sought desperately to assure naturalization officials of his marital probity, swearing of the other Romanian woman, "I left her *pour complètement pour toujours*."[43] Despite—or perhaps because of—his fervent protestations, officials pursued a further inquest into the precise nature of Goata's marital and familial situation. This investigation revealed that he had also left behind three children in Romania. In the final analysis, however, police officials determined his Romanian children were produced "by a *concubine* whom he left due to her poor conduct." The choice to refer to his Romanian partner as a *concubine* is not without significance: as a "concubine," she was divested of all marital prerogatives to, and thus all legal claims on, Goata. Moreover, it characterized their previous liaison as an informal domestic arrangement, null and void in the eyes of the law. Finally, the assertion that she was "of loose morals" was an official strategy to both rhetorically *and* legally dismiss the claims of this unnamed Romanian woman, thereby clearing the way for Goata's more perfect union with a Frenchwoman on French soil.

In a shocking passage that suggests local police officers actually confronted Goata with information from the "family inquest," the note concluded, "He will have no further news [from them], neither from the mother nor from the children." With familial bonds thus permanently severed with his foreign family, Goata could finally be eligible for not only the marital duties owed to his French wife, but the national obligations owed to the French nation. He was thenceforth endowed with the status of husband-citizen. Indeed, the officer who led the inquest opted to naturalize Goata "given his familial situation."[44] In so doing, officials put paid to Goata's messy marital situation, making it clear that in foreigners' domestic affairs, it was *French* families—and French *wives*—that mattered most.

"Deliver to Me My Husband": Frenchwomen Bargaining with Bureaucrats

The naturalization process afforded French wives an opportunity to bargain with officials in ways their foreign-born husbands could only dream of.[45] The rhetorical strategies they employed in these encounters reveals the latitude afforded to French women who presented themselves in terms male officials could recognize—as patriotic wives and republican mothers issued from distinguished French families. Of course, at times, their participation in the process was simply necessary, and thus immigrant husbands came to depend on them. Eugénie Guyard, a native of the Côte d'Or region, was a concierge married to Swiss baker Guillaume Sandmeier. Because Sandmeier was illiterate, Guyard had to write to the minister of justice in 1924 on his behalf requesting his naturalization. Vouching for her foreign husband, she swore, "He is French at heart" and closed her missive with the following statement: "I remain at your disposal for all other verbal references regarding our patriotic French sentiments."[46] In this instance, Guyard's intervention was the product of the husband's illiteracy: the silent Sandmeier was given voice by his literate French wife. But her assurances about her foreign-born husband's patriotism was no doubt influenced by the doctrine of republican motherhood, demonstrating her faith that she had indeed instilled the proper patriotic virtues in her immigrant husband.

On other occasions, Frenchwomen intervened more forcefully on behalf of foreign husbands in ways that had less to do with republican motherhood and more to do with their rights as French women. Spaniard Esteban Hom, a Barcelona-born cabinetmaker, sought naturalization in 1929. The prefect wrote, "Good information . . . but is a bachelor and is without serious qualification [*titre*]." This was far from the final word on the subject once Esteban Hom's French fiancée got involved. As usual, French bureaucrats attempted to use their power to encourage Hom to marry as a condition of receiving

French naturalization. In fact, they decided "to temporarily close the file until proof of marriage." At his convocation a year later, Hom was still unmarried, but he had brought his French fiancée, Jeanne Autheval, with him to plead his case. Autheval stated the following to the officials who received them: "She would like for the postulant to be naturalized before marrying him. *It is the case that she* has children *from a previous union with a* Frenchman who do not wish for her to marry a foreigner. I told her that from the other side the Adm. envisages his naturalization upon the condition that he marries." Although this naturalization official tried admirably to exercise state power, Jeanne Autheval held her ground, demanding the naturalization of her Spanish fiancé before the marriage would be concluded.[47] Hom was, indeed, naturalized by January 1930. The absence of a record indicating either Jeanne Autheval's naturalization or reintegration would suggest that she triumphed over meddlesome bureaucrats. As middlewomen between foreign men and the French state, then, Frenchwomen acted as brokers for French nationality, withholding marriage until naturalization was won from the state.

Hom and Autheval were not alone, though at times it seemed as though some Frenchwomen opted to play foreign partners and the French state against one another, leveraging nationality and marriage deals to their advantage with both opponents. Like Autheval above, Angelina Josephine Thalus, the French *amie* of Belgian Florent Vanderkelen, insisted to authorities that she "will only marry a Frenchman." She had, in fact, previously been married to a certain Monsieur Thalus who had "abandoned" her and their twelve-year-old son years ago. Upon learning of her first husband's death in 1925, Angelina Josephine set the wheels in motion for both Vanderkelen's naturalization and their marriage. According to Vanderkelen, "Being free she would like to regularize our situation, but, wants to remain French." In fact, Vanderkelen claimed that his partner's wishes alone motivated him in his request, since he was fifty years old and saw no need for French nationality at his age.[48] Such examples, then, indicate that the French *amies* of foreign men may have been able to exert a certain power in dealings with both foreign husbands and the state in one fell swoop.

Frenchwomen's influence on officials was most indispensable during moments of national catastrophe, when national sentiment hardened against foreigners and officials sought to keep them at bay. When states moved to separate husbands from wives, fathers from children, conditions were ripe for a tug-of-war between Frenchwomen and state authorities. During the First World War, French Camille Mecking attempted repeatedly to leverage her gendered power as a Frenchwoman with the government in favor of her husband and her family. Theirs was a long odyssey to citizenship due to deep anti-German hostility during and after the war. It was not enough that her husband Guillaume Mecking was repeatedly refused French naturalization, but the entire Franco-German family of five were uprooted and sent to a camp in the Loiret on September 5, 1914. Immediately, Camille Mecking, too, mobilized.

Writing to the minister of justice, Camille Mecking identified herself as the daughter of a father from Bayonne and a mother from Paris. Next, she wrote that she married a German in 1905 "with the condition that he would naturalize [and become] French," a process he began in 1912 after the obligatory six years of residence in France. But with the commencement of the war, their naturalization plans came to an abrupt halt and the Mecking family found themselves in a "drôle de situation," as she put it. Officials evicted them from their home on rue Titon in Paris, sending them to "an unknown destination." "I found this type of proceeding very odd," Camille Mecking wrote, "since my husband has done everything in his power to become French," for instance, volunteering for the French war effort. Guillaume Mecking was then removed once more, his wife continued, this time to an "ursuline convent in Herlois . . . in a house that resembles a prison and where one finds people of all categories." She closed the letter recounting her family's wartime misfortunes with a plea that was at once impatient and imploring: "After having been subjected to every possible vexation, I seek recourse in the benevolent intervention of your Excellency to obtain satisfaction on the subject of naturalization and to deliver to me my husband as soon as possible."[49] She renewed her pleas again in 1916 after learning that foreigners fighting for France were awarded nationality.[50] In the end, anti-German feeling was too powerful to overcome, and it would be a decade before the Meckings—now a family of six—received naturalization. Nevertheless, Camille Mecking's insistent and persistent pleas indicated that she believed herself entitled to lobby fiercely on her husband's behalf.

While Frenchwomen themselves played a central role in bureaucratic dealings, occasionally their family members became embroiled in their private affairs. Indeed, a handful of foreign men claimed to pursue naturalization for the sole reason that the French families of their future French wives strongly encouraged it. Russian-born Meyer Rotbourg claimed in 1921 that his request was motivated by "the desire of the family of my future wife."[51] Marie Marcelle Antoinette Buttafoco's mother was rather more interventionist than Rotbourg's in-laws. In 1920, the formidable widow Buttafoco decided she had had enough of the minister of justice's refusal to grant her would-be Armenian son-in-law, Abel Yegparian, French naturalization, a "favor" he requested as early as 1914 when he enlisted in the Foreign Legion.

Underlining emphatically throughout her letter, she wrote, "For *five* years he has waited to marry [and] he would be very happy to be able to *fix a date*." She closed her stern missive with the following: "In the hope that you, Monsieur, would take into consideration *his voluntary military engagement*, rest assured that his naturalization is above all to permit *his marriage* with a Frenchwoman *who wishes to remain French* and who has been waiting for *five years*." Lest her copious underlining be lost on the official in question, a postscript dispelled any remaining uncertainty: "This Frenchwoman is my daughter and I have had the immense sorrow (glorious, it is true) of giving my only son and sole provider Antoine Buttafoco, military class of 1910, to France and beg your mercy if I must see, before dying myself, my task unfulfilled in leaving my daughter in the sad situation that the law makes for us?"[52] Needless to say, the emotion-laden letter was effective: Abel Yegparian was French and married to his French fiancée before the end of the year.

As Madame Buttafoco's letter demonstrates, the rhetorical strategies of Frenchwomen in their dealings with bureaucrats, ministers, and administrative personnel followed a few key patterns. Certainly, the invocation of male family members who had perished in the First World War was an effective strategy. But Frenchwomen shored up their credentials as worthy citizens of the French nation in other gendered ways, too. Take, for instance, Aline Kaplansky, Paris-born wife of Romanian furniture polisher Leiba Tiseler. The Tiselers began the naturalization process in July 1929, but it was Aline Kaplansky who took the lead in propelling the request forward, past administrative obstacles. She wrote to the minister of justice the very day she submitted the application. The letter documented her French family's many contributions to the glory of France. First, she referenced her brother, a decorated railway employee in the North for over forty years; her mother, winner of a gold medallion *de famille nombreuse* for birthing eleven children for the *patrie*; her five brothers who fought valiantly during World War I only to return home "frightfully wounded"; and finally her own Romanian husband, who also fought for France during the war and, like her brothers, returned "wounded in the face."[53] She thus located herself at the center of a nexus of honorable family relations in the hopes that it would accelerate her family's naturalization process.

When the summer of 1929 passed without news from the Chancellery, and facing the substantial sum of 250 francs to renew the couple's identity papers, Aline Tiseler took up her pen once more. Though just three months had passed, Tiseler adopted a decidedly less confident tack, choosing instead to portray herself as poor, sick, self-sacrificial, and in desperate need of help. Excusing herself for the impertinence of addressing a man of his stature,

Tiseler nevertheless sought to "explain my situation" to the minister of justice. In her words, "Being a mother of three young babies issued from consecutive pregnancies one after the other, I am quite weak, I rested several months at the hospital, [and] I have just left quite enfeebled." Thus did she both highlight her reproductive services to the French nation while making clear the ways in which those services had ravaged her body and threatened her physical health. After establishing her poor state, she explained, "My husband makes but very little [which is] insufficient to meet the needs of his family." Positioning herself as the indigent wife of a foreign man, she repeated her family's eminent credentials, invoking once more her status as a Frenchwoman issued from a long line of French progenitors who had all contributed mightily to the French nation. She included only one small variation, mentioning that she was an orphan (that her parents had passed away some five years previous was of little consequence in the first letter, apparently). Tiseler entreated the paternalist state to lend her succor, closing with one last supplication: "A mother of three children kneels down before you so as to obtain mercy from a dignified man for the needy." Her groveling paid off: the Tiseler family was naturalized within months.[54]

The invocation of reproductive services rendered and dedication to republican motherhood was a frequent rhetorical strategy that Frenchwomen employed in their letters to male officials. If Tiseler softened her tone in order to request paternalist intervention, other Frenchwomen did precisely the opposite, sharpening the pitch of their pleas when they seemed to fall on deaf ears. One need only remember Emilienne Goata, who wrote to officials in 1933 after her Romanian husband's naturalization requests had gone unheeded. Throughout her letter she invoked the possibility of her foreign-born husband's itinerance, the specter of her imminent abandonment, which, combined with the large family's depression-era impoverishment, would leave her with no other choice than to confer her children to Public Assistance. Whether her husband Nicolas Goata would truly have left the family and returned to Romania is debatable. But Emilienne Goata was no longer willing to await a bureaucratic decision on which the fate of her family hinged. She proved herself more than willing to resort to threats with the intent of provoking a reaction from bureaucrats.[55]

When words failed, some Frenchwomen engaged in even more confrontational tactics during the naturalization process, for instance, appearing at the steps of the Chancellery to bargain with officials in person. Deals were often struck over the cost of naturalization, which, while prohibitive, was nevertheless negotiable, especially for working-class families. Such haggling began when the foreigner in question offered one amount, and officials—

based on the family's income—parried with another. Occasionally, the naturalization process stalled at this crucial step. But more often foreigners either agreed to the sum proposed by officials, or counteroffered, usually with desperate invocations about the ill health of various breadwinning family members. Marie Levine, a French dressmaker born in Paris in 1894, was the wife of Russian-born Peissak and mother of their two Paris-born children. When the Bureau de Sceau demanded nearly eight hundred francs for the husband's naturalization, Madame Levine marched into the office of the Chancellor one June day in 1925. In the words of one official, "The wife of the postulant declared that the sum of 64 francs constituted the maximum pecuniary effort possible." Without bothering to claim either ill health or ill fortune, Levine simply refused officials' monetary request outright. Such an act of rebellion was rare indeed, and even more rarely recorded in naturalization dossiers. Receipts from her file indicate that the Levines paid 120 francs in the end. It was not a total victory for Marie Levine, but it was something.[56]

Of course, it was unique to Frenchwomen that they could bring their gendered power to bear so flagrantly in their dealings with state officials. Invoking, variously, threats, honor, reproductive service, and republican motherhood in supplication letters to male bureaucrats, intrepid French fiancées and wives showed remarkable resolve, standing up to authority and demanding that bureaucrats take their foreign husbands' requests seriously. While foreign men tended to tread softly, their French female spouses marched ferociously into bureaucratic battle, experimenting with rhetorical styles and narrative self-presentations that they believed would most effectively sway bureaucratic sympathies. They drew especially on their venerable French lineage, which, of course, immigrant men and women could not. However, they also capitalized on their reproductive services to the nation, which, immigrant men did, too, though perhaps with less success. Significantly, however, some Frenchwomen willfully cast themselves in a desperate, vulnerable, not to say pitiable light to get what they needed, and that gendered form of self-presentation and interaction achieved tangible results with middle-class male officials. This vulnerability vis-à-vis foreign-born partners, both presumed and performed, as well as the official male protection it would require, played an especially important role in French officials' dealings with nonwhite colonial men during and after the First World War.

The State, Race, and Intermarriage

Though the French state brought nearly a quarter of a million colonial and Chinese men to the metropole during the Great War to keep munitions factories operating briskly, it was not a decision taken lightly. The large-scale presence of nonwhite men on French soil posed certain challenges to employers and the state, among them racial conflict between French and colonial workingmen. To prevent discord that detracted from the war effort, the state created an elaborate disciplinary surveillance system to monitor colonial and Chinese men, the Colonial Labor Organization Service (SOTC). The SOTC grouped colonial workers into battalions arranged by nationality, assigned them employers, and made arrangements for their housing, transportation, and food provision. Although designed explicitly to prevent racial conflict (and, less explicitly, to derive maximum productivity from nonwhite labor), SOTC *contrôlleurs* were likewise tasked with the duty to police the morality of colonial workers. Frequently, contrôlleurs interpreted this mandate as a directive to discourage cross-cultural social and sexual encounters between nonwhite men and Frenchwomen, and especially between North African men and Frenchwomen. In fact, the very organization of colonial workers into army-style battalions was, in part, an effort to segregate them from their French female co-workers.[57] But for those colonial men who managed to evade the state's disciplinary reach, romantic possibility flourished and, indeed, interracial sexual encounters in the metropole between nonwhite men and Frenchwomen were more numerous than ever before during and immediately after the war.[58]

While interracial unions alarmed state officials greatly, and even prompted some to take preemptive measures to prevent their formation, they remained, in the end, powerless to stop them. Barring the introduction of harsh legal measures forbidding interracial unions categorically and punishing those in violation of the law as was the case in the United States and Nazi Germany during this period, not even the ever-watchful, disciplinary French imperial nation-state could eliminate interracial couplings altogether. On the contrary, debates surrounding the passage of the 1927 Law of Independent Nationality revealed an acute awareness of intermarriages concluded between Frenchwomen and colonial male subjects in France. Although proponents of the law claimed that it would protect Frenchwomen from "brutal" and "barbaric" colonial spouses, the very passage of the law is revealing.[59] The parliamentary debates surrounding the 1927 law indicated the (albeit, reluctant) willingness on the part of French jurists, parliamentarians, and lawmakers to extend the concept of marital assimilation "even" to colonial subjects, ranked at the bottom of the French civilizational hierarchy.

In spite of officials' fantasies of disaster over miscegenation on French soil, they were in reality faced with their own powerlessness. Unwilling to adopt the harsh measures required to put an end to interracial unions altogether, French colonial and state officials instead accepted and even sanctioned marriage between Frenchwomen and colonial men as a solution to the only other possible alternative—*illicit* unions between them. When confronted with interracial couples and, more importantly, their métis children, officials opted to shore up families in the name of familialism and out of a desire to protect both Frenchwomen and half-French children. Thus, in the twin interests of protecting children and alleviating the economic strain on single French mothers, ministers came to encourage marriage between Frenchwomen and colonial male subjects by the end of the war. Above all, officials refused to undermine families on French soil—even mixed-race families.

Official awareness of mixed-race unions on French soil first appeared as a result of close monitoring of colonial soldiers' and workers' correspondence via the Postal Control Service. Established in 1915, Postal Control served as a means of surveilling the colonial population on French soil, to oversee their mores and behaviors, and exercise corrective measures, if need be. Along the way, French contrôlleurs learned a great deal about how colonial soldiers experienced life in Europe. As historians have documented, colonial soldiers wrote frequently and with great feeling about their displeasure with the cold European climate, poor quality of food, meager rations, and low wages. Above all, however, they longed to return home.

Amid the sea of monotonous complaints, contrôlleurs soon caught wind of more titillating tidbits. North African, Madagascan, and Indochinese men wrote to friends and family in the empire often about their sexual escapades with white women while stationed on French soil. Consequently, contrôlleurs began to monitor colonial correspondence with ever-greater assiduity. While their disciplinary gaze was at first fixed on what they perceived as illicit sex and sexuality—the frequenting of prostitution, the sending of pornographic material, and especially the "rampant" trade in nude photographs depicting white women—contrôlleurs soon had bigger fish to fry.[60]

At first, contrôlleurs classified colonial subjects' "marriage plans" with Frenchwomen in the same category as "ephemeral relations," code for prostitution or sexual flings of a temporary variety.[61] They also monitored the development and progress of relationships between Frenchwomen and colonial workers and soldiers, determining a veritable "geography" to these liaisons, located mainly in the south of France, especially around Marseille where many colonial officers were stationed.[62] As early as November 1916, bureaucrats in the Postal Control office designated a portion of their monthly surveillance reports to "Franco-Annamite Liaisons," then later "Morality, Liaisons, and Marriage Proposals [*Projets de mariage*]," and finally

"Franco-Annamite Marriages."[63] The section consisted of a numerical summary of how many new liaisons between Frenchwomen and "Annamite" men appeared each month, followed by a number of racy excerpts from the correspondence of Indochinese men reporting home to their friends about their sexual exploits. Eventually, a section monitoring the growing number of pregnancies between Frenchwomen and "Annamite" men appeared, followed, at last, by a growing list of métis children. By late 1918, officials had located a whole community of these mixed-race children in the Saint-Médard region of southwestern France.[64]

Although initially classified as illicit interracial sex, bureaucrats could not deny mounting evidence that Indochinese soldiers had, on the contrary, formed very real attachments to French women and their families. As one bureaucrat and interpreter for Postal Control, Sergeant Lacombe, wrote to his superiors in 1917, "In addition to letters from women having voluntarily tied their existence to an indigene worker, there are also sometimes letters from parents or family members who indicate to what extent the affection of the entire family was acquired by the smooth-talker [*enjôleur*]."[65] Lacombe also noted that these women were not prostitutes from "particular milieus," but female correspondents "from the very best society."[66] In other words, what officials had originally considered illicit interracial unions began to look disconcertingly like licit familial bonds. This was all the more so when parents and family members of Frenchwomen gave sanction to these couples. And the French colonial administration in charge of monitoring colonial soldiers and workers were powerless to stop these unions. In the words of Lacombe, while they constituted "evidently grotesque liaisons, . . . we cannot prevent them."[67] While bureaucrats at the Postal Control, Ministry of War, and Ministry of Colonies experimented with possible methods of preventing the formation of such unions—proffering solutions that ranged from repatriation to imprisonment to "discretely" notifying the families of Frenchwomen who cavorted with colonial men—no programmatic solution was ultimately adopted.[68]

By the end of the war, many of these relationships deepened, and Indochinese soldiers grew more enmeshed with the families of their lovers and the local communities. In light of these developments, even the surly Lacombe came around to the notion that marriage was necessary, if not desirable, in order to guarantee the protection of French *filles-mères* and to stabilize newly formed, mixed-race families on French soil. As 1917 wore on, Lacombe's monthly reports betrayed a not-so-subtle shift in attitude, moving from horror at "evidently grotesques liaisons" to a solution-oriented approach for the rapidly increasing number of unwed mothers and illegitimate mixed-race children in certain regions of France. In a typical introductory passage, Lacombe began, "Each month furnishes new facts regarding the complex problem of liaisons between Frenchwomen and Indigenes," declaring, "Sincere or not, the attachment that some Annamites feel for our [female] compatriots appears quite great."

Lacombe then ruminated on the disastrous consequences of disintegrating these de facto, if not de jure, families rapidly forming on French soil: "When they leave their military encampment, entire families are plunged into desolation and when there is a pregnancy, [or] children, the most insistent steps are taken to obtain their return." In other words, either the Frenchwomen, their families, or both were deeply aggrieved to see colonial soldiers removed from their military camps, especially when they left in their wake unwed mothers and fatherless children. Consequently, Lacombe posed a rhetorical question to his superiors, "Should we not respect these free unions, above all those that are consecrated by a birth?" answering, "The protection that we owe to children [*l'enfance*] seems to plead in favor of this idea."[69] In other words, the crisis of depopulation afflicting the Third Republic compelled state officials to act in the best interest of children—even mixed-race children. And if marriage between Frenchwomen and colonial male subjects provided the best means of achieving a stable family life for those children, then so be it.

Of course, racial (if not racist) considerations played their part in Lacombe's thinking. "One knows the importance of blood connections in the country of Annam," he stated, explaining, "The father is not accustomed to disowning his child, [because] he is too frightened of the posthumous consequences that it could have, for his soul, the brutal abandonment of the being that he has procreated, above all if it is a son." In other words, Lacombe suggested, quite remarkably, that the French state capitalize on this cultural belief system by tying colonial fathers irrevocably to their métis children. But on the whole, such culturalist reflections were eclipsed by Lacombe's fixation on the fates of both métis children and their unwed French mothers. "In terms of the unfortunate filles-mères, their situation finds itself always aggravated by the departure of he who should help them," he claimed, adding, "Their moral distress is horrifying." In other words, mandating or even permitting Indochinese men to leave was actually the greater of two evils: not only did his absence destroy would-be families, but it left behind French women and half-French children deprived of a much-needed male breadwinner.

Having thus couched his reflections in a paternalist, protectionist language, Lacombe drove his point home: "Should we not anticipate then in certain instances the regularization of the union by marriage?" He supported this bold assertion by reasoning, "Assimilation occurs so much from one day to the next, that the step [of marriage] could be easily overcome by a great number of indigenes, if their stay in France was prolonged by long months."[70] Marriage to a Frenchwoman, in other words, would accomplish the messy business of assimilation. In essence, then, marriage really solved three interrelated problems at once: it provided women with breadwinners, it provisioned children with fathers, and it sufficiently assimilated even colonial men.

More than one lone bureaucrat found this line of reasoning appealing. In fact, Lacombe's thinking appeared in official decision-making circles after the war. With the end of the Great War, the number of interracial unions between Frenchwomen and colonial soldiers did not abate. As even Lacombe remarked, with uncharacteristic wit, "From the point of view of liaisons, many leave behind these unfortunate women who pursue them, out of love or out of hatred."[71] These scores of Frenchwomen, jilted and abandoned, according to Lacombe, prompted further conversation on the matter of marriage among French governmental ministers. Although the majority of colonial workers and soldiers were rapidly repatriated after the war, officials were at last confronted with the dilemma Lacombe and other low-level bureaucrats in the Postal Control had witnessed throughout the war. Simply put, should the French state repatriate colonial subjects who had established *foyers*, fathered children, and "liaised" with Frenchwomen out of a commitment to "racial hygiene"? If the experience during the war was any indication, Frenchwomen and their families would simply not accept the repatriation of colonial soldiers who had become, if not husbands, at least fathers, partners, and accepted members of the family and local community. While there were isolated cases of repatriation and even imprisonment of colonial subjects, on the whole, officials adopted another plan of action.

In 1919, a small interministerial debate erupted over the situation of colonial soldiers and workingmen who had established relationships with Frenchwomen or had children with them. Clemenceau, minister of war at the time, declared via a confidential circular dated April 4 that all colonial workers and soldiers were to be immediately repatriated to their countries of origin according to the "delays fixed by their engagement contract." However, there would be four exceptions to this rule:

1. If they wish to improve their knowledge of a specialized industry necessary in their colony of origin.
2. If they wish to engage in higher education for which they are recognized as being sufficiently prepared.

3. *If they are legitimately married to a Frenchwoman.*
4. *If they are fathers of a child born or about to be born of a regular or irregular union with a French woman.*[72]

If colonial soldiers and subjects fell into one or both of the latter two categories, Clemenceau further stipulated that they had to present a certificate of approval from the mayor of their canton "about the regular or irregular unions that the indigene would have contracted or would propose to contract with a French woman, the children born or conceived in these unions, the social or familial situation and the morality of the woman, [and] the indigene's relations with the local population." Clemenceau demanded absolute secrecy about these stipulations to the "indigenes," perhaps to limit the number of mixed households and unions established out of convenience.[73] Yet, despite the secrecy surrounding the circular, the requirement of a mayoral certificate, and even the further amendment that colonial subjects would have to provide proof of "sufficient" financial resources in order to stay, the spirit of the measure was nevertheless clear: those colonial male subjects who married or established families in France would be absorbed into the French nation.[74] This logic was applied to foreign-born men of all nationalities a decade and a half later as the state sought to off-load dead social weight—that is, nonreproductive foreign bachelors.[75]

There was some initial blowback, of course. That same month, Josselme, an interpreter and the head of the Postal Control for colonial workers from Indochina and Madagascar, fiercely disagreed with the course adopted by the administration. "The *confidential* circular concerning Franco-Annamite marriage is welcomed with joy," he reported dismally, explaining that "the correspondents announce the great ease of unions and the Indochinese are very happy." He quoted from one such letter, written by Sergeant Hue posted in Saint-Auban, who wrote jubilantly, "The Minister has arrived at a confidential decision 28.932 5/8 concerning the marriages between Frenchwomen and Annamites, [and] they are letting us take a wife, it is no longer forbidden."[76] Josselme concluded that the administrative decision would encourage a great many Indochinese workers and soldiers to remain in France now that the war was over. He even opined that, with the easing of restrictions, colonial subjects would seek to form new attachments with Frenchwomen, then "marriages will follow, or at the very least cohabitation."[77] He was not alone in his disappointment.

In June 1919, the governor-general of Indochina, Maurice Antoine François Montguillot, similarly expressed alarm at Clemenceau's circular. He complained to the minister of colonies that "indigenes" who formed relationships with Frenchwomen may very well have wives and children back in their home country. Montguillot claimed that immoral colonial subjects would abuse these stipulations in order to flee their spousal and paternal responsibilities back home, in the empire: "It could be the case in effect, that the postulant while being the father of a child borne or about to be borne of a regular union with a French woman already has one or several legitimate wives in the Colony and one or several indigenous children." Montguillot proposed a solution whereby indigenes with French wives or "concubines" in the metropole would first have to obtain a notarized letter from the minister of the colonies of their respective country attesting to their bachelor status. Thus, Montguillot sought to frame his opposition to the bill as a question of ensuring the morality of the indigene in question for, "the aforementioned interministerial circular would consecrate the definitive abandonment by indigenes of their legitimate families and would render definitive an absolutely immoral situation."[78]

In this manner, we see a stunning counterexample to officials who favored French over foreign wives and children in the case of European men like Romanian Nicolas Goata: such murky transnational marital and familial situations were less tolerable where colonial men were concerned. Despite Montguillot's ethical posturing, in the end, he proposed shoring up colonial families simply to prevent interracial unions from taking root in France. Months later, the minister of colonies agreed to the wisdom of Montguillot's logic, proposing to extend a formal investigation into the "familial backgrounds" of all colonial subjects, to ensure that the French state did not inadvertently "consecrate an immoral union."[79] Again, the possible "abandonment" of foreign wives and families had not entered the official calculus where European men were concerned. Foreign attachments of this variety were, however, a deal breaker for colonial men wishing to marry white French brides and put down roots in France.

It was not only the desire to provide material support to half-French children and unwed French mothers that motivated ministers to adopt intermarriage as a solution. Racist fears of what would become of Frenchwomen whisked away to the furthest corners of the empire, without the protection that marriage afforded them, also played their part. For this reason alone, officials permitted Algerian Barka Ould Matala—married to a Frenchwoman during the war—to remain in France thereafter. Essentially, ministers felt compelled to naturalize him lest they condemn his wife, their compatriot, to a more horrible fate. Taking Matala's union into consideration, the minister of colonies reflected in August 1919, "I esteem, in effect, that those indigenes whom we have allowed to contract marriage with Frenchwomen, should not return to their colony of origin, and that [should persist] as long as the union shall last." He followed his statement with the following: "It would be disastrous, in my opinion, to see those of our compatriots who, ill-informed or abused, have married indigenes, called to endure a terrible life, in a necessarily hostile milieu, to finish almost inevitably, in the lowest prostitution."[80] Such arguments would reappear throughout the decade, surfacing notably in debates regarding the 1927 passage of the Law of Independent Nationality.[81] In short, even those officials most opposed to the intermarriage of Frenchwomen and colonial men believed that it was ultimately better for colonial subjects to marry their "concubines" and remain in France than to permit illicit unions between them that exposed Frenchwomen to even greater danger (whether that danger was real or imagined, however, is debatable). For the sake of Frenchwomen, then, marriage was the best option.

The results of this informal intermarriage policy pertaining to colonial men and Frenchwomen rippled through the 1920s, taking on new dimensions as conditions on the ground changed.[82] And by all accounts, the circular did indeed have an impact. In a June 1920 report, Josselme wrote suggestively, "The month of May has been fecund in liaisons," adding, "To that effect I believe it necessary to call the attention of the Central Administration to the fact that many of the liberation requests [of colonial soldiers] in France are inspired by feminine reasons."[83] According to Josselme, Indochinese soldiers continued to rejoice at their ability to marry Frenchwomen years later. In November 1923, officer Viên stationed in Grasse wrote to his friend Vo Hoang Phát, "If one wants to be happy one only has to marry a Frenchwomen," though Viên added the major caveat that doing so required a lifelong separation from one's homeland.[84]

Another interpreter of the Postal Control, Jolin, discovered similar sentiments among Indochinese soldiers in his department between 1923 and 1925, during the French occupation of the Ruhr Valley in Germany. There, as before in France, Indochinese soldiers experienced a great deal of "luck" with women—this time with German women. As before, they boasted plenty about loose German women, whom they described as "prettier than French girls."[85] Although they realized that many German women were in dire straits due to the staggering hyperinflation afflicting the country, they rejoiced in the sexual opportunities this allotted them: German women desperate for food and supplies engaged in prostitution in order to survive. Some soldiers even likened the situation of these German women to that of Indochinese women who, in search of an economic savior, became concubines of Frenchmen in the empire. In the colonial context, the term *concubine* bore a more sexual and illicit connotation than it did in the metropole, where, as we have seen, it denoted merely informal domestic arrangements that approximated conjugal households. In the words of one Indochinese soldier, "German women, in the manner of Annamite women who marry Frenchmen to have a better life, take Annamites as their lovers so that they have something to eat."[86] This astonishing passage revealed a stark role reversal on metropolitan soil, inverting both race and gender relations to be found in the empire.

More problematically, from Jolin's perspective anyway, "considerations of a feminine order" destabilized the sexual, racial, and international order in the Rhineland. "The question of liaisons with German women and the births which follow may be causes of attachment that the Governor-General of Indochina would have an interest in avoiding if possible." Moreover, he claimed that sexual liaisons between French colonial subjects and German women eroded at the former's sense of duty and obligation for the *patrie*. Instead, it replaced colonial soldiers' reverence for France with a false admiration of the German *volk*, by way of the German woman. Jolin even believed that Germany could manipulate the affections of Indochinese men through German women and thus turn these colonial soldiers against the French.[87] For his own part, Josselme reminded French administrators, "The white woman exercises over Asiatics a great attraction" and warned that "the Indochinese [man] may be drawn by diverse contingencies and come to establish themselves in Germany just as so many established themselves in France after the war."[88] And both Jolin and Josselme were right: just as "Franco-Annamite" households appeared in France during and after World War I, so too did "Germano-Annamite" households develop along the Franco-German border.[89]

In fact, the sexual liaisons between colonial soldiers and German women provide one last illustrative example of the power of the marital assimilation model for French bureaucrats. In 1924, one Annamite soldier wrote home to a friend that, indeed, some of the colonial men preferred German women to Frenchwomen for reasons both personal and political. Although he found German women "elegant," "polite" and "prettier than the girls in France," he and his friends were interested in only transitory amusements with them: "We think that with the German girls we can have fun because, when they become pregnant we are not obliged to marry them; whereas with the young French girls who might accidentally find themselves in the same situation, we would be obliged to marry them." He concluded by reasoning, "We would be thus condemned to remain in Europe our whole lives taking care of them."[90] In the hierarchy of desirability, then, this Indochinese soldier placed German women above French women because, should they become pregnant, soldiers were off the hook. On the contrary, if the same situation arose with a Frenchwoman, colonial officials would most certainly force them to marry and thus condemn them to a miserable fate in Europe.

Although bureaucrats complained mightily about the racial unsoundness of interracial unions between Frenchwomen and colonial men, eventually they came to consider marriage an adequate solution to the problem of unwed pregnancy, fatherless children, and poor single mothers. The iron grip of colonial authorities over colonial subjects in the metropole in fact worked to enforce marriage rather than prevent it. Well before the adoption of the Law of Independent Nationality in 1927, officials on the ground had made their peace with marriage as the solution to the "problem" of mixed-race intimacy on French soil. In other words, even in the colonialists' worst nightmare, marriage still emerged as a solution to secure the safety of Frenchwomen, to provide fathers for métis children, and to perhaps in time assimilate "even" the colonial subject into the French nation via marriage and the French family.

Bureaucrats in institutional settings at local, municipal, and national levels emerged as gatekeepers to the French nation between the wars. In their various dealings with immigrants and colonial subjects, officials shored up the institution of marriage as they expanded the boundaries of the French national community progressively outward. They enforced marriage among naturalizing bachelors, policing heterosexual masculinity and employing "carrot and stick" tactics when necessary; and they imposed marriage on colonial male subjects who had begun romantic and sexual relationships with Frenchwomen, especially when those relationships yielded children. Marriage was not only a means to fix mobile foreign-born men and contain their unstable sexuality; it was also a means of provisioning unwed French mothers and their children with breadwinners, even at the relative "expense" of shoring up mixed-race families on French soil. In so doing, bureaucrats occasionally privileged French wives and families over foreign wives and families, at least where European husbands and fathers were concerned. Try as they might to refuse to marry (and try many certainly did), foreign-born men seeking naturalization were ultimately at the mercy of marriage-minded bureaucrats, and colonial subjects even more so.

Through these strategies, bureaucrats successfully sculpted the body politic, molding foreign-born men and French and foreign women into conjugal families before allowing them to gain entry into the French national community. This conjugal politics forwarded by bureaucrats was just one manifestation of the disciplinary paternalism affecting men, and foreign-born men more specifically, in the context of the French depopulation crisis. But it also depended on a supportive orientation toward those Frenchwomen who sought to join their fates with those of foreign-born men. After all, naturalization offered Frenchwomen an opportunity to bargain with bureaucrats, as well, sometimes positioning the state and their immigrant husbands against one another in order to get what they wanted. In this, they turned French officials' dedication to protecting patriotic wives and republican mothers to their advantage, using heterosexual femininity and its pillars—marriage and motherhood—to maximum advantage in the process. Whether and to what extent they exaggerated their despair is less relevant than the fact that state officials were inclined to hear them out and that these women themselves knew this to be true. While immigrants—men or women—rarely stated so forthrightly and so forcefully what they desired from officials, the state's familialist orientation and officials' paternalist attitudes toward women did open up one avenue for foreign-born women who could, like Frenchwomen, position themselves as the very wives and mothers the state increasingly yearned to protect and provide for. Like Frenchwomen, many immigrant women would also learn to use the paternalist orientation of the state to their advantage in dealings with both officials and immigrant husbands.

CHAPTER 3

Wives, Wages, and Regulating Breadwinners

In Yolanda Foldes's 1937 novel about a Hungarian family in interwar Paris, the youngest of the family, Klari Barabas, inadvertently stumbles into the middle of a lovers' quarrel involving Greek Christos, a friend of the family, and his French wife. "The Frenchwoman is pushing me to my grave," complains Christos of his wife's nagging to find work. But "the Frenchwoman" complains at great length, too:

> You don't know what it is like to marry a foreigner, Mademoiselle Barabas. . . . You don't know a foreign man until you have lived with him. Foreign men are bizarre, Mademoiselle, they have their heartaches that one does not understand, and that gnaw at them. Christos is like that. . . . If I leave him be, he will stare in front of himself all day long, gloomily, and he would never work. . . . So, tell me, mademoiselle, can someone accept such a thing? When I tell him to go to work, he grows angry with me. But what, one cannot die of hunger, after all.[1]

Unable to deal with the complexities of adult life, young Klari hurries away, concluding, "This visit taught her something that she would remember . . . that life is hard, not only for a foreigner, but also for the being who associates with one of the uprooted."

As the misfortunes of fictional Christos and his French wife suggest, men's work, missing wages, and marital discord were indeed intimately intertwined in the mixed and immigrant working-class households sprouting up throughout France after the Great War. Because of the twin middle-class ideals of the male breadwinner and the *femme au foyer* that governed early twentieth-century economic and social life, women in France, whether French or foreign, were often unable to find and keep well-paying work allowing them to feed their families.[2] Instead, they and their children relied on the strong and steady wages that men alone were capable of procuring. Consequently, by the early twentieth century, marriage had become the most reliable legal means of securing access to a male breadwinner and his wages, especially in the event of the union's demise. Should a marriage dissolve, divorced and separated wives with children to care for had a variety of legal means at their disposal to secure *pensions alimentaires*. These alimentary pensions were to be paid regularly by estranged husbands, and officials scrupulously enforced these laws where immigrant husbands were concerned, often at the behest of French and foreign wives themselves. Thus, while French employers, naturalization officials, and colonial administrators attempted to use marriage to force immigrant men to participate in the *patrie* as upstanding husband-citizens, the French and foreign women who tied their fates to the "uprooted" had their own reasons to insist on it, as well.

Although marriage and divorce laws provided indispensable financial assistance to wives and mothers, an array of antidesertion legislation had also evolved over the late nineteenth and early twentieth centuries in recognition of other marriagelike formations, particularly those that produced children. This variety of family law—above all, *recherches de paternité*, or paternity suits—aimed to protect women from so-called seducers, would-be betrayers, and alleged abandoners while also providing for the children born of these broken and ephemeral unions.[3] Not only did immigrant wives and mothers learn how to use these legal tools; many grew adept at navigating the multifaceted French state and its many resources, often with the express aid of officials themselves. In this, male officials in several corners of the government demonstrated once more the lengths they would go to police foreign-born men who, it was believed, were only too willing to neglect their marital and familial obligations. Officials also demonstrated just how far they would bend the system in favor of wives and mothers, whether French or foreign-born.

This chapter explores the lives of working-class French and foreign men and women residing in Paris who joined their fates to one another. Whether immigrant men were swept away by war, revolution, economic venture, or extramarital adventure, the French and foreign women they left behind would go to great lengths to find them, bringing the policing power of French and foreign states to bear, if need be. In so doing, they took advantage of the state's increasing propensity to police foreign male mobility as well as foreign male sexual morality and marital probity. As they worked to track down men they described as fickle lovers, abusive amis, and hard-hearted husbands, both French and immigrant women found allies in middle-class male officials who peopled the growing policing apparatus of the state, availing themselves of its paternalist inclination to protect "vulnerable women" and its colonialist inclination to protect white Frenchwomen, especially. French and immigrant women's style of self-presentation also drew on raced and gendered categories that lay at the heart of regulatory systems in modern France. That is, local police officials charged with applying family law and gendered social policy as well as enforcing law and order were primed to "see" in immigrant husbands a yearning for flight, to perceive in colonial male subjects a propensity for sexual violence. Mixing fact and fiction, just as the law and its officials encouraged them to do, French and foreign women showed themselves quite proficient at presenting themselves as in need of paternalist intervention and at using the state to regulate former and future breadwinners, alike.

Of Wives and Wages

While in the preindustrial period, married women throughout Europe could combine market-oriented activities and domestic work, the arrival of industrialization precluded such easy reconciliations. Although Frenchwomen, both married and single, worked at higher rates in France than elsewhere in modern Europe, they dropped to the lower rungs of the occupational ladder during the era of industrial transition.[4] This trend accentuated during and after World War I, when women who were first called to munitions and wartime factories found themselves pushed out of the workforce after the war to make room for returning veterans. Those women who remained active in the labor force endured the contraction of employment opportunities, the deskilling of their occupational sectors, and concomitant pay cuts and job insecurity.[5] The Great Depression drove home the gendered economic lessons of the era—namely, that work was a male prerogative. Employers, state officials, politicians, and benevolent bourgeoises from across the political spectrum appealed to workingwomen to yield their jobs to men, and above all for married women to return to the *foyer* where they supposedly belonged. There, the female obligations of childbearing and child-rearing took precedence and the nation depended on them to carry out the duties of republican motherhood.[6]

Throughout the 1930s, the French state also enacted social policies that propagated the male breadwinner ideal, though perhaps less insistently than their British counterparts.[7] Above all, the state linked entitlements to the employment status of male heads of household, incorporating assumptions about women's presumed dependence on men in the process. These were the same groups that supported unwaged mothers' allowances and argued for the primacy of women's maternal roles throughout the 1920s.[8] As a result, during the interwar decades, French and foreign women found marriage and marriagelike household formations increasingly necessary to support themselves financially. While of course many wives had little choice but to work considering the economic realities of their working-class lives, their wages were typically low, unstable, and largely supplemental to the household income. By contrast, the male wage—heftier and more stable—became central to the survival of working-class households.

In Paris, mixed and immigrant households that relied on a foreign breadwinner were no exception to this general trend in the history of marriage, work, and women in France and elsewhere.[9] Of course, there were specificities to their situation. The French wives of foreign men were more likely than immigrant wives to work, and they were more likely to work outside of the home, at that.[10] But even among those immigrant wives who did not work, husbands' expectations about wives' proper place could take priority over the economic realities of the household. Although Spanish Manuela Martinez worked in Spain before her migration to Paris in 1928, her husband Vicente grew tired of her occupational distractions, claiming that she did not spend enough time keeping house and caring for their five-year-old son. Though she worked for a time selling oranges and bananas at a stall in the center of Paris, Vicente eventually forbade her to work, citing "the negligence and disorder" of their household as the primary cause. Instead, he demanded that Manuela, "devote herself uniquely to her [household] interior and to her child."[11] When confronted about her supposed negligence and the household's reputed disorder, Manuela Martinez justified herself thusly: "I was always worried about keeping my house in order. But at one time, we needed money, and I went to sell oranges at the door of a café. That is what explains why, sometimes, everything was not perfectly in order in my home."[12] In fact, the economic pressures on the household were so great in 1931 that, unbeknownst to her husband, she started taking in laundry from the neighborhood to supplement the household's income.[13] That she hid her economic activity from her husband underscores that some husbands saw the realm of work as their unique prerogative in the household, an attitude supported by the wider economic, social, and political climate.

FIGURE 3.1. A photograph of Polish-born Gendel Scher who became Russian after marrying Simon Mass in 1907. In 1922, when the photograph was taken, she had lived in Paris for five years with her husband, a woodworker, as well as her three children. Gendel Mass née Scher, Application de carte d'identité, March 2, 1922, in Simon Mass and Gendel née Scher, I/A 138, Archives de la Préfecture de la Police.

If husbands declared waged work their province, some French and foreign wives nursed financial expectations of what husbands ought to provide. Naturally, these expectations were most visible when they were not met. Rachel Lewinsky, a Pole, rebuffed a marriage proposition from compatriot Jean Swiderski whose breadwinning potential she seriously doubted. Lewinsky explained, "Since he did not want to give me money and since I am not the kind of woman who provides for a man [*entretenir un homme*], I threw him out."[14] When marital discord reached a fevered—not to say murderous—pitch, friends, neighbors, and community members often cited husbands' failures to financially provide for their wives and children as a primary irritant in the relationship. It was well-known by her intimate acquaintances on Cité Industrielle in Sainte Marguerite that Emilia Violina's Italian husband beat her for failing to use precious household resources like coal sparingly. Neighbor women considered Violina stingy, not "frugal" as he was described in official reports. Jacques Violina told a different story, however, claiming that his Luxemburg-born wife beat him because "she reproached me for not giving her enough money."[15] Alice Plourde, too, testified that her friend Suzanne Genevrier complained often of her Algerian husband's miserliness; for his own part, Arezki Slimani found fault with a wife who "spent all my savings and then wanted to leave me."[16] While political and economic pressures worked to increase wives' dependencies on husbands, wives too came to have certain financial expectations of husbands on whom they relied to maintain and replenish household coffers.

The material importance of the male income was laid bare in cases of adultery, when wives less often expressed a sense of sexual or emotional betrayal, but rather immense frustration and resentment at the loss of wages. This was as true for French as for immigrant wives. When Greek confectioner David Botton left his French wife and their four children to take up with his mistress, Yvonne Botton worked hard to remain in close contact with him in order to access his wages. Her estimate of the financial loss his absence inflicted on the household was quite specific: "At the start of our marriage, he gave me seventy francs a day to buy clothes for the children or fix their shoes . . . since meeting Mademoiselle Malfatti, he will not give me more than thirty francs a day and he has innumerable difficulties participating in the maintenance of the children." Rather than spend his wages providing for his legitimate family, Yvonne Botton claimed that her adulterous husband spent his money on his new mistress.[17] A friend of a brother-in-law summarized Botton's financial situation drily: "It is certain that with a wife, four children, and a mistress, Botton has monetary needs."[18]

When Italian Henri Ferrari left his family for a French mistress, his wife, Emilie, needled him incessantly for financial help, even enlisting the aid of his boss in her campaign to extract money from the wayward spouse.[19] His failure to send a portion of his wages back to the wife and children he left behind was the substance of the complaint Emilie's mother, the widow Dimascio, sent to police officials. Specifically, she reproached Henri, "who had never sent a *centime* to support his four small innocent children."[20] Indeed, wives considered the disappearance of male wages a sure sign that funny business was afoot. Although Russian Antonine Smaguine did not know for sure that her husband was cheating on her, she had begun to have her suspicions "since for three months he did not give me money for the household." He left her for his French mistress a few months later, in December 1930.[21] Thus, wives experienced extramarital affairs not merely as emotional strains on the family, but primarily as financial burdens on the household.

In households organized around an immigrant male breadwinner, the fragile health of these men also posed an ever-present threat to the financial security of the entire family. Illness and death impinged on mixed and immigrant working-class households to a perhaps greater degree than French households. After all, throughout the interwar decades, immigrant men increasingly worked in the most unhealthful industries (for instance, chemical and metallurgical plants and refineries) and the most arduous trades (construction, agriculture), which French workingmen had deserted.[22] Moreover, as we will see in further chapters, immigrant families overall lived in spaces more cramped and crowded than their French counterparts, spaces in which diseases bred and claimed victims with relative ease. While there were significantly more female widows than male widowers in France generally at the start of the twentieth century, the immigrant wives of foreign men were likely more impacted by the premature death of spouses than other segments of the population. In 1926, French statisticians noted that immigrant widows were responsible for the largest families in France, proportionately speaking, an outcome that could only result from the premature death or unexplained disappearance of a breadwinning husband.[23]

Of course, husbands suffered from the illness and death of wives, too. Considering the gendered division of household labor, though, a wife's illness or death deprived him of childcare provider, cook, seamstress, maid, laundress. When Michel Polycar's wife died of pneumonia three years after the Turkish family's arrival in Paris, he moved quickly to fill her position. After trying and failing to woo his niece, he set his sights on a Turkish neighbor and wed her six months later. According to social workers investigating familial discord between the new stepmother and her three stepsons, "Monsieur Polycar only considers his second wife as a domestic servant charged with household responsibilities."[24] The judgment might seem unduly harsh were it not for the fact that the new Madame Polycar concurred with their assessment.[25] While the death of a wife incurred certain inconveniences, it did not imperil the husband's livelihood in quite the same way as the death of a husband imperiled the wife he left behind.[26] In other words, the death, illness, or absence of wives and husbands impacted households in materially different ways.

The onset of the Great Depression only exacerbated the fragility of working-class households, especially those dependent on immigrant male breadwinners. As the Depression deepened, the French state enacted restrictive measures to protect native labor against the immigrant workforce. Consequently, employers began to dismiss immigrant employees at a rapid pace.[27] Foreign workingmen, especially bachelors, were repatriated.[28] By contrast, women's work was not as severely impacted, in part because women's jobs were already so deskilled and low paying.[29] In mixed and immigrant households of Paris, the French and foreign wives of out-of-work foreign men increasingly went to work to support children who depended on them and husbands who would have to do so as well. When Polish Dimitri Wandiak lost his job as an electrician in 1932, his wife, Anne Bugajsi, was forced to find regular employment in France for the first time. But mindsets do not change overnight, even if markets do. From the start, Bugajsi made it very well known both to her spouse and all her intimate acquaintances at the clothing workshop where she found employment that she resented supporting him. According to the concierge of her building, "In the month of June 1932, the wife left him because he no longer worked and she did not want to continue feeding him."[30]

With foreign husbands down on their luck, French and foreign wives thus emerged as the fragile breadwinners of depression-era mixed and immigrant working-class households. But just as some wives struggled to adjust to their new role, so too did husbands experience difficulty coming to terms with the sudden role reversal. In certain instances, the inversion of gender roles at home proved a considerable source of shame for them. Amerigo Brunetti, an Italian sculptor, allowed himself to be baited by a compatriot named Bertolucci, "who said he [Brunetti] had not been happy since he lost his job and since his wife had to provide for him." Deeply offended, Brunetti responded, "You know nothing, young man, of how I have worked in my life and you do not have the right to speak about my wife like that." A scuffle between the men ensued shortly thereafter at the *débit* on rue Hallé in the 14th arrondissement.[31] In February 1939, Algerian Mohamed Salah also beat and killed his prosperous cousin who dared to mock his unemployment in front of a room full of acquaintances at a restaurant in the 18th arrondissement.[32]

Of course, in the midst of a Depression, neither French nor immigrant wives found easy, stable employment. By and large, they simply increased the frequency of their participation in unstable, sporadic economic pursuits to make ends meet. Above all, immigrant women found themselves cleaning houses in the neighborhoods. When Italian Jean Cauda lost his job as a mechanic, his wife was suddenly thrust into the job market. Tellingly, officials registered surprise at the lack of marital discord given the absence of a male wage, indicating how tethered the two factors were even in the official mind. According to a stunned Police Inspector Lasigne, "Despite his unemployment, the household seems to get by without apparent difficulty, probably thanks to the aid furnished by unemployment funds and the salary of Madame Cauda, employed in cleaning houses in the neighborhood."[33]

In worst-case scenarios, married immigrant women might engage in prostitution to support husbands and families in the 1930s. For instance, when Polish Jean Schwiderski, an out-of-work baker, fell on hard times, he pimped out his wife, Fajga, to support the household. For a brief time, he even sent her to work at a *maison de tolérance* in Tunis, collecting her wages from Paris.[34] But this is an admittedly extreme example. What is important is the way in which macrolevel shifts in the economy initiated subtle and not-so-subtle shifts in gender relations between spouses. While French and foreign women of mixed and immigrant households may have found themselves increasingly responsible for providing for their households, the larger political and economic climate made it impossible for them to match the earning potential of men. Working wives and mothers were poor substitutes for male breadwinners, especially immigrant male breadwinners.

War, too, swept husbands away, sometimes temporarily, sometimes permanently. Countless immigrant women such as, for instance, Russian Rachel Goichman had lived in France well before 1914 and, like French wives, were widowed by the war their husbands fought on behalf of France.[35] Still others found themselves "abandoned" by husbands called away by business or pleasure—or both. This was the case for Sophie Malkine, a native of Odessa, Russia, whose husband, an employee at Standard Oil in Bakar, had some years earlier left for the United States on business. She was not to hear from him again, thus it fell to her to support her mother, her brother, and her two Paris-born sons.[36] Others may have instead heeded the siren song of adventure, which had the same effect of removing the all-important breadwinner from mixed and immigrant households altogether. Although the dissolution of households removed the male wage, as long as legitimate husbands could be located, a breadwinner could in fact be won.

Locating Men: Women Using Consular and Colonial Authorities

A fluid sexual atmosphere had long reigned in the *quartiers populaires* of Paris, but for women these liaisons always carried with them the potential for grave danger. From sexual violence to the possibility of pregnancy, the risks of amorous encounter were especially great for single migrant women from the countryside without the benefit of male kinfolk to preserve their honor and thus to whom the men they slept with owed nothing. During the interwar decades, sexual dalliances between French and immigrant women, on the one hand, and foreign men, on the other, only heightened the dangers of "abandonment" since many immigrant men were indeed here today, gone tomorrow. Moreover, as an immigrant, he was unknown to friends, family, and the wider community, who traditionally brought community standards to bear on "seducing" parties by forcing marriage in the case of pregnancy.[37]

Indeed, the image of the foreign man who seduced women with abandon then left them high and dry once pregnant became something of a trope for maternalist social service organizations in the capital during the interwar period. Germaine Besnard de Quelen, founder and director of the League for the Protection of Abandoned Mothers (LPAM), spun one such tale to her audience of social workers and supporters in 1937: a young girl from the provinces met "a handsome foreigner" who "seduced her with his promises." Finding herself pregnant and abandoned, she suffered further disgrace when her parents disowned her. Like other single mothers that Besnard de Quelen imagined, "She wandered, aimlessly, this immense and devouring Paris that she knew not, [when,] directly in front of her: she arrives at the Seine." There, in her bleakest moment, she contemplated suicide.[38]

The trope of the *fille séduite* throwing herself into the Seine to end her misery was well-known to nineteenth-century Parisians.[39] The image of the fille séduite remained alive and well during the interwar years. In Eugène Dabit's *Hôtel du Nord*, set in a seedy hotel of Paris populaire in the 1920s, several such women make a pitiable appearance—most notably, Renée, a sweet country bumpkin who takes up with the louse Trimault once arrived in Paris. The residents of the hotel watch as the young Renée falls under Trimault's spell, only to find herself abandoned when he leaves her pregnant. Mere pages later, two more filles séduites—one of the Pellevoisin sisters and the *bonne* Jeanne, both from the provinces—find themselves in similar predicaments. As Renée puts it, with a pathos verging on pathetic, "La vie à deux use le coeur d'un homme [Life together wears out a man's heart]."[40]

Despite such harrowing tales, certain women proved themselves less despairing and more deft when they found themselves in similar situations. And there were many such women. Of the thousands of unmarried and pregnant Frenchwomen who found solace and sanctuary at the LPAM during the interwar years, several singled out foreign men as the offending parties. For instance, Suzanne Balivet, a seventeen-year-old housemaid abandoned by her Serbian fiancé. Although he "led her to believe that he was happy with his impending paternity," he left without a word after she presented him to her mother who lived just outside of Paris, in Seine-et-Oise.[41] Isaline Bron, a thirty-four-year-old housemaid also living in the 16th arrondissement, admitted with "much chagrin" that she had loaned her Armenian lover more than five thousand francs for his naturalization with the expectation that he would marry her. She was sorely disappointed when he disappeared from their home only a few weeks later.[42] In the neighborhood of Sainte Marguerite, French Marie Anne Léontine Goasdaiff, a resident of 35 rue Richard Lenoir, had a similar experience with an Italian man who returned to his country after their tryst, leaving her five months pregnant.[43] Indeed, such stories abound in the archives.[44] Of course, fingering a mysterious foreigner, vanished without a trace, may have been a convenient and far less shameful narrative choice for unmarried, pregnant women who were left alone to bear the stigma of unwed pregnancy. Indeed, when a young French girl, Simone Gaudinot, claimed to have been "raped by an Italian," the social worker handling her case dismissed it as "a fairly improbable story" fabricated in light of her imminent medical examination and what it would likely turn up about her sexual experience.[45] Yet, the fact that many women took additional action to locate foreign men suggests that, for a number of them, these claims were more than mere fabrications.

Certain French and foreign women found ways to bring state powers to bear on recalcitrant foreign lovers, fiancés, and spouses in France, often with the assistance of female social workers. For instance, League personnel frequently connected married foreign women and immigrant mothers to consular authorities when their husbands left them. When twenty-three-year-old Czech Roza Albertilikova, a factory worker in Argentueil, was abandoned by a compatriot and the father of her child, social workers recommended that she pay a visit to her Czech consulate.[46] Madame Michel counseled Spanish Vicenta Dasi, a thirty-eight-year-old domestic servant in the 16th arrondissement whose husband and compatriot left her in 1930, to drop by the Spanish consulate as well.[47] Did immigrant women and French social workers believe foreign consulates would simply aid in locating foreign husbands or go one step further, perhaps provide assistance—material or otherwise—to the jilted foreign wife in question? Though the precise nature of expected assistance remains just out of focus, there was clearly an expectation of *some* assistance.

Though social workers, lawyers, and legal consultants on hand at social service organizations frequently recommended taking up matters of marriage and desertion with foreign consulates, some women arrived at this conclusion on their own, turning to consular authorities on their own initiative for help locating a man who had left them in the lurch. Take, for instance, Yvonne Lecoz, a twenty-one-year-old factory worker. In 1931, Lecoz's partner, "an Italian lift-boy," abandoned her eight months pregnant. Even before she sought help from the League, she had already gone to the Italian consulate "to obtain some information about him."[48] Lecoz's behavior suggests a certain economy of information shared among Frenchwomen who knew where to go and who to talk to when romance with foreign partners went awry.

Frenchwomen might also approach consular authorities if they even nursed suspicions about the moral (and marital) probity of their beloved. As we saw in chapter 1, the marital status of Italians in France was a particularly problematic one after Mussolini outlawed divorce in 1928. In France, the banning of divorce in Italy cast suspicion on Italian men who did not act quickly—or quickly enough—in the eyes of their *amies*. This was the case for Pascal Fenile, a thirty-four-year-old entrepreneur who did indeed leave his wife behind in Italy when he came to France. Soon after his arrival, he began courting a young Frenchwoman, Suzanne Lurin, all the while "carefully dissimulating his familial situation," as prosecutors would later put it. Court officials noted that he promised her marriage in order to "win over her resistance," a euphemism indicating that he lied to her in order to lay with her. They moved to Paris together, but months and years passed and still the young Suzanne remained unmarried. In July 1931, Suzanne Lurin and her mother, "wearied by the inexplicable eternalization of an irregular and humiliating situation," appeared on the doorsteps of the Italian consulate in Paris to look into the background of this mysterious foreign beau. There, it was at last revealed to mother and daughter that Fenile did indeed already have a wife in his home country.[49] Thus, Frenchwomen learned to maneuver international regulatory systems to their own advantage, gaining information about former and would-be spouses from consular authorities. In this sense, Frenchwomen accommodated themselves to a new age in which family, friends, and neighbors could no longer be relied on to either vet a potential spouse or to ensure that he remained in the event of an unplanned pregnancy. In an era of mass mobility, then, Frenchwomen found recourse in international and state powers whose officials embraced them in return.

Married and unmarried immigrant women employed similar methods when dealing with their foreign spouses and partners in France. For instance, Emilia Leon, a native of Luxemburg, developed a very close friendship with her French concierge, a relationship mostly cemented over her ongoing domestic troubles. Leon regarded her husband, an Italian locksmith named Jacques Violina, as an endless source of trouble and her concierge concurred. The official inquest, however, yielded a different story. Despite her complaints, officials determined instead that the household was marred by Leon's violence against her husband, Violina. The abuse her husband was subjected to, so the story went, prompted him to quit the marriage in 1935, after seven years of marriage. When he departed, he also took with him their six-year-old son. In the hopes of learning their whereabouts, Leon immediately sought out the Italian consulate. In this particular instance, foreign consular authorities even acted as informal marriage counselors for the Violinas.

According to official reports, "The Vice-Consul [of the Italian Consulate] attempted a reconciliation, but in vain."[50] Although Emilia Leon's search for husband and child was not fruitful in the end, her actions suggest that, at the very least, some foreign women, like many Frenchwomen, believed they would find a sympathetic ear in official circles.

French and foreign women who suffered from domestic abuse regularly filed their complaints with neighborhood authorities, recording their suffering at the local police station.[51] Considering the thick networks of information among workingwomen in the capital, it is rather unsurprising that immigrant women would have also taken advantage of the local police as a regulatory apparatus. Yet, both French and foreign women involved with North African men used a special policing division in the capital aimed at monitoring the mores and behaviors of colonial subjects: the North African Brigade, or the police arm of the Service des Affaires Indigènes Nord-Africaines (SAINA), established in the summer of 1925. The North African Brigade was a special division of the Paris Prefecture of Police vested with the authority to surveil and otherwise harass North African migrants in Paris. The creation of the office in the 7th arrondissement was the outcome of political consensus across the board on the issue of North African "criminality."[52] Although the service was intended to investigate major crimes involving North African colonial subjects, like murder, the French and foreign women of Paris used these policing institutions for their own personal ends. That is, immigrant and French women at times sought recourse to the North African Brigade to protect them against men whom they considered, successfully portrayed as, and/or rightly described as violent North African lovers and spouses. That colonial men could move seamlessly from one category to another gave both French and foreign women a measure of latitude when registering their claims with French officials.

Blanche Sadoun, a Tunisian Jew who migrated to Paris in the 1920s, worked as a dancer in a *café maure* called El Maghreb in the 5th arrondissement. In 1929, she married Moroccan Mohamed ben M'Barek Cheradi "selon le rite musulman" in Marrakesh. Their union later disintegrated due to "discord" between the two partners. When she became the object of domestic abuse, Sadoun chose to address herself not just to the local police, but to SAINA. There, she claimed that her husband treated her savagely, no better than "a slave that one beats, at his pleasure, without end." "My life as you have recorded is in perpetual danger," she told them. Later reports mixed pronouns, making it difficult to separate Sadoun's own voice from that of officials. Nevertheless, documents recorded: "She knew that she would be spared any danger only if the Service des Affaires Indigènes from whom

I solicit protection, agrees to look after me."[53] Sadoun thus invited police intervention into her relationship, a relationship she characterized as violent. In so doing, she portrayed herself—and was portrayed as—a (female) victim in need of (male) protection from an abusive husband. Given the colonial context, she necessarily portrayed herself—and was portrayed as—an indigenous woman in need of white protection from a violent colonial male subject. As we will see in chapter 6, many immigrant women adopted similarly gendered and raced rhetorical strategies when filing local police complaints signaling domestic violence, although the mobilization of neighborly networks often yielded better, quicker results. In this particular instance, however, that Cheradi later murdered Blanche Sadoun points to the limits of police power even for women who tried to harness and direct the gendered surveilling and raced policing bodies of the state.

While women like Sadoun used police power to try to protect themselves from nonwhite male colonial subjects, white Frenchwomen more successfully turned state and local power to their own advantage, misrepresenting details of their acquaintanceship with North African men in the hopes that officials would intervene on their behalf. In so doing, they highlighted both gendered and racial dimensions of their relationships with colonial men that remained implicit in Sadoun's statements. French Victorine Louise Morot was the hotel-operator of a small pension in Villecomble during the 1920s where she had occasion to meet one of her lodgers, a young Algerian man by the name of Touhami Boubeker. Boubeker entrusted her with his money because, by his own admission and that of others, "not knowing French and unable to get by [*se débrouiller*] in Paris, he found recourse in her."[54] According to another testimonial drawn from Boubeker, this was something of a pattern for him, since, "Knowing neither how to read or write, saving his money in case of unemployment or sudden illness, he entrusted his money voluntarily to this or that one of his employers or *hôteliers*." Boubeker and Morot agreed that once he had accumulated ten thousand francs, she would help him open a savings account.

By all accounts, Victorine Morot hoodwinked Touhami Boubeker. After several months of collecting his money, she suddenly became difficult to locate. According to Boubeker, whenever he did manage to find her and question her about his savings, she would "always threaten to have him arrested if he did not leave her be." Sometime later, Morot made good on her threats, filing a complaint against him on March 12, 1934, with the North African Brigade. In it, she claimed "that she was the object of death threats on the part of Boubeker and demanded to be protected."[55] She even told her employer, Jean Gervet on rue Amelot, that an Algerian whom she used to do laundry for was coming around, threatening her "for incomprehensible and futile motives" and that she had gone to the North African Brigade out of fear.[56] While there were rumors of a love affair between them, Boubeker adamantly denied them and insisted that he sought her out solely in the interest of seeing his small fortune returned to him.[57] Morot, on the other hand, let friends, neighbors, and employers intuit a vague romantic connection between the two. By insinuating the existence of a sexual relationship, Morot invited a particularly interested form of police intervention, taking advantage of the state's disciplinary predisposition to surveil colonial subjects in the metropole, above all when a sexual relationship with a white woman was concerned. Morot used the state's gendered and racist policing logic in her private dealings with Boubeker, indicating that at least some Frenchwomen learned to use state and police powers against foreign bachelors and colonial subjects. Moreover, they knew to insinuate something torrid even when sex, marriage, and pregnancy were not at issue.

Both Blanche Sadoun and Victorine Morot turned to colonial police units of the Paris Prefecture—the North African Brigade—to find what they themselves termed as "protection," but that should not obscure the fact that Morot had distinct advantages. The colonial state, ever fearful of the fates of Frenchwomen, bent to protect them from what it perceived as violent, predatory, colonial male subjects. From an official standpoint, then, white Frenchwomen like Morot had the upper hand when it came to relationships with and accusations against nonwhite colonial men. Significantly, in the end, Morot's false claims against a colonial male subject were more effective at "protecting" her than Sadoun's true claims against her violent spouse, suggesting a contrast between the paternalist and colonial state's efficacy when co-opted by white versus nonwhite women. It also serves as an important reminder that, through state officials, white Frenchwomen wielded a particularly acute kind of gendered power vis-à-vis men with whom they were intimate.

Working the (Legal) System: Breadwinners, Families, and the Law

For French and foreign women, the battery of family laws and legal practices they sanctioned at the start of the twentieth century provided yet another effective means of bringing state power to bear on spouses through what Michael Willrich has termed "breadwinner regulation."[58] Family law and social policy had gradually expanded over the course of the nineteenth and early twentieth centuries, allowing women greater flexibility in the claims they made. According to these laws, marriage was no longer essential, but children born of the union—even illegitimate unions—were. This was the outcome of over half a century of legal reform and courtroom battles that finally crystallized at the dawn of the twentieth century into a legal system that would favor women and children in France for the sake of rebuilding the population and restoring the nation.

Although the Napoleonic Code had enshrined male power within the household at the head of the family, during the late nineteenth and twentieth centuries French law steadily eroded male hegemony within the home. In the latter half of the nineteenth century, new paternalist concerns over seduced girls duped by predatory bourgeois men welded with growing populationist angst over the demographic state of the country. Together, these twin concerns—paternalist sentiment toward women and pronatalist interest in improving children's welfare—ushered in a wave of social legislation intended to meet the new realities of the demographically depleted French nation.

In addition to enacting measures that regulated and policed the moral, sexual, marital, and parental scruples of men, the state also increasingly took their place as husband to unwed mothers and father to illegitimate, abandoned, and orphaned children. Consequently, these laws represented a broader shift toward state intervention in family matters of all varieties, especially where women and children were concerned. Paternity suits, alimentary pensions, and family abandonment claims (*abandons de famille*) all belonged to this fin-de-siècle and belle époque swing toward regulating male sexual behavior and moral probity in the interests of women and children and, ultimately, in the interest of improving the quantity and quality of the French national community.[59] But what began as protective measures to shield married and unmarried mothers and their children from deadbeat dads, capricious lovers, and shady spouses came to empower French and immigrant women greatly in their dealings with both state officials and their sexual partners, especially if they were foreign-born.

The most ubiquitous of these resources was the paternity suit, since it was available to both married and unmarried women. It was the outcome of nearly three decades of protracted parliamentary debate, finally sanctioned by the law of November 16, 1912. The 1912 law amended Article 340 of the Civil Code, which had aimed: first, to protect men from slanderous accusations by loose women, specifically bourgeois men from accusations by their female employees; second, to protect heterosexual conjugal families from unwed working-class mothers; and finally, to sidestep the thorny issue of inheritance, lineage, and filiation that came with the birth of illegitimate offspring. Under very specific conditions, filiation could now be established by the mother, construed by the law as the custodial agent and caretaker of a child. This measure thereby endowed even unwed mothers with the power to take the fathers of their children to court and demand alimentary pensions. Failure to do so resulted in either *déchéance paternelle* (according to the Law of July 24, 1889) or else possible fines and even imprisonment (according to the Law of April 19, 1898). In some sense the law merely codified what judges had already been doing since the mid-nineteenth century—namely giving women the right to confront adversaries and demand just retribution, often in the form of financial compensation for unplanned pregnancy, unjust desertion, and subsequent economic hardship. Yet, the 1912 law, as well as the fin-de-siècle laws establishing the alimentary pension, represented a radical legal departure from the patriarchal spirit of the Napoleonic law that had reigned in France during the previous century.[60]

A variety of social service organizations in the capital, pronatalist and maternalist in orientation, worked to make paternity suits available for both French and foreign working-class women in France. In Paris, several organizations provided free legal counsel to women, helping them to locate the fathers of their children, lodge a paternity suit with the aid of love letters, and obtain alimentary pensions from them in the interest of both mother and child. Foremost among these organizations were Sauvons les Mères et les Bébés (Let Us Save Mothers and Babies), L'Union Féminine Française (French Women's Union), and of course, the LPAM, which we have already encountered.[61] From the moment of its founding in 1925, LPAM offered "juridical consults" with their legal team (lawyer Maurice Garcon and his secretary Yvonne Netter) whom they kept on hand every Monday.[62] By 1928, Mademoiselle Michel, a lawyer who worked on behalf of the LPAM, boasted that eighty requests for "judiciary assistance" had been "favorably received" by officials, the majority of which constituted paternity suits and family abandonment complaints.[63] Rachel Goldstein, a Turkish Jew, living on rue Béarn in the 3rd arrondissement, was one such complainant whose paternity suit was hampered by her lack of letters from the putative father.[64]

While social service organizations certainly spread the word, many immigrant women sought out this form of help of their own volition, yet another example of the circulation of information in working-class communities. Polish Ryvka Bester, a twenty-two-year-old seamstress living on 6 Cité Lesage Bullourde in the 11th arrondissement, formulated a complaint against Bernvelzwerg, a man she described as an abusive former lover. According to her official statement, "He abandoned the defendant when pregnant." For his part, Bernvelzwerg "denied having beaten the complainant, and threatened to kill her."[65] The deepening of the Depression may well have played an important role in rendering paternity suits necessary, placing as it did a tighter squeeze on immigrant households and especially on female-headed households lacking a primary breadwinner. Records of the Commissariat of Police in the neighborhoods of Sainte Marguerite and La Roquette record a number of women seeking to file paternity suits against former lovers in 1933, a steep rise from 1926 (a year of relative economic prosperity, by comparison).

If paternity suits formally empowered unwed mothers from 1912 onward, other legal provisions were reserved for the lawfully wed. Family abandonment suits, established by the Law of February 7, 1924, and modified by the Law of April 3, 1928, aimed to protect the conjugal family from the desertion of one or the other spouse. Specifically, it condemned the deserting party to a prison sentence of three months to a year for failure to pay alimentary pensions ranging from one hundred to two thousand francs for at least three months. Repeat offenders could expect automatic imprisonment. Moreover, those accused of *abandon de famille* could be shorn of their paternal rights (*déchéance paternelle*).[66] While this latter stipulation applied to both fathers and mothers, the former aimed primarily to protect wives from deadbeat husbands, since it was, if not impossible, then highly unlikely, that a wife would pay her husband alimentary pensions. Essentially, the law gave teeth to what had been merely a civil law, disregarded at a whim. It criminalized family abandonment by fathers in a straightforward manner and provided avenues of financial compensation for wives.

Immigrant wives and mothers registered family abandonment suits at their local police stations during the interwar years. Italian Marie Caputo, a seamstress living on 20 rue de la Roquette in the 11th arrondissement, filed such a suit against her ex-husband Tomasso Di Iacano in 1933.[67] So too did Russian Andréa Garimberg née Stengel, who submitted a formal police complaint that same year against the ex-husband who owed her a thousand francs.[68] Polish Mathilde Kanterowitz, a thirty-seven-year-old typist, also filed an abandonment complaint against her ex-husband, Adolphe Eundewell. Condemned by the court to pay Kanterowitz 400 francs per month, Eundewell had fallen behind on payments and owed her nearly 2,760 francs, or approximately six months of alimentary pensions, by December 1933.[69] Indeed, some immigrant women pursued ex-husbands tirelessly until they received their due. Rachel Gostynsky, also Polish, first lodged a complaint for failure to receive alimentary pensions from her ex-husband, Levine, in February 1933, but returned to the commissariat periodically throughout the year to request their continued help haggling for payments with her former spouse. By December, he owed her a thousand francs and claimed that he was unable to pay at that time.[70] Foreign women thus showed themselves to be not just savvy, but persistent when using the French legal system, a system increasingly designed to support women like them with children to provide for.

Foreign husbands whose wives and lovers brought suit against them coped the best they could, but the law left them little room to maneuver. As the 1930s progressed, the French state improved its ability to track their every movement. To start, the state mandated that foreigners renew identity cards (replete with current addresses and other identifying information) on a constantly evolving "regular" basis: first every three years, then every year, then every three to six months by the mid-1930s. Officials also stepped up their policing of earlier laws. For instance, the number of foreigners arrested for violating the law of 1926, preventing them from changing occupations within a year of entering France, increased five-fold. This law was intended explicitly to prevent foreigners' mobility in France.[71] Foreigners in Paris also had to register each change of address twice: first at the local police station from which they departed and next at the police station of the quartier where they arrived. By the eve of the Second World War, foreigners whose identity papers were not in order risked fines of one hundred to one thousand francs and prison sentences of one month to one year.[72] Thus, the breadwinner regulation of foreign men took place not only against the background of populationism and paternalism, but also against the background of hardening official attitudes toward foreign mobility more generally in the 1930s. Unless they wanted to evade discovery entirely by ignoring the many constraints placed on their mobility, and incurring the severe penalties such behavior entailed, foreign men were forced to make their whereabouts known during the interwar years—both to the state as well as the women and families they perhaps sought to avoid.

Like the penalties for failing to pay alimentary pensions, the stakes of family abandonment could be quite high for men—and higher still for immigrant men than Frenchmen. By the 1930s, family abandonment resulted in the expulsion of a handful of foreign men from France. For instance, in 1930, two foreign men residing in Paris were expelled on these grounds, as well as one foreign man in 1931 and another in 1934.[73] Still, it is difficult to say whether these men were expelled for family abandonment *tout court* or if, more probably, police officials picked them up on minor charges then subsequently used family abandonment as a justification to deport out-of-work foreign workingmen in the depressed 1930s, as the timing of these expulsions would suggest. Either way, it is clear that crimes against one's family was construed as a violation to the French national family, more largely, and that such transgressions could sever a man's ties with France altogether.

As the state leveled its disciplinary gaze evermore at *both* breadwinners and foreign male mobility, immigrant husbands and lovers were less able to avoid paying former wifely intimates. At the same time, however, immigrant men were squeezed hard by the Depression, leaving them with little income to devote to their former partners or their offspring, legitimate or otherwise. This was a tricky balancing act, and they rarely fared well. The fortunate among them could, like Romanian butcher Ozias Hesel, simply provide proof of payment by showing police officers the receipts for alimentary pensions rendered, in the hopes that this would ward off future inquiries.[74] Others, like Romanian Léon Sapsa, an upholsterer living on 20 rue des Taillandiers, claimed that he had paid his ex-wife the first four months of alimentary pensions owed to her as outlined by their nonconciliation ordinance, but pleaded that he would be unable to pay more for the time being.[75] This was a recurring theme in 1933: foreign wives demanded more at a time when immigrant husbands could give less.

Fathers might also position themselves as the more effective caretaker by maligning the mother of their children. In 1926, police attempted to force Abdallah Bagdadly, an Algerian street vendor living in La Roquette, to pay his Algerian ex-wife, Boudia Fatma Merad, an alimentary pension, presumably on her request. Defending himself, Bagdadly claimed that, although he used to send his ex-wife seventy-five francs per month, he stopped when he saw what state his children were in: "Mistreated by the mother, covered in vermin, half-naked, beaten, malnourished." Although both his son and daughter suffered from this mother's neglect, Bagdadly only removed the former from Algeria, taking the son with him to France. Protesting against the recommencement of alimentary pensions, Bagdadly adamantly refused to pay his former wife, but did volunteer to take custody of their daughter, thus proving that he was willing to make certain paternal sacrifices in lieu of others. The Bagdadly affair provides a rare instance in which a father, and a colonial male subject, at that, managed to avoid the payment of alimentary pensions, and he did so by undercutting the indigenous mother and undertaking the full-time care and custody of the children in her place.[76] Few men adopted this tack, however.

The submission of an abandon de famille could also be the first step in procuring a divorce, the right to which reappeared in France only in 1884 as the Naquet Law, so-called after its most vigorous supporter, Gustave Naquet. According to Article 310 of the Naquet Law, after three years of separation, either partner could sue for divorce, a stipulation contravening entirely

Napoleonic law wherein men had been given a clear advantage over their wives when it came to divorce.[77] Rachel Meller, a Polish stitcher of men's trousers, recorded at a police commissariat in 1934 that her husband had left her and that she had been searching for him for nearly three months. By thus establishing her abandonment as a legal fact with a juridical life of its own, she needed only to hunker down for a little less than three years before she could finally sue for divorce.[78] Of course, these legal maneuverings were particularly complicated for Italian women since, once again, divorce for them was forbidden. Those complications were magnified when husband and father were not one and the same. Madame Osnandi, an Italian workingwoman at a paper factory outside of Paris, found herself in quite a predicament as a result: although her Italian husband had left her and she was pregnant by another man, she could neither divorce the first nor claim alimentary pension from the second. Social workers at the League hoped for the best when they sent her to a legal consult with Yvonne Netter in 1931.[79]

Although not conventionally considered part of the expansive social legislation at the turn of the century, the *constat d'adultère,* or adultery statement, proved of great use to French and foreign wives looking to sue for divorce. The constat d'adultère is intimately tied to the history of divorce in modern France. When the Naquet Law reintroduced divorce in Third Republic France, one of the many ways it diverged significantly from Napoleonic law was by allowing for divorce on more expansive grounds, including adultery by the wife *and* adultery by the husband. Until adultery ceased to be peremptory grounds for divorce in 1975, French men and women would struggle to prove their spouse had cuckolded them through recourse to the constat d'adultère. It was therefore a formal recognition of infidelity, verified by local police officials, and recorded for all of posterity.

Despite its pretense to formalism, many constats d'adultère have the delicious feel of tawdry melodramas, replete with all the sensationalism necessary to transform private drama into public spectacle. To begin with, one or the other partner had to have cause to believe that they were being cuckolded. After declaring their suspicion at the local police station, officials orchestrated "sting" operations intended to catch the spouse who had strayed from the conjugal bed in the act. Arriving early in the mornings to these *"faux ménages,"* or "false households," police officers first knocked then pushed their way through doors, taking care to note each individual's state of dress (or undress), looking for signs of fresh coital activity, and extracting confessions from guilty parties about the length of the affair. All details were then recorded with great ceremony at the station, constituting colorful entries couched between more mundane offenses—robberies, petty thefts, and other criminal misdeeds—and exposing unapologetically the private lives and travails of foreign men and women in the capital.[80]

In October 1926, for example, Josse Priem, a thirty-eight-year-old Belgian wine merchant, left his wife Annette to take up with a Belgian dressmaker named Marie Vandenboosche. Looking to catch the miscreants unawares, police officers knocked at their door on Passage Saint Bernard at six-thirty in the morning. The officer on duty recorded that Vandenboosche answered the door and was, alas, "dressed." He then pushed his way through the door to catch a glimpse of the sleeping arrangements before anyone had sufficient time to "rearrange themselves." At that moment, he saw Priem in bed along with a small child, described as "the child borne of their false union." The officer then pressed both Priem and Vandenboosche until he had succeeded in extracting the following confession: "We recognize having lived together for over seven years."[81] That Priem and his mistress had lived together, borne children, and established a household of at least seven years' duration suggested that this was no casual "fling." Rather, the "accused" had begun a life together that Priem's wife had likely known about for some time. It seems probable, then, that the constat d'adultère was an effective means by which she could ensure that the divorce was pronounced in her interest, thereby permitting her to demand alimentary pensions. This is all the more plausible considering that adultery siphoned off male income from working-class households, income that a divorce pronounced in favor of the wife could restore to the legitimate household.

This was a common strategy among wives, both French and foreign. Later that year, police also caught up with Russian tailor, Israel Kramarche and his Polish mistress, Pessia Slowik (also a married woman). Both stood accused of "Adultery and Complicity." According to the police report, the two had taken up residence together on 18 rue Sedaine. On the morning of December 29, 1926, officials showed up at their door just before eight o'clock in the morning, again hoping to catch the lovers unawares. They noted that Slowik, who answered the door, was "summarily dressed" and that Kramarche slept in the bed along with their eight-year-old daughter. "An examination of the place indicated cohabitation," officials recorded. The couple admitted to having lived together for some three years, which was all Kramarche's spurned wife needed to demand that he pay rent for the family he had left behind.[82] While the constat d'adultère might have proven a means of emotional catharsis, it also presented cuckolded wives with an opportunity to demand financial compensation of many varieties. That many adultery statements and stings were organized against husbands who appeared to have cohabited and even fathered (not very young) children with their "mistresses" further suggests that the injury of adultery was not fresh to these wives. The constat d'adultère was, in short, more than soap opera; it involved real stakes. As a juridical document with legal standing in the courts, it served several purposes: it reestablished immediate access to male wages by abandoned wives; later, it gave cuckolded spouses (both male and female) the peremptory grounds for divorce legally required to pronounce the separation in their favor; finally, for women, it provided justification for their access to the alimentary pensions on which they increasingly relied during the interwar period.

Although the criminalization of adulterous spouses in France between 1884 and 1975 was, in theory, gender neutral, the organization of the social, economic, and legal system in France (as elsewhere) penalized male breadwinners to a greater extent. Thus, it remained in each partners' interest to ensure that the divorce was pronounced in his or her favor. According to Article 299 of the Naquet Law, "The spouse against whom the divorce will have been pronounced will lose all the advantages that the other spouse provided for them, whether by marriage contract, or since the marriage."[83] In other words, the cheating wife risked losing her alimentary pension if she was caught; similarly, the cheating husband, if caught, could be more severely punished through the alimentary pension he owed to his cuckolded wife. The constat d'adultère, then, had teeth, which accounts for why French and foreign husbands *and* wives made use of it. Moïse Philiba, a merchant at 114 rue du Chemin Vert, filed a constat d'adultère against his wife Sarah who, he claimed, left him five years earlier to take up with another man. He sought to use this juridical statement as sufficient grounds for divorce in his favor.[84] Thus, both men and women participated in this particular legal practice because they each had something to lose to—or gain from—the other.

If foreign women showed themselves more than willing to use the state by engaging in these legal practices, it was no less true that the French state was quite simply willing to be used. That is, officials deployed their power by intervening on behalf of foreign women whose husbands had left them. When Romanians Faïga Moïse and Ozias Hessel divorced, he reneged on his agreement to pay two hundred francs per month to support his wife and four children. He claimed that she refused his payment, but French state officials demanded that he make good on his payments regardless.[85] Years later, in 1933, they were still haggling over the exact amount he owed her, a fact which proves that these financial and legal arrangements could have long shelf lives.[86] On other occasions, it appeared that French state officials, though eager to help, believed themselves to be hamstrung, for instance by French marriage laws that recognized only civil ceremonies, not religious customs. For instance, Romanian Ida Sura Goldstein lived (perhaps as a lodger) with the Agolis on 52 rue Basfroi. She also worked as a dressmaker for "Neimon," who ran a confection workshop from home at 3 Passage Rauch. A mother of two, Ida Sura demanded that her husband help in the provision of child support, in this case, by paying the wet nurse two hundred francs per month. Though she claimed they were separated, police officials noted that the couple had been married in a religious not a civil ceremony, thus neither the marriage, nor the separation, nor even the familial ties, among them were recognizable according to French law. Though she could file a paternity suit as an unwed mother, Ida Sura Goldstein was legally unrecognizable to the French state as a married woman.[87]

As Goldstein's case demonstrates, marriage worked as a protection against abject poverty in the (rather likely) event of the union's collapse by providing wives unfettered access to breadwinners. Although there were other legal measures that the unmarried mother could rely on, particularly the paternity suit, she was barred from the benefits reserved for the lawfully wed, such as those the abandon de famille or divorce could procure. Both spousal regulation and breadwinner regulation, then, opened up myriad possibilities for immigrant wives and mothers, who implicitly demonstrated both their reproductive utility to the French nation and explicitly demanded paternalist intervention from the state in return.

Like their French female counterparts, immigrant wives and widows turned to the state for aid and protection, harnessing the paternalist and familialist orientation of state structures, legal practices, and bureaucratic sympathies in order to police foreign partners and extract financial assistance from them. Although Frenchwomen could draw on a long and storied past in France in ways that immigrant women could not, both French and foreign women—as wives and mothers—managed to get results when dealing with international, state, and municipal officials. From international embassies and consulates to local police officials and social workers, French and immigrant women adopted and performed the at times quite authentic parts of jilted lover, abandoned spouse, struggling widow, and so on in order to get help from the state, whose emissaries, middle-class male officials, were eager to help them on matters where the nation's very future was at stake. In the process, immigrant women learned to speak French in more ways than one: while they certainly had to speak at least enough French to bargain with state officials in the first place, they also had to adopt a rhetorical stance that positioned them variously as spurned women, as abandoned mothers, and by extension, as vulnerable female clients of the French nation in need of paternalist protection. They thus adopted bureaucratic narrative forms that made middle-class Frenchmen more likely to help them, portraying themselves as or being portrayed as one of several female archetypes (scorned wife, self-sacrificing mother, abandoned lover, desperate divorcée, forlorn widow) that the law had been constructed to recognize and support against one of many male archetypes (cheating scoundrel, abandoning spouse, feckless father) the law had been constructed to identify and discipline. In part, then, the state's growing propensity to regulate both foreign male mobility and negligent breadwinners combined to afford the French and immigrant wives of immigrant husbands maximum protection. And nowhere was the state's logic of supportive maternalism more inclusive of foreign-born wives and mothers than within the dynamic world of social assistance.

Chapter 4

Mothers, Welfare Organizations, and Reproducing for the Nation

In his 1933 *Down and Out in Paris and London*, George Orwell describes a local drunk, Charlie, who, needing to provide for his French *amie* Yvonne, suddenly remembered the many Paris maternity wards "where women who are *enceinte* [pregnant] are given meals free and no questions are asked." Charlie explained to his audience of amused onlookers what many of them most certainly already knew: "It is done to increase child-bearing." In the end, he convinced his *amie* to pose as a pregnant woman in order to secret away food for the both of them in her pockets. Their scheme worked. *"Mon Dieu,"* exclaimed Charlie, "if only I were a woman I would have eaten at one of those places every day."[1]

As Charlie and Yvonne's scheme suggests, France had emerged not only as a safe haven on the continent between the wars, but as a maternal haven with Paris its undisputed capital. This was yet another outcome of widespread demographic angst and pronatalist zeal that gripped French decision makers in the early Third Republic, encouraging population-minded state officials and benevolent bourgeoises of private charities to join forces for the sake of the future of France. While the state provided ample financial assistance to pregnant women, new mothers, and large families, local municipalities offered them numerous public health and childcare establishments dedicated to safeguarding and improving their well-being and that of their children. Public assistance was then richly fleshed out by scores of private charitable organizations run by middle-class Frenchwomen that had emerged over the course of the nineteenth century.[2] Social workers of these welfarist organizations not only provided French and foreign mothers financial, social, and emotional assistance with the tasks of childbearing, child-rearing, and household management, but served as crucial intermediaries between them and the state. Together, public and private assistance networks forged a wide-ranging maternalist and familialist welfare world in France. It was a charitable landscape that immigrant women in the family way learned to navigate, often with the guidance of female social workers who lobbied on their behalf.

Although immigrants enjoyed generous access to public benefits in the 1920s, by the onset of the Depression, access was no longer assured. Immigrant mothers thus turned increasingly to private charitable organizations and their trained social workers for assistance. At a time when the relationship between immigrants and the state, particularly immigrant men and the state, was shot through with xenophobia and hostility, immigrant women found solace and support in social workers. After all, unlike immigrant men, immigrant women had been valued exclusively for their reproductive rather than productive service, and though French state and society no longer had use for the latter in the depressed thirties, the former was still very much needed. If, as we saw in the previous chapter, benevolent paternalism allowed immigrant women to find a small but critical opening in their relationship with the state as wives and mothers, those roles allowed an even greater opening when it came to their interactions with middle-class female social workers in maternalist and welfarist organizations throughout the capital. Through the supportive maternalism rife in the mixed domain of social assistance, immigrant mothers reaped the rewards of generous state and social sponsorship of motherhood, even into the otherwise xenophobic 1930s.

Although public assistance emanated from the state, it was disbursed at local welfare offices, or *bureaux de bienfaisance*, throughout the country. And although many private charities were national in size and scope, they were committed to meeting women, children, and families where they were, typically at home, in the working-class neighborhoods where they dwelled. As a result, welfare was a profoundly local experience, and one best observed through a local lens. Through an exploration of three organizations in the capital, then, this chapter moves us squarely to working-class Paris and up to the very edges of Sainte Marguerite and La Roquette. Each organization reveals a different face of social assistance available to immigrant families in *Paris populaire* during the interwar decades: first, the Foyer Français, an immigrant aid society; second, the League for the Protection of Abandoned

Mothers (LPAM), a maternalist philanthropy touched on in the previous chapter; and finally the Social Service for Children in Moral Danger (SSCMD), a child welfare organization whose assistantes sociales made regular house calls to French and foreign families throughout the capital. Founded within just two years of one another, between 1924 and 1926, all three organizations were united in their commitment to bolster France's population—the first through the introduction and assimilation of new "foreign elements," the second through the preservation and protection of poor mothers and their newborns, and the third through the surveillance over and solicitous engagement with working-class families and "problem" youths. In their shared goal to increase the French population, they are representative of the panoply of associations that proliferated in France during the interwar years. Together, they demonstrate how the politics of populationism in interwar France enabled struggling immigrant families balanced precariously on the edge of poverty to survive, especially in the turbulent 1930s.

Paris and Public Assistance

For both French and foreign, access to state and municipal social programs varied from one locality to the next, the result of conflict between national directive and local initiative.[3] But foreigners also contended with a host of binational treaties structuring their access to welfare provisions.[4] By 1936, France had concluded such treaties with Italy, Czechoslovakia, Poland, Belgium, Luxemburg, Romania, Austria, Switzerland, Spain, and Yugoslavia. These were primarily arrangements relative to foreign workers and the degree of assistance available varied by country.[5] Treaty stipulations determined access to free medical care and hospitalization as well as state and municipal services and entitlements. Generally speaking, Italians, Belgians, and Poles received the most favorable treaty terms and, consequently, the most generous welfare assistance from the French state. Those foreigners who could not invoke a treaty had no right to state benefits, though as many contemporaries of the period pointed out, this was hardly how it worked in practice.

In the 1920s, most foreign workers received free medical care and hospitalization, though not without considerable consternation from the French public. Throughout the interwar period, references to foreign populations crowding French hospitals abounded, concerns crystallizing around the medical and hygienic threat to the French "race" posed by a rapid, unregulated influx of immigrants who were not properly screened before crossing the frontier.[6] Undoubtedly, these critics were rather less populationist than pronatalist in orientation, wishing to increase the French population through an increase in specifically French, rather than foreign, births. But they represented the minority opinion throughout the interwar decades, even in the xenophobic thirties. Rather, most municipal leaders in charge of local welfare bureaus saw a potential payoff in the population boost that large numbers of foreigners afforded a French nation laid low by demographic woes. G. Fabius de Champville, secretary-general of Paris welfare bureaus in 1926, lamented the stream of diseased foreigners and applauded the healthful effect of their presence on French natality in the same breath.[7] But with the onset of economic crisis in the 1930s, flexibility in welfare provision all but disappeared. Even those foreigners whose reciprocity treaties guaranteed them unemployment aid found a French state more willing to repatriate than negotiate.[8]

According to treaties concluded in the 1920s, Belgians, Italians, Spaniards, and Poles were entitled unequivocally to the same unemployment benefits as French citizens as long as their papers were in order.[9] By 1930, Romanians, Austrians, Yugoslavs, Czechs, Swiss, and Armenian and Russian refugees could also request lesser unemployment aid by invoking diverse treaties.[10] But as the crisis deepened and the ranks of the unemployed swelled, foreigners, among the first to lose their jobs, called in their assistance to varying effect.[11] Many were unceremoniously repatriated unless they could prove they had formed family attachments in France.[12] In Paris, certain municipal leaders called for an unequivocal end to unemployment benefits to all foreigners, regardless even of length of residence or family size.[13] This was a far cry from the open-armed welcome paid to fecund immigrants in the first few decades of the twentieth century; then again, that had been a time of prosperity.

During the interwar years, family allowances constituted one welfare provision especially common among foreign families who tended to have *familles nombreuses*, or large families of three or more children. According to their reciprocity treaties, Italian, Polish, and Belgian families were entitled to large family pensions as long as they could prove at least five years of residence in France; however, they received only half that of a French family.[14] Foreigners who were not covered by treaties occasionally sought naturalization as a means of becoming unequivocally eligible for these benefits. Both Selig Gallner, an Austrian canner and father of five, and Isaac Tcheskiss, a Russian cabinetmaker and also father of five, sought naturalization in 1914 and 1922, respectively, to secure family allowances for their large households. In fact, their "avowed motives of assistance" so imperiled their naturalization requests that they received "decidedly unfavorable recommendations" from both the police commissioner in their neighborhoods as well as the police prefect of Paris.[15] That said, the Bureau de Sceau disregarded police counsel on both occasions, opting to naturalize precisely on the basis of Gallner's large family.

By contrast, foreign mothers had considerable state resources available to them. As with all state aid, access to those resources ebbed and flowed in tandem with economic circumstances. But as late as 1933, most pregnant foreign women were eligible to receive *secours de grossesse*, or pregnancy benefits, from local welfare bureaus. Like French women, they needed only to be in their fifth month of pregnancy and to prove one year of uninterrupted residency in Paris, though it is likely that this situation changed as the 1930s wore on and municipal resources evaporated. Evidence suggests that women of "certain nationalities" became subject to more stringent residency requirements.[16] Apart from Polish women, for instance, many Eastern European women in Paris in the 1930s were permitted neither pregnancy benefits nor family allowances.[17] Though access to state entitlements waned in the depressed thirties, foreign women still had a number of municipal hospitals, maternity wards, women's shelters, and convalescence homes to turn to in Paris, all remnants of the vast maternalist aid networks that had developed over the course of the nineteenth century. By the interwar period, few public hospitals in Paris had nationality restrictions, although most, like local welfare bureaus, had residency requirements.

Certain private hospitals also attracted foreign women in spades. The Rothschild Hospital, founded in 1852 expressly for the city's Jewish inhabitants, was unique in its markedly foreign clientele as compared to other municipal institutions. In 1914, the renovated Rothschild opened its doors on rue Santerre in the 12th arrondissement, not far from the large foreign Jewish populations in the neighboring 11th and 20th arrondissements. After the war, it was also equipped with a brand-new maternity ward. In a 1930 report on the maternity's operations, Doctor Henri A. Victor recorded, "Before 1914 and the war, our clientèle was constituted almost exclusively of Jews [*Israélites*] residing in France for generations, a large proportion were of Alsatian origin . . . [and] those Jews having lived in Eastern Europe and the Balkans, even North Africa and Turkish Asia." But the war had dramatically transformed the capital. He continued, "We know how numerous, after the war, were the emigrations from Poland, Russia, Hungary, [and] Salonica. Many of these emigrants settled in France, and particularly in Paris."[18] In other words, the war ushered in demographic transformation that had significantly altered the demographic composition of the maternity ward's clients on rue Santerre.

A relatively "open-door" policy toward foreign mothers also reigned in other municipal establishments that provided shelter and meals to pregnant women and new mothers, such as the Ledru-Rollin, Michelet, Pauline Rolland, and George Sand refuges.[19] The city maintained records of the women who came to find solace at these institutions between 1914 and 1931. Of the more than 93,000 women served during this period, 7,150 of them, or about 8 percent, were foreign. Polish, Italian, and Belgian women were the most highly represented, perhaps reflecting their greater presence in the capital as compared with other national groups.[20] The Asile Michelet in the 13th arrondissement was particularly popular among foreign women who represented nearly 19 percent of all mothers who sought sanctuary there in 1928.[21] Between the wars, the Baudelocque mothers' hospital in the 15th arrondissement also regularly welcomed a diverse immigrant clientèle, although Polish mothers predominated. These foreign mothers tended to be unwed as well.[22]

State entitlements and municipal institutions, then, provided dual, reinforcing systems of assistance to foreign families and foreign mothers, especially, in the capital. But access was not always assured and grew increasingly unreliable in the Depression years. While state-run mother-care centers in Paris continued to offer services to foreign women, they nevertheless enacted diverse nationality and residency restrictions that grew more stringent as the 1930s wore on. As the state turned away from them, immigrant mothers living in Paris increasingly turned to the dense web of private organizations that crisscrossed the capital.

Immigrant Aid Societies: The Foyer Français

Founded in February 1924 by radical leftist Paul Painlevé, the Foyer Français boasted an executive board featuring some of the period's most ardent pronatalists, among whom were Roger Olchanski, Paul Raphael, and the indefatigable André Honnorat, cofounder and president of the Alliance pour l'accroissement de la population française.[23] Its stated goals were to ease the assimilation process of foreigners by advocating on their behalf in their dealings with the French state, particularly when filing naturalization requests, and by providing free French language classes. Although it was dissolved a mere eleven years later, the Foyer Français was extremely active for the decade or so that it was in operation, functioning, in theory, as an early immigrant aid society.[24] In practice, of course, it was an advocate network that sought to "franciser" those foreigners considered most useful and desirable to the French nation: that is, large families and young foreign men on the verge of both military service and marriage with French women.

Honnorat often framed the mission of the Foyer Français in populationist terms. In 1926, he explained to members the arduous work that lay ahead of them: "You all know that among the problems that exist in France, the most grave is that of population: on the one hand we have, for extremely unfortunate reasons, too few children, thus too few Frenchmen, and, on the other hand, because many foreigners came to replace our dead and unborn, they came precipitously and they will have trouble assimilating if the Foyer Français does not help them."[25] In other words, the Foyer Français had two objects: to combat French demographic decline and to alleviate the difficulties of assimilation experienced by foreigners. And there was no reason that both could not be resolved at once, especially through the naturalization of large families. As Honnorat himself pronounced in his opening remarks at the members' first meeting in 1925, "They are whole families who disembark at the frontiers and head toward the large city centers, and it is these families that we must make French [*franciser*]."[26] Indeed, in regard to their naturalization services, Secretary-General René Lisbonne even boasted, "We have the satisfaction of dealing with families with ten or more children: these are notably Italians, Turks, and Poles; often we have families of six, [but] families of three are rare." He added too, "We concern ourselves frequently with single men who impatiently await their naturalization to be able to contract marriage with a young French girl."[27] Essentially, the Foyer Français and its members were not just pronatalists, but populationists who, like most of their French contemporaries, showed a very clear preference for large foreign families and the family-minded.

Not only did Foyer members demystify the impenetrable naturalization process, helping foreigners to compile dossiers and complete forms, but the organization even subsidized, in whole or in part, the fees associated with the naturalization itself. In the early days of their operations, they attended to nearly 160 naturalization dossiers per week. By January 1926, they had prepared 1,307 dossiers representing 5,712 foreign men, women, and children.[28] It helped, too, that they held the ear of bureaucrats in high places. The organization guaranteed that any naturalization dossier assembled by them and submitted to the Ministry of Justice and the Paris police prefect would be "studied with great interest and resolved as soon as possible."[29] In 1926, realizing the great boon the Foyer represented, officials at the Ministry of Justice even began referring foreigners loitering about its headquarters at the Place Vendôme to one of several Foyer Français offices in the capital.[30]

To get the word out, Foyer Français members engaged in active, even aggressive, campaigns of self-publicity. From the start, the organization took great pains to, as one member put it, "seek out foreigners among themselves [*chez eux*]." Olchansky elaborated, "We have, for every nationality, councilors who know in which quarter of Paris the Italians dominate, in what other quarter the Armenians, etc." Indeed, advertisements for language classes presented a promising pedagogical opportunity in and of themselves. Olchansky described, "We have drafted leaflets in the respective languages of these foreigners, taking care to print just opposite the French translation, so as to allow them the opportunity to translate the leaflet themselves; they see thusly which word of their own language corresponds to which French word." This was only the beginning. Foyer members went to foreign religious leaders in Paris; they publicized themselves in the foreign-language press; they posted advertisements in the cafés and bars that foreigners were known to frequent; they distributed pamphlets outside of synagogues patronized by Polish immigrants on religious holidays—all in an effort to advertise their organization to a broad spectrum of immigrant communities.[31]

Foyer members divided themselves into nationality-specific "sections," teams geared toward outreach among specific communities, whether Russian, Polish, Romanian, or other Eastern European "Israelites."[32] In 1926 the association even requested and was granted approval from the Prefecture of the Seine to put up posters advertising its free services in all twenty *mairies*, or town halls, of Paris.[33] The Garde de Sceau, seeing in the fledgling organization an opportunity to lighten his load, wrote to the prefect of the Seine, "[The Foyer Français] renders precious services, avoiding, most of the time, the Bureau de Sceau, so encumbered with affairs at the present, in giving necessary information to those interested."[34] The Foyer Français, in other words, acted in concert with, and with the tremendous support of, those in power to aggrandize the French nation one foreign *famille nombreuse* at a time.

And there is evidence that they were successful in their endeavors, both in getting their name out and in advocating on behalf of immigrants. In the working-class quarters of the 11th arrondissement, the Foyer Français had established one of three offices they called, rather optimistically, "assimilation centers."[35] Immigrant families in the neighborhood were aware of its services and sought recourse there when displeased with the sluggish ministerial response to their naturalization requests.[36] In 1927, Bassi Tcheskiss, a Russian housewife and mother of six went to the Foyer Français to follow up on her application, which she had submitted on behalf of her husband and herself over two years ago. Dire economic circumstances moved her to act after the long years of ministerial silence. She explained in a letter to the minister of justice that her husband could no longer work, having succumbed to a work accident that left him blind four years ago.[37] This left only her eldest son, Simon, as the sole financial provider for the family, and he was away completing military service. Simon, she explained, could not be liberated from his military obligations until he could present "a paper proving that we have become French." She ended her letter, "Since my son's absence, which is to say for the last year, I can hardly manage to feed my small family, finding myself in very great need, and I assure you, Monsieur le Ministre, that you would do me a great service if you could help me in these punishing circumstances."[38] The Foyer Français successfully intervened on her family's behalf and the Tcheskisses were naturalized just three weeks later. Undoubtedly, her "small family" of eight motivated, at least in part, the Foyer's speedy efforts.

While the aid and preparation of naturalization requests for large families and family-minded foreigners was the Foyer's primary goal, the provision of free French language courses came a close second. Since 1924, the organization provided courses at six schools in and around Paris.[39] Classes met two to three times per week in the evenings for a total of eight to ten hours a week. They were divided along national lines and taught by volunteer teachers, the lower levels by the most advanced students themselves or else naturalized foreigners; the higher levels by a teacher who did not speak the same language as the students.[40] In 1925 they counted just 250 students, but by 1926 they had 801 enrolled students in Paris alone, and over 1,600 throughout France.[41] Most of their Parisian students were of Russian, Polish, Romanian, Armenian, Hungarian, Czech, and Greek origin.[42] By 1927, they expanded their services into three more schools in Paris so that by 1928, they could claim 1,084 enrolled students in the capital.[43] Of note, the Société Générale d'Immigration, discussed in chapter 1, funded Foyer Français language courses for immigrants.[44]

Classes were held at public schools in Paris. Besides already being equipped with the necessary pedagogical accoutrements (that is, desks and chalkboards), classes held at public schools yielded other unforeseen benefits in the quest to make as many immigrants French as possible. Foyer representatives found themselves "in close contact with the school directors and teachers who then familiarized themselves with our policy relative to naturalization." Members were shocked to find that "many of them were ignorant of the disposition permitting foreign parents, by simple declaration before a judge of the peace, to renounce in the name of their French-born children the right to opt, at the age of adult, for their country of origin." This was a reference to the practice of French naturalization by declaration, whereby parents guaranteed that their children born on French soil could not reclaim their foreign nationality at age twenty-one.

By informing foreign parents and applying subtle pressure, French public school teachers could join the ranks of the Foyer's army, fighting "to enrich this country with intelligent and industrious future citizens," one foreign child at a time.[45]

French language classes also promoted the Foyer's familialist politics in another way. Members often waxed philosophic on the indispensability of the French language in assuring harmony and promoting friendship between French and foreign, thrown suddenly together in the same neighborhoods of Paris. In an interview published in a Jewish newspaper, cofounder Olchansky contended that learning French "removes between them and the inhabitants of France all the barriers that separate them."[46] Besides greasing the harmonic wheels of neighborhood life, speaking French opened immigrants up to a world of romantic opportunity. As Raphael put it, through language instruction, foreigners increased their opportunities "to frequent our compatriots" and, "in orienting the instruction of single foreign men in this direction, we provide them access to French families."[47] That is, foreign men who spoke French could woo in French and wooing Frenchwomen begat evermore French families, or so the logic went.

Although there was much ado made about foreign bachelors, the Foyer Français did reach out specifically to immigrant women in at least one known campaign. In April 1925, Madame Justin Mayer spearheaded and organized an Assistance Committee that worked in conjunction with Paris Public Assistance. This committee was comprised of assistantes sociales borrowed from Public Assistance as well as foreign female students who served as interpreters. Together, they paid regular visits to the maternity wards of Paris where they endeavored to convince pregnant foreign women "that they can and should make their children French, by simply signing before a Justice of the Peace from their neighborhood a renunciation in their children's name, to decline French nationality in the future." In 1926, these *équipes de femmes*, as they called themselves, expanded the scope of their operations to the private maternity wards of Paris, the likes of which were evidently familiar to Orwell's fictional characters. Their first year, they credited themselves for assuring the French nationality of ninety children born on French soil of foreign parents and initiating at least fifteen naturalization requests through their solicitous engagement with foreign women. Additionally, René Lisbonne worked closely with Louis Mourier of Assistance Publique to ensure that abandoned mothers would be given ample opportunity to naturalize the children they consigned to this public institution.[48] How did those interactions unfold? Though Foyer records are scant on details, those of maternalist organizations patronized by foreign mothers allow for a fuller understanding of those negotiations and offer a more complete glimpse into the lives of foreign women.

Maternalist Philanthropies: The League for the Protection of Abandoned Mothers (LPAM)

As in Great Britain, Germany, and the United States, middle-class Frenchwomen were the first to identify the needs of women and children as worthy of social welfare initiatives.[49] They set themselves to the elaboration of those welfare programs, developing over the course of the nineteenth century an overlapping web of maternal aid societies throughout France. These private charitable organizations did indeed improve poor mothers' lives, though as part of a wider effort to lower infant mortality and increase birthrates.[50] The League for the Protection of Abandoned Mothers belongs to this maternalist genealogy. Founded one year after the Foyer Français, in 1925, the League was the brainchild of Germaine Besnard de Quelen. Unlike the Foyer Français, however, it enjoyed more than fifty years of uninterrupted activity before its dissolution in 1978.

The League first opened its doors in a tiny "barrack" along boulevard des Lannes on the far western outskirts of the city at the edge of the bourgeois 16th arrondissement. By 1928, it had moved to a more central location, 154 rue du faubourg Saint Honoré along Place Philippe du Roule in the 8th arrondissement, making it more accessible to the workingwomen who came by foot, bus, and metro "just nearby [*tout proche*]."[51] Officially, the League had three defined goals: to provide immediate aid to all pregnant women and new mothers, regardless of nationality or religion; to help these women find jobs that would allow them to keep and provide for their children; and to undertake the guardianship of abandoned children. Not long afterward, the League expanded its range of activities to include an adoption section and a service to place children with wet nurses in the provinces.[52]

Like the Foyer Français, the League was unabashedly pronatalist in its ambitions and enjoyed the support of those in power of a similar mind, including former statesmen and municipal leaders (figure 4.2). At the first meeting in 1926, Wenceslas Huet, a representative from the Ministry of Labor, commended League volunteers on "coming together and working to remedy the most distressing crisis that exists for the future of a country such as our own: that of natality."[53] And this was indeed the vision of its founder, Besnard de Quelen, who rallied her volunteers with the following maternalist battle cry: "Let us do everything possible, to help the mothers, so that the children will not be abandoned. Let us help [mothers] during pregnancy, let

MOTHERS AND REPRODUCING FOR THE NATION

FIGURE 4.1. The League's first published pamphlet cover reads: "The League for the Protection of Abandoned Mothers welcomes all abandoned mothers, married or not, without distinction to religion or nationality." LPAM brochure, 1926, in D84Z/228, Archives de Paris.

us help them during childbirth. Let us protect the child even at his mother's breast, just as we will protect him, afterward, so that he can grow up and become a man."⁵⁴ But mothers were more than simply vehicles by which the French nation would enrich itself with new citizens. They were deserving of assistance in their own right. Quelen reasoned, "We no longer want a mother, in these times, to wander the streets, to sleep on the sidewalks, with a tiny babe in her arms, or for a young girl [to be] terrified by what she

FIGURE 4.2. "March 2, Paul Strauss, former minister, visiting the temporary children's shelter accompanied by M. Couturier and M. Kirsch." Kirsch is identified as "mayor of the 11th arrondissement." LPAM brochure, 1931, p. 54, in D84Z/228, Archives de Paris.

considers a catastrophe, all because no one is there to help her." In lending succor to new mothers, it was true that the League would thwart a more formidable opponent, "the decline in birthrates"; but the League and its social workers were also driven by an imperative to improve women's lives and foreign women numbered among its foremost beneficiaries.[55]

The League's wide-ranging assistance made it a popular destination for poor French and foreign women during the interwar years. By 1930, one secretary declared that the League was in the throes of "such rapid development," its numbers swelling with "unfortunate creatures" arriving daily "from Paris, from every corner of the provinces, and even from abroad . . . worn out by material and moral suffering."[56] From the moment it first opened its doors in 1925 until 1935, the League had already assisted as many as 12,781 women in Paris—both French and foreign. Of the 8,800 whose nationality was recorded, 822 were foreign-born women.

Aside from the first year of its operations (1925) when foreign women represented nearly 14 percent of the League's clientele, the greatest numbers of immigrant women patronized the League in 1933 and 1934 when they accounted for 10.1 percent and 9.3 percent of clients, respectively. These years roughly correspond to foreigners' highest concentration in the capital, as well. The foreign population of Paris reached an all-time high in 1926, accounting for 10.34 percent of the city's total inhabitants, dipping only slightly in 1931 to 9.8 percent.[57] Moreover, because the French state pulled away from foreigners in the 1930s, it forced them to turn to charitable organizations, like the League, for assistance. These years, which coincide with the deepening of the Depression, reflected the growing need of foreign families, and especially foreign women, in the capital.

According to League records, between 1925 and 1935, they had assisted 191 Poles, 83 Belgians, 82 Italians, 74 Swiss, 46 Algerians, 45 Russians, 35 Romanians, and 35 Spaniards, among others. In my own analysis, these were the nationalities most represented, as well.[58] What is striking immediately about those figures is the large number of Polish women assisted by the League as compared to all other foreign women. Polish women accounted for more than twice as many Italian or Belgian women, the next largest groups of foreign women patronizing the League.

The image of the poor, struggling Polish mother must have been so commonplace to League volunteers that she soon featured in the lightly fictionalized accounts of "poor mothers" come to find solace at League headquarters. In this rendering, she was described as "a large, ruddy redheaded girl" who "spoke French with some difficulty." Come to Paris on her own to make her way as a domestic servant, she was soon led astray by a compatriot who seduced her with promises of marriage. Trusting his honeyed words, she quit her job, took up with him, then proceeded to give birth to one child after another. Pregnant once more, she awoke one day to find herself in the following situation: "The father, weary of the rapid and incessant pregnancies, tired of these mouths to feed and the cries, the tears [that] exasperate him when he returns home exhausted from his punishing work as a mason, leaves her." According to this tale, for some six weeks she and her children wandered the streets of Paris, living off the charity of strangers until she at last learned of the League.[59] Though this dramatized account may have exaggerated certain details, many elements actually ring rather true.

To begin with, like the Polish unfortunate in this tale, foreign women who sought help from the League were concentrated in female-dominated sectors of the French economy: domestic service, needlework, and the confection trades, as well as factory work in the expanding manufacturing sector. These trades had long been the province of young women arriving new to the capital, whether from the countryside or further afield.[60] These were also traditionally the least remunerative professions; foreign women in this sample made an average wage of about twenty francs per day. Although they ranged in age between eleven and sixty-eight years old, foreign clients were about twenty-nine years old with one or two children at their side when they arrived on League doorsteps. More than one-fifth arrived pregnant, like *la Polonaise*. Unsurprisingly, they tended to live in either the poor outlying regions of the Parisian *banlieue* or else the working-class districts of northern and eastern Paris—that is, in the 11th, 18th, 19th, and 20th arrondissements. A significant number could also be found in the 16th arrondissement, where they worked as live-in domestic servants for bourgeois families. Although the length of residency in France was only recorded for twenty-three foreign women, those few had been in the metropole for nearly eight years. The length of time spent in Paris was recorded for almost half of foreign women and, on average, they had lived in Paris for slightly over six years when they came to the League. Then again, a handful showed up at the League having only arrived in Paris the day before or even that very morning.[61]

Though termed "abandoned mothers," the reality was less straightforward, and in some cases, foreign women could hardly be called abandoned at all. The classic scenario is of course one in which foreign women sought to flee physically abusive relationships, and there were many such stories.[62] While abused women often sought shelter with relatives, many foreign women living far from home did not have that option. Other foreign women came to the League because their household simply could not survive on the male breadwinner's meager salary. In these instances, foreign women sought help in finding well-paying jobs to buttress the household economy.[63] Contrary to the image of victimized wives and mothers forwarded by French officials and occasionally immigrant women themselves, it was sometimes these women who made the decision to quit the household because of their partners' inability to financially support the family.[64] In 1938, Friedel Steiner, a twenty-five-year-old Polish worker living in the 14th arrondissement, explained that although she was "not completely abandoned by her partner [*ami*], both of them are out of work and she prefers to live by herself."[65] The desire to strike out alone was probably more than a little informed by a yearning for one less mouth to feed.

Economic fragility, limited familial support, unstable domestic arrangements—these were the circumstances that framed the lives of immigrant working-women in Paris, and these circumstances pushed them to seek assistance. As the tale of *la Polonaise* demonstrated, foreign women often did appear on the doorsteps of the League in a pitiable state. They came hungry, impoverished, in need of medical assistance, and frequently laid low by a streak of bad health that left them no longer able to financially support their children. Upon entering League offices, women were promised basic and immediate material assistance: clothing, food, drink, even money in exceptional cases (figure 4.3). The League also procured jobs for them—waged work allow-

FIGURE 4.3. The office of the League for the Protection of Abandoned Mothers, 1928. LPAM brochure, 1928, p. 54, in D84Z/228, Archives de Paris.

ing mother and child to remain together. Ideal occupations for unskilled, foreign women were, as before, domestic service, particularly for bourgeois families living in large homes where mother and child alike could be housed. But other jobs, as nursemaids, cooks, or laundresses, were also common. This was in line with the League's overarching goal to permit struggling mothers without economic resources to retain guardianship of their children.

Job placement remained one of the most important services that the League continued to provide foreign women well into the 1930s. Ever mindful of women's own burdens, Besnard de Quelen often commented on the state's fixation on male unemployment during the thirties. As early as 1930, she reminded League volunteers that, contrary to popular belief, the Depression affected women, too, perhaps with greater consequence. "We often talk about the male worker," she declared, "but do we speak of the mother whose wages decrease while the wet-nurse's fees do not? . . . Do we speak of the mother who will bring her child to Public Assistance so that there, at least, he can eat?"[66] Consequently, League members dedicated themselves to procuring employment for their French and foreign charges, often in domestic service, an industry that remained largely untouched by the crisis.[67] But if both French and foreign women were affected by the Depression, they were not affected in equal ways. In 1934, League agents tried to place

Hélène Colowiec, a twenty-eight-year-old Polish woman, as a maid with a certain Madame Quiry only to find that the lady "would not take a foreign woman."[68] Moreover, the precarity of foreigners' access to state aid during these years meant that many foreign women could not rely on unemployment benefits like their French female counterparts.[69] Remarkably, League volunteers remained committed to foreign women's right to work when, at the same moment, foreign workingmen encountered resistance at all levels of state and society for the same prerogative.

The legal clinic was another popular service which, as we have seen, foreign women availed themselves of to track down lovers who were the objects of their paternity and family abandonment suits. While some may have hoped to hunt down wayward *amis* in the hopes of extracting marriage concessions, most used this legal tool to demand child support.[70] Some foreign women also sought guidance in procuring divorces from husbands with whom they had come to France, but from whom they now sought to separate.[71] The League also used legal consults in one very particular way in relation to immigrant women and their children: to initiate naturalization proceedings. In the first year of the League's operation, the legal clinic oversaw the successful naturalization of ten foreign children.[72] Though a modest start, naturalization became an increasingly popular tool for League volunteers in their dealings with foreign women and families.

Though rarely clear on whose initiative naturalization was undertaken, League volunteers certainly played a decisive role. Given the material benefits French citizenship entailed, foreigners may have looked favorably on the idea of naturalization, though perhaps only at the gentle urging of a League volunteer. In 1929 a forty-year-old Russian, André Martehouck, came to the League on behalf of his wife who had just given birth to their seventh child. Martehouck came expressly to find out how to obtain a family allowance. The League informed him that, being Russian, he was not eligible for this pension, then advised him that naturalization would be a sure means of securing it.[73] On some occasions League volunteers did more than raise the idea. In 1932, Nathalie Alexandroff, a twenty-eight-year-old Russian seamstress, came to the League for help sending her sick infant to a children's convalescence home that only accepted French children. Rather than find another institution, the League telephoned the offices of the Oeuvre de l'Enfance to advance her the ninety francs necessary for the child's naturalization and he was soon on his way.[74] While League volunteers were not always so proactive, naturalization was certainly a measure they advocated and facilitated.[75] However, if like the Foyer Français, the League underwrote the naturalization of foreign families and children in the spirit of populationism, its members were also motivated by a genuine desire to provide relief to foreign mothers and their children. This maternalist mandate led them to petition on behalf of mothers, regardless of national or ethnic background, in their effort to secure financial assistance from the state. Often, this mission placed them squarely at the center of immigrant women's struggles with officials.

While Italian, Polish, and Belgian women were generally well served by Public Assistance thanks to reciprocity treaties, their nationality was not always enough to ensure favorable treatment, even in the years preceding economic crisis. In 1927, this was the problem Maria Fronteuska faced. A twenty-year-old Polish domestic servant living in the 3rd arrondissement, Fronteuska learned of the League via another client. Upon leaving the hospital with her newborn daughter Hélène, a League member noted, "She finds herself refused Public Assistance aid because she is Polish and does not know what to do now." The League recommended her to a convalescence home and meanwhile busied itself with procuring Fronteuska's aid.[76] But if this was the case for protected nationals in the 1920s, the going was less easy for unprotected foreigners in the intransigent 1930s. In 1934, Anna Brodetzky, a forty-one-year-old Russian housemaid living in the 11th arrondissement first came to the League for advice on which sanitarium to send her sick children. In the ensuing years, she returned for clothing, meals, and medical consultations as well as the placement of her three children with wet nurses. In 1937, after undergoing surgery at the Saint Antoine Hospital, she found herself unable to work. Though receiving eighty francs a month in unemployment aid from her local welfare bureau, she was denied a family allowance on the basis of her Russian nationality. To add to her problems, her foreign work papers had expired. In both matters, the League intervened, procuring her a family allowance from Public Assistance and renewing her foreign papers to allow Brodetzky to remain in France.[77] Indeed, during the 1930s, League ladies busied themselves with ensuring foreign women's access to unemployment aid, family allowances, and pregnancy benefits from a state less willing to provide it to foreigners, even those whose treaties supposedly protected them.[78]

Over the course of the interwar years, League members on the frontlines became well versed in "the hassle of foreign papers" and adapted accordingly.[79] They learned to navigate the morass of procedures that foreigners were subject to in the interwar years. They helped women apply for and renew foreign identity cards and work papers—necessities for any foreigner wishing to remain in France at a time when the state increasingly sought to repatriate them.[80] On several occasions during the 1930s, League volunteers even lobbied the police prefect to prevent foreign mothers from being deported.[81] Indeed, throughout the interwar years, League volunteers grew adept at negotiating the intricacies and inconsistencies of the French state's policies toward foreigners, even intervening on behalf of foreign women during the 1930s.

The League's foreign clientele forced members to work closely and in coordination with foreign aid societies in Paris. Various charitable associations worked in concert with the League to provide a supportive infrastructure for diverse groups of foreign women in the capital: the Société héllenique de bienfaisance de Paris for Greeks; the Comité tchèque for Czechs; Bienfaisance des dames polonaises for Poles; and diverse charities for both Russians and Armenians. Eastern European Jews received frequent support from the Comité de bienfaisance israélite as well as the Association israélite pour la protection de la jeune fille.[82] Additionally, social workers from the Rothschild Hospital corresponded often with League members in the interest of foreign Jewish women. Finally, the League worked in concert with immigrant aid societies, especially the well-known Service social d'aide aux émigrants.[83] Even the wife of Roger Olchansky, cofounder of the Foyer Français, personally referred a client, suggesting links between the Foyer and the League.[84] The picture that develops, then, is one of overlap, for if the League sought out certain groups, so too did diverse charitable organizations seek out the League. Essentially, an ensemble of organizations grew close knit and cross-referential via their dealings with foreign women. In Paris, a dense web of charitable societies built up around foreign women at a time when nationality increasingly marked some out for exclusion from the French state and its provisions.

Child Welfare Organizations: The Social Service for Children in Moral Danger (SSCMD)

While maternalist groups established a physical presence in the capital in the hopes of attracting needy mothers and their newborn children, other welfarist groups were decidedly more interventionist in approach, inserting themselves directly into working-class families in the straightforward interest of protecting children. These child-centered organizations sent armies of assistantes sociales from their central headquarters in Paris into the darkest recesses of the city where working-class families resided. In part, these groups arose in response to new pronatalist legislation appearing in the fin-de-siècle and belle époque periods, varieties of which were recounted in the previous chapter. In addition to laws that sought to protect mothers in the interest of their children, however, a substantial number of laws took direct aim at the health and welfare of children, sidestepping parents altogether, even removing them if they were deemed harmful to the child's best interests. As a result, although French and foreign mothers could develop close relationships with SSCMD social workers, differing ideas of what was "best" for children could also drive a wedge between them. Consequently, relations between mothers and social workers of child welfare organizations were more ripe for conflict than those between mothers and social workers of immigrant aid societies and maternalist philanthropies.

The Law of July 27, 1889, introduced the measure of déchéance paternelle, a juridical process that removed paternal rights over children from parents judged unworthy and incapable by the courts. The Law of July 19, 1898, then entrusted both these mistreated children as well as delinquent youths to charitable institutions.[85] An entire arsenal of laws put in place in 1912 also affected children in direct ways. For instance, the Law of July 22, 1912, instituted a special Tribunal pour enfants et adolescents de Paris, where minors were tried for both petty and major crimes with an eye to rehabilitate rather than punish. The same law also mandated that judges presiding over the Tribunal pour enfants arrive at their decisions with the aid of both a formal inquiry and medical examination of the child in question. Yet, no intermediaries existed to undertake this monumental task. The SSCMD arose in response to the lack of coordination among judicial, legislative, and policing bodies that coalesced around the Tribunal pour enfants.[86]

Founded in 1923 and operating to this day, founders designed the SSCMD to serve as an intermediary to the judiciary, local police, working-class parents, and "problem" adolescents.[87] Like the Foyer Français and the League, it enjoyed financial backing from the state and official support from those in power, as a glance at both the official budget and member list of the organization reveals.[88] The SSCMD first opened its doors at 36 quai des Orfevres in the 1st arrondissement, a building that now serves as the current site of the Tribunal pour enfants et adolescents de Paris. It moved from one building to another throughout Paris in the 1920s before finding a more permanent home at 19 rue du Pot-de-Fer in the 5th arrondissement in January 1932.

Initially, the organization was funded by the largesse of its primary benefactress, Olga Spitzer née Wolfsohn, a Paris-born philanthropist married to a successful French-naturalized Hungarian banker. In addition to Olga Spitzer, the SSCMD had four other founding members: Chloe Owings, an American social worker who completed her dissertation at the Sorbonne; Paul Fauconnet, a French sociologist and student of Durkheim; Marie-Thérèse Vieillot, a French social worker; and finally, Henri Rollet, lawyer, then judge, and only much later a *juge d'enfants* from 1914 until his retirement in 1930. Rollet, in particular, had maintained a pronounced interest in children's welfare issues from the start of his law career, advocating heavily in favor of the laws above. Rollet was also the cofounder, along with Jules Simon, of the Union française pour le sauvetage de l'enfance in 1887 and, in 1890, of the Patronage de l'enfance et de l'adolescence, veritable hospices for mistreated and delinquent children. Rollet served as the president of the SSCMD from 1923 until 1934.[89]

The SSCMD instituted an American-style version of casework designed to meet the needs of the French judicial system and "the crisis of the French family," despite the fact that many of the families in question were not, in fact, French. Out of 103 households in the neighborhoods of Sainte Marguerite and La Roquette treated by the SSCMD between 1929 and 1940, 28, or more than one-fourth, of them consisted of one or two foreign parents. French, foreign, and half-foreign (or half-French) children were signaled to the SSCMD either by authorities (juges d'enfants, the prefect of Paris police, or other social organizations involved with the family) or individuals. In most cases, children's involvement in petty crimes of theft, public indecency, breach of trust, even prostitution brought them to the attention of first the French legal system, then the SSCMD.[90] In some cases, however, social workers at diverse organizations in the capital were appalled by the bad behavior of their clients' children and approached the SSCMD of their own volition. For instance, a certain Madame Enos of the Comité de bienfaisance israélite contacted the SSCMD regarding the Russian Friedlanders, whom she described thusly: "The mother has no authority over the children; these children are ill-mannered and say disconcerting things for their young age."[91]

In other instances, however, it was the parents themselves who identified their own children as in need of *correction paternelle*, or judicial intervention on behalf of parents to correct a child's indiscipline as sanctioned by Article 375 of the Civil Code.[92] French and foreign parents alike used the *demande de correction paternelle* to request that the juge d'enfants put an end to the adolescent shenanigans of their misbehaving children. French Madame Vallès, for instance, sought intervention of behalf of her son Henri because of his "laziness and bad conduct" in 1929, as did Turkish Michel Polycar for his son Marcel citing his "difficult character" as the culprit for family disunity.[93]

On still other occasions, neighbors might band together to demand the removal of parental rights (or déchéance paternelle) on behalf of a wronged child. Neighbors at rue Popincourt in the 11th arrondissement, for instance, gathered together to sign a petition "against the alcoholism of the parents and the negligence of the children" belonging to the French Millons.[94]

Elsewhere in the same neighborhood, neighbors singled out sixteen-year-old Polish Isaac Morgen as in need of protection from his father who subjected him to "mistreatment" and five-year-old Hungarian Paul Frischka whose father also "brutalized him."[95] As the welfare of children emerged as a high priority for statesmen, municipal leaders, politicians, and social service workers during the interwar years, the failure of parents to sufficiently provide for and take care of their children was increasingly criminalized. In fact, immigrant parents risked potential expulsion for maltreatment of children. In 1926, twenty foreign parents received expulsion notices due to "mistreatment of children."[96]

Once a child had been identified by the judicial system, by frustrated parents, or by concerned neighbors, the work of SSCMD assistantes sociales truly began. They had three mandates: first, to complete inquiries into minors aged thirteen years or younger, taking into account a total "social and familial investigation" rounded out by thorough medico-psychiatric consultations; second, to propose solutions to judges, such as educational measures, medical treatments, or changes in "milieu," which magistrates and government officials then relied on in order to decide whether a child should be removed from their parental household; and finally, to execute those measures adopted by the judiciary all the while exercising an "amicable surveillance" and "educative influence" over the family. Social workers sought the causes for delinquency "in the complexity of the familial history of each youth, in the intricate relations of the family with its neighbors, and by an extensive study of the physical and moral conditions of the youth." Above all, SSCMD social workers saw their job as achieving a reconciliation between parents and children, and they intervened to find the best solution for working-class Parisian families, whether French or foreign.[97]

To permit working-class French and foreign parents to keep their households afloat, social workers obtained the necessary financial resources from local welfare bureaus and diverse charitable organizations. In this, SSCMD assistantes sociales mirrored the activities of LPAM social workers. For instance, when investigating the possible mistreatment of young Paul Frischka, they concluded not only that they should monitor the family's situation, but that "there is on the other hand pecuniary aid to furnish, the family being deprived of what is strictly necessary since the unemployment benefits were refused for a reason that we have yet to discover."[98] The "first step," according to one SSCMD social worker, was to "signal the family to the Oeuvre de secours aux hongrois," a charitable organization for Hungarians, "where we sent the mother." When they could do nothing, the SSCMD gave the family one hundred francs for groceries and clothing, then sent them to the minister of labor to regulate their foreign papers so as to ensure uninterrupted access to unemployment benefits. They further alerted the social workers of two other Catholic philanthropies in the capital, the Sisters of Saint Vincent de Paul and of the Church of Saint Ambroise in the 11th arrondissement where the Frischkas lived. Soon, SSCMD social workers learned the reason that *père* Frischka had been denied unemployment aid: the proud locksmith had rather imprudently told the bureaucrat at the *caisse de chômage* that he "would not take just any job." The ladies of the SSCMD urged him to reconsider his position. All this they did within the first month of interaction with the Frischka family, in January 1933.[99]

Because children were the primary focus of SSCMD social work, they spent most of their energy procuring the placement of French and foreign children within the vast childcare infrastructure of the capital. Like the newborns whose mothers arrived at the doorsteps of the LPAM, SSCMD social workers sent the very young off to *nourrices*, or wet nurses in the countryside; to *pouponnières*, or full-time nurseries where working-class mothers could still visit their babies from time to time; or else to *crèches*, or neighborhood nurseries where, for a small fee, mothers deposited babies and toddlers during the day and retrieved them in the evening.[100] They enrolled very young children such as Hungarian Paul Frischka in *écoles maternelles*, or neighborhood preschools, and they registered primary school children in *cantines scolaires* programs, or free school cafeteria service for indigent youngsters.[101]

Adolescents caused both their parents and SSCMD social workers the greatest consternation, for they contributed most to the lack of familial harmony. To restore concord to French and foreign families, social workers frequently involved the children in activities that necessitated their temporary absence from the home—with requisite adult supervision, of course. They sent them to *colonies de vacances*, or children's camps in the healthful countryside away from the urban ills and immoral distractions that abounded in Paris.[102] They also involved youngsters in a variety of scout movements that began to appear in France during the interwar years, such as the Eclaireurs de France, the Eclaireurs israélites, or the Auberge de jeunesse.[103] Finally, social workers placed them in apprenticeships as well as trade and professional schools. In October 1932 SSCMD social workers engineered the placement of Turkish Robert Gabaï in an apprenticeship at the Ecole de Commerce et Industrie in Versailles; the placement of Romanian Ladislas Kohn at the Ecole des Chausseurs-Bottiers in October 1934; and the placement of Italian Victor Maiorano at the Ecole de Saint Hilaire where he left with an apprenticeship contract as a mechanic in 1935.[104] Thus, SSCMD social workers concerned themselves not only with the welfare of youngsters, but also nurtured the career ambitions and professional success of their older siblings as well. This mission placed them well beyond their mandate of simply attending to "problem" adolescents and assuring familial harmony.

On those occasions when social workers recommended the removal of children from a harmful home environment, they ideally sought to place them with relatives or else interested parties and guardians.[105] When no relatives could be found (as was often the case for foreign families), children might be sent to a neighborhood *foyer des jeunes*, or adult-supervised youth hostel.[106] If parents were deemed wholly unfit to provide for their children, SSCMD social workers might place them in refuges, such as the Saint Anne Refuge and the Argonne Association, or even orphanages, in the worst-case scenario.[107] Young girls, by contrast, were often sent to religious institutions, churches, and nunneries, such as the Patronage Sainte-Thérèse, the Church of Bon Pasteur, or the Sisters of Saint Vincent de Paul in Paris.[108] There were special institutions, too, for the mentally-disabled, such as the Oeuvre de l'enfance déficiente and the Asnières Institute where Turkish siblings Marcel, Salomon, and Joseph Gabaï were sent in the 1930s.[109] If the parents were deemed fit, but the environment unhealthful, children might be temporarily sent to sanatoria and "preventoria" in the countryside, or other healthful rural locales, such as the Aérium Saint Joseph in the northwest department of Ille-et-Vilaine.[110] And in 1929, the SSCMD purchased a château in Brunoy, in the department of Seine-et-Oise, where they established "a center for observation and triage," called the Foyer Soulins. Problem youths, typically adolescents, were sent to the Foyer Soulins so that social workers could get to know them better and thus easily place them in the institution most suited to them. Meanwhile, children adhered to a strict regimen of "class, gymnastics, games, and chores in the house and in the garden" to occupy them until SSCMD social workers arrived at a conclusion regarding their future.[111] Despite social workers' best efforts to portray the Foyer Soulins as a fun-filled youth camp, it is doubtful that children experienced it as such. Moreover, the children sent to the Foyer Soulins tended to exhibit more extreme misbehavior. Half-Spanish André Pacaud was sent to Brunoy after caught stealing again, and the eldest son of the Turkish Gabaïs was placed there because he had developed the nasty habit of physically assaulting his mother.[112] Thus, the Foyer Soulins was more likely a detention center for children with a (criminal) record of misbehavior.

Still, the Foyer Soulins was undoubtedly the best alternative that difficult children, or children in difficult circumstances, could hope for in terms of existing public welfare institutions. The Service des Aliénés was one unpleasant destination for French- and foreign-born minors if mental illness was suspected.¹¹³ For those children whose parents either could not or would not care for them, with no relatives or potential guardians, the Service des enfants assistés, an office of Public Assistance, was their likely destination.¹¹⁴ Indeed, one need only recall the threats formulated by Emilienne Goata, the wife of Romanian ex-soldier Nicolas, who, at the mere mention of depositing her children at Public Assistance forced officials at the Bureau de Sceau to rethink withholding naturalization from the struggling family. While this state repository for orphans and "morally abandoned" children had improved much by the interwar years—lowering rates of mortality, abuse, and illiteracy among wards of the state—the adults it churned out were hardly much better off than the families that had been forced to abandon them there in the first place. Even for parents living on the edge of poverty, consigning their children to Public Assistance was truly an option of last resort, often reserved for those so plagued by disease, alcoholism, or poverty that they had few alternatives left.¹¹⁵ Parents' reluctance to give up their children stemmed in part from the fact that they were forbidden from contacting their sons and daughters again until the children had reached legal adulthood. Thus, surrendering children to Public Assistance was a potentially permanent act reserved for the very desperate.¹¹⁶ If French and foreign parents sought to avoid Public Assistance, the specter of this state institution was equally frightening to children. When Franco-Algerian Sabine Halimi was informed that she would be sent to Public Assistance in conformity with a court order, "she made a scene of desperation and absolutely frightening fury" at her school."¹¹⁷

The SSCMD was not a maternalist organization per se, but female social workers did target mothers as those key figures on whose health and fitness the future of the family most depended on for survival. When they encountered the Belgian Warinier family, they immediately noted that the mother was "suffering" from a multitude of ailments: from "violent and frequent asthma attacks" such that she "cannot remain standing and appears extenuated." They engineered her hospitalization at the Hôpital Saint Antoine.¹¹⁸ And when they met Turkish Arira Gabaï, the first order of business was fortifying the ailing pregnant woman. Social workers sent her to the Baudeloque Maternity in the 15th arrondissement and thereafter arranged for her to be seen regularly for shots at a dispensary in the nearby 20th arrondissement. Months later, they also arranged for Gabaï to rest at a convalescence home with her newborn Henri after his birth.¹¹⁹ The interaction points to the degree of assistance that immigrant mothers in the capital could rely on, even from welfare organizations that prioritized children.

Since mothers often emerged as figures of tremendous importance in their work with families, SSCMD social workers developed close personal relationships with their charges. Consequently, foreign mothers came to them when they found themselves in dire straits. After weeks of denying that her husband beat her, Hungarian Elisabeth Frischka appeared to social workers one day in March 1933 to ask for help with her husband who had grown "so unkind to her." She explained at length: "He is horribly jealous, goes to join her at the homes of her employers where she works [as a domestic servant] in order to see that she is not deceiving him; he cannot tolerate to see her sick or tired and even though he does not do anything all day he leaves her in charge of the household and the child." The discovery of his infidelity was the last straw. After confronting her husband, Elisabeth Frischka ("who is normally very sharp and perceptive," noted social workers) had become "pitiable." To separate the woman from her husband, social workers engineered her employment (not for the first time) with a *colonie de vacances* in the countryside. Weeks before she was scheduled to leave, she came to the SSCMD seeking refuge from his violence and social workers found a cheap hotel where she could stay for the night. The following day, they met with the abusive spouse and did not mince words: "It is still understood that Madame Frischka will leave for the *colonie de vacance* with Paul [her son], and that from now on if she suffers from the ill humor of her husband, she will come to find us so that we can protect her."[120]

While the development of these sorts of protective relationships might be readily expected of maternalist organizations in which mothers were the direct recipients of aid, it is telling that they were also a common feature of child welfare organizations. Most cynically, we might conclude that social workers of child welfare organizations could not deny that the welfare of children ultimately depended on the welfare of mothers; less cynically, we might conclude that the protective surveillance social workers exercised over families could lead to friendly relations and relationships with the mothers. Of course, relations between representatives of child welfare organizations and working-class mothers were more likely to assume an adversarial quality than those between mothers and immigrant aid societies or maternalist charities. After all, parents and welfare agents of organizations like the SSCMD could clash over what constituted a child's best interests. Still, as the example of Elizabeth Frischka above demonstrates, the SSCMD nevertheless provided the conditions in which relationships between social workers and some immigrant mothers flourished, and on which a handful of immigrant mothers even came to rely.

Although not adhering to a strict maternalist mandate like the LPAM, SSCMD social workers nevertheless undertook much of the same work as League ladies in their interest to improve the health of working-class families and children. In the process, they too leveled their gaze on French and foreign mothers at the center of working-class households. Moreover, the more frequent interaction among female social workers of the SSCMD and their French and foreign working-class charges allowed for supportive relationships to grow. Social workers of child welfare organizations such as the Social Service for Children in Moral Danger connected immigrant mothers to important resources in the capital that ultimately improved their health and unburdened them of some of the heaviest responsibilities of working-class motherhood. Thus, in addition to what was often a generous state and local welfare program, immigrant mothers could find both moral and material support from French social workers of child welfare organizations even if they were not, ostensibly, anyways, the primary targets of intervention.

The Nature of Conflict

No philanthropic work is entirely devoid of class antagonism and condescension, moralizing sentiment and surveillance efforts, and in fact the moments of conflict between immigrant women and French social workers are just as instructive as moments of harmony.[121] Although Foyer Français sources give no hint of antagonism between immigrant clients and organization members, class and, more rarely, culture, divided benevolent French ladies of the leisure class in both the LPAM and SSCMD from their foreign working-class charges. This could manifest itself in a suspicion of foreign women's comportment. In 1928, the Social Service Section of the Paris Police Prefecture referred a Belgian worker by the name of Léontine Stouf to the League. When she arrived, League volunteers remarked that she appeared dirty and disheveled. Although Stouf claimed that with her partner's twenty-five francs per day and her own thirteen francs a day wage she could not manage to provide enough food for her children or even pay rent, League ladies were not persuaded. They concurred, "We have the impression that there exists an absence of good conduct in this household where they cannot manage to eat despite a reasonable income." In the end, they still gave her a meal ("because the woman is enfeebled by her hunger"), but the suspicion that she was not managing her household economy well prevented them from doing more.[122]

If foreign women sometimes experienced social workers' disapprobation, they were not all content to remain passive in their suffering, and in some instances, foreign women gave as well as they got. In 1933, Béatrix Fox, an Irish nurse with two children and another on the way, came to the League "complaining about Public Assistance" and expecting the League's intervention on her behalf and help placing her children with wet nurses.

But League ladies felt she produced "a very bad impression, saying that she will not make a Frenchman of her son and that she does not like France, [the country] that shelters and nourishes her." Remarking that both she and her son were "richly dressed" and that "she does not appear to suffer much from the economic crisis," they proclaimed, "We will wait until she has better sentiments toward our country before we help her."[123] Indeed, while foreign women came to the League for aid and assistance, they had to walk a fine line between proper comportment and self-advocacy without appearing pushy, lest they disrupt League members' view of them as docile clients. After all, middle-class social workers saw themselves as bestowing favors on worthy charges. They, too, brought their own mix of expectations and biases to their charitable works.

Given the particularly interventionist nature of SSCMD social work, mutual frustration and occasional conflict between agents and clients were rather more common. Indeed, while many French and foreign parents at first welcomed the help of SSCMD social workers, some later came to resent the overbearing style of these middle-class busybodies. In 1934, after several years of intervention in favor of the Belgian Wariniers, social workers were shocked to learn—through the concierge, no less—that "the family is very hostile towards us," and "it will no longer be possible to penetrate [the household], even to take care of the young girls."[124] Although social workers were eager to place children in healthful milieus, French and foreign families greeted their suggestions with varying degrees of approval. Italian Adèle Coletta berated social workers for sending her daughter Simone away to the Sisters of Saint Vincent de Paul, claiming that it was a burden on the family budget to pay the pension. Moreover, considering that her husband was the abusive alcoholic, she questioned the wisdom "of placing the child when it was the father who was guilty."[125] Indeed, the majority of conflicts between SSCMD agents and clients were waged over what truly constituted a child's best interests, as foreign mothers and fathers grew resentful watching their parental privilege quietly usurped by nosy social workers. In this, however, they were not so different from French parents who voiced similar reservations about SSCMD social workers.

On rare occasions, social workers manifested cultural, even racial biases in their dealings with immigrant parents. For instance, one social worker struck a decidedly anti-Semitic note when describing Polish Jew Abraham Grossman, recording, "Monsieur Grossmann is a strange man who appears to have escaped from some faraway ghetto. He lives in a world of his own, one completely inadaptable to French life. The only laws that he knows are those of the Israelite religion which he observes with devotion."[126] Several social workers may have believed that different cultures produced different parental norms and expectations, some of which were antithetical to French customs of child-rearing. Of Michel Polycar, social workers declared, "He has conserved of his Turkish origins a rather strict notion of paternal authority," which manifested itself through harsh parenting and a "brusque manner" with his sons that caused them "to withdraw unto themselves." Consequently, they sought to remove his children in order to "place them under a better masculine influence."[127]

Arab North African men were the frequent targets of racist comments. While SSCMD social workers acknowledged that "Monsieur Ghersa is a hard-working, serious man who appears attached to his children," they nevertheless qualified their statement thus: "Of Arab origin, he is hardly adapted to French habits, speaks the language poorly, and appears rather simple-minded." Despite their harsh judgment, Algerian Abdallah Ghersa was, in fact, married to a Frenchwoman, Angèle Lebrun and nothing in their file suggests that the couple spoke any language apart from French with one another. Moreover, the opinions of social workers were decidedly contrary to those of the local community: French concierges and neighbors offered only words of support on behalf of Ghersa, agreeing, "The father loves his children." If anything, they censured his wife whom they described as "fundamentally bad" and "a cruel mother to Roger and Madeleine."[128] And while social workers commented on the "brown" color and "exotic" look of mixed-race children like the Algerian Ghersas and Halimis (and also half-Spanish André Pacaud), these impressions did not ultimately prevent them from helping the families in question.[129] Only once did I find clear-cut evidence of discriminatory behavior by a social worker of the LPAM, and it concerned the potential adoption of a half-French and half-Algerian infant. The League volunteer handling the case recorded, "We spoke to the woman about our reservations concerning the adoption of the child because the father is a mulatto [*mulâtre*], consequently the child will probably be born black, in these conditions adoption will be very difficult."[130] While undoubtedly disturbing, such comments constituted the extreme and hardly add up to a persistent pattern of prejudice on the part of social workers. Apart from this lone example, social workers' racial, ethnic, or religious biases do not appear to have obstructed the flow of aid to either immigrant women or foreign and *métis* children.

Of all the factors that obstructed interactions between social workers and clients, the language barrier was the most recurrent. At the League, for instance, not all foreign women could communicate in French, making it far more difficult to plead their case.[131] In 1934, League volunteers noted with dismay that Gisala Seekar, a twenty-three-year-old Yugoslav, "cannot explain herself, [she] speaks French very badly." In the end, they understood only that she was trying to designate the father of her child. Without understanding what she needed from them, though, they could do no more than send her to La Maternité for the night.[132] This was more or less what they did years earlier, in 1927, for Yohanna Popelka, a twenty-one-year-old Czech girl who, besides managing to relate that she had been "abandoned by the father," could offer League volunteers no further information. She, too, was sent to a convalescence home and League members later spoke with the Czech embassy to inquire as to Czech assistance organizations that would be more linguistically equipped to handle Popelka's case.[133] Although several foreign women braved the encounter with League volunteers without sufficient French fluency, others thought it best to bring an interpreter. In these instances, it was often female friends, family members, or French neighbors and concierges who accompanied them to the League and translated for them.[134]

While perhaps frustrating for both parties, communication difficulties never constituted an impenetrable obstacle. Children and younger relations might serve as interpreters on behalf of their parents. For instance, Georges Kiradi translated the questions of SSCMD social workers for both his Hungarian parents as did Suzanne Friedlander, the eldest daughter of Russian widow Rachel Friedlander.[135] When no relatives were on hand, social workers and immigrants simply made do. And although SSCMD social workers often remarked that foreign-born men and women spoke French poorly, it is telling that they nevertheless managed to obtain copious amounts of information on these families, suggesting a measure of exaggeration on their part. After all, in addition to speaking with families directly, they retrieved their information on households by culling page after page of "testimony" from French concierges, neighbors, teachers, employers, merchants, grocers, and bakers in the neighborhood, indicating the extent to which immigrant men and women successfully made themselves understood by the local community on a daily basis. While foreigners may have spoken in heavily accented French, it was still French that constituted the lingua franca of melting-pot Parisian neighborhoods in the first decades of the twentieth century.

While the state provided immigrant mothers and families with generous benefits during the interwar decades, in the context of the depressed 1930s, foreigners found themselves increasingly forced to seek additional support in an overlapping web of populationist aid societies, maternalist philanthropies, and pronatalist welfare organizations throughout the capital. Despite their disparate methods, all such organizations were eager to help large families and struggling mothers. Importantly, foreign mothers were especially supported during this period. Even child welfare organizations that made the well-being of children the first priority provided material and moral support to foreign mothers in distress, recognizing implicitly that the welfare of children depended first and foremost on the welfare of mothers. If at times class, culture, and language divided social workers from their foreign clients, on the whole national, ethnic, and confessional difference mattered little. In comparison to French clients, only naturalization and the regulation of foreign papers were marked out uniquely for foreign women and families, usually as part of a battery of weapons employed by social workers in the 1930s to enable foreigners to procure more social provisions from an increasingly miserly French state. Consequently, immigrant women figured prominently in the disbursement of welfare aid by both the state and private organizations, collecting the wages of motherhood for their reproductive service to the French nation.

The early welfare state was deeply embedded within neighborhoods and communities throughout France. While each arrondissement of Paris distributed state and municipal assistance through local offices staffed by city workers who became well acquainted with residents' lives, private charitable organizations were either headquartered in working-class neighborhoods, or else sent their armies of social workers marching from headquarters out to the furthest reaches of Paris *populaire*. The following chapters follow these social workers and their immigrant clients back home, to the melting-pot neighborhoods of working-class Paris where French and foreign converged. In the end, it was these neighborhood solidarities that would serve as the ultimate bulwark against moral and material deprivation during the interwar period, and even worse to come during the Second World War.

CHAPTER 5

Neighborhood, Street Culture, and Melting-Pot Mixité

In January 1933, following a heinous murder in *quartier* Sainte Marguerite, unemployed Polish delivery boy Jankiel ("Jacques") Kaczurynski was asked to report on his whereabouts on the day in question. In the process, he recounted to court officials an ordinary day in his life. He and his French mistress, Raymonde, started their morning at a café at the corner of rue de Charonne and rue Godefroy Cavaignac. From there, they parted ways—Raymonde to do her laundry at the washhouse on rue Basfroi and Jankiel to another café on rue du faubourg Saint Antoine for a *rendez-vous* with his friend André Herlin, a French butcher who lived on the same street. After another coffee, they ambled over to Les Halles in the hopes of finding day work "collecting wood from the old crates." With no wood or work to be found, they made their way to the Office de Placement in the center of the city, on rue Jean Lantier, to have their unemployment papers stamped. Now midday, they walked back to café Rey where they had met earlier and chatted for a half hour until Jankiel left to find his *amie*. The pair returned home together for lunch and, while eating, Jankiel learned from Raymonde who had heard from the baker that a murder had taken place in their building that morning.[1]

Through the peregrinations of this Polish *flâneur*, the contours of quartiers Sainte Marguerite and La Roquette as well as its mixed community of inhabitants come into sharp focus. Despite administrative borders separating the two neighborhoods from one other, French and foreign inhabitants blurred those boundaries through their daily habits and chores, their relationships and routines. As they came and went between the two, their meanderings knit together of intersecting streets and alleyways a *quartier vécu*, or lived quarter.² So too did their daily routines knit together a melting-pot community in which the lives of a multicultural bunch of French- and foreign-born inhabitants coalesced. Social histories of migrant communities in Paris have long been attentive to how these urban dynamics of mixed residential life eased the assimilation of foreigners into local society, in notable contrast, of course, to the residential segregation and immigrant ghettoization to be found in the American case.³ Yet, while the fact of urban mixité in working-class neighborhoods of Paris is now well-established, scholars still know far less about how sex and gender contributed to the formation of these cross-cultural solidarities. Drawing on the rich literature exploring gendered urban dynamics among Parisians in the eighteenth- and nineteenth-century capital, this chapter and the next address that oversight.⁴ In the process, they demonstrate how the gendered dynamics of working-class life furnished cross-cultural networks and solidarities that contributed to immigrants' lived experience as reproductive citizens.

This chapter moves us into the tumult of the neighborhoods of Sainte Marguerite and La Roquette, the contiguous Parisian quartiers located in the 11th arrondissement where foreigners of all national and colonial stripes settled in greatest numbers in the first decades of the twentieth century.⁵ Court documents, social worker files, and police sources reveal the texture of gendered sociabilities, especially among men, unfolding in their workplace and lodgings, flowing out onto street corners and into cafés, restaurants, debits, and bars. They show clearly the role of gender in forging cross-cultural solidarities among French and foreign, with particular attention to how working-class life wove immigrant men, especially husbands and fathers, into the very fabric of neighborhood life in interwar Paris, as it had done for countless Limousins, Auvergnats, Bretons, and other provincial migrants drawn to these quartiers since the mid-nineteenth century.⁶ More specifically, these sources shed light on how neighbors drew on preexisting gendered norms of working-class life to assess both French and immigrant itinerants and residents who converged in these quartiers, frequently favoring permanence over transience, the rooted over the uprooted, families and family-men over bachelors and the unattached. In contrast to migrant bachelors, immigrant families who settled en masse in these quartiers and quickly adapted to the gendered rhymes and rhythms of urban working-class life in the capital came to form an integral part of the local Parisian community, rather than a community apart. Even in the depressed 1930s, foreign families did not constitute a caste of outsiders, relegated to the fringes of French society. Rather, they were buoyed and buffered by the close social ties they had long formed—and continued to form—with French and foreign neighbors in local communities, and gender played a decisive role in that process.

Sainte Marguerite and La Roquette: A Portrait of the Neighborhoods

Legacies of popular insurrection dating all the way back to the heady days of the French Revolution dot the history and landscape of the onzième. Most notably, in July 1789, a motley crew of Parisians stormed the Bastille, an ancient prison and a hated symbol of royal despotism. Although they "liberated" embarrassingly few prisoners, the day was nevertheless duly memorialized and proclaimed a national holiday. The next generation of Parisians would participate in the uprisings and barricades of 1848, and their children after them the Paris Commune of 1870, the last great Parisian revolt of the nineteenth century. Communards, as these revolutionaries were called, began their revolt with an act of dramatic defiance, burning the guillotine on

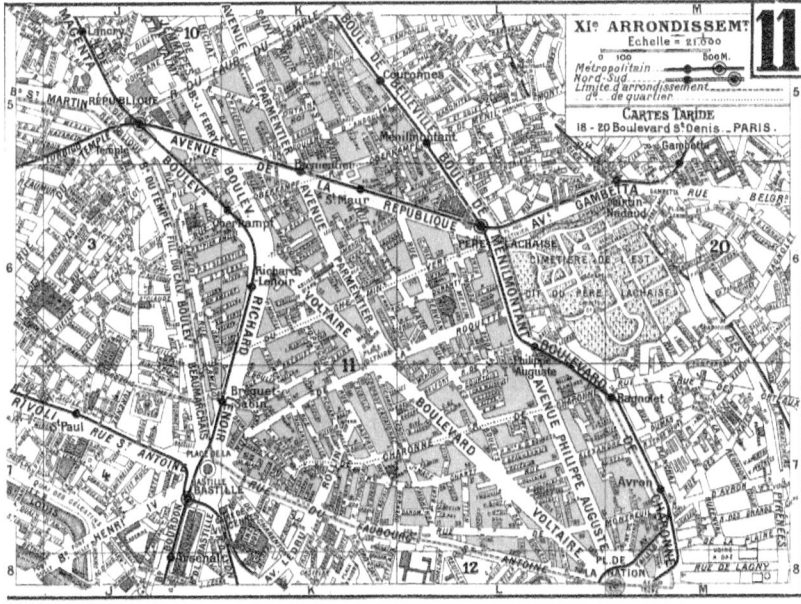

FIGURE 5.1. The 11th arrondissement, 1926. Author unknown, published by Cartes Taride. Paris: Alamy.

the steps of the town hall of the 11th arrondissement. Their demise was no less dramatic: less than a year later, in May 1871, the last of the Communards were lined up against a wall in the Père Lachaise cemetery at the easternmost end of La Roquette and brutally executed by Marshal MacMahon's forces. The *mur de fédérés* remains a vital landmark for all who wish to pay tribute to the city's violent, revolutionary past. The onzième's history is a potent mix of working-class radicalism, revolt, and repression that receded only gradually over the course of the twentieth century.

Physically, the quartiers of Sainte Marguerite and La Roquette radiate eastward out of the Place de la Bastille, a "desert," one moneyed tourist recalled, "where the east-end working class quarter, the vast nameless abode of Labour begins."[7] But the onzième was anything but nameless. Indeed, a panoply of people's champions lend their names to the streets comprising these neighborhoods, a testament to the political legacy of this part of the capital and its notoriously unruly inhabitants. The sheer combination of *rue, boulevard, place,* or *cité,* which memorialize famed *philosophe* Voltaire is but one impressive feature of these quartiers. On the whole, however, street signs pay homage to great political men, veritable icons of the popular classes. Rue Godefroy Cavaignac and Avenue Ledru-Rollin, named after Eléonore Louis Godefroi-Cavaignac and Alexandre Auguste Ledru-Rollin in 1884 and 1879, respectively, pay their due to stalwart republicans and self-proclaimed defenders of the working classes who participated in the revolutionary struggles of 1848. Ledru-Rollin in particular organized the first elections in 1848 after the granting of universal male suffrage. The twentieth century, too, contributed its fair share of left-of-center radicals to the landscape of the onzième. Significantly, Place Léon Blum, formerly Place Voltaire and the current site of town hall, was renamed in 1957 to commemorate the Socialist leader of the short-lived Popular Front government so reviled by the far right, as much for his politics as his parentage (he was Jewish and nearly paid for it with his life under Vichy). The streets baptized in honor of Blum and the rest represent a formal acknowledgement by municipal powers of the leftist political heritage of the onzième, past and present.[8]

While Communists never held absolute sway in this district, as they did in the neighboring 19th and 20th, residents were nevertheless solidly left-leaning and socialist in their voting patterns from about 1901 onward.[9] Lucien Besset, an industrialist and moderate-left radical elected deputy in 1932, was, in the words of one historian, "more representative of the average opinion of the 11th arrondissement than the communists elected in 1936."[10] And there is reason to think that Besset was an influential presence in the neighborhood, well-known and respected by French constituents and immigrant inhabitants. Besset was something of a go-to man for many foreign families in the quartier on whose behalf he frequently wrote to the Bureau de Sceau from his office on rue des Immeubles Industriels. His letters sped up the naturalization process for worthy immigrant pères de familles; indeed, he was always keen to point out that these men were "pères de familles *nombreuses.*" Besset wrote, for instance, four separate letters on behalf of Polish Jew Maurice Bergman, a father of five, between January 1932 and February 1933.[11] In 1931, he not only wrote on behalf of Italian Camille Perron, but even went so far as to offer to pay his naturalization fees.[12]

Although elected deputies like Besset reflected the center-left tradition of the onzième's inhabitants, the political associations of immigrants residing in these quartiers remain less clear, not least of all because it was so dangerous for immigrants to be outwardly political between the wars.[13] Interwar Communist activism entailed severe consequences for foreigners, which would only become clear decades later under Vichy. In 1933, Frenchman Léon Dubois and his Spanish friend José Gimenez were hauled in for plastering "propaganda" along boulevard Voltaire about the First World War, or what their tracts derided as "the 19th anniversary of the world-wide slaughter [*la tuerie mondiale*]" advertising also "a regional demonstration against war and fascism."[14] Ten years later this blemish on his record would come back to haunt Gimenez when Vichy officials eyed him suspiciously as an "active propagandist of the Communist party of the 11th arrondissement."[15] Not even naturalized immigrants were safe under Vichy if they engaged in obstreperous political activism between the wars. In 1941, Vichy officials initiated the denaturalization of Leiba Marcu, a Romanian tailor who came to France in 1912 with his wife, Riva Matas, and their three sons (figure 5.2). The cause: he was a known member of the Socialist party and, of course, Jewish.[16] That same year, French-naturalized, Polish-born Jew Chaïm Bromberg was arrested, denaturalized, and deported by Vichy officials as a "communist militant" and "propagandist" who engaged in "revolutionary activity."[17] While neighborhood street signs gesture at a staunch leftist tradition, participation in that tradition came at tremendous personal cost, especially to well-known, foreign-born radicals during the Vichy period.

The vast majority of remaining streets in these neighborhoods pay homage to the craftsmen, tradesmen, and small time manufacturers who made their fortunes in this district throughout the eighteenth and nineteenth centuries: for instance, rue Keller, after the successful foundry of a goldsmith; rue Richard Lenoir, after the fabric manufacturer; rue des Taillandiers, literally "street of the edge-tool makers," who practiced their trade there; and finally rue de la Forge Royale, deriving its name from a sign that once

Figure 5.2. A photograph of Romanian Riva Hena Marcu née Matas who lived on rue de la Forge Royale with her husband, Leiba, and her sons Meyer, Herman, and Jacques. Riva Hena Marcu née Matas, Application de carte d'identité, October 18, 1921, in Leiba Marcu and Rebecca née Matas, I/A 136, Archives de la Préfecture de la Police.

advertised the services of a forge to the inhabitants of the quartier long ago.[18] When interwar Catholic social reformer Jacques Valdour visited this network of streets branching off of the faubourg Saint Antoine, he identified it as "metal-workers' own personal domain," for, "they swarm there, invading the courtyards, the rear courtyards, [and] passageways." He noted too the panorama of signs advertising the many small trades of its craftsmen, hung all about "on plaques of stone, wood, leather, [and] zinc, sculpted, engraved, enameled, hooked up nearly everywhere above the doors or atop the pillars of the doorways." One abridged list of the trades listed on these plaques gives a flavor of the rich and variegated world of small crafts as well as the universe of specialized skill in which these craftsmen of the interwar quartier participated:

> Metal Shaving—Tube Fabrication—Artisanal Brasswork—Metal Slabbing—Bronzework—Gold and Silver Plating—Bronze-Worker, Varnisher and Polisher—Fine Hardware—Lighting Fixtures—Tools—Nails—Tin

Plates—Shower Fixtures—Artisanal Locksmith—Plumbing Fixtures—
Zinc-Worker—Mechanical Modeling—Electroplating—Drilling—Bar
Turning—Foundry—Tubes—Electrical Fixtures—Glazing and Shaving—
Bronze Imitation.[19]

In fact, Valdour's list is a good sample of the professional backgrounds of many of the French and foreign male inhabitants of these quartiers, as well as a good indication of how the socio-professional profile of the neighborhood had entered a period of transition. For over a century, the faubourg Saint Antoine had been nearly synonymous with a thriving craft culture centered on cabinetmaking, furniture making, and woodworking, transitioning also toward metal- and glass working. Located in the southern extremities of the onzième, the faubourg Sainte Antoine still preserved its workshop atmosphere and labor traditions but was entering a slow decline after the war. Already, the introduction of steam-powered machines and the more general mechanization of small trades in the late nineteenth century had reduced the number of necessary employees and led to more streamlined designs.[20] As the furniture-making industry tapered off in the last half of the nineteenth century, the metallurgical trades that dominated Valdour's list soared. By the early twentieth century, the growth of manufacturing and factories in the north of the neighborhoods also changed the occupational profile of residents, attracting more unskilled factory workers, for instance, to the "gas factory" at 104 rue de Charonne.[21]

The political cast and occupational character of these neighborhoods shaped the migrant waves that settled there. In the nineteenth century, they were Auvergnats and Bretons, skilled masons and artisans. By 1863, enough Protestant Belgian construction workers and their families had settled in Sainte Marguerite to justify the erection of a small chapel on 97 rue de Charonne, as well as a Lutheran school on rue des Taillandiers for the children of German and Alsatian migrant workers, and the Temple de Bon Secours on rue Titon, which stands still. From the 1880s onward, immigrants from Italy, Switzerland, and Luxemburg began to cluster in faubourg Saint Antoine, overflowing into La Roquette. By the early twentieth century, Eastern European Jews of Russian, Polish, Romanian, and Greco-Turkish origin, sometimes called "Levantine Israelites," were also spilling out of the Marais, past the Place de la Bastille, and eastward into these neighborhoods. According to painstakingly gathered municipal statistics, not only did the onzième boast one of the largest immigrant populations in Paris from 1881 to 1926, but the quartiers of Sainte Marguerite and La Roquette, in particular, attracted the lion's share of foreigners. In 1921, foreigners accounted for between 10 and 11 percent of residents; by 1926, that figure was closer to 16 percent.[22]

As immigrants extended into the 11th arrondissement in the early decades of the twentieth century, they brought with them their traditional *métiers*, mostly the confection trades in leather, furs, and fine fabrics. Their tradition of confection *à domicile* further transformed the socio-professional fabric of the neighborhood, pushing it toward textiles, an industry that predominates still in the Popincourt network of streets today. By the end of the 1920s, nearly one in seven residents of Sainte Marguerite and La Roquette was foreign-born, which led Valdour to remark during his masquerade as a lathe-turner in La Roquette, "The number of foreigners living in my neighborhood is considerable." He continued, "The abundance of foreigners is such that I frequently pass people in the street speaking a foreign language: one day, on rue Popincourt, I met two Chinese persons; and, another day, two Italian workers; another time, I took my meal next to a Portuguese man; one evening, I passed four Spanish workers in the street, then two Italian workers."[23]

Patterns of chain migration influenced immigrant settlement patterns, not least of all because French and foreign networks of assistance eased the pain of transition. These neighborhoods were rife with mutual assistance organizations, particularly those organized and operated by Italian immigrants who had lived there for at least a generation, such as the Mission Catholique italienne on 46 rue de Montreuil.[24] Several Jewish mutual aid organizations also catered to residents in the area, including the Comité de secours aux anciens combattants russes, which maintained a local section, and the Comité de secours aux juifs russes, devoted to the material aid of Jewish women and children.[25] Significantly, however, these neighborhoods bustled with French welfarist activity trained on working-class mothers, children, and families, and these private efforts augmented in the 1930s. With the deepening of the Depression, a *soupe populaire*, or soup kitchen, opened its doors on 23 rue Basfroi and attracted a regular immigrant clientele. In order to receive their free meal, immigrant workingmen braved the considerable risk of being caught up in the police dragnet during the 1930s, when police roundups at soup kitchens targeted foreign male indigents in violation of work visas.[26] By contrast, maternalist organizations in the 11th arrondissement continued to draw both French and immigrant families through the 1930s unabated and, it should be noted, unmolested.

Between the wars, immigrant women constituted about 45 percent of the foreign population of these two neighborhoods, a rate that mirrors their overall presence in the Seine Department as well as their presence in interwar Paris.[27] In addition to gender ratios suggesting the large number of foreign-born families in these neighborhoods, matriculation records show that more foreign children attended schools in the 11th arrondissement than any other district in Paris.[28] Conforming to the neighborhoods' demographics, the children were predominantly Italian, Russian, Polish, and Ottoman Greek and Turkish. All things being equal, about 5 percent of all foreign children in Paris should have attended school in each of the twenty arrondissements of Paris; instead, 15 percent of all foreign children in Paris were matriculated in schools in the 11th arrondissement, three times what one would expect.[29] That trend persisted at least until 1929.[30]

Of course, some immigrant women and children lived in boarding houses, which given the onzième's tradition of attracting migrants, were common in Sainte Marguerite and La Roquette during the interwar years. The Ruche parisienne on 20 boulevard Voltaire, for instance, was billed as "a hostel for young Swiss women in Paris temporarily." For twenty francs per day, the nuns of Saint Vincent de Paul received these young Swiss women, between the ages of eighteen and twenty-six, and operated a restaurant on the premises providing meals for just five francs each.[31] A certain Foyer de Jeunes, or youth hostel, at 151 Avenue Ledru-Rollin also provided dormitory-style shelter for children, though not all of their pensioners were orphans.[32] Another Foyer des Jeunes is also likely to have existed at 20 Passage Charles Dalléry, though most pensioners were young Frenchmen.[33]

The Palais de la Femme, one of the foremost sites of accommodation for migrant women in Paris, was also located in these neighborhoods, on 94 rue de Charonne. It first opened its doors in 1910 as the Hôtel populaire, part of the Groupement des maison ouvrières. Initially, it was a workingmen's hostel, though in 1911, the Abbé Mainguet made a point to distinguish the Hôtel populaire from the average "garni for the poor" that was "so often insalubrious." Unsurprisingly, its boarders were about 11 percent foreign workingmen in the few years it existed.[34] In 1914, at the start of hostilities, the Hôtel populaire was converted into a Foyer des soldats, or a soldier's hostel where men assembled before their mobilization. After the war the structure lay in disrepair until 1926 when the Salvation Army bought the building and repurposed it instead as the Palais de la Femme, essentially a boardinghouse for women who, due to the "penury of lodgings" in the capital were in "great moral and physical danger."[35] One approving visitor commented thusly:

> In the middle of working-class Paris, on rue de Charonne, populous and teeming, that ascends from Bastille to Père Lachaise . . . in faubourg Saint Antoine where each ancient building could recount tales of battles of yesteryear, where each street-corner has seen a barricade, where the revolutionary spirit simmers under the cinders, because

poverty there is always great. . . . in the middle of these black apartment buildings, of these sordid courtyards, of these narrow streets, there you will find this enormous building and its many windows.[36]

In this manner, one visitor tied the appearance of this boardinghouse to its surroundings and so too might we. On the plaque that still stands before the structure today, it states: "Throughout the years, the Palais de la Femme has welcomed, without distinction to culture, religion or civil status, every woman needing to secure accommodation in Paris." The foreign-born women and, especially foreign-born mothers, who found shelter in the Palais de la Femme thus joined a revolving cast of characters, French and immigrant, who created a home for themselves in these neighborhoods between the wars.[37]

A Geography of Neighborhood Vice: Crimes of Transience, Crimes of Permanence

To live in Sainte Marguerite and La Roquette during the interwar decades was to navigate a rough and tumble working-class neighborhood. Still, neither quarter was among the most dangerous neighborhoods in Paris. The rate of violent death, while not low per se, never achieved the heights of Grandes Carrières or Clignancourt, contiguous quarters in the 18th arrondissement that ranked among the most unsafe in Paris. Murder and violent crime such as physical assault or rape accounted for just 3 or 4 percent of cases filed in *mains courantes*, or neighborhood complaints, for Sainte Marguerite and La Roquette in this sample. The 1933 murder of the Tokars, an old Russian couple who had lived on 78 rue de Charonne for more than two decades, rocked the entire Franco-foreign community, including Jankiel Kaczurynski and his French *amie*, in part because murder was such an uncommon occurrence.

Rather than headline-grabbing crimes, then, these neighborhoods were rife with more everyday offenses. Theft, especially petty theft, accounted for over half of all offenses recorded in 1926 and 1933. Pickpocketing, too, was a common form of subsistence and middle-class visitors to the neighborhood made easy targets for foreigners looking for quick cash. Francisco Clementi, a Spanish cabinetmaker, picked the pocket of Georgette Graux, a Frenchwoman come to visit the 11th arrondissement from her home in the bourgeois 7th arrondissement. She was sampling the wares of a street merchant on Place de la Nation near the corner of boulevard Voltaire when Clementi made off with her purse and wallet.[38] Fraud and "breach of faith" (*abus de confiance*), particularly in business dealings and informal loan agreements, followed, though at a great distance. Disorderly conduct (*rebellion et outrages*), vagrancy, and assault also ranked regularly among the top ten most common transgressions in these neighborhoods. While disorderly conduct was a charge commonly employed against residents making merry on a Saturday night, vagrancy charges typically targeted the itinerant, and itinerant men at that.

Although many immigrants eventually settled in these neighborhoods, a more mobile bunch occasionally found their way to Sainte Marguerite and La Roquette. Place de la Nation, rue de Montreuil, and boulevard Voltaire were common meeting grounds for vagabonds and tramps, driven there by hunger and poverty. Swiss Auguste Gysin was arrested on rue Saint Sabin for vagrancy because, in the words of his arresting officer, "He cannot work, he has no money, [and] he stole a garbage bin to procure for himself some money and bread." This officer added, as though an afterthought, "He has no family in Paris."[39]

Men rather than women were arrested for vagrancy, which is not to say that there were not also plenty of poor and desperate foreign women trying to make their way in Paris. Their methods, however, were different. On the whole, foreign women were written up for very petty offenses and minor violations. Only in rare instances were they arrested. Although prostitution accounted for a very low percentage of crime in these neighborhoods, immigrant women were arrested for prostitution at high rates. Despite the deepening of the Depression, the number of prostitution cases in both Sainte Marguerite and La Roquette plummeted in 1933 as compared to 1926: in Sainte Marguerite, a mere five *filles insoumises* were arrested throughout 1933 and only one was foreign. That there would be but a handful of prostitution cases in a working-class quarter during the depressed thirties seems unlikely.

French and foreign prostitutes worked the same network of streets in these neighborhoods during the interwar years: rue Amelot, rue Daval, and Place de la Nation.[40] And yet, very few of those foreign women arrested were residents of Sainte Marguerite or La Roquette. Rather, they tended to reside in the northern part of the 12th arrondissement, near faubourg Saint Antoine. A far cry from the romanticized images of primped women working in nineteenth-century *maisons de tolérance*, these unlucky women led a less spectacular existence. They were often arrested after finishing with a john in some dark alleyway or *passage* late at night. When Yvonne Kumen, a nineteen-year old waitress from Luxemburg living on rue d'Austerlitz in the 12th arrondissement, was arrested on rue Amelot for prostitution, she explained her offense with alarming candor: "Having arrived three months ago and finding herself without work she prostituted herself in order to survive."[41]

If prostitution was not strictly regulated in the 1930s, the illegal sale of goods by foreign women certainly was. They were typically caught selling illegal wares along rue de la Roquette, Avenue Ledru-Rollin, and rue Popincourt. They sold books, clothing, flowers, and other assorted knickknacks. Some also sold foodstuffs, such as garlic, pears, melons, grapes, parsley, and peppers. Immigrant women appear regularly among those written up on this charge in part because street vending and peddling was a common form of subsistence among them throughout the 1920s and 1930s. From the 1880s onward, Eastern European Jewish workingwomen from the neighborhood toiled away as street merchants at the nearby Carreau du Temple in the Marais. Russian Jews Anna Tchervonogour and Frida Goldenberg as well as Romanian Jew Adèle Brodski animated this marketplace in central Paris through their bustling commerce, selling, hawking, and haggling with customers everyday but the Sabbath, which they scrupulously observed.[42] The sudden appearance of immigrant workingwomen in police registers in the 1930s suggests not the appearance of a new trade, but the clamping down of the police apparatus on unregulated traders that competed with local business interests. Some women were repeat offenders and not all were residents of these neighborhoods: for instance, Algerian Françoise Dsai and Italian Marie Tomasso were both listed as street peddlers residing in the 18th and 19th arrondissements, respectively.[43]

Arrest records also suggest patterns of sociability among these foreign vendors. Given the clustering of the arrests, it appears exceedingly likely that foreign vendors grouped together on a single street to hawk their wares at once. On February 14, 1933, Serbian Joseph Stachler, Algerian Sadek ben Salsbe Chahmini, Italian Salvatore Gusmini, and two Frenchmen were arrested for the illegal sale of items.[44] Stachler and Gusmini lived on the same street, Passage Deschamps. As we will soon see, proximity of lodging often suggested overlapping social links—in this case, overlapping social links aside from their shared "commercial activities." Arrest records for women, too, reveal networks among immigrant women. On March 6, 1933, the above-mentioned Françoise Dsai (Algerian) was hauled in along with three Italian women who lived in the neighboring 19th arrondissement: Jeanne Verrucchia, Antonia Di Masero née Rongione, and Marie Tomasso née Di Masero.[45] That at least two of these three women share patronymics also points to the overlap of kinship and commercial networks. Thus, street peddling, like vagrancy and prostitution, reveals a world of itinerant foreign men and women who occasionally found their way to La Roquette and Sainte Marguerite.

Among residents, the most common petty offenses (*contraventions*) recorded were public drunkenness, disturbing the peace (*scandale*), brawling (*rixe*), and "mild violence" (*violences légères*). Together, these categories accounted for nearly two-thirds of all minor offenses recorded in these neighborhoods in 1926 and 1933. Relationships between inhabitants of the quarter and the police could often be strained. It was not uncommon for insults like "idiot," "bastard," "scum," "dirty good-for-nothing," and other salty phrases to be hurled at police officers by delinquents trying to beat a fast retreat.[46] Confrontations between French and foreign residents and police officers often took place on Saturday nights when men of all nationalities came together to celebrate the end of the workweek. Police officers occasionally intervened to temper these boisterous evenings and received punches, kicks, sometimes bites as their reward.[47]

Then again, violence directed toward police officers was part and parcel of the, at times, rough culture of working-class male leisure. Men in the neighborhood participated in their fair share of bar brawling and street fighting with one another quite regularly; such episodes are too numerous to count.[48] Depicting one such "jolly evening" typical of a Saturday night in his working-class neighborhood, Orwell paints a pretty picture of dart-playing, bottle-throwing, binge drinking, and loud living, concluding, "For many men of the quarter, unmarried and with no future to think of, the weekly drinking-bout was the one thing that made life worth living."[49]

Although men were visible in the streets, French and foreign women, too, participated in Parisian street theater. Their voices could also be heard among the chorus, singing, chanting, yelling, and quarreling with one other. Two Italian women (who were probably related given their shared patronymic, Thozzi) drew a crowd of one hundred neighbors when they began hurling insults at one another on rue des Immeubles Industriels—a narrow cobblestone pathway lined with furniture shops owned by foreigners like Russian Motel Mozeur.[50] According to police records, the two women had to be pulled apart and the crowd of workers who gathered to watch them forcibly dispersed.[51] In October 1925, another "discussion" turned violent between two neighbors, the first a French galosh maker, the widow Marie Guichard, and the second a Belgian maid, Marie Virginie Drocourt. Their public dispute embroiled several residents in their building at 110 rue de Montreuil.[52] Foreign women were also involved in the occasional bar brawl, though that was a form of bellicosity usually reserved for men. In late August 1933, Romanian Aurélie Schwartz swung at her countrywoman Dora Frai with a string bag containing a liter of wine at the café Rey. The wine bottle broke on Frai's face and she was taken to the nearby Saint Antoine Hospital. Witnesses at the café on rue du faubourg Saint Antoine included a relative of Aurélie Schwartz, Joseph Hermann, as well as a Russian neighbor, Rebecca Silverman.[53]

Some troublemakers were well known to the community because of their immoderate (and immodest) behavior. Neighbors of Giuseppe Costamagna on rue des Boulets complained that when drunk the Italian day laborer "criait à tue-tête" out in the street.[54] On New Years' Day in 1926, Said Ahmed Chaïd, an Algerian metalworker living on rue Sedaine, caused quite the rumpus in a bar on rue de Charonne. French and foreign patrons complained that he had consumed too much drink, insulted them, and to top it off, "opened his pants and exhibited his sexual parts in front of everyone!" After he sobered up, Chaïd shamefacedly admitted to the first two accusations, but vigorously denied the last.[55] Then there was "the Boxer," who, as his nickname suggested, was renowned throughout the neighborhood for his combativeness, as poor Joseph Diener, a Polish cabinet worker living on rue Godefroy Cavaignac, discovered one summer day in 1926. In fact, the Boxer's real name was Marcel Bergermann, a Polish cabinetmaker himself who lived with his mother in a small apartment on rue du faubourg Saint Antoine.[56] Residents knew Costamagna, Chaïd, and "the Boxer" because they worked, lived, and socialized with them every day in the quartier.

To be sure, the twentieth-century quartier vécu was larger than the small network of streets it had once been for nineteenth-century residents of the capital. Early twentieth-century Parisians strayed further, but rarely beyond the neighboring arrondissements. In the case of residents of Sainte Marguerite and La Roquette, a handful worked in the 12th and the 20th arrondissements, to the south and to the east, respectively. By the 1930s, however, the search for work in the capital could send French and foreign scurrying all over the capital, as it did Jankiel Kaczurynski. Kaczurynski's winding trajectory through the city on a typical day also reminds us that the experience of foreign workingmen could be one of constant mobility, particularly when work was scarce. Even the act of settlement masked a certain ongoing transience that hung about foreign bachelors like a rotten smell.

Immigrant Workingmen, Habitats of Transit, and the Social Consequences of Male Mobility

Though the search for work constituted the immediate cause of mobility, finding a job did not necessarily entail "settlement" for immigrant workingmen, nor did it put an end to the ongoing search for affordable accommodations. The combination of frequent work shortages and unstable wages proved a constant source of dispute between foreign workingmen and their *hôteliers* and *logeurs*. Failure to pay rent, in full and on time, was the most common source of conflict between French landlords and their foreign working-class male tenants.⁵⁷ Sometimes this offense was coupled with other accusations. Belgian De Villa's lodger claimed that his wayward tenant slipped out one morning, making off with sheets and bed covers.⁵⁸ Similarly, the *hôtelière* of a building on Place de la Bastille accused Polish Joseph Schulberg of both failing to pay rent and stealing room amenities.⁵⁹

Complaints suggest that foreign workingmen were, indeed, frequently on the move and that more than a few did at least attempt to sneak off without paying full rent. Such behavior nourished an atmosphere of suspicion between lodgers and workingmen and sometimes spurred informal negotiations between them. Giuseppe Biglione and his French *hôtelier* on rue Mont Louis had no luck coming to such an agreement. The Italian chimney worker wanted to let his room to another tenant in the mornings when he was away at work and pay only his share of the rent for the evenings. Lodger René Pelegry, however, saw in this proposal a means by which Biglione could make off with all his belongings without paying any rent so he demanded to hold on to Biglione's bags until the room was adequately paid for.⁶⁰ Other foreigners, too, tried their hand at subletting under the nose of French hotel owners with limited success.⁶¹ In Orwell's description of his time in Paris as a foreign workingman, he recalled an episode involving a young Italian whom his hôtelière, a certain Madame F., "did not like the look of" and "made him pay a week's rent in advance." True to form, the Italian paid the rent, stayed six nights in the hotel, then, "on the last night, robbed a dozen rooms including mine."⁶² Dealings between foreign male lodgers and French hotel owners sometimes created such tense situations that police intervention was required. French concierge Marie Bouger at 8 rue Popincourt felt herself so "menaced" by her Turkish tenant, Sabateye Nahmias, that she lodged a formal complaint against him for the repeated insults he dealt her.⁶³

Conflicts and negotiations between foreign tenants and French lodgers like Biglione and Pelegry are reminiscent of Orwell and Boris's elaborate plot to evade the French *patron* of a rundown hotel where they had roomed with a third foreigner, identified in the text only as "the Jew." In fact, they suspected their Jewish roommate of giving both the *patron* and them the slip, leaving the two friends to foot the bill for the room in his stead. Determined to "foutre le camp" first, Boris suggested they sneak out their belongings bit by bit and, so as not to alert the attention of their vigilant hotel owner, fill their suitcases with stones foraged from the Seine. If the *patron* suspected anything, claimed Boris, "He will do what he always does, the mean sneak; he will go up to my room and feel the weight of my suitcase. And when he feels the weight of stones he will think it is still full. Strategy, eh?" As for the suitcase, it would have to be abandoned because, as the Russian ex-general reasoned, "One always abandons something in a retreat. Look at Napoleon at the Beresina!"[64] Although told with characteristic wit, the episode recounted by Orwell pointed to a moral economy of suspicion and a culture of intrigue that existed between single foreign workingmen and their Parisian hôteliers.

Foreign workingmen of the same national, ethnic, or confessional affiliation often roomed together as a result of economic necessity and as a strategy to lower the cost of rent, a pattern that was, in comparison, less common among French workingmen, whether of Parisian or provincial origin.[65] Then again, the benefits of cohabitation were perhaps more obvious for foreign rather than French workingmen. After all, cohabitation allowed them to enjoy the comfort of cultural camaraderie and to buffer themselves against the shocks of uprootedness in an alien environment. Living with a compatriot may also have been thought to guarantee personal safety and provide a modicum of security in a hostile and alien city. Ironically, we know how common cohabitation among foreign men was because of how much theft occurred between male roommates. Rarely were men robbed of expensive valuables for, truth be told, they rarely owned anything of value. If, in the western arrondissements, residents registered the loss of pearl earrings, gold watches, and fine jewelry, in the eastern arrondissements, inhabitants lost rather less-valuable items.[66]

Among foreign workingmen in Sainte Marguerite and La Roquette, everyday items were most commonly stolen: clothing, shoes, suitcases, and other possessions more banal besides. Algerian laborer Belaïd Ouaksel was robbed of a watch, a razor, and a pair of shoes by "a compatriot by the name of Akli Zalah who slept for eight days in the same room and left last night."[67] In La Roquette, Czech construction worker Jan Kluchy was robbed of a shirt and razor by countryman and roommate, Pavel Semain.[68] Two Romanian men, who had shared a room in a hotel on rue des Taillandiers for five months, fought one evening and the next morning one made off with the other's clothing.[69] That clothing was the most common item stolen indicates a certain economy of want that existed among foreign workingmen in these neighborhoods. The loss of one pair of trousers could halve a wardrobe.

Groups of foreign men might take over a single *garni*, or hostel, the likes of which mushroomed throughout the capital during the interwar years. Variously referred to as *chambrées*, *hôtels meublés*, or simply *meublées*, garnis were cheap, dirty, and cramped, packed together and stacked atop one another in buildings that approximated dive hotels. Their occupants were overwhelmingly young, single, male, proletarian, and by the interwar years, foreign.[70] Indeed, although foreigners only ever accounted for, at most, one-tenth of the Parisian population, they comprised roughly half of garni residents (see table 5.1). There was a particular geography to garnis in the capital; they clustered in the city's most working-class areas and its most recently incorporated districts at that.[71] Consequently, garnis were characterized by a culture of transience and impermanence both shaping and shaped by the demographics of their occupants who were, above all, liminal characters. During the nineteenth and twentieth centuries, there was a cultural association between garnis and all that was seedy, criminal, and subversive about the city. For interwar Parisians, garnis were the shadowy sites of lovers' trysts, criminal characters, and sexual vice of all sorts. As sociologists Claire Lévy-Vroelant and Céline Barrere have shown in their work on garnis as a *lieu de mémoire,* the garni was "a space of degradation and of promiscuity, of social danger in need of reform . . . along with the cabaret, the bistro, or the street." It provided a place "for those without roots or anchorage in the city."[72] Contemporaries in the capital inextricably tied the presence of an immigrant underclass of workingmen to these transitory spaces of the capital. The respectable residents of apartment buildings, where women and families were far more numerous, existed in a world apart from these so-called subversives.[73]

The garni was truly the bachelor's housing option and gave rise to a particularly masculine subculture, something that was not at all the case for apartment buildings. Relationships between foreign workingmen and garni operators strained under the pressure and, in the worst cases, they resembled two opposing factions with each party sticking to their own. A group of Czech day laborers staying together in a garni on Cité Beauharnais purposefully hid the robberies committed by one of their own for months rather than turn him in to the police. The Czech workmen endured thefts of their foreign papers, clothes, money, and other valuables because, "not wanting to denounce a compatriot, they hoped that he would return to his senses of his own accord." In fact, it was only after their compatriot stole from the garni operator, Monsieur Valibus, that the police were finally called in. Despite the mountain of goods he had siphoned off of his compatriots over the weeks, it was the comparatively negligible sum of ten francs taken

Table 5.1 French and foreign population of Paris residing *en garni,* 1926 and 1931

YEAR	FRENCH	FOREIGN	TOTAL
1926	1,111,745	1,140,121	2,251,866
1931	1,798,936	1,008,295	2,807,231

Source: "Population étrangère en garni," Annuaire Statistique de la Ville de Paris, 1925–26, 483; "Population étrangère en garni," Annuaire Statistique de la Ville de Paris, 1929–31, 296.

from the Frenchman that did him in.⁷⁴ Another Czech laborer, Jospeh Vik, attempted to file complaints against his hôtelier on multiple occasions, but officers did not take his charges seriously, reasoning, "Vik appears haggard, speaks French poorly, [and] speaks sentences that seem to make no sense." Not only did officers refuse to follow up with the French hotel owner Vik identified, but they sent the foreign workingman to an infirmary, pending possible institutionalization.⁷⁵ Although extreme, this example throws in stark relief the risks run by foreign workingmen should their complaints fall on unsympathetic, even hostile ears at the local police station.

A culture of mistrust reigned between single foreign men on the one hand and local police and landlords, on the other. Although single immigrant women occasionally landed in hot water with their landlords, those instances were few and far between.⁷⁶ Despite foreign bachelors' residency and settlement in these neighborhoods, French lodgers continued to see them as transients liable to depart without even a moment's notice. Consequently, French hôteliers developed strategies of their own to monitor them, to ensure that rent was paid regularly, and to make certain that no property was damaged or stolen. In this, the local police presence worked in French and propertied interests, more apt to penalize and investigate mobile foreign bachelors than French landlords, who were their fellow countrymen and presumably "known quantities" in the neighborhood. It is possible, too, that certain landlords in the area were not especially keen on renting to immigrant men and especially not to immigrant bachelors, considered a roving population that changed hotels with impunity, left debts in their wake, and were generally less dependable than families. This low-level, interpersonal hostility may account for the limited extent of single foreign male settlement in these two quarters where foreign families, instead, took their place.

Networks of Cross-Cultural Male Sociability

Some foreign men who found themselves in these neighborhoods after the First World War knew one another in the old country, reproducing their small villages in departments throughout France.⁷⁷ In Paris, patterns of chain migration played a part in the development of male networks of sociability as well. For instance, nearly half of all naturalized Romanians in these neighborhoods were born in Jassy, and the rest in one of three cities: Falticeni, Piatra, and Bucharest. Similarly, the majority of naturalized Turks, hailed from Constantinople. Of course, once in Paris, coincidence, too, played its part. Two natives of Palazzalo, Italy, and childhood acquaintances named Salvatore Infantino and Salvatore Musso reconnected years later in Paris as adults when they ran into each other on the street.[78] Since roughly 10 percent of foreign men naturalized before 1930 benefited from the Law of August 5, 1914, which gave French citizenship to those foreign men (and, by extension, their wives and children) who volunteered in the Foreign Legion during World War I, a handful may have met in the French armed forces. Jean Vizner, a Hungarian iron fitter living on rue de Charonne with his wife and daughter, served in the Foreign Legion for six years in the 1920s. There, he met a compatriot, Giza Sezentmihalgi, "with whom I continued to have friendly relations in Paris, after our liberation."

Though Sezentmihalgi lived in the neighboring 20th arrondissement, he was a frequent guest in the Vizner home and was often accompanied there by his "French mistress." These soirées sometimes included other foreigners, as well, like Vizner's friend Antonio Ongaro. The Hungarian iron fitter and Italian mechanic met in the changing rooms of the Société Générale des Voitures on rue d'Aubervilliers in the 19th arrondissement where they both worked and where Ongaro lived. Describing how they struck up their acquaintance, Vizner explained, "About two months ago, I lost or someone stole my caliper and I spoke to Ongaro who spontaneously offered me a tool of this sort. I wanted to pay him, but he refused and to compensate him, I told him that he should come over one day and eat lunch at my home."[79] Thus was it that the Hungarian Vizner family, Italian Antonio Ongaro, and Hungarian Sezentmihalgi and his French mistress all enjoyed a meal of beef and potatoes served by Jean Vizner's wife, Gisèle, one April afternoon in 1930. They were the very picture of family life, illustrating how entirely the gendered rhythms of working-class domesticity could weave French and foreign into the fabric of local life.

The workplace, then, was a key site of multicultural sociability for French and foreign men, whether they spent their days in the garage, like Ongaro and Vizner, or the factory, the butcher shop, the woodshop, or one of the many furniture and cabinet workshops that employed the majority of workingmen in these neighborhoods. Very successful immigrants, of course, owned and operated workshops in Sainte Marguerite and La Roquette. These foreign-born owners employed both French and foreign workers, a fact recorded with some consistency by interested French officials seeking to gage the "Francophile sentiments" of successful foreign entrepreneurs.[80] Ovcei Tessller, a Russian cabinetmaker, employed a dozen men, both French and foreign, from the neighborhood while most of Romanian cabinetmaker Avram Lavner's thirteen employees were French.[81] Other foreign employers in the neighborhood had an even larger pool of employees: Aran Bahr Lubtchansky, a Russian manufacturer of beds and bedsteads, employed some forty workers at his factory on rue Mercoeur.[82] The Haentges, a pair of brothers from Luxemburg (married, it would appear, to a pair of sisters from Suresnes) owned and operated a furniture factory on rue Titon where they employed nearly fifty French and foreign workers.[83]

Of course, foreign entrepreneurs and manufacturers might also cause minor disturbances in their local communities by employing shady tactics to compete with local merchants. There was no small amount of hostility on the part of French shopkeepers who did not appreciate newly implanted foreign competitors who failed to adhere, deliberately or otherwise, to commercial guidelines recognized by the rest of the neighborhood. Ber Moskowitch, a Russian baker living on rue de la Forge Royale, kept one of his employees working all night. When asked by the police why he did not release his employee sooner, Moskowitch admitted that he needed the young man's expertise because "I wanted to have fresh bread to fight the local competition [*la concurrence voisine*]."[84] Other immigrant entrepreneurs experienced—or invited—similar difficulties on themselves. In 1933, police officers penalized Polish Moschek Gotainer for keeping his furniture store open on a Sunday in violation of a 1925 decree.[85] Perhaps Gotainer had not yet adapted to the local rhythms of commercial life in the neighborhood, but the frequency of such incidents invites less generous interpretations. In 1933, many Eastern European Jewish butchers elicited local resentment (and official sanction) for keeping their butcher shops open on Mondays, when local butcher shops in the neighborhood traditionally closed.[86] In fact, Polish Abraham Lis, a butcher at 160 Avenue Ledru-Rollin, was written up no less than seven times in 1933, suggesting that willful ignorance and the spirit of commercial rivalry may have inspired him more than sheer naiveté.[87] Of course, foreign shopkeepers who engaged in risky tactics to compete with local French business interests risked alienating their clientele and stirring up resentment in the neighborhood.

By contrast, foreign women's workplace sociability was more limited. While some immigrant women, particularly those married to French men, may have found blue-collar employment as factory workers and even white-collar employment as typists and secretaries, most immigrant wives and mothers of foreign households did not work. When they did, it was typically employment that kept them near kith and kin, as seamstresses and garment workers doing piecework at home with family members and compatriots, or as maids for well-off compatriots and coreligionists of the neighborhood rather than French households of the quartier.[88] These forms of at-home work, including domestic service in the neighborhood, provided more flexible hours, permitting foreign women to reconcile their reproductive and productive lives. For instance, Turkish Mercado Ojalvo served as a domestic worker for Hélène Barouch on boulevard Voltaire, and Arira Gabaï (a mother of eight by 1940) worked for Madame Lévy on Passage Folie Régnault.[89] Unlike their husbands who participated in the dynamic culture of the workshop, then, immigrant women did not experience such vibrant, multicultural workplaces nor their spillover into local street life. But, as we will see in the next chapter, being "at home" in the apartment buildings of working-class Paris furnished its own lively multicultural atmosphere in which French and foreign women partook.

Workplace sociability for French and foreign men flowed outward from the workshop into neighborhood cafés, *débits de vin*, restaurants, and bars after hours. In her 1937 novel, Hungarian author Yolanda Foldes drew on her own experiences in Paris between 1921 and 1930 to depict the immigration, implantation, and integration of one fictional foreign family. The novel revolves around the Hungarian Barabas family living on the narrowest street in Paris, la Rue du Chat qui Pêche. It is narrated from the perspective of teenage Anna Barabas, who occasionally accompanies her father to the neighborhood bar. Through her character, the reader eavesdrops on the heated political discussions that took place among some of the novels' other principal characters—Lithuanian socialist Liiv, Russian ex-general Bardichinov, and Spanish republicans Alvarez and Maura. Meeting regularly at the neighborhood café to argue politics well into the night, the men shared conflicting political outlooks, amusing and frustrating one another in equal measure. Importantly, too, they spoke in French, for it was the only language common to them all.[90]

Drawing on his own experience eavesdropping on workers' conversations at local bars, Valdour painted a rather different picture of working-class indifference to the rise and fall of political fortunes throughout Europe. Exasperated, Valdour fulminated, "Would that the parliamentary regime in Spain ends tomorrow after having ended in Italy [first], these workers could not care less. They continue, as is their custom, to detail minutely the pleasantness of the women and young girls who pass by."[91] According to Valdour trivial matters were of at least equal, if not greater consequence to workingmen who were, outside of the workshop, content to involve themselves in meaningless chit-chat. But it was a rich and pointless chatter that constituted the very sediment of homosocial interaction among working-class men.

As literary sources suggest, public spaces did indeed serve as important sites of multicultural sociability between French and foreign men, making merry and causing trouble. A little after midnight on September 5, 1926, an international group of friends did just that. One Luxemburger, two

Germans, and one Italian, all workers who lived on rue Keller, went out for a drink at the neighborhood débit several buildings down. After a few glasses of wine, they grew rowdy, broke a window, and were picked up and detained at the local police station for the evening at the request of the *débitant*, Monsieur Bourbon.[92] Polish and French hatmakers, David Hersz Plomik and Gaston Borrely, instigated a near riot against the police in the quarter of Sainte Marguerite. It began in the early evening at a débit on Avenue Ledru-Rollin where the owner, Madame Camure, tried to send away these two merry makers for "causing a scandal in the establishment." When police attempted to intervene, Plomik and Borrely "excited the crowd against the officers," and it was only thanks to the intervention of a handful of policemen dressed "en bourgeois" that the crowd was eventually contained and dispersed. The next day, when asked to explain themselves, Plomik and Borrely admitted "they drank a little more than [was] reasonable," but nevertheless pled their innocence in the whole affair.[93]

If the workplace and public spaces of the neighborhood produced and cemented friendships, so too did they nurse rivalries. As workplace tensions boiled over, disgruntled co-workers fired the occasional shot at one another at the doors of the *atelier*, though that degree of violence was extreme.[94] A simple brouhaha at the door of the workshop to settle some score or another was more common. French René Humbert and Italian Mattéo Pignalo waited until the end of the workday to finish a fistfight they had begun earlier, in the workshop. Onlookers assembled on the street to watch, many of them co-workers of Humbert and Pignalo, but they remained silent when officers questioned them as to the nature of the dispute.[95] Thusly did the life and culture of the workshop ripple out into the streets and surrounding neighborhoods.

At work and afterward at the bar, French and foreign employers and employees came to know the most intimate details of one another's lives. They complained to each other about their wives, bragged about their sexual exploits, confided in their fellow workers about their mistresses. In part, this male culture of workplace intimacy was possible because of the thin separation between home life and work life. Lovers, spouses, and partners sought out one another at the steps of the workshop, at the factory door, and at local cafés, to publicly denounce the wrongs done unto them, to advertise their suffering to the entire community, or simply to claim their due. The figure of the working-class woman waiting for her man at the door of the workshop in an effort to lay her hands on the family's wage before it was frivolously spent on drink had long been a fixture in French popular culture. Conversely, men might try to intercept their women at the end of the workday to claim their own portion of her wages, as Paul Paillet, the French husband of Polish Marie Didocha, was wont to do. On numerous occasions, Didocha's foreman, Gabriel Poncerf, and fellow co-workers at an automobile factory in the 12th arrondissement had observed this sad sight.[96] Thus, street life, work life, and home life were not discrete. One bled invariably into the other.

Street Life and Community

Social historians of eighteenth-century Parisians long ago uncovered a popular work culture deeply embedded within the life of the quarter where so-called domestic concerns impinged often.[97] For early twentieth-century French and foreign men and women in the capital, home and work life continued to intermingle, the street forming the backdrop to "private" confrontations. Jilted lovers presented their case to the court of public opinion, confronting wayward spouses out in the open so as to curry neighborhood opinion. Italian factory worker Emilie Ferrari confronted her cheating husband, Henri, when he left her and their four children to live with his French mistress in a shabby hotel near his furniture workshop on rue Saint Sabin. She went to the workshop determined "to remind the fugitive husband of his duties as spouse and father." The quarrel escalated and Emilie, "consumed by desperation," as she later put it, shot her husband in the street before a group of his co-workers, neighbors, and passersby.[98]

In the course of the ensuing investigation, it became clear that co-workers were well aware of this Italian furniture-maker's domestic situation. Co-worker Jean Signorini, an Italian furniture deliveryman working at the same workshop, knew intimately the details of the Ferrari's marriage and, like many others, witnessed the attack. While he thought his friend Henri "a good worker," he nevertheless reproached his behavior of late as "abnormal for a married man."[99] Henri's French employer, Edouard Boutier, was similarly aware of the Ferraris' domestic troubles, for Emilie had approached him several days earlier and persuaded him to intervene. After the tearful tête-à-tête, Boutier called Henri into his office and chastised him thusly: "What you are doing is not right; you have abandoned your wife, but the two of you had four children, [and] you must feed them." During this meeting, Henri disclosed to his boss every detail of his new relationship and in the end agreed to send money to his spurned wife in the interest of the children he had left behind.[100]

Even neighborhood folk who did not work in the same shop knew of the tawdry affair, a reminder of how workplace gossip spilled out into nearby cafés, débits, and restaurants where workers mingled with other neighborhood inhabitants. Etienne Masson, a French mechanic who worked for the cabinet manufacturer located just across from Henri Ferrari's own workshop, felt acute personal responsibility for the crime because, he explained, the affair was public knowledge throughout the quarter. "For some time," Masson began, "Ferrari's conduct has been scandalous. It was common knowledge that he had a mistress; he often went to the café with her, kissed her on the mouth and rode with her on the back of his motorcycle."[101]

Cafés, bars, débits, and restaurants were sites of neighborhood sociability where residents came to unwind with neighbors, friends, and co-workers at the end of the day. They were also social spaces where residents struck up new acquaintanceships. In the boisterous atmosphere of the débit, many experienced fleeting romantic and sexual encounters; other relationships took firmer root. Foreign-owned establishments provided newly arrived immigrants information about local work and housing opportunities.[102] So too did they provide spaces for revelry and amusement. Men played cards and gambled away their pay into the early morning hours at any one of the several French- and foreign-owned and -operated débits lining rue de Montreuil, rue Sedaine, and other streets throughout the quarter.[103] Men and women enjoyed impromptu dances, for instance at Italian Giuseppe Aurora's débit on rue Merlin, the "bal Delloi" on 45 boulevard de Charonne, or just about anywhere along rue de la Roquette.[104] In the years immediately following the First World War, numerous cafés, debits, and late-night bistros disappeared along rue de la Roquette, rue Godefroy Cavaignac, rue du faubourg Saint Antoine, and Place Voltaire, and none too soon, in the opinion of some self-appointed moralists and urban reformers.[105] But as long as these establishments could avoid detection by municipal authorities, they provided the requisite space for French and foreign residents of the quarter to *s'amuser* with impunity.

One street in particular drew a regular clientele of residents out for a good time: rue de Lappe. Located near the Bastille at the point where La Roquette and Sainte Marguerite adjoin, this street was lined then (as now) with bars, débits, and public dance halls that drew young people all night and into the wee hours of the morning. In fin-de-siècle Paris, public dance halls like those on rue de Lappe attracted French provincials who came for the music, the people, the social and sexual thrill, and sometimes even initiated a courtship with a like-minded partner.[106] Rue de Lappe continued to draw a large French and foreign clientele during the interwar years, a fact revealed by how often foreigners registered the loss of their foreign papers and wallets there, presumably after a night of drinking and debauchery.

NEIGHBORHOOD, STREET CULTURE, AND MELTING-POT MIXITÉ

Rich depictions of rue de Lappe appear in travel writing, literature, and memoirs of the period. Paul Cohen-Portheim, a well-to-do Austrian travel writer, recorded his observations of this sordid little street in the 1920s. His detailed portrait of rue de Lappe vividly reveals the social and sexual culture of the street:

> Close by the Place de la Bastille, a few steps from the great whirlpool of traffic, lies one of the most unusual streets in Paris, the rue de Lappe, a short, narrow, dirty little lane, full of incredibly ancient, blackened, and dilapidated houses, which suggests Marseille or some other big port more than Paris. In nearly all of them, there is a dancing-place or *bal-musette*, where the music is still in many cases provided by a barrel-organ. These places are patronized partly by respectable working people and little shop assistants, partly by down-right criminals. Each has a narrow passage where the bar is and a big room behind. It only takes a couple of policemen to bar the way out of the street, and hardly a week passes without a raid, when green motor-cars haul the entire company off to appear at the police station. Here, rather than in Montmartre, one may still find a touch of the romance of apachedom—pimps and their women, homosexuals of both sexes, sailors genuine and otherwise.[107]

By contrast, Léon-Paul Fargue, self-appointed "pedestrian of Paris," thought rue de Lappe had lost something of its mystique by the late 1930s. Referring to it as "the former jewel of the 11th arrondissement," Fargue bemoaned its increasingly seamy character: the blinking electric signs, "oozing pavements," blaring music, and seedy clientele. He disapproved especially of the "hoodlums" and rough types who liked to "make 'sport'" and often "took a long piss in the building doorways." Nor did he look kindly on middle-class men, those "specimens of *haut snobisme*," out looking for a good time while slumming with the riffraff.[108] To be fair, Fargue's characterization is not entirely off the mark. The *bals-musettes* on rue de Lappe were, according to Cohen-Portheim, "a degree lower on the social scale" than comparable establishments in the fashionable districts of Paris.[109] Indeed, the incoherent drunk lying listless on the cobblestones of rue de Lappe was a common sight, and more than a few were rudely awakened by police officers.[110] Officers, too, knew the kind of seedy subculture that thrived along rue de Lappe and, as Cohen-Portheim mentioned, executed random sweeps to curb "degenerate" behavior.[111] Whether revered or reviled, rue de Lappe remained in the opinion of most "a remarkable little ghetto of vice."[112]

First- and second-generation sons and daughters, in particular, availed themselves of these exciting opportunities to "s'amuser dans la rue," as they called it.[113] In addition to the lively social scene on display at public dance halls, bars, and débits, moviegoing was a common pastime for adolescents, whether foreign- or Paris-born. The interwar popularity of concert halls and cinemas in Paris was so evident that it led Valdour to comment cynically, "The needs of the imagination are better served than those of the soul . . . or those of the body."[114] Valdour's verbal slight regarding deficient standards of working-class hygiene aside, it was true that moviegoing exploded during the 1930s, not least of all because it brought young men and women together in public spaces and permitted them to socialize. The most popular cinema of the neighborhood, le Ciné Magic on rue de Charonne, became a common meeting ground for those interested in being seen, meeting new people, or getting away from the stresses of home life.[115] Young Chaja Edelsztejn, a Polish seamstress, agreed to see a Russian-language film with her Romanian neighbor, Elias, at the theater in Pigalle, though her husband Seyba was irate when he discovered her indiscretion.[116] Even cinemas, then, were potential sites of multicultural mixing, Franco-foreign flirtation, and sexual experimentation.

Anonymity and revelry were part of the thrill, but they also posed certain dangers, particularly to foreign women in the capital. Young Jeanne Mikulska, a twenty-year-old Polish domestic servant living with her employers at 104 Avenue Ledru-Rollin, learned the hard way that foreign women made for easy targets in the capital. Having met a young man at the bal Noygues on rue de Lappe, she left with him because he promised to take her for a drive in his brother's car. Enticed, she followed him only to discover that he had lured her to an isolated location where he and a friend robbed her of the paltry ten francs she possessed.[117] Mikulska was not alone. Several foreign women in the neighborhood played the unsuspecting dupe to ill-natured men, sometimes mistaking a romantic prospect for what turned out ultimately to be a swindle. On other occasions, fast-talking men approached foreign women in the neighborhood, claimed to be officers, and made off with their foreign papers and work visas.[118] Fictional Anna Barabas endured a similar encounter with a young Frenchman in her quarter whom she suspected of stealing her wallet, particularly when she saw his studied look of "elegant indolence" and his taunting smile.[119] This is not to say that foreign men did not suffer their share of indignities—and petty thefts, more specifically—at the hands of French and foreign women.[120] But men could avenge themselves on these women through the use of violence, the exercise of which was deemed socially acceptable by many in the community.

Throughout Sainte Marguerite and La Roquette, foreigners interacted and socialized with their French co-workers, employers, and neighbors, just as they battled and bargained with merchants, hôteliers, and police officers. Indeed, foreign men and women were woven into the very tapestry of neighborhood life for the most ordinary of reasons: they lived and worked there; they drank and dined there; they partook of the vibrant culture of leisure and sociability that animated everyday life in these neighborhoods. These gendered patterns of sociability were established not only between French and foreign, but also among foreigners of disparate origin. Of course, neighborhood life was not always the perfect picture of harmony. Familiarity bred both conflict and community among neighbors. Yet, even in those instances of discord, it was as fellow neighbors, not as outsiders, that immigrant men and women were maligned.

There was but one exception to this general rule of concord: that of immigrant workingmen, above all foreign-born bachelors, who, in their everyday dealings with hotel, cafe, and bar owners as well as other residents of the neighborhood were more likely than others to elicit hostility. Though the working-class culture of interwar Paris could accommodate quite a lot of male vice, residents had difficulty getting accustomed to the ways of uprooted foreign-born bachelors who periodically appeared on their streets. It was just one way that disciplinary paternalism surfaced as a social logic in local communities, organizing the most everyday of interactions and shaping the terms on which foreign men engaged with their neighborhoods.

Private dramas, public conflicts, and a profusion of relationships bound French and foreign residents of these working-class neighborhoods together. Just as "private" affairs impinged on every aspect of street life in flagrant fashion, so too did domestic life and the daily management of households propel French and foreign women into their surrounds and into this vibrant street culture. Like their menfolk, wives and mothers had their own geography within the quartier. Above all, they enjoyed the dynamic culture of Parisian apartment life and built within it a colorful world of sociability for themselves that would sustain them through trying times.

Chapter 6

Motherhood, Neighborhood, and Nationhood

Although Jankiel Kaczurynski was interrogated for the murder that took place in his neighborhood, he was ambling about Paris looking for work when the drama occurred. Instead, it was the neighbor women who shared the apartment building on 78 rue de Charonne who sprang into action on the morning of January 17, 1933, when they first heard shots fired. Shortly thereafter, Hana Wolf, a Polish maid, found the bodies and called for help. Sixteen-year-old Rebecca Ricichi, an Italian schoolgirl living with her parents on the second floor, responded to her cries. Horrified by the scene, Rebecca fled, nearly knocking over Madame Antonos, her Greek neighbor on the same floor, to whom she relayed the news. Once informed, Madame Antonos rushed downstairs to the first floor to confirm the incident then hurried out into the street. She explained what she had seen to the neighborhood grocer, Abraham Ickowicz, a Polish Jew who lived around the corner on rue Saint Bernard and worked just below the apartment of the slain Tokars, an elderly couple of Russian Jews. Ickowicz left his store to notify an officer walking the beat on rue Basfroi who then informed the Police Chief of quartier Sainte Marguerite.[1]

The murder of the Tokars in Sainte Marguerite provides a remarkable window onto the social dynamics of apartment house life in Paris. News of the tragedy traveled quickly, rippling through a tight network of French and foreign neighbor women whose lives ran up against one another in the cramped apartment building of the quartier. It offers a rare glimpse of the social world of workingwomen, and most significantly, a sense of the female community they built in the dark hallways, crowded courtyards, and hidden recesses of the Parisian apartment building. It was precisely at home where foreign wives and mothers spent their days—tending to the household, caring for children, scrimping and saving, cleaning and laundering, all in the company of their French neighbors. In court cases and police files, social service records and dossiers, traces of marital disputes, family frays, and neighborly brawls involving immigrant wives and mothers blend with the everyday history of the neighborhood and its predominantly French-born inhabitants. A working-class culture of want and privation thrived in the diseased and dilapidated, close and crowded apartment buildings of the 11th arrondissement. Consequently, the material conditions of everyday life brought foreign wives and mothers into daily contact with their French neighbors and local community. This was a culture of apartment-dwelling that bound women of French and foreign origin engaged in their common tasks running households, caring for children, regulating disputes, and managing their daily lives. In addition to the vibrant and generous world of welfare, it was these social ties that insulated them against the strains of working-class life in the capital and, from the 1930s onward through the Second World War, from the increasing animus of the French state.

While the apartment house was certainly a social universe unto itself, it was not a bounded entity; its boundaries were porous and permeable, blurring with the goings-on unfolding in the streets down below. The rhythms of household management and motherhood propelled French and foreign wives and mothers out of doors and structured their geography within the neighborhood, bringing them into contact with grocers, merchants, *débitants*, and *cafétiers*; residents of their building, street, and quartier; bureaucrats from local welfare bureaus, social workers from maternalist organizations, doctors and nurses of public health and hygiene offices; and finally nurses, teachers, and *directrices* at neighborhood *crèches*, *écoles maternelles*, and primary schools. In other words, French and foreign mothers shared the social and spatial experience of motherhood in these neighborhoods, rendering motherhood at once a local neighborhood experience shared by friends, neighbor women, and community members as well as an increasingly national public duty bringing them into regular contact with agents of the state—French social workers, welfare agents, and school teachers.[2] Supportive maternalism, then, was both a state and social logic that embedded French and foreign women into the local community as reproductive citizens. And it was so-called private spaces—above all the apartment house—that brought them all together.

"Airy Graves"

Throughout the nineteenth century and the first half of the twentieth, the 11th arrondissement was among the most populous, overcrowded, and diseased neighborhoods in Paris. In 1891, it was surpassed in population density only by the 19th and 20th arrondissements. During the interwar years, the number of inhabitants in the onzième soared, making this district the second-most crowded in the city.[3] Consequently, public health threats were numerous. In 1911, there were more fires in the 11th arrondissement than anywhere else in Paris.[4] If, in 1911, the neighborhoods of La Roquette and Sainte Marguerite had the most "dangerous, insalubrious or incommodious establishments" in all of Paris, it was a state of affairs that did not much improve after the Great War. Apart from stray quarters in the 18th and 20th arrondissements near the burgeoning industrial belt, all four neighborhoods of the onzième figured among the ten least hygienic neighborhoods throughout the interwar decades. Of all eighty quartiers of Paris, La Roquette contained the greatest number of "dangerous" and "insalubrious" establishments.[5] The 11th arrondissement also harbored its fair share of *îlots insalubres*, though the locus of disease was already shifting decidedly toward the northeast of the city by the end of the twenties, to the 18th, 19th, and 20th arrondissements.[6]

Of course, some noxious neighborhood buildings never made it into the official record. In 1925, for instance, a packaging factory located on Cité Popincourt spewed dust into the dilapidated buildings surrounding it.[7] Near rue Popincourt, too, a factory belched out vapors and pollutants into the air, causing concern among social workers for the welfare of residents in the area who breathed in these "unhealthful fumes."[8] Even the chimney smoke from Italian Luigi Morati's sawmill factory on rue Godefroy Cavaignac carried with it little bits of paper into the air, as did Swiss Alexandre Saggi's own factory, located on the same street.[9] And dirt and disease walked hand in hand.

These grimy neighborhoods boasted some of the highest mortality rates in the capital. Tuberculosis and smallpox spread rapidly in close and crowded apartments. In 1921, La Roquette and Sainte Marguerite contained no less than twelve *îlots tuberculeux* affecting 219 apartment buildings and their nearly ten thousand residents.[10] The scourge of the French working classes exacted its toll on foreign newcomers in the capital. Exhausted by the disease, Isaac Rubin, a Russian Jew and locksmith living with his large family on rue Guénot, eventually quit his job and instead helped his wife sell fruits and vegetables in the local open-air markets.[11] Polish tailor Zelman Fajgenman sought treatment at a sanitarium, but eventually chose to die at home on rue

Neuve des Boulets with his wife and children.[12] In working-class apartments, death was disconcertingly close to all. The whole building of residents at rue des Taillandiers heard Russian Friedlander cry out in the night for months as he lay suffering.[13] Illness was not only a matter of discomfort, pain, and suffering; it prevented foreign men and women from working, leaving them unable to pay their debts. When their French concierge brought a complaint against them for failure to pay rent, the Russian Liopines acknowledged the 130 francs debt they owed, but, with Madame Liopine seriously ill, they could not pay it off.[14]

Overcrowding, poor living conditions, and high rates of illness likely accounted for the higher rate of suicide that pervaded these neighborhoods as compared to others in Paris. While the number of suicides in Sainte Marguerite between 1911 and 1931 approximated the city's average, even falling below on occasion, almost twice as many suicides took place in La Roquette as elsewhere in the capital.[15] Polish carpenter, Monsieur Owezarzyk, committed suicide in his room on rue de Montreuil because, as his concierge informed police, his illness had left him in devastatingly low spirits.[16] When Hungarian Ladislas Molnar's wife, Térer, threw herself from the window of their fourth-story apartment on rue Keller, the police learned from her French and foreign neighbors that she was "of sickly constitution, [and] suffered from stomach and chest pain." Neighbors had overheard her on numerous occasions threatening to "commit suicide to put an end to her suffering."[17]

Children below the age of nine were in particular danger of contracting measles, chickenpox, scarlet fever, diphtheria, and other diseases that affect primarily the very young. Children in the 11th arrondissement tended to fall prey to these diseases during the summer months, perhaps because the weather was warm enough to play outdoors, and interaction with other children in the neighborhood allowed for the rapid spread of germs. While infant and child mortality rates in France fell overall during these decades, some unlucky mothers in these neighborhoods would never have suspected as much.[18] Three of Rachel Friedlander's nine young children had perished by 1934.[19] Disease took away eight of French Angèle Brugnon's babies, leaving her with one lone daughter, Gabrielle.[20]

Public hygienists, municipal officers, and social workers all identified these features and documented with due diligence what they found when they penetrated these dark, disease-ridden recesses of the capital. Of course, social workers' observations concerning the health and hygiene of inhabitants were often wedded to middle-class fears of lax working-class morals and subpar standards of hygiene, and were perhaps also inseparable from "voyeuristic curiosity" provoked by the "titillating squalor of the slum."[21]

With these caveats in mind, the notes taken by SSCMD social workers nevertheless provide a detailed portrait of French and foreign living quarters in these neighborhoods of interwar Paris.

A number of the French and foreign families whom SSCMD social workers encountered in these neighborhoods resided in small rooms on the sixth and seventh floors of their respective buildings. A product of Haussmannization, these upper stories were (and still are) referred to as *chambres de bonne*, or maids' quarters, a gesture toward their original, historic purpose. Constructed to provide living quarters for live-in domestics in the late nineteenth century, these rooms were repurposed as cheap, affordable housing for migrant newcomers by the interwar years. On the indirect correlation between the top stories of Parisian apartment buildings and the low social status of their occupants, Orwell provides a descriptive allegory based on Bouillon Zip, "a mixture of slops and synthetic soup" that cost about twenty-five *centimes* per packet in the early 1930s. Asserting, "People who drink Bouillon Zip are starving or near it," he then observed that "the vile, sour odour" of it intensified around the sixth flight of stairs and, more generally, "as one got higher."[22] Depicting his fictional seven-storied Hotel Savoy, Joseph Roth, too, declared: "Poverty make its home in high places, and those who lived on high were in the depths, buried in airy graves."[23]

What Roth termed "airy graves," SSCMD social workers called to these neighborhoods described simply as "small," even "miniscule" and "atticlike."[24] Of the seventy-four SSCMD reports that mention household size, most indicate that families lived in a one- or two-*pièce*—that is, one- or two-room apartments, toilet and kitchen not included. Such rooms lodged around four or five people, and foreign households more besides. By 1926, French statisticians had taken note of large foreign families, finding that while French and French-naturalized families averaged just 1.98 children per household, foreign families averaged 2.17.[25] In Sainte Marguerite and La Roquette, foreign households were indeed larger than French and mixed households, family size often reflecting reproductive behaviors that immigrants carried from their home countries. Among foreign families, those migrating from Luxemburg and Belgium were the smallest, averaging 2 and 2.2 children, respectively. By contrast, Russian, Greco-Turkish, and Polish families in these neighborhoods boasted the largest families, averaging 2.76, 2.83, and 2.91 children per family, respectively. Foreign families in these quartiers with the greatest number of children tended to come from those countries with the highest birthrates during the interwar period; conversely, the smallest foreign families came from those countries with correspondingly lower birthrates.[26]

Of the nine families who occupied apartments with three or more pièces, most lived in *habitations à bon marché* (HBM), or low-rent municipal housing reserved for large families. In 1937, families with approximately 3.4 children inhabited HBMs throughout Paris, far fewer children than the large *familles nombreuses* that officials intended to house in these eyesores dotting the Parisian landscape.[27] Not so the HBMs of these neighborhoods located on rue Henri Ranvier. On average, families of five lived in each of these nine French and foreign households. While foreigners averaged 1.25 pièces for an average of 4.8 persons, their French counterparts had 1.72 pièces for an average of 4.3 persons.[28] In short, given their large families, foreign-born households simply had less space in which to lodge more people.

In some instances, social workers were loath to call foreigners' living quarters rooms or pièces, at all, but rather "cubbyholes."[29] Because foreign families had to make do with less, they were creative in their sleeping arrangements. In a two-pièce apartment occupied by the Romanian Kohn family on rue de Charonne, SSCMD social worker Mademoiselle Perret wrote of the rooms, "The one serves as a kitchen, dining room and bedroom for the parents, the other, furnished with only a bed and a divan, serves as a bedroom for Ladislas and his sister."[30] Obsessive documentation of sleeping arrangements like this was a staple of social worker reports from many organizations. It stemmed from middle-class fears of working-class promiscuity and incest when families were crowded together in beds and atop mattresses in haphazard fashion.

Household interiors were portrayed as microcosms of the old, "dilapidated" apartment buildings that contained them.[31] Social workers noted with dismay the inadequate housekeeping routines of French and foreign charges, frequently depicting rooms as dirty, unkempt, and disorderly. In fact, "disorder" was a word frequently invoked to refer not simply to household cleanliness but apartment conditions. "Disorder" signified the presence of broken doors and furniture, holes in the walls and ceilings, as well as "narrow kitchens" and "somber entranceways." Insufficient aeration was also great cause for concern, though social workers acknowledged that, in some cases, it could not be helped. In an apartment on Cité Popincourt, Mademoiselle Perret noted, "The windows look onto the courtyard of a packaging manufacturer [and] more dust than air enters."[32] Another remarked with deep disgust on the "nauseating" odors emanating from "blackened sheets" covering the bed of one family.[33]

Olfactory revulsion was a common theme, for social workers frequently commented on the prevalence of "unbreathable," "detestable," "insalubrious," and "disagreeable" odors.[34] To enter the families' homes, social workers first had to navigate down "dark, obscure and malodorous stairwells."[35] They were also sensitive to aesthetic details, remarking that while one apartment might be "poorly furnished" with only a "miserable-looking crib" for the children, in another "there was a real desire to render the lodging attractive (tables, pottery, etc.)."[36] If they noticed furnishings, they also noticed the absence of furnishings and imputed meaning to its absence: "There are still several items of furniture that denote a certain affluence long past, but great empty spaces have been left behind by those [items] that must have been sold in moments of difficulty."[37]

While the biased impressions of middle-class social workers are questionable, working-class inhabitants of these neighborhoods themselves readily acknowledged the inadequacies of their living situations. When Mademoiselle Lacheret called on the widow Friedlander and her six children to investigate the Russian family's apartment on rue des Taillandiers, she registered with some surprise that the entire family occupied a single room which, though "well-ventilated" and "fairly clean" was nevertheless "miniscule," asking, "one wonders in a practical sense how all these people can sleep and live in such a small space."[38] The Friedlanders and their French neighbors agreed with her assessment. Suzanne, Rachel Friedlander's eldest child, verbalized what this social worker had already seen for herself: "Her siblings only traipse about the streets because of how cramped the apartment is, [in order] to finally get some fresh air, by playing in the courtyard when they can."[39] The Friedlanders' neighbors, too, chimed in, volunteering that living space limited the degree to which mothers, whether French or foreign, could supervise their children during the day. One French neighbor in the building told social workers, "When one has such a small room as the one occupied by this family, it is impossible to keep the children calm all day or even in the evenings."[40]

But cramped living spaces had another outcome that historians of the working classes in Paris have long been attentive to: they created conditions of forced intimacy among neighbors. Neighbors knew the most personal details of one another's lives, a phenomenon Eliza Ferguson has described in a late nineteenth-century Parisian context as the daily acquisition of "neighborly knowledge."[41] When foreigners came to populate these buildings in the early twentieth century, they merely joined an ever-expanding cast of newcomers, blending in seamlessly with the vivid diorama of French working-class life so beautifully painted by social historians of eighteenth- and nineteenth-century Paris.[42] Each day, French and foreign neighbors exchanged salutations in stairwells and hallways, greeting one another with the customary "bonjour" and "bonsoir"; each evening, they heard one another through the thin floor boards and panels separating their cramped rooms; the more daring among them spied on their neighbors through keyholes, hoping to catch a glimpse of something sordid. Neighbors knew intimate and, surely to our minds, meaningless idiosyncrasies about one another. Monsieur Wurmser on the third floor of his apartment building on rue Sedaine knew that his elderly upstairs neighbor, the crotchety Madame Manévy, walked about her room in slippers and "liked to sing while she cleaned."[43]

If little separated one room from the next, so was it true that very little separated working-class apartments from the streets below. Historians of Paris have demonstrated the permeability between the "domestic interior" of Parisian apartments and the "urban exterior" of the streets below.[44] The windows of individual apartments served as portals into the lives of others, providing a visible connection between building residents and passersby in the street. Madame Tarragon, though not on speaking terms with her mother, the aforementioned Madame Manévy, was nevertheless reassured each time she walked along rue Sedaine and caught a glimpse of her through the window puttering about.[45]

French and foreign residents were connected to the life of the quarter through open windows, as news circulated and conversations wafted up into buildings.[46] More than permitting the circulation of information, windows allowed foreign residents at home to be a part of the action from the safety of their own homes. Testifying in a case involving a bar brawl that transpired near her apartment, Polish Hélène Bruszczywski explained to court officers that she had a full view of the entire fisticuffs between the Frenchman and Algerian from her kitchen window.[47] Similarly, Italian Lina Bertolucci knew her husband Pietro was assaulted by a countryman in the débit across the street from their home because she had a perfect view from her apartment building in the 14th arrondissement. She heard his cries reverberate throughout the street through her open window.[48] Porous boundaries between apartment life, street life, and even family life were a feature particular to working-class culture in Paris made possible by inadequate housing conditions.

In some cases, interiors and exteriors were so thoroughly confounded that neither window, nor wall, nor roof served as effective barriers. French Georges Cressot caught two Italian bandits red-handed when he surprised them in his third-story lodging one afternoon in August 1926. As he ran into the street to call for help, the two robbers took advantage of the opportunity, "saving themselves by fleeing through the room's window which looks out onto the rooftops." The simple heist suddenly transformed into a mad caper through the buildings of the neighborhood as first the thieves, then police officers, headed straight for "the attic of Monsieur Waring's workshop [at] 23

Passage Etienne Delaunay" then "traversed the kitchen of Monsieur Rezungues, on the third floor, 35 Passage Bureau, breaking and toppling over the dishes without this person being able to intervene." At last, Victor Bazzani and Cesari Senafonte took to the rooftops through the windows once more before the officers, alas, seized them.[49]

Such permeability between the life of the apartment and the life of the street allowed the entire neighborhood of Sainte Marguerite and La Roquette to witness simple family disputes. In September 1926, when the weather was still warm enough to keep the windows open, the Cohens, a Turkish Jewish family living at 23 bis rue Popincourt, caused a ruckus. According to police reports, the family "discussion" drew some two hundred neighbors and passersby from the street below. Curious onlookers watched with bated breath as the four family members—Haïm and his three children, Moïse, Rachel, and Ventura—tore viciously into one another. How long had the discussion raged before one among the crowd thought it sufficiently "threatening" to warrant police intervention? In the end, officials recorded for posterity, "It was established that the cries were let loose inconsiderately by the father Monsieur Cohen who declared that he was frightened by the menacing attitude of his children." Of course, the crowd in thrall to the drama playing out above them found the whole episode rather more entertaining than "inconsiderate," as police documented.[50] Similarly, when sixteen-year-old Isaac Morgen insulted his father, David, a Polish cobbler, at the bakery on Cité Lesage Bullourde, the incident created grist for the rumor mill among French and foreign inhabitants of the neighborhood.[51] Even private family disputes were, then, a public affair in the quartier and in the apartment house.

The Social World of Workingwomen (1): In the Neighborhoods

While of course both men and women were drawn into the life of the quartier unfolding at cafés, débits, bars, and restaurants described in the previous chapter, women had a unique microgeography within the neighborhood. Immigrant women experienced the neighborhood while running their endless household errands, which brought them to the baker, the local grocer, the nearby *fruitier*, and to their children's schools.[52] In *La Rue du Chat Qui Pêche*, Foldes once again beautifully captured the experience of foreign women slowly habituating to the rhymes and rhythms of the Parisian neighborhoods in which they lived. With her younger brother and sister away at school and her mother and father working long hours during the day, teenage Anna Barabas was left alone to run the household. Her daily chores pushed her out of doors, into her quartier, and into the arms of her French neighbors—merchants, vendors, mailmen, police officers, her siblings' schoolteachers, regulars at the various cafés lining rue de la Huchette, adjacent to where she lived. "Anna spent a great part of her time on the streets of Paris," wrote Foldes, "and the street was a good teacher." Foldes continued, "Anna understood now the slang of the taxi drivers and the fruit and vegetable merchants, the pleasantries and the insults, the loud, joyous, raucous, frank life of the streets of Paris."[53]

While feeding and fending for a family pushed French and foreign women alike out of doors and into the shops of neighborhood merchants, grocers, bakers, and butchers, many other neighborhood sites catered exclusively to this motherly clientele. These were, above all, a rich and overlapping network of municipal welfare offices, immigrant aid societies, maternalist organizations, and child welfare groups, which, as we saw in chapter 4, provided generous aid and support to immigrant mothers throughout the interwar period. While such institutions drew French and foreign mothers to this or that neighborhood of Paris, the local presence of many of these municipal offices and private philanthropies in Sainte Marguerite and La Roquette structured the geography of immigrant women within these neighborhoods,

FIGURE 6.1. The marketplace at rue Richard Lenoir, where the 4th and 11th arrondissements meet, in 1922. Bibliothèque nationale de France.

both catalyzing the movement of mothers and shaping the contours of their motherly mobility.

All working-class French and immigrant mothers knew the local welfare bureau situated in Place Voltaire well: it was there that they solicited diverse maternal benefits, including *secours de grossesse*, maternity leave, state-provisioned milk bonuses, and *allocations de familles nombreuses*. More than twenty times as many widowed or divorced women than widowed or divorced men received family allocations in the 11th arrondissement during the interwar years, as was the case throughout much of Paris between the wars.[54] Consequently, the municipal staff of the Office Public Maternel et Infantile in the 11th arrondissement came to know some French and immigrant mothers and their families quite well, for instance, the French-born Dufresnes or the foreign-born Rubinzstains.[55] By contrast, foreign fathers such as Hungarian Paul Frischka and Romanian Nicolas Goata were more likely to appear at local welfare offices in search of unemployment benefits and were less likely to elicit favorable responses from taciturn bureaucrats.[56]

Several public and private hospitals as well as municipal hygiene offices were also located in Sainte Marguerite and La Roquette, providing mothers in the neighborhood with ample medical options when pregnant or ill. The Saint Antoine Hospital, located on the border between the 11th and 12th arrondissements, offered a "consultation maternelle" in the infirmary, where French and foreign mothers could obtain medical help and advice for themselves and their newborns. Polish Rachel Morgen did just that in the 1930s, which is how social workers at the hospital came to know the family so well.[57] Jewish women might however opt for the social services of the maternity ward at the Rothschild Hospital, located just south in the neighboring 12th arrondissement. During these years, the Rothschild maternity ward appealed to an increasing number of foreign Jewish mothers in these neighborhoods, such as Turkish Arira Gabaï.[58] When children fell ill, which was no rare occurrence in the moldering apartments of eastern Paris, French and foreign mothers took them to the local municipal dispensary on rue Omer Talon or, even closer to home, the clinic on 70 rue du Chemin Vert.[59] For her own part, Arira Gabaï preferred to receive shots from the dispensary on rue Croix Saint-Simon in the 20th arrondissement because it was nearer to her home on the eastern border of the onzième.[60]

The mobility of French and foreign mothers in the neighborhood also conformed to the extensive maternalist geography of charitable organizations within the 11th arrondissement. A *cantine maternelle* opened in 1912 at 76 rue des Boulets and another at 3 rue Crozatier in the nearby 12th arrondissement. Both provided cheap meals to mothers residing in the neighborhood

FIGURE 6.2. A photograph of Turkish Djoya Abouaf who, in 1923, lived in La Roquette with her husband, Moïse, and their three children depicted here. Djoya Abouaf, Application de carte d'identité, September 6, 1923, in Moïse Abouaf and Djoya née Baralia, I/A 1, Archives de la Préfecture de la Police.

who, volunteers noted, suffered acutely from the unemployment crisis of 1926.[61] Another *foyer-restaurant féminin* also opened up on 74–76 rue Amelot where French and foreign mothers could find both food and shelter for just four francs a night.[62] The Charité Maternelle on 16 rue Basfroi, the Mutualité Maternelle at 185 rue de Charonne, and the Société d'Aide Maternelle nearby also offered both food and shelter to Polish Dina Rubinsztain and other new mothers in the onzième.[63]

Like the SSCMD, a number of organizations, such as the Ligue Française des Mères de Familles and the Société Protectrice de l'Enfance, employed loyal cadres of *inspectrices, enquêteuses,* and *dames visiteuses* charged with the task of conducting home visits in the 11th arrondissement to ensure the health and well-being of working-class mothers and their children.[64] The former even established a permanent office at 185 rue de Charonne, the site from which they loaned linens to mothers in the area.[65] The Société de Charité Maternelle, too, opened three consultation bureaus in the 11th arrondissement of which two were located in these neighborhoods, one on 140 rue du Chemin Vert and the other on 16 rue Basfroi.[66] Emilienne

Goata, French-born though Romanian by marriage, patronized a number of these establishments as did Dina Rubinsztain, Polish-born but French by marriage.[67]

The rich array of municipal offices, public and private hospitals, and charitable organizations in and near Sainte Marguerite and La Roquette underscores the powerful familial character of the neighborhood. The prevalence of maternal institutions and charities inspired and shaped motherly mobility in the quartiers. Tending to sick children; registering for welfare benefits; obtaining free clothes, linens, food and milk for newborns—all these activities regularly propelled mothers out of the household and into the vibrant life of the local community. Moreover, if household errands and responsibilities brought foreign women into contact with the neighborhood, so too did their daily routines bring them into contact with one another. In the course of going about their respective business, two immigrant women living on the same street in the neighboring 4th arrondissement struck up a close friendship. Hungarian Jenny Ziszovitz explained of Czech Veronika Dererova, "I used to talk to her sometimes when I ran into her on the street and she sometimes came to see me when her work allowed it." Since neither had yet mastered French, they spoke to one another in cobbled-together bits of Hungarian and German.[68]

Although officials and some social workers frequently commented on immigrant women's lack of French fluency, foreign-born women managed well, perhaps better than their foreign-born husbands. In 1929, questions regarding immigrants' French fluency first appeared on naturalization forms. Though bureaucrats primarily showed interest in foreign-born men's mastery of the French language, they noted foreign-born wives' French fluency in about one-third of the cases. Though a fairly restricted sample size, clearly officials considered a greater proportion of foreign wives (63.64 percent) to be very fluent or fluent in French than their foreign husbands (55.74 percent).[69] Although unlike their husbands they did not tend to work, and certainly did not work very far from home, the apartment building and the neighborhood nevertheless served as their entrée into local French culture and society. Though immigrant men enjoyed the multicultural sociability of the workplace, immigrant women experienced the multicultural sociability that apartment living, household management, and the duties of motherhood in urban Paris entailed.

Motherhood between the wars was not only a social experience knitting together a loose, multicultural circle of friends, family members, and neighbor women in the common interest of child-rearing; motherhood was also a profoundly spatial experience that set women on well-worn paths to well-known coordinates interspersed throughout the neighborhoods. In addition to welfare offices, charitable organizations, and both public and private health clinics, schools constituted important coordinates in mothers' neighborhood geography, simply because the schooling of children fell within their maternal purview.[70] French and foreign mothers circulated from one day nursery, preschool, or primary school to another in their neighborhoods, always with children in tow. Between the wars, the 11th arrondissement boasted two crèches, or day-nurseries for infants: the Crèche Charles Floquet on 8 rue St Maur and the Crèche laïque du quartier Sainte Marguerite on 38 rue St Bernard.[71] After their children had reached age two, mothers then shepherded them to écoles maternelles, or preschools in the neighborhood. For instance, the Russian widow Friedlander sent her daughter Renée to the école maternelle on rue Taillandiers, as did Polish Dina Rubinsztain her son Henri.[72] Meanwhile Hungarian Elizabeth Frischka sent her son Paul to the preschool on Cité Voltaire.[73]

The simple act of picking up one's children from the neighborhood école maternelle or crèche brought foreign women of the quartier into contact with French school *directrices,* teachers, nurses, and assistantes. Like SSCMD social workers, their impressions of foreign women were often mixed. While one school social worker claimed that Turkish Arira Gabaï was a good mother "who was very attached to her children," another wrote of Russian Rachel Friedlander that she was "negligent" and sent her children to school "dirty" and "unkempt."[74] Like SSCMD social workers, however, they recognized the constraints placed on foreign working-class parents in the capital. Although one school social worker on rue Keller thought the Bajrochs to be "hard-working, honest, and *braves gens,*" she nevertheless acknowledged that the pair of Polish confectioners were often forced to send their four children out to play in the street in order to work without interruption in their small living space.[75] Though impressions were certainly mixed, they were nevertheless borne of familiarity, repeated interactions, and conversations between female school officials and foreign women.

Schools also brought foreign mothers into contact with one another. Then, as now, mothers crowded around the entrance of primary schools waiting for their little ones to come marching out at the end of the school day. While standing about, foreign women struck up conversations with one another and those conversations could sometimes lead to unexpected friendships. In the neighboring 20th arrondissement, Polish mother Fajga Dyzenchantz found a supportive friend in Haver Goldseigel, another Polish housewife, in whom she confided that her husband beat her. Though living a few streets away from one another in Belleville, they only became acquainted with one another because their children attended the same school on rue Tourtille.[76]

When children were old enough, mothers then sent them to the French republican primary schools in the neighborhood along rue Keller, rue Trousseau, rue Godefroy Cavaignac, and rue des Boulets, among others.[77] It is likely that they did not accompany their children at this late age, especially if children were already accompanied by older siblings. However, it is significant that mothers sent their daughters to French republican primary schools along with other little French girls, on rue Servan or rue Titon, for example.[78] Rarely did foreign parents in these neighborhoods send their children to non-republican institutions. When they did, it was to religious schools, instead. Turkish Jew Israel Mechoulam and his Bulgarian Jewish wife, Zimboul Machiah, sent their daughters Sahra and Ye'a to the Jewish école Rothschild on 60 rue Claude Bernard in the 12th arrondissement, to the considerable consternation of police officials compiling information on the family for their naturalization dossiers.[79] Indeed, by the late 1920s, children's enrollment in and attendance at republican schools had become another indication of the assimilability of the foreign-born. The question "Are the children instructed in French schools?" began to feature on the naturalization form from then on. That the preponderance of French, foreign, and naturalized mothers sent their children to laic schools in the neighborhoods suggests their adoption of French (and republican) child-rearing practices.

The welfare office, maternalist charity, day nursery, and primary school, like the butcher shop, the bakery, and the grocery store, constituted the local coordinates of French and foreign mothers' geography in their neighborhoods. So too did the local welfare agent, social worker, nursemaid, and teacher as well as the butcher, the baker, and the grocer form the social coordinates of mothers' daily interaction with members of the local community outside of the home. Motherhood thus embedded immigrant mothers spatially and socially into the urban fabric of the neighborhood. It also shaped the nature of their interactions with neighbor women at home.

The Social World of Workingwomen (2): In the Apartment House

While the business of motherhood and the lure of the neighborhood brought them into the streets, French and foreign women also spent a great deal of time together at home, in cramped and crowded apartment buildings when their husbands and children were away during the day. As in other places at other times, or indeed in Paris in centuries past, the many lives and households contained within apartment buildings ran up against one another in ways both ordinary and routine. What was missing in one woman's household could, for instance, be pinched from another's. The Bullers on rue du faubourg Saint Antoine loaned a pair of sheets to their neighbor, Adjala Ratz, a Polish woman and mother of two.[80] A Swiss woman borrowed a sewing machine and her husband some tools for his trade as cabinetmaker from their Italian, Eastern European, and French neighbors in the same building at 10 rue de Charonne.[81] In working-class communities where resources were scarce, borrowing was a fact of life, and it brought residents together.

Neighbors circulated freely in one another's homes. Though *mains courantes* paint a portrait of theft, the complaints often involved people who had ready access to one another's homes. Polish Olga Leibowitz reported a gold watch stolen from her one Saturday night after the departure of two neighbors, Meyer Chiffon and Meyer Leighneniff.[82] The Klopps, a couple from Luxemburg, noted with alarm that they were missing a thousand francs after a dinner at their home with friends.[83] Marcelle Rabuf, a Polish street peddler living on rue Gonnet, reported to police that her fourteen-year-old sister-in-law, Marcelle Litwack, made off with seven thousand francs one evening in 1926.[84] For better or for worse, friends, family members, and neighbors came and went with ease from one room to the next.

Daily household routines within the home also brought immigrant women into contact with their French and foreign neighbors. Even the simplest of housekeeping chores triggered interaction and, given the proximity of lodgings, one woman's cleaning routine could be the scourge of her downstairs neighbor. Jacques Carasso, a Turkish hosier living on the third floor of the apartment building at 106 rue de la Roquette, flagged down a neighborhood police officer when he returned home one evening to find that his laundry, which he had left drying all day out the window of his apartment, was sopping wet. The culprit was his upstairs neighbor, Sarah Palleussia, a Turkish housewife who, while cleaning, had dumped a bucket full of water from her fourth-story window.[85]

Palleussia was written up for violating the municipal ordinance of June 22, 1904, part of a sanitary code designed to protect the public health of Parisian inhabitants. Of the thirty-seven articles comprising the code, the French and foreign women of this neighborhood were overwhelmingly found in violation of the central proscription against the jettisoning of items from windows into the streets below during certain hours of the day. Subject to broad interpretation, this article also came to include the prohibition of shaking out sheets, blankets, clothing, and carpets during those hours. Foreign women of all national stripes were written up by officers for this offense, usually between the hours of eight and eleven o'clock in the morning. Because foreign women were so often cited during the morning hours, it is likely that shaking out the sheets the family had slept in the night before formed the first of their daily chores.[86] Banal though they are, these write-ups reflect the daily rhythms of immigrant households, providing a brief glimpse of foreign women in Paris going about their everyday business.

This innocuous chore, in particular, was a common source of conflict between neighbors, and especially between neighbor women. In October 1937, Belgian Germaine Lambrechts was shaking out her sixteen-year-old daughter's coat from her third-story window on Passage Montgallet in the neighboring 12th arrondissement, when her downstairs neighbor, French Hélène Plisson, remonstrated furiously. Plisson screamed out her window that Madame Lambrechts "was sending dust into my home," unloading her "microbes" onto her downstairs neighbors. According to Plisson, Lambrechts responded, "Shut your mouth! [*Ferme ta boîte!*]" Receiving this indelicate response, Plisson demanded that their concierge, Madame Mangeard, intervene. However, once Mangeard realized it was only a child's coat that her Belgian tenant had shaken out, and not the carpet her French occupant claimed, she upbraided Plisson "for accusing other residents without any reason" and promptly sent her back to her room. Unwilling to accept defeat, Plisson shouted insults up the stairwell in the hopes that her jibes—"old whore! dirty tramp!"—might reach the ears of her adversary. In that, she succeeded: the whole building of women heard her cries.[87]

Though trivial, these episodes could metastasize into all-out warfare between residents. A similar conflict initiated a long-lived rivalry between two women in the 4th arrondissement. On rue des Lombards, fifty-two-year-old French street vendor Léontine Dumaine reviled her fourth-story neighbor, Fatah Ben Salah, an Algerian prostitute. Whenever the latter watered her plants or shook out her clothing, sheets, and bedcovers, she soiled the room of her third-story neighbor. The conflict escalated from verbal barbs and injuries hurled at one another from windows into the streets below, to spitting at one another when they crossed in the street. Their implacable hatred was only resolved when Dumaine's Algerian lover, Mardoché Oliel, and Ben Salah's French lover, Marcel Pannier, fought it out in the street.[88]

While proximity could, at times, foster discontent, nourish pettiness, and culminate in ruthless rivalries, conditions of forcible proximity encouraged expectations of mutual reliance, a sense of community, and a shared sense of responsibility among French and foreign women in these neighborhoods. In addition to borrowing and sharing goods, women also offered services to one another, especially childcare. While foreign women in immigrant households worked at significantly lower rates than either French or foreign women in mixed households, it was not uncommon for immigrant women to work odd jobs sporadically during the day, often cleaning apartments in the neighborhood. If possible, they could leave their small children under the supervision of older daughters or other female family members. Turkish Esther Maoul, mother of two, managed to provide for her household despite their abandonment by cleaning houses in the neighborhood while her mother watched over the little ones.[89] More common among those separated from family members, however, was the supervision afforded by neighbor women. Although Polish Dina Roubinsztain did not often have work, when she did, she invariably relied on her French friends and neighbors on 3 Passage Thiéré to look after and feed her two children.[90] The neighbor women at 76 boulevard de Charonne also admitted that they gave little Madeleine Ghersa something to eat when she was hungry, which occurred quite often, according to them.[91] Rywka Lustmann, a single Polish mother living on rue Bisson in the 20th arrondissement, also frequently left her nine-year-old daughter Anna with the Franco-Algerian couple living downstairs when she cleaned houses in the quarter. After all, Lustmann had been in the same building as Ramdane Kacide and his wife Denise Guillerme for nearly six months. Kacide described how little Anna would "sometimes run around our room, [and] have a bit of food, complaining that she did not eat well at her mother and stepfather's." Significantly, while police later believed it necessary to engage the services of a Yiddish-speaking interpreter to question Lustmann, no language barrier impeded the development of her acquaintanceship with this French- and foreign-born couple, a couple she felt close enough to entrust her child to.[92]

Unsanitary living conditions, crowded rooms, and insufficient household resources pushed children out of their homes, into the homes of others, and out onto the streets. Along the cobblestone pathways, they, too, met, played, and made mischief with other French and foreign children from the neighborhood. When fictional Anna Barabas called out the window to her younger siblings Jani and Klari to return home for supper, she remarked casually, "They mill about in the street with little black, Algerian and French children."[93] As parents the world over know well, children are socializing agents unto themselves. Madame Lenoir, the French concierge of the apartment at 137 rue Chemin Vert, shooed away young Nachma Frydman, the son of her Polish tenants, when he brought his friends Charles Van Santvoort and Pierre Louis Colson to play in the courtyard of the building. The three friends, certainly not all Polish, continued their games in the woodshops of Bernard Roux just next door. When Nachma fell and hurt himself, all the parents were called to account.⁹⁴ Similarly, when neighborhood friends and schoolmates Polish Charles Pomeranc and Romanian Ladislas Kohn stole a bike, their parents were forced to interact with one another to protect their misbehaving children from being sent to Public Assistance.⁹⁵ Thus, French- and foreign-born children not only interacted with one another, but brought their parents into contact with one another through their own interactions and indiscretions.

Family conflict also created opportunities for multicultural mingling when children sought recourse and sympathy outside the home. When Turkish-born Marcel Polycar's mother passed away and his father quickly remarried, the fourteen-year-old "sought to remain at home with his family as little as possible." Consequently, he began to spend a great deal of time with a Franco-Serbian couple who lived down the street on rue des Taillandiers. The Mitsketches ran a small clothing workshop and, though Marcel was an apprentice leather craftsman, he nevertheless lent them a hand from time to time. Though working for the Mitsketches, the relationship between the couple and the young man was more social than economic. Rather than pay him wages, the couple preferred to take him to the cinema from time to time. French-born Madame Mitsketch spoke often with Marcel while he worked and thus knew about his distressing home situation. When his father eventually threw him out of the house, Marcel was forced to find a room *en garni* along the faubourg Saint Antoine. Still, he continued to dine with the Mitsketch couple every evening.⁹⁶

Foreign children were considered part of the community and neighbors intervened to protect them from their parents. Mixed-race children were no different. French Nancy Sauvadet, the one-time lover of an Algerian man with whom she had had two children, was not well-regarded by her neighbors in the building on rue Asile Popincourt. Rumors of her intemperance circulated throughout the building. In reference to her premature aging, many inhabitants even referred to her as "la vieille." During one drunken spell in 1934, Sauvadet locked her son Maurice out of the home, and he was forced to sleep in the stairwells and the building's toilets until a French neighbor, Madame Rouchard, took pity on the boy.⁹⁷

A certain amount of suspicion hung about Frenchwomen who consorted with North African men, though it is unclear whether it is the opinion of neighbors or official bias that we detect.⁹⁸ Sauvadet denied that she was a prostitute, though when confronted by social workers, she admitted to "having [Algerian] friends other than Halimi," the father of her children. Regardless of what precisely she meant with these carefully chosen words, social workers believed her statement denoted "an absolute immorality in speaking of her successive liaisons."⁹⁹ Considering how disliked she was by her neighbors, it is possible that this impression was reinforced by the testimony of Sauvadet's less forgiving acquaintances. It is also possible that transitory male "friends" of North African origin were less tolerated by the local community than the more permanent presence of North African husbands and fathers. In August 1940, an SSCMD social worker wrote disdainfully of Madame Dumur who occupied with her son François "a shady hotel" where Algerian laborers were the primary lodgers.¹⁰⁰

By contrast, the social dynamics of neighborhood life mitigated in favor of North African fathers, even to the detriment of their French wives, if need be. Recall, for instance, the Ghersas: when the seven children of Algerian subject Abdallah Ghersa and his French wife Angèle Lebrun appeared malnourished and mistreated, suspicion fell on the French stepmother not the Algerian father. In fact, concierges and neighbors offered only good words on behalf of Ghersa, agreeing that "the father loves his children." On the subject of his new wife, however, they remained skeptical. "His wife is fundamentally bad," they claimed, "and is a cruel stepmother to Roger and Madeleine." In addition, social workers recorded, "Many witnesses attest to the nastiness of the stepmother and to her mistreatment of the two children."¹⁰¹ The case was similar for Algerian Amar Benedis and his French wife, Geneviève née Trezenem. In December 1943, Geneviève left, taking her three children, claiming they were "brutalized by the father." Though police officers were inclined to protect the mother and children, social workers arrived as a different conclusion based on neighborhood observations. "In the neighborhood, they say the mother is abnormal and beats [her son] Michel." Concluding that Madame Benedis was "lazy," "of dubious morality," and "very dirty," they further averred that "in her absence, [the youngest son] Jean is well cared for; the father does not mistreat the children."¹⁰² In both mixed-race households, then, neighbors and social workers perceived the cause of mixed-race families' dysfunction in gendered rather than raced terms, placing responsibility squarely on the shoulders of bad French mothers rather than hard-working colonial fathers.

If the case warranted, neighbors might bring police power to bear on those who did not conform to community standards regarding the proper raising of children. As we saw in chapter 4, in 1933 neighbors submitted a letter to the police commissariat denouncing Paul Frischka, a Hungarian locksmith living on rue Neuve des Boulets. According to this band of neighbors, he regularly "brutalized" his son. When confronted, he acknowledged that "he beat the child when he deserved it, but did not however brutalize him."¹⁰³ When, in 1933, Arira Gabaï, a Turkish woman and at that point a mother of six, struck her son Léon so hard that he momentarily lost consciousness, her neighbor, Monsieur Landolph, denounced her to the Comité de l'Enfance, claiming that a group of neighbors had to intervene to prevent her from doing further harm to the child.

This Monsieur Landolph took a special interest in Léon Gabaï. He was very detailed about the exact nature of the parents' shortcomings: while "the parents were certainly attached to their children," they nevertheless provided their brood of six with "insufficient" and "at times unhealthy food." Landolph related that Bension Gabaï only bought "the least expensive" food and "did not concern himself as to the freshness of the foodstuffs." He then called the mother's cooking practices into question, doubting her method of "boiling vegetables without oil or butter."[104] Indeed, if neighbors showed a willingness to aid and assist one another, so too, did they feel entitled to involve themselves in one another's family affairs. It was the proverbial trade-off in which mutual aid necessarily entailed expectations of mutual involvement. In this, foreign mothers were treated no differently than the French mothers with whom they shared the building, the street, and the neighborhood.

The Moral Economy of Apartment Life

While of course the exchange of material assistance and reciprocal services brought neighbors together, it was the emotional bonds between French and foreign women that are particularly telling. Frenchwomen informed their foreign female neighbors about important resources in the capital intended expressly for the aid and uplift of women and their children. These were the diverse charitable organizations that provided material support to mothers, regardless of ethnic background, since the late nineteenth century. During the interwar years, Frenchwomen not only furnished foreign women with information about the existence of these organizations but led them right up to the doorsteps of various charities. Social workers from the League for the Protection of Abandoned Mothers remarked on several occasions that foreign women were brought to their offices in the 8th arrondissement by neighbors.[105] Conversely, when Yvonna Piech, an "ailing and trembling" Polish housewife living on rue de Charonne with her husband and three children, showed up at League doorsteps uttering incoherent phrases, social workers accompanied her home by taxi and inquired as to her well-being with her neighbors and husband.[106] Thus, Frenchwomen not only provided invaluable information about resources in the capital, but even more intangible moral and emotional support leading all the way up to the steps of charitable organizations and back home again.

When disaster struck, French female neighbors proved an indispensable resource. They protected one another from brutal spouses and partners and provided shelter to fellow employees, neighbors, and friends chased away from home by violent circumstances.[107] In one court case after another, immigrant women filed formal complaints against violent spouses at their neighborhood police station, but sought refuge with other friends and neighbors swiftly thereafter.[108] In other instances, French neighbors did even more to provide solace and companionship to one another in times of need. When Mariana Musso, an Italian woman living in the 18th arrondissement with her husband and five children, began to suffer from complications following a hasty abortion, her sixty-year-old French concierge, Madame Millet undertook the daily supervision of the Musso children, checked in periodically on the sick mother, and repeatedly called the doctor on her behalf—all for a foreign woman she had only known for scarcely a year. Although Mariana's husband, Salvatore, maintained that his wife "does not speak any French," she clearly spoke well enough to make herself understood to her French concierge.[109]

Indeed, the concierge was a figure of central importance in the lives of foreign women, wielding as they did a significant amount of social power. Although appearing on the urban scene only in the late eighteenth century, the concierge became a fixture of the Parisian social landscape as the next century wore on.[110] It was to them that police turned when they needed information about inhabitants of the quartier for, indeed, concierges knew every detail of their residents' lives.[111] Each one of the 108 court cases in this study as well as all 103 social worker files investigating families in these neighborhoods includes the testimony of concierges who were in a privileged position to provide information so sought after by officials. Caretakers of the apartment building (and typically older Frenchwomen), concierges were often home all day. More than just informants, then, concierges could play an integral role in the lives of their immigrant residents, forming a core social support for those so far from home.

Interpreting and translation were among the most common favors asked of French concierges by their foreign residents. Most often, this meant reading mail from and writing letters to French recipients. When Russian Elie Leib Levitetz's former French mistress accused him of sending her "menacing letters," Levitetz refuted her charge, claiming that he could neither read nor write in French, and that it was his concierge whom he enlisted for those very services.[112] For more than thirty years, the Tokars, an elderly Russian couple living at 78 rue de Charonne, obtained the aid of successive concierges who would read to them their mail. Désirée Attry, a sixty-one-year-old French concierge, recalled that she read one letter a week for Hana Tokar, which is how she came to know that Hana served as a matchmaker for the neighboring community of foreign Jews.[113]

Some relationships between foreign women and concierges assumed even more importance. Concierges were deeply involved in the lives of their *locataires*, and this was all the more so given that the concierge was recognized by all as the individual vested with the moral authority to arbitrate in disputes between women in the same building. In many ways, this is unsurprising. After all, cohabitation within the same apartment building was a natural channel by which relationships formed. And concierges were more than childcare providers, adjudicators in disputes, gossipmongers, and busybodies. Some concierges and their foreign female tenants came to know one another surprisingly well through the simple fact of cohabitation. For more than a decade, when the youngest son of Fanny Ronban, a Romanian widow and mother of three, periodically succumbed to fits of epileptic seizure, it was her French concierge, Marie Louise Vax, whom she called to help her restrain the boy until his shaking subsided.[114] At home all day in the same apartment building on rue de Charonne, Ronban and Vax learned about one another's lives, sharing burdens and lending one another succor. A similar thing occurred for Arira Gabaï, a Turkish housewife whom we have encountered before and who lived with her many children on rue Mont Louis. When Gabaï suspected she might be pregnant with her seventh child, she was so dismayed that she shared her grief with her French concierge. The relationship between the two women grew so close that one day Gabaï, particularly exasperated by the behavior of her youngest son, confided to her concierge his dubious paternity.[115] Concierges, then, were emotional confidantes in whom immigrant women at the end of their rope trusted.

French concierges also played a central role in helping women manage their stormy domestic lives with spouses and partners. Virtual gatekeepers to apartment buildings, concierges had the power to aid and abet women looking to surreptitiously leave when partners were away at work. Edouard Ikler, a Hungarian road worker, returned home one evening to a vacant room and realized that "the woman with whom he had lived *maritalement* for three years," Josephine Hosinger, had left him, "taking with her all of the furniture: dresser, kitchen cabinet, iron and leather bed frame, two tables, eight chairs, a canapé, a sofa, bed sheets, pots and pans, a sewing machine, all worth 1000 francs." A feat like this was unimaginable without, at the very least, the tacit approval of the concierge. In this case, approval was more than tacit: the concierge herself arranged a buyer for all the furniture and even accompanied Josephine on a visit to the potential buyer some weeks in advance to handle the negotiations.[116] Polish Louis Swinsky, a chauffeur living at 132 rue de la Roquette, was similarly dismayed when he returned home one evening to find his *"amie"* Olga vanished. The woman with whom he had lived for six years and fathered a two-year-old son had also taken with her all of their furniture. To add insult to injury, it was clear that the concierge and various inhabitants of the building (especially a certain Madame Pitois and Olga's own mother) had aided in her "escape."[117] Indeed, the practice of French and foreign women leaving men and taking the household valuables with them was a common sight throughout Paris during the interwar decades and concierges played a central role.[118]

Some French and foreign women came to care quite deeply about one another. As we learned in chapter 3, Emilia Léon, a maid and native of Luxembourg, was unhappy with her husband, an Italian locksmith. Since her marriage to Jacques Violina in France in 1927, the couple had continued to have a notoriously stormy relationship that their neighbors often bore witness to. Their raucous marital disputes forced them to move often between the 10th and 11th arrondissements, for police presence was constantly summoned at their various addresses. In 1935, Emilia confided in her French concierge, Yvonne Hiernard, how miserable she was with her husband, though Hiernard needed little confirmation. "She did not give the impression of being happy in her household," explained Hiernard, adding, "She frequently cried." Later that year, when Emilia's husband took their son out of school and sent him to stay with his parents in Italy, the concierge told officers that Emilia was "completely despondent" and "demoralized." "I comforted her the best that I could," the concierge explained, adding, "I did everything possible."[119]

Neighbors and residents looked down on a concierge who refused to involve herself with the domestic business of the *maison*, especially where abused women were concerned. When neighbors suspected that the Italian bellboy Lorenzo Richiardi was having "relations" with his young daughter, the concierge recalled, "The residents of the building reproached me for not going to the police," despite her protestations that it was "a delicate matter" and she had no proof.[120] Yet, residents' recrimination against this concierge suggests that they were an integral part of this working-class social system in which all residents, French or foreign, were required not only to conform to community standards for acceptable behavior, but also permitted to share in the advantages of neighborly intervention on their behalf. Those advantages were particularly forthcoming where women were concerned.

French and foreign women of the neighborhood banded together to shield one another from violent men. When Madame Kholendenko, a Polish widow, grew "tired of the brutality" of her partner, Zemeilchstern, she left with the help of two neighbor women.[121] When Turkish Arira Gabaï left her husband and children from 1927 to 1929 because she could bear "la grande misère" no longer, her French neighbor, Madame Georges, a laundress on the same street, watched over the Gabaï children and "looked after the family's affairs" in Arira's absence. Having known Arira since 1925, Madame Georges took her side in the domestic dispute. She recalled disapprovingly to SSCMD social workers that during his wife's absence, Bension could often be found drinking "in good company," a comment insinuating the dubious morality of the husband and intimating a word of support in favor of the wife. Even once Arira returned, Madame Georges continued to rally around her cause, fixing her disapproval squarely on Bension, "a drunk," and *les enfants* Gabaï, "very difficult children" in her estimation.[122] Thusly did the community of neighbor women periodically ban together to protect their own.

In more extreme cases requiring official intervention, the neighborhood petition was a common tool used by the community to mobilize in defense of one among them. According to the French and foreign residents at 65 rue Sedaine, Madame Manévy (whom we have met at several turns in this chapter) was unfairly imprisoned after a particularly noisome quarrel with the wife of a police officer in the building, Madame Eischberg. Though the residents agreed that Madame Manévy was certainly "peculiar," if not downright persnickety, they still banded together to protest police abuse of the old woman. Her proponents from the building signed a petition where they called the arrest of Manévy "a shame," "unjust," "scandalous," and declared, "what has happened to Madame Manévy cannot go unpunished." The prosecutor for the quartier, Monsieur Camille-Renault, drew a starker assessment of the situation, painting a veritable portrait of police conspiracy. Eventually, Madame Manévy was released.[123]

Neighborly rallying through the petition was a common practice adopted by French and foreign members of communities in other neighborhoods in and around Paris, as well. In 1931, Spanish *fruitière* Manuela Talavera shot and killed her husband, Vicente Martinez, in self-defense in her apartment on rue Saint Honoré in the 1st arrondissement. An entire community of supporters and sympathizers, exclusively residents of the quarter, came out in her defense, sending the following letter to the commissariat of Les Halles:

> The undersigned attest that Madame Martinez née Talavera has always shown herself to be serious and correct and that she enjoys among all those who know her the best reputation from a moral point of view. They declare that she has always taken good care of her little boy, [who

is] always well-kept by her. They know that Madame Martinez was unhappy in her household, her husband was known as brutal, above all when he was drinking. They permit themselves to ask *Messieurs* the Judges to be kind toward this poor woman and to return her quickly to her little baby who has great need of her.[124]

In the end, Manuela Talavera was found innocent of three counts of aggression against the husband she shot.

A small community of Frenchwomen throughout Paris and several Armenian women living in Seine-et-Oise just outside of the capital were similarly outraged when rumors began to circulate about Anna Iskendarian, a woman they held in high esteem. After her husband Vitchen shot and killed her in a jealous rage, rumors surfaced that she had had an affair and thereby incited her husband's murderous fury. Her French and foreign supporters defended her good name even in death, sending police officials a flurry of letters "to protest against the calumnies addressed against Madame Iskendarian, the victim."[125] They underscored her virtuous conduct as wife and mother and dwelled especially on the sacrifices she made for her young daughter. Two Frenchwomen, in particular, played an important role in Anna's life: Aimée Lerat, her former French concierge in Enghien, now living in the 4th arrondissement of Paris, and Marie Le Roy, the French débitante of the café in the apartment building on rue de Flandre (19th arrondissement) where she had once lived with Vitchen. Aimée and Anna had reconnected years earlier in Paris, and Marie Le Roy kept in touch with Anna after she left Vitchen. As Le Roy recalled, "Even after she left our street Anna continued to visit me from time to time" and "the young woman often told me her sorrows."[126] On the day she was shot, Lerat and Le Roy accompanied Anna to her meeting with Vitchen and cautioned her against speaking with her husband because of his menacing air. Though ultimately they could not spare her from his violence, the unanimous defense of Anna by her French and foreign friends and neighbors posthumously left little doubt as to Vitchen's guilt. He was summarily condemned by the court.

To be a mother in interwar Paris was to become, quite simply, French. In the Parisian apartment house, working-class French and foreign women created a social world of their own characterized by strong networks of mutual reliance and female solidarity. Apartment life permitted foreign women to build extensive networks with their neighbors, especially Frenchwomen who recognized in them fellow wives and mothers who shared their everyday struggles as well as their day-to-day diversions, as colleagues in the common tasks of running households, raising children, and managing lives.

Consequently, the daily demands of the household and reciprocal expectations of material and moral assistance overrode ethnic and cultural distinctions between French and foreign women. Motherhood, in particular, served as a powerful social, even spatial sediment, tying immigrant mothers forcefully to other neighbor women and rooting them to their neighborhood. The demands of motherhood propelled women to specific neighborhood sites where they interacted with a common set of local community members and state agents, individuals who recognized them and supported them as reproductive citizens of the French nation. With the coming of the Second World War and the Occupation, this uniquely working-class female culture of housekeeping, child-rearing, and apartment-living held up under terrible strain, and neighbors would once again be called on to look after their own.

Chapter 7

Neighborly Networks and Welfare Work under Vichy

On May 10, 1940, the French mobilized halfheartedly for a battle against the Nazis that would end in catastrophic defeat. A mere six weeks later, German occupiers entered the country victoriously and remained there for the next four years. In this manner, "les années folles" of the 1920s receded into distant memory and "the hollow years" of the 1930s gave way to the "dark years."[1] In the chaos of defeat and the agony of occupation, Marshal Pétain, the grandfatherly "hero of Verdun," promised the French a return to social order. Despite claiming to act as a "shield" between the French people and German occupiers, his Vichy government collaborated considerably with the Nazis, meeting and exceeding Nazi expectations where the arrest, deportation, and persecution of Jews was concerned.[2]

During the German Occupation of Paris, the 11th arrondissement emerged as a sustained official target of *rafles*, or Jewish roundups, given the massive settlement of foreign Jews. German authorities, in collaboration with Paris police forces, orchestrated two especially large rafles during this period, one of which was centered on the onzième. It occurred on August 20–21, 1941, when officials encircled the neighborhood, stopped French and mostly foreign Jewish men on the streets, asked for their identity papers, and arrested them. In other cases, Jewish men aged eighteen to forty-five were taken directly from their homes. They were held either at the Paris police station or the Gymnase Japy, located just off boulevard Voltaire in La

Roquette, then transported to Drancy, a transit camp located in the Paris suburbs. The extermination camps in Eastern Europe would be, for many, the final destination. Sporadic arrests continued in the weeks that followed, until some 4,279 Jews had been interned in Drancy by September 1. The second large roundup, occurring on July 16–17, 1942, and remembered as the "Vel d'Hiv roundup" after the bicycle stadium used as a holding center, affected the entirety of Parisian Jewry and included women and children for the first time. It swept up primarily Jews living in the 3rd, 4th, 10th, 11th, 12th, 18th and 20th arrondissements. In these two roundups combined, more than 17,000 Jews—many inhabitants of the 11th arrondissement—were apprehended and later deported by the French state.[3]

While this arrondissement certainly constituted a prominent site of official terror and persecution directed toward Jews in Paris, it also witnessed the appearance of France's first Jewish resistance organization. Called variously the Comité Amelot, the Groupe Amelot, or the Rue Amelot, the organization was founded in June 1940 and took its name after the street on which it was located, where quartiers Sainte Marguerite and La Roquette met. While the Groupe Amelot often features as one of several Jewish organizations that pursued social assistance as opposed to political resistance during the war, rarely have the daily activities of its large and nameless corps of assistantes sociales been studied.[4] More rarely, still, have their activities been viewed as part of the extensive world of local welfare that preceded the Occupation. This has as much to do with the ways in which resistance historiography evolved to distinguish "rescue work" from "resistance work" as it does the ways in which women's contributions to the resistance have been sidelined.[5] This chapter explores the activities of the Groupe Amelot and its social workers—young, professional, French, and more often foreign women who were embedded within larger rescue networks throughout France involving Jewish and non-Jewish assistantes sociales. It demonstrates not simply the continuities between interwar welfarist activity and wartime resistance work undertaken by female social workers but rather argues that interwar welfare work—particularly child placement *en famille, en pension,* and *en nourrice* in the French countryside—served as the blueprint for rescue work to come.

Because Amelot's ongoing reproductive mission centered in no uncertain terms on mothers and children, France's first Jewish resistance organization managed to hide in plain sight from a regime that, while viciously anti-Semitic, was no less ferociously devoted to the procreative obligations incumbent of all members of French society. And though the Comité Amelot presents a clear case of institutional continuity from the interwar years through Vichy and beyond, it is nevertheless representative of the many Jewish and non-Jewish social service organizations run by cadres of trained assistantes sociales who similarly undertook rescue work on behalf of Jewish families during the war as an extension of their daily social assistance work. Although the French state appeared to have changed priorities overnight, this was not at all the case for mother- and child-oriented welfarist organizations that continued to mobilize on behalf of mothers, children, and families, including those of immigrant Jewish origin. Through the prism of Occupation, their daily work took on subversive dimensions. When they could not help, mixed communities of French and foreign neighbors, Jew and Gentile, stepped up, protecting their own from the murderous encroachment of an intrusive state.[6] Though neighborly relations could, of course, pull in different directions during the war just as they had before the war, the fates of foreign-born Jewish families in Sainte Marguerite and La Roquette reveal the strength of relationships cemented over the previous decades. Significantly, the focus on social assistance, on rescue work, and on women's participation within neighborhoods and the wider world of welfare explains not one but two French "enigmas" that have long vexed scholars: first, how 75 percent of Jews in France survived the war, the highest percentage in all of Nazi-occupied Europe; and second, how so many Jewish children, in particular, survived in France as compared to the rest of Europe.[7]

Vichy and the Limits of Familialism

The Vichy government made manifest the worst elements of what had been brewing just below the surface of the Third Republic for decades—antirepublican forms of anti-Semitism, antisecularism, and antiliberalism as well as republican forms of racism, misogyny, and xenophobia. Yet, because France had become home to thousands of foreign-born Jewish women, children, and families by 1940, tearing Jews, even French-born Jews, out of the fabric of French society was no easy task. It forced Vichy officials to continuously strike a balance between anti-Semitism, a key feature of the new regime, and populationism, a longtime feature of the Republic. Prior to the summer of 1942, the tension was largely resolved by the state's persecution of nonprocreative Jews, on the one hand, and its protection of Jewish breadwinners and their families, on the other. Early deportation and internment policy bears out this observation. In 1941, one social worker working with detainees of an internment camp in France noted that "fathers of needy families with five children" could obtain release, following the logic that they were "in need of the father's work to survive."[8] Later, during the summer

1942 roundups, bachelors and couples either without children or with grown children were not even taken to Vel d'Hiv: they were sent directly to Drancy.[9]

The Vel d'Hiv roundups targeted women and children for the first time and marked a significant turning point wherein the interwar familialist logics governing Vichy deportation policy shifted. From then on, even the procreative with families would find themselves in the crosshairs. Perhaps because of this stark shift in policy, following Vel d'Hiv, the head of the Service Social des Etrangers (SSE) thought it wise to issue clarifying instructions regarding who was to be deported. On August 26, 1942, he circulated among SSE representatives a telegram recapitulating information relayed in weeks previous to the Ministry of the Interior as well as regional and departmental prefects throughout France. The instructions contained a list of criteria regarding target nationalities (primarily Eastern and Baltic Europeans) and deportation categories as well as "exceptions concerning all targeted categories" and "the Fate of Families of Exempt Individuals." Those immigrant groups singled out for deportation harkened back to Depression-era logic, mostly targeting those of recent arrival. Yet, significantly, stipulation "g" went so far as to single out *"bachelors* arrived in France since 1933 and aged 16 to 40 years." In addition to granting exemptions to the elderly, the "untransportable," and distinguished former soldiers who served in the French Army, the policy also spared children under sixteen years of age (stipulation a), pregnant women (d), fathers and mothers with children under two years (e), and those with French spouses or children (f).[10] In other words, the instructions coupled antibachelor elements with familialist exceptions, showing greater leniency for children, families, and those with French attachments. While Third Republican officials had used similar criteria in the 1920s and 1930s to mark some out as more worthy of social rights and privileges than others, Vichy's use of the criteria carried lethal consequences in Hitler's Europe.

In hindsight, subsequent roundups and deportations would not entirely conform to these instructions. In this, the Vichy state followed the same murderous trajectory as the rest of Occupied Europe, definitively shifting their persecutory gaze from men to women, children, and families in summer 1942. But these instructions do reveal the extent to which officials relied on and amplified interwar familialist criteria to both reach and exceed German quotas for Jewish deportations. They did so primarily by ridding themselves of ethnically undesirable dead social weight—foreign-born Jewish bachelors and the nonprocreative. Even with these official instructions, however, after summer 1942, such "easy" reconciliations were no longer possible, at least not where the policing apparatus of the state was concerned.

By contrast, the realm of social action showed more continuity with republican populationist and pronatalist ideology that could, in fact, benefit procreative immigrant Jews. Where family policy was concerned, Vichy bore a remarkable resemblance to the French Third Republic—extending interwar family policy, hardening the Republic's tough approach to abortion, divorce, and adoption in ways that shored up families, but rarely innovating new policies altogether. As a result, officials made only slight modifications to the 1939 Code de la Famille, for instance, canceling family allocations to households with just one child but increasing payouts to households with two or more children. Such modifications stood only to benefit large immigrant and immigrant Jewish families further. The extension and continued application of Third Republican family policy resulted from a combination of administrative in-fighting, budget and personnel constraints, as well as the realities of the moment (war, occupation, social unrest). It was also, in many ways, the inevitable outcome of a growing technocratic state in which the reproductive family was at last enshrined as the central building block of French society despite an otherwise fluctuating series of political regimes.[11] Significantly, Vichy officials themselves recognized that families were well-provided for by a variety of state and parastate social actors, including welfare officials, employers, and charitable associations who operated together and apart in a decentralized but vibrant welfare world. Vichy simply did not have to innovate when it came to social action; they merely rationalized and systematized the abundant social services that had already come into being by the 1930s.[12]

Interactions between private Jewish charitable organizations in the capital and the Vichy administration underscore how unique social assistance was among other government offices in its continued provision of Jews. In 1943, correspondence between social workers, municipal authorities, and Vichy administrators revealed a tacit expectation that the Union Générale des Israelites Français (UGIF)—the Jewish umbrella organization under the Commissariat Général aux Questions Juives (CGQJ) that centralized and monitored all Jewish social service activities—would liaise with Public Assistance, the Direction of Social Service, and the local *bureaux de bienfaisance* on behalf of their Jewish clients. In fact, the director of Public Assistance reminded the prefect of the Seine that "the agreement has thus been well-established" for some time.[13] The conversation had been prompted by an initial inquiry from the president of UGIF to the CGQJ about whether the Jewish organization should consider augmenting its social assistance or if it could continue to rely on the French state. In January 1944, the prefect of the Seine issued a telling reply: "In the present state of the legislation, none of the constitutive texts in the form of assistance, that one could call 'legal' ("Obligatory assistance to pregnant women, to families, medical assistance, assistance to interned families, to refugees, etc. . . .), *carry a trace of racial discrimination.*" He continued, "As a result, as long as government authorities do not engage in modifications of the texts in question, one should take from the present situation, in legal terms, the double conclusion that each individual, *no matter what his race,* who meets the conditions fixed for each type of 'legal' assistance has the right to benefit from those allocations."[14] In other words, as late as 1944, the CGQJ was assuring the UGIF in no uncertain terms that social assistance was provisioned to all, regardless of race, as long as they met all other reproductive criteria. UGIF did not need to increase social assistance, then, only aid Jews in their quest to secure it from public officials. For Jews who avoided getting ensnared by the police, social assistance remained one—perhaps the only—official realm in which familialism trumped anti-Semitism. Many foreign-born Jews would not take that risk, though, and instead turned to charitable welfare organizations to survive.

The Groupe Amelot: Women, Welfarism, and Gendered Resistance Work

Before it would play a vital role in the Jewish resistance, the Rue Amelot group was a *colonie scolaire,* or philanthropic organization, devoted to the care of primarily foreign Jewish children and families. Founded in 1926 by Jewish activists David Rapoport (a Ukrainian) and Juda Jacoubovitch (a Pole), the *colonie scolaire* provided complementary Jewish schooling to immigrant children in the neighborhoods. It also set up a network of *colonies de vacances* in Berck-Plage for working-class children. In 1930, the founders added a medical service for mothers, which offered free consultations and, several years later, in 1933, the dispensary adopted a new name to better reflect services rendered: La Mère et l'Enfant, or Mother and Child. It was precisely as a maternalist social service organization that the Groupe Amelot, as it has been remembered, continued to act in the interests of French and especially foreign Jewish families and children during the Occupation.[15]

Given the melting-pot character of the onzième, it is hardly surprising that "a crowd" of foreign Jews—including Russians, Poles, Romanians, North Africans, and "Juifs d'Orient"—found refuge at La Mère et L'Enfant, both before and during the war.[16] What is more surprising is that, given the scope of its resistance work, it evaded detection by German authorities for so long. Although the CGQJ had nursed suspicions about "secret funds" "of unknown provenance" used for more than mere "public assistance," it was not until 1943 that German officials learned of La Mère et L'Enfant and definitively brought it to heel under the UGIF.[17] It was an official surveillance that Rapoport and the rest of Amelot's leadership feared and avoided as long as possible. As one contemporary later reflected, "We succeeded in camouflaging our existence under the cover of our Dispensary's sign, which passed unnoticed with both the Police and the German Gestapo."[18] Significantly, the language of "masking," "camouflaging," and otherwise working "under the purely philanthropic cover" of the dispensary suffuses both historical and scholarly accounts of the Comité Amelot, suggesting how successfully maternalism would cloak Jewish rescue-as-resistance work.

Until their discovery in 1943, Jacoubovitch wrote of only a few brushes with authority, Amelot emerging each time unscathed because of the organization's focus on mothers, children, and families. In 1940, when interrogated by two Feldpolizei, "We simply replied that we were 'an aid organization.'" The following year, the French police received an anonymous denunciation informing them that Amelot members had secretly sent money to Moscow, but the police concluded "that it was certainly an act of revenge by someone to whom we had refused our help." And in 1942, when they faced more acute danger as French police inspected their offices, even Jacoubovitch was amazed they survived in one piece. "It is surprising that more questions were not asked about the activities of the Comité," he later reflected, considering that perhaps the officers themselves had wondered, "How an organization [that] specialized in children's aid could also concern itself with adults?"[19] Even when the rue Amelot office periodically fell under official scrutiny, they simply moved to another maternalist dispensary, dispensaire Tiomkine in the Belleville neighborhood of the 20th arrondissement, before eventually returning home on rue Amelot.[20]

As a social service organization, the Rue Amelot group engaged in a wide range of mother-, child-, and family-focused activities from its founding onward and relied predominantly on an army of Jewish female social workers to carry out its fieldwork (figure 7.1). The war was no exception, though Amelot's *assistantes sociales* are rarely mentioned in official histories of rescue and resistance work. In fact, according to the organization's wartime records, they were at the heart of daily operations and tended to the two largest projects: the administration of the four *cantines populaires*, or soup kitchens, and family assistance, which housed all social service and rescue activities.[21]

Three of Amelot's four cantines populaires were located in the heart of the old Jewish districts of Paris in the neighboring 3rd and 4th arrondissements. Miraculously, all four remained open throughout the war despite the successive arrests and deportations of their Jewish, foreign-born *directeurs*

FIGURE 7.1. The personnel of the Groupe Amelot, ca. 1940–42. From left to right: (*front row*) Dora Liberboïm, Mademoiselle Mandelstamm, Mademoiselle Libman, Madame Youchnovetski, unidentified boy, Isidore Vladimirowski, Madame Dobrinski; (*back row*) Madame Rapoport, Dr. Leibovici, Madame Losice, Jenny Caraco, David Rapoport, M. A. Cremer, Jules Jacoubovitch, Monsieur Charavner, Monsieur Kouliche, Monsieur Ischlonski, I. Byl, Judkowski, Z. Salomon, Tcherechna. Dossier 1c, DLXXXIV, Mémorial de la Shoah.

and, more often, *directrices*. Situated just blocks from the onzième, each soup kitchen maintained its own distinctive character. The cantines at rue Béranger, run by Russian-born Judith Topcza, and at rue Vieille du Temple, run by Polish-born Esther Rivka Richter, drew many Jewish families from Sainte Marguerite and La Roquette, and foreign Jews and refugees, at that.[22] Both directrices had emigrated to Paris before the war, participated in left-wing radical politics, contributed to the wartime founding of Amelot, and were arrested during the war for their efforts.[23] Jacoubovitch described them as a "colossal" presence, not merely overseeing the distribution of food, but providing comfort and community in dark times. At rue Vieille du Temple, Richter, known more familiarly as Madame Ika, "was a real mother" to her patrons, "exercised a strong [*fantastique*] influence over them," and made the soup kitchen "a real *chez soi*." After her arrest in 1941, Jacoubovitch paid her successor, Monsieur Nathan, the highest compliment he could, praising him for "[knowing] how to safeguard the spirit of Madame Ika."[24]

According to one estimate, assistantes sociales and directrices like Topcza and Ika oversaw the distribution of over 850,000 free meals during the war.²⁵ The cantines populaires kept poor immigrant Jews, especially women and children, from starving during the war, particularly after July 1942 when municipal soup kitchens stopped serving Jews.²⁶ It also supplied a space in which assistantes sociales could learn about the evolving needs of families. "Thanks to the information furnished by the directors of the cantines," remembered Jacoubovitch, "our organization could rationally and effectively organize its activity." The cantines, then, provided social workers with a daily opportunity to serve as liaisons and go-betweens with Jewish families, and thus helped them shape a coherent family assistance program for the organization.

Madame Youchnovetzki, a Jewish woman born in Bialystok, directed Amelot's family assistance and social services sector along with Jacob Byl, a Polish Jew and cofounder of the colonie scolaire, and Enéa Averbouh, an energetic assistante sociale from the Oeuvre de Secours aux Enfants (OSE) who collaborated closely with Amelot's social workers throughout the war.²⁷ Like other interwar and wartime welfare organizations dedicated to women, children, and families, Amelot's family assistance program bore a few standard features. First, Youchnovetzki spearheaded efforts to establish a *vestiaire* during the war, usually housed in Paris with non-Jewish families already providing safe harbor for hidden Jews.²⁸ During the war, assistantes sociales distributed over 26,000 pieces of clothing to women and children in Paris as well as to internees in France's concentration camps.²⁹ Second, the ongoing provision of direct assistance to Jewish families was a key part of Amelot's mission. As during the war, it entailed a great many visitations, placements, payments, and donations, as well as follow-up correspondence and documentation.³⁰ Third, like all maternalist organizations, Amelot offered employment services for mothers, a medical dispensary, under whose name it operated, and a legal office, which took on everything from emigration and repatriations to divorce cases.³¹ In other words, throughout the war, Amelot's social workers continued and accelerated their efforts to provide aid to Jewish mothers and their children, furnishing them with material, medical, and legal assistance—everyday acts of social assistance that took on subversive dimensions under Vichy.³²

As the Occupation wore on, the organization became an increasingly important source of relief for the capital's most impoverished Jewish families, especially immigrant mothers and their children. After all, the state had initially targeted Jewish men between the ages of eighteen and forty-five, whisking away fathers, husbands, and sons with impunity and leaving mothers, wives, and daughters to fend for themselves. Turkish-born Suzanne Obadia received seven hundred francs per month from UGIF to help support her seven children after her husband Raphael was deported from Drancy in 1942.[33] And when Russian-born Herzlik and Perla Chenochowitcz were deported in 1941 and 1942, respectively, their two daughters, sixteen-year-old Fanny and thirteen-year-old Simone, lived off "savings left by their parents and the aid accorded by official Jewish organizations."[34] Indeed, by 1944, only 7 out of 230 families assisted by Amelot were French.[35] Certainly, their workload increased over the course of the war as the state stepped up its persecution of Jews and foreign Jewish families came to increasingly depend on charitable social services and family assistance. In many ways, this was a familiar dynamic, reminiscent of the depression years when public assistance shrank for immigrant men and, to a far lesser extent, women and families. But the workload also increased because family assistance itself became the organization's means of pursuing rescue work throughout the war.

As French and foreign Jews were rounded up in camps throughout France, social workers extended assistance to camps where families were imprisoned. Over the course of the war, social worker Madame Dobrinski directed the preparation and delivery of over nine thousand *colis*, veritable care packages filled with food and clothing.[36] Originally prepared for the neediest Jewish families in the onzième, colis were increasingly rerouted to Jewish internees in Pithiviers, Beune-la-Rolande, La Tourelle, Drancy, Compiègne, Poitiers, and Tours. Social workers also served as intermediaries between deportees and their family members and other loved ones, relaying information and serving as go-betweens to ensure that those left behind, particularly children, were cared for.[37] Madame Moszkowicz, for instance, living on Cité industrielle in Sainte Marguerite wrote to Amelot for help in 1941 when she found herself interned in Drancy with sick children.[38] As late as May 1944, they were still sending colis both to Jewish families in the neighborhoods as well as to state and private institutions and facilities where Jews both hid and were hidden, for instance the Rothschild Hospital in the neighboring 12th arrondissement, Maison Blanche in the 13th arrondissement, and the Asile Saint Maurice at the edge of the 20th arrondissement.[39]

In extraordinary cases, Amelot's social workers sought and even succeeded in liberating Jewish children from detention and internment camps in France. In May 1941, Amelot staff worked through two non-Jewish social service organizations who were, as Jacoubovitch noted, "known by the occupier for undertaking social action, the first in favor of immigrants, the second in favor of children." Staff of these French social service organizations, very likely the SSAE and the Red Cross, successfully intervened with local prefectures to help secure the release of Jewish children from the camps.

Several months later, under the cover of their mother- and child-centered interests, emboldened Amelot social workers participated more openly: Madame Valensi, one of Amelot's most active assistantes sociales, obtained the liberation of 120 children imprisoned in Poitiers in September 1941.[40] Valensi also traveled to the southern zone in March 1942 and helped with the release of 21 Jewish children from the Vienne province, as well as 80 others under age fifteen in the following weeks.[41] Thus, family assistance undertaken by Amelot social workers extended old elements of interwar welfare aid for mothers, children, and families to new wartime settings.

The rescue of Jewish children followed this pattern of continuity and adaptation, and eventually came to form the backbone of family assistance work. Though involving the largely female personnel of numerous social service organizations focused on the survival of women, children, and families, rescue efforts remained all but invisible to French and German officials who saw little more than the everyday world of welfare run by countless unassuming assistantes sociales. Within the Groupe Amelot, it was again Madame Youchnovetzki and her social service team who coordinated these activities. Though rescue work took place uninterrupted throughout the war, it was very much tied to the various rafles that periodically sent ripples of terror throughout the Jewish community.[42] The roundup of Jewish children in July 1942, who accounted for nearly one-third of those raffled, unleashed a sense in the Jewish community that no one was safe. In the days following the rafle, Amelot headquarters were flooded by foreign-born Jewish mothers and fathers looking to hide their children before the next dreaded roundup.[43] Indeed, summer 1942 was a sort of turning point for Jewish welfare organizations: both UGIF and Solidarité, a Communist Jewish resistance group, created children's services sections that summer.[44]

As before the war, tucking away Jewish children in corners of the French countryside took place under the guise of straightforward social assistance, outwardly no different than placing children en famille or en nourrice as had become the norm over the previous five decades.[45] Little surprise then that sister organizations developed a similar set of prescribed steps: first, they secured each Jewish child a placement in Paris or, more often, in the French countryside; second, they prepared children for transit and transported them to their new home; and, third, they closely managed and monitored the placement, making adjustments as necessary. Social workers thus drew on accepted social blueprints for child-rearing and caretaking rooted in pre–World War II welfare systems and their institutional processes. Throughout, the participation of non-Jewish organizations and female colleagues were key to the rescue of Jewish children.

As the terror of persecution heightened over the course of the war, Jewish parents began to hand their children over to social service organizations in the capital with little argument. When deported Jewish parents were sent away, leaving children behind, it was often friends, neighbors, and concierges who would take them in before alerting Amelot's *assistantes sociales*.⁴⁶ Once brought to their attention, social workers went about finding these children a permanent refuge, drawing on suggestions made by their non-Jewish colleagues who occasionally dropped in to tip them off to families in Paris and the provinces interested in taking in children.⁴⁷ Although some non-Jewish Frenchwomen spontaneously turned up at Parisian headquarters offering to take in Jewish children during the war, social workers tended to prefer *familles d'accueil* in the provinces who attracted less attention since, to the official eye, they appeared simply as *nourrices*.⁴⁸ They sought out especially small farms, as isolated as possible, where the presence of a Jewish child was a boon to the household, both for the pension as well as the labor they might furnish.

As social workers pulled together networks of shelters in the provinces, some enterprising *paysannes* wrote to them of their own volition and offered to take in Jewish children. After learning that "[Amelot] distributes children *chez des particuliers* in the province," the widow Hergaux, from the Vendome region of Loire-et-Cher, wrote to social workers in December 1943 asking if "it might be possible for you to send me two youngsters of three to five years [age]."⁴⁹ The widow Vaucelle from la Vallée de Montfort in the Sarthe province also wrote to Amelot to take in a child "même tout petit." She even mentioned that her neighbor, Madame Aubry, would be interested in taking one in, as well.⁵⁰ Of course, social workers recognized that these offers could be motivated in equal parts by good will and material need given the realities of wartime privation throughout France. In fact, when Madame Le Laire of Noisy Le Grand wrote that she would be willing to take in a "young boy of 12 years," she stated explicitly that she expected him to "run and go and fetch [*cour et aller et venir*] my two cows." Nevertheless, she was adamant that "he will be fine with us and I will take care of him like he was my own."⁵¹ Others were more forthright in their demands. Dispensing with all pretense, a certain Madame G. Puchère from Vignieux stated explicitly: "I write to let you know that I accept the two children that you have proposed to me. . . . My conditions are as follows[:] for children aged six to seven years: I will take 700+ [francs] per month and for children aged nine to ten years[:] 800+ [francs] per month. If you would be so kind as to let the parents know to furnish me with one sheet per child." She concluded the negotiation by reminding Amelot's social workers that, "as a result of the difficulty finding food provisions, I must ask that their *cartes d'alimentation* are complete."⁵²

While some French families in the countryside knowingly took in Jewish children, even, like Madame Puchère, turning the offer of assistance to their own material advantage, on the whole social workers tended to withhold the identities of Jewish children from host families with whom they were placed, suggesting they did not entirely trust in the good will of provincial *paysan-n-e-s*.[53] Jewish resistance fighters too remembered how difficult it seemed at times to move rural opinion in favor of rescuing Jews. In their efforts to persuade French families in the countryside to take in Jews, the Jewish section of the Main d'Oeuvre Immigré went so far as to appeal to readers of its underground publication through well-worn populationist arguments, pleading, "Can we stand aside and be indifferent to the depopulation of our country, to all of the young people who are threatened with deportation."[54] For his own part, Jacoubovitch drew a contrast between the French of Parisian neighborhoods and the French of the provinces, claiming, "In the Paris region, the child services section could act with Jewish collaborators aided by Christians. But in the provinces, the situation was different," recalling "We were not able to find in the provinces permanent Christian collaborators like in Paris."[55]

Indeed, decades of living and working in the close quarters of melting-pot neighborhoods had forged a civil society in Paris more inclined to help Jewish neighbors than in the more homogeneous regions of the French countryside. This was certainly the case elsewhere in Occupied Europe, including Belgium and the Netherlands, where mixed working-class neighborhoods assured the survival of Jews at higher rates than more segregated environments which, instead, intensified Jewish isolation.[56] For instance, while 37 percent of Jews in residentially integrated Brussels were deported over the course of the war, more than 67 percent of Jews who clustered in ghettolike concentrations near the railway in Antwerp suffered the same fate.[57] Though the melting-pot neighborhoods of Paris favored the circumstances under which Jews might find aid and assistance from non-Jews, as the police dragnet ensnared them in increasing numbers, it was the very isolation of rural France that seemed to promise newfound security. In the end, Jewish families and social workers weighed the growing likelihood of official persecution in occupied Paris against the at times unclear motives of provincial peasants, and many came to believe the latter offered them their best chance for survival.

Once receiving households in the countryside had been located, social workers transported children to their new homes, a task complicated by the need to camouflage the identity of Jewish children and themselves. While members of the Groupe Amelot fabricated false identity cards on site with help from Rapoport's city hall contacts, some *assistantes sociales* preferred more homegrown methods.[58] Recalling her mother's participation in rescue efforts, the daughter of Madame Flament, a non-Jewish social worker who worked in a dispensary in the Marais, remembered her mother creating fake identity papers for Jewish children at home in the kitchen before later accompanying them to their new homes.[59] Still others called on their personal and professional networks in Paris, relying on bureaucrats they knew and had worked with in previous years in the police prefecture, local *mairies*, even the Post Office and Ministry of Public Health for help falsifying birth records, identity papers, and *cartes d'alimentation*.[60]

It was dangerous work, made more so by the fact that most of the Jewish children Amelot rescued were very young, born predominantly in the 1930s. While many were French- and even Paris-born, others were recent refugees from Poland, Romania, Czechoslovakia, and elsewhere in Eastern and Central Europe.[61] Consequently, stories abound of the difficulty social workers had getting children to remember their new names, to say nothing of their parents or backgrounds, to refrain from speaking Yiddish or their accented French lest they give themselves and the rest of their traveling companions away. Social workers were keenly aware that a simple "anatomical investigation" by Vichy or German officials could reveal circumcised Jewish boys and thus condemn them all.[62]

In the early war years, Jewish social workers transported children themselves, considering perhaps their credentials as assistantes sociales of maternalist organizations protection enough. As the persecution of Jews stepped up, however, "passing Gentile" became increasingly important. While some like OSE social worker Celine Vallée were protected by "French-sounding" last names, others were volunteered for duty because they "looked Aryan."[63] In 1943, Rapoport even encouraged an Amelot social worker, Berthe Zysman, to "contract a fake marriage with a Russian-born Frenchman" to avoid arrest.[64] With the introduction of additional *statuts de juifs* constraining Jewish mobility, Jewish assistantes sociales increasingly relied on their non-Jewish colleagues at sister organizations to take children to safety, whether by train, bicycle, or foot. For instance, Lucie Chevalley-Sabatier, founder of the SSAE, used her official clout both to furnish fake identity papers for Amelot's social workers as well as to transport Jewish children to the countryside herself.[65]

While Amelot's assistantes sociales always worked collaboratively with other Jewish social service organizations, including UGIF, OSE, Sixième, and Solidarité, they increasingly relied on non-Jewish French social workers from a variety of organizations to undertake the third and final step: follow-up visits with placed children, which often yielded new *familles nourricières*.[66]

Mademoiselle Papinos, who directed Amelot's secretariat for child placement from her own apartment, regularly called on Madame Corbet, a French social worker with another charitable organization, to undertake visitations on her behalf.[67] Monitoring placed children also entailed the vast busywork of paying pensions, handling correspondence, coordinating the delivery of shoes, pants, and handkerchiefs from the *vestiaire*, and administering the growing number of hidden children in their charge. To better manage the resulting glut of paperwork, Amelot's social workers created an intricate anonymous filing system to document each child's "social situation" in his or her placed home in order to make the best "match" possible. Nearly identical to the records of interwar maternalist organizations, Amelot's wartime files included notes from home visits, observations on physical and moral well-being, opinions about the child's relations with the *famille nourricière*, and detailed accounts of pension payments.[68]

Marthe Laborde, a non-Jewish French social worker employed by the Seine prefecture through the Créteil hospital, was particularly involved with Amelot throughout the war. The scope of her participation underscores the increasing importance of enlisting non-Jewish social workers and illustrates how the wider world of welfare mobilized to protect Jewish children. First contacted in 1942 by Madame Getting, the head of UGIF's Child Placement Services, Laborde was asked to help place several Jewish children in La Manche, Ille-et-Vilaine, and La Mayenne where rural French families who often took in Créteil's convalescing young wards lived. Getting reached out to Laborde because they had been colleagues during the 1930s, when Getting served as the founder and president of hospital social services in the Seine before she was removed under Vichy's race statutes. Through UGIF, Laborde learned of Amelot and placed herself in their service.

As a non-Jewish social worker with connections to rural French families, Laborde was a valuable asset. Explaining how she reconciled her day job with Jewish rescue efforts, Laborde recalled simply, "[Because] my absence [was] justified by my service, each time I was accompanying one or two children to their convalescent home [in the provinces], I took the opportunity to bring several Jewish children." Through secret telephone calls, Laborde and Amelot's social workers arranged regular *rendez-vous* at train stations where she could pick up groups of six or seven Jewish children and travel with them to their new home in the countryside. When she needed an extra pair of hands, she recruited her sister-in-law. In time, she became an integral part of the Amelot team during the war, directing the orphanage in La Varenne that Rapoport had acquired in 1940 in order to hide Jewish children. Along with several non-Jewish social workers who, like her, were natives of

Saint-Maur, Laborde watched as La Varenne's charge grew from just eight Jewish orphans to over thirty within the first year of the war.[69]

In addition to revealing the extent of coordination among Jewish and non-Jewish social workers, Laborde's participation in Amelot's rescue work is a reminder of the thick web of female associational activity that hummed along in a welfare world comprised of multiply affiliated social workers. After all, Laborde was officially a municipal worker associated with a public hospital in the Seine who became involved in rescue work thanks to professional contacts from the interwar years. As a non-Jew, she leveraged opportunities to travel in the countryside to find homes for Jewish children and transport them there. When she needed assistance, she drew on local networks of family, friends, and colleagues to get the work done. While the war and Vichy's persecution of Jews certainly increased the stakes of her participation, in nearly every way it was an organizational collaboration reminiscent of the interwar years and representative of what social workers throughout France were doing on behalf of Jewish children. Though rarely acknowledged, French and foreign, Jewish and non-Jewish female social workers formed the nucleus of extensive child rescue networks radiating out of Paris and into the countryside. Consequently, female participation in Jewish rescue work in wartime France was quite high, women accounting for as many as 86 percent of resistant-e-s in the southern zone.[70]

Although typically folded into the broad category of "non-Jewish social assistance," the familialist and maternalist world of welfare and their all-female staffs furnished Amelot with reliable institutional partners in Paris and the provinces, a reminder of how the rescue of children was of a piece with their interwar mission to support families and mothers, whether French or foreign, Jewish or non-Jewish, unmarried and married, widowed and divorced.[71] Familialist organizations like the SSCMD also worked closely with Amelot during the war such that several characters reappear in different guises throughout this welfare-cum-rescue world: for instance, the esteemed Dr. Minkowski, an SSCMD psychiatrist as well as a doctor at the Rothschild Hospital, who most notably founded the OSE and by his own account came to resistance work through Rapoport's entreaties.[72] In Paris, the League for the Protection of Abandoned Mothers continued to help French and foreign working-class mothers, some of whom they had first made contact with during the 1930s who then returned during the war for material aid after finding themselves in all too familiar circumstances. For instance, Sura Cukier, a Polish Jew who came to the League for help nine times over the course of 1937, reappeared in March 1941 after her French husband had left her and her two French-born children.[73] That said, women also showed up with more extraordinary requests borne of wartime circumstances, asking for assistance in evacuation, flight, and repatriation or following the mobilization, deportation, or imprisonment of the fathers of their children. Sura Ryka Ilotogorski, also a Polish Jew and mother of two, came in March 1942 to secure allocations for herself and her children following her husband's detention in Pithiviers.[74]

Jewish and non-Jewish charitable organizations offered many options for Jewish children orphaned by the war. Amelot's orphanage in La Varenne or UGIF's juvenile dormitory on rue Lamarck in the 18th arrondissement were two well-known shelters for Parisian children whose parents had been arrested and deported, to say nothing of the vast network of shelters that OSE and Jewish scouting groups had raised before the war and repurposed under Vichy.[75] Homes, orphanages, and others facilities for children and adolescents run by religious groups as well as non-Jewish maternalist and familialist organizations also adapted under the war's exigencies. For instance, Amelot's social workers availed themselves of SSCMD's Foyer de Soulins in Brunoy, an observation facility for children with behavioral problems, as well as SSAE's children's centers, which served as hideouts for Jewish children during the Occupation.[76]

Astonishingly, the multiple fates of French and foreign-born Jewish children reveal that, while many found safety through private charitable organizational networks, many others hid within the vast network of public institutions for children that had multiplied in France since the late nineteenth century. From local health clinics, public hospitals, sanitoria and convalescence homes to orphanages, summer camps, youth homes, and Public Assistance itself, the entire infrastructure put in place by Third Republican statesmen to safeguard the health of working-class children provided ready-made shelters for French and immigrant Jewish children for the duration of the war.[77] It may even have been an open secret that these shelters were safe havens. After the war, Albert, the son of Polish Jews, recalled that a certain Madame Destant had eventually helped his sister Pauline find shelter in the countryside by first tucking her away temporarily in a psychiatric center outside of Paris.[78] In fact, hiding Jewish children in hospital sick wards became a favorite strategy of social workers who bargained that the specter of contagion might put off French and German officials long enough to get children to a more permanent shelter in the countryside.[79]

Of course, working with public institutions was not a foolproof strategy.[80] But state- and municipally run centers could better shield Jewish children from the state's persecution than the centers run by Jewish charitable organizations, which, to some, had begun to approximate traps as the Occupation wore on. This lesson was made clear on February 10, 1943, when French and German officials for the first time targeted Jewish children, ransacking Jewish *regroupements d'enfants* throughout Paris and the surrounding region, including UGIF children's centers, the Rothschild Orphanage, and the Amelot orphanage in La Varenne.[81] That the Vichy state and Nazi officials would target Jewish youth centers is perhaps not surprising; but that it would take three years to hit on the strategy underscores Vichy's softer approach toward Jewish youth, at least for the early part of the Occupation.[82] Ultimately, Jewish children's high rate of survival in France attests to how successful social workers were at protecting them from the state by paradoxically using the state and its public institutions to hide them.[83]

The near-total dependence of Jewish mothers and families on social service organizations during a period of unrelenting state terror gave a distinct flavor to the difficulties social workers encountered when working with the families of rescued children. Catching wind of a rumor about impending rafles, mothers might demand their children back. Jacoubovitch described in heart-rending detail these desperate scenarios, as social workers sought in vain to soothe terrified parents who periodically showed up on their doorstep demanding to know where their children were hidden. Seeking to be reunited with their children, parents might learn the address of their child's nourrice and, locating them, blow their child's "cover," effectively "outing" them as Jews to the whole village.[84] In some cases, parents might even attempt to join their children en nourrice, perhaps seeking refuge themselves. Such scenarios made Amelot's assistantes sociales fretful: "Certain hunted parents [*parents traqués*] (such as the Rubensteins *chez* Madame Thuault) have moved in with their nourrices. I insist on a rapid departure [because] the women's chatting [*bavardage*], their accents, could draw attention to them and the tranquility of the children would be compromised." In this particular instance, the parents remained for another three months, a reminder that, while a robust infrastructure supported, sheltered, and hid Jewish children, their parents and older siblings were another matter.[85]

While social workers did find ways to extend child placement services to Jewish adults, they were more costly to place and there was a general sense that, as Jacoubovitch wrote, "They could manage [*se débrouiller*] better than children."[86] Though Jewish charitable associations continued to provide some material relief, they and their staff encountered increasing danger as the Occupation dragged on. With the arrests of Amelot's top leadership in 1943 and its ensuing absorption by the UGIF, the organization's social workers grew more circumspect about their activities, relying increasingly on non-Jewish officials and social workers to undertake the riskiest clandestine work. They also began to advise families to stay away from the dispensary and, to prevent them from coming to their offices on rue Amelot, they distributed aid in person to individuals, quarter by quarter.[87] As social service organizations fell under greater suspicion, Jewish men and women turned increasingly to their neighborhoods and communities, which offered them the best, perhaps their last and only, chance for survival.

Jewish Families, Neighborhood Culture, and the Struggle for Survival

In 1940, the Vichy government began its attempts to purge foreign elements from the French nation by establishing a Commission de Revisions de Naturalisation (CRN) to review naturalization files of the interwar decades, root out Jewish "undesirables," and legally remove them from the national community through denaturalization.[88] The investigative reports produced by Paris police as a result provide a sobering portrait of foreign-born families encountered throughout the previous pages. Certainly, some families were made, like that of Haïm Goldenstein, a Romanian hatmaker naturalized in 1928 who had since married Polish Sara Frajlick, fathered four children, and put down roots on rue Keller.[89] And many foreign-born Jewish families remained in the neighborhood throughout the war, like the Russian Gourevitches on rue Montreuil, the Greco-Serbian Camhis on rue Chanzy, or the "Ottoman" Esperances on boulevard Voltaire (see figure 7.2).[90] But other foreign-born Jewish families were clearly unmade by the war. The Polish-born Handkans, the Turko-Bulgarian Mechoulams, and the Russian-born Khenkines fled Paris during *l'exode*, leaving their belongings behind as they made their way to the Free Zone, confounding police officials as to their whereabouts (see figure 7.1).[91] Some, like Russian-born Shiffra Kreis, left her husband behind and took their son Lazare to safety in southern France during the exodus, while others, like Russian-born Czina Schenkermann, could only be persuaded that the danger was real once her Romanian-born husband Nissim was interned in Drancy in August 1942.[92] Flight was a particularly wise strategy for those with even a hint of radical leftist politics in their background. Sophie Lachminovitch, the French-born daughter of Russian emigrants, landed on the official radar due to her Communist activism in the 1930s. When she fled to Dordogne in March 1944, CRN officials denaturalized the whole family.[93]

To remain in these neighborhoods throughout the war was to risk arrest, deportation, and, though they may not have known it yet, death. Many of the immigrant, foreign-born, and mixed Jewish families of these quartiers

FIGURE 7.2. Though Serbian Jew Sol Camhi died of natural causes in 1942, her husband Mentech and their four children were among those foreign-born Jewish families who remained in Sainte Marguerite during the war. Application de carte d'identité, February 14, 1923, in Mentech Camhi and Sol née Colonomos, I/A 34, Archives de la Prefecture de Police.

were torn apart in the early years of the war by the deportation of fathers and sons, later by the deportation of mothers, daughters, and young children.[94] On the whole, foreign-born Jews of La Roquette and Sainte Marguerite survived by adhering to the proliferating *statuts de juifs* preventing them from owning businesses, from practicing law or medicine, from entering public spaces outside of officially sanctioned hours.[95] While some, like Russian-born Adolphe Kraousmann, attempted to circumvent the system by avoiding the 1940 Jewish census and adopting instead a fake identity, if caught, as he was, immediate arrest, imprisonment, denaturalization, and deportation were to be expected.[96] In rare instances, some foreign-born Jews dared to push back against Vichy's denaturalization campaign, invoking familialist claims reminiscent of the interwar years.[97] When Romanian-born

FIGURE 7.3. Elsa Manachem, born in Poland in 1892, arrived in Paris in 1920 with her husband, Jacob Handkan. They and their daughter escaped to the provinces for the duration of the war. Application de carte d'identité, March 19, 1926, in Jacob Handkan and Elsa née Manachem, I/A 92, Archives de la Prefecture de Police.

Joina Rabinovici learned that he had been summarily denaturalized in 1941 for "lack of military service" to France, he wrote back in February 1942 that he was "stupefied" by the news given that he had always lived "simply, and *en famille,*" citing his French-born wife and Paris-born daughter as evidence of his clear attachment to the French nation and the necessity of reintegrating him at once. The prefecture convoked him again in August 1943 and undertook an investigation that December.[98]

Foreign-born Jewish families relied on their friends, neighbors, and community to survive the war years. When both his parents were deported, Turkish Jew Maurice Sasson turned to his half-siblings and employers in the neighborhood of La Roquette to help him make ends meet until he managed to flee to the southern zone in the summer of 1944.[99] Given the embeddedness of local welfare offices and other social service organizations, neighborhood social workers were also crucial to the survival of Jewish families in these quartiers. When Noël Kuperman's father, a Polish Jew, was arrested at his home on rue des Boulets and sent to Pithiviers, she and her older brother would have been left to their own devices once their mother fell ill had a neighborhood social worker from the mairie not intervened, obtaining for the father a very rare weeklong release during the mother's hospitalization.[100] Similarly, Nelly Scharapan, the Paris-born daughter of Polish immigrants living on rue de la Forge Royale, recalled with gratitude Mademoiselle Le Clézio, the directrice of a dispensary on nearby rue Ordener, who helped the family stay afloat during the Occupation by giving her grandmother work caring for neighborhood children and securing them new lodgings when police came looking for them in 1942.[101]

The abundant postwar accounts of Jewish children in France are dotted with stories of being taken in spontaneously by neighbors, and especially neighbor women. David, eleven years old at the start of the war, was a Paris-born son of Greek Jews from Salonica living in La Roquette. After the war, he recounted having watched his father, an electrician, interviewed and taken in by French police on rue Sedaine in August 1941 before later being interned in Compiègne, sent to Drancy, and finally dispatched to Treblinka where, as David learned after the war, he perished. He and his pregnant mother remained, fed by Amelot's soup kitchens and sustained by ongoing Jewish cultural life organized by UGIF on nearby Passage Charles Dallery. When, in November 1942, roundups targeting Greek and Turkish Jews tore through the neighborhood, claiming his mother and grandmother, a neighbor woman took him and his newborn brother in for eight days. "She did not ask questions," he recalled, "she understood what had happened. She took care of us as if we were her own children." Corresponding with his cousin, she engineered his placement with peasants in the Nièvre where he finished out the war disguised as an Alsatian refugee and orphan.[102] Noël Kuperman, above, had a similar experience: her mother's neighbor, Madame Viamant, "a Catholic," was so used to watching the children while their mother was away at work that, with the financial assistance of Amelot, she played an active role in the family's survival during the Occupation, helping to get the children to safety in the countryside. Though Kuperman's mother had wanted to take them to the train station herself, Kuperman recalled that, "Madame Viamant—who saved us—told [my mother] that it had become too dangerous for children in Paris, that my mother wore the yellow star, that there were Germans in the metro and that she should not come with her to Montparnasse." Viamant sent the Kuperman children away to her own family in Bretagne, a vivid testament to the depth of bonds forged between some French and immigrant neighbor women before the war.[103]

Of course, the Occupation also allowed non-Jewish neighbors, intimates, and acquaintances the opportunity to settle scores with Jews in the quartier through denunciations.[104] But there is little evidence suggesting denunciations were common in these neighborhoods. The lone example concerns Turkish Jew Samuel Almozinos whom Paris police investigated in February 1942 after receiving an anonymous letter that he was involved in "communist propaganda." In the end, police determined it a "calumnious denunciation" and left Almozinos, his French wife, and their two children in peace on rue de la Roquette.[105] Apart from this single instance, though, it is neighborly solidarity that stands out.

Concierges once again played a significant role in neighborly networks of support and assistance, opening their doors and providing sanctuary to persecuted Jewish families in their buildings during the war. When children like Maurice, Noël, Nelly, and David above found themselves orphaned, concierges took them in, cared for them, and fed them. Drawing on their extensive information networks, they could even warn Jewish families in the apartment building of impending roundups and help them escape.[106] Not only were they a valuable source of information within the neighborhood and within resistance networks, but they were an important source of misinformation to officials.[107] When police inquired as to whether Jews lived in her building in the onzième, Nelly Scharapan, above, recalled that their concierge, "*Brave* Madame Pretet," told them there were not, then came to warn Scharapan's grandmother that the family was in danger.[108] Even a small bit of feigned ignorance could make the difference between life and death. In December 1940, police inquired with the concierge at 9 rue Trousseau about the Marcu family, a Romanian-born, French-naturalized family of five. Though police learned that the family had left Paris in early June 1940, the concierge claimed herself "without news since their departure" and that she knew nothing of "what has become of the three sons who had been mobilized in 1939."[109] Given her extraordinary centrality to daily apartment life, it is unlikely that this concierge was quite as uninformed as she claimed.

From an official standpoint, neighborly networks could also spare the lives of naturalized Jews.[110] When assessing whether a foreign-born family merited denaturalization—thereby removing the first obstacle to arrest and deportation—officials scrutinized closely family members' "fréquentations." A bureaucratic category of measurement assessing French assimilation, *fréquentations* appeared in naturalization dossiers before the war, resurfacing during the war to evaluate how embedded foreign-born families had become within their local community. When officials discovered that the *fréquentations* of naturalized Jews were "mixed," "varied," or skewed toward "our nationals," as was the case for the Franco-Romanian Aizensteins, the Polish-born Brams, and the Serbian-born Widow Levy, assimilation was judged to be complete and they were left untouched.[111] By contrast, naturalized Jews whose social networks officials did not deem sufficiently French or at least "mixed" paid a heavy price. Take, for instance, the Arditiis who, officials recorded, "frequent more especially foreign Jews from Turkey," and represented just one family among numerous others whose ongoing preference for "foreign *milieux*" served, in official eyes, as grounds to strip them of French citizenship.[112] Even, as in the case of Russian-born Rachel Baitschmann, when officials acknowledged that she "appeared assimilated," they nevertheless were concerned that she continued to "frequent more particularly her foreign coreligionists in the neighborhood."[113] For foreign-born Jews naturalized during the interwar decades, then, mixed social networks with French non-Jews provided not just material benefits, but could shield them from denaturalization and perhaps deportation.

As Jewish men were arrested and deported, the wives, widows, and mothers they left behind found themselves in dire financial straits. In addition to relying on neighborly good will and addressing themselves to Jewish charities, they also, as Russian-born widow Friedland did, sometimes had to sell furniture, clothing, and any other goods that could provide a small income.[114] Surprisingly, they also found recourse in local authorities. In the wake of roundups, Jewish contemporaries observed that some Jewish wives went to their neighborhood police stations to not only seek information about their husbands' whereabouts but request financial assistance feeding their families. In fact, during the first years of the war, the wives of internees received an allocation of 7 francs per day for themselves as well as 5 francs per day for each child.[115] Bizarrely, it would appear, the state took away loved ones and breadwinners with one hand, then provided for those left behind with the other.

Some immigrant Jewish families in Sainte Marguerite and La Roquette may have intuited that social assistance was a unique exception to the state's overall campaign of Jewish persecution and continued to engage frequently and productively with their local welfare office. For instance, Russian-born Abraham and Sisla Kouperschmidt, still residents of Passage Lepeu, received 245 francs per month from the mairie of the 11th arrondissement throughout the war, the last documented payment occurring as late as February 1944. Moreover, their twenty-year old daughter Marguerite had been placed by the onzième's social workers in Pau, where her older brother Maurice lived with his family.[116] The same went for Turkish-born Ora Perez who, between the wars, came to *vivre maritalement* with once-widowed, once-divorced Saul Veissid, a French-naturalized Turkish Jew who had been deported to Auschwitz in 1941. According to a February 1944 police report, Perez continued to live with Saul Veissid's four children on rue Sedaine, receiving 400 francs from the UGIF every month and 98 francs every two weeks from the local welfare bureau for "her interned *ami.*"[117] On just one solitary occasion was there evidence that Jewish families on public assistance might have been courting danger. In August 1942, a French social worker associated with the internment camps wrote to inform Amelot's Valensi that "the Prefects have the power to send women and children who make a request for allocations to concentration camps"; she further urged Valensi "to warn these women so that they no longer insist on their inscription in the local welfare offices."[118] But given the variety of allocations distributed throughout the war to women and families, there is no indication that social workers or their Jewish clients heeded this warning nor that local welfare or police officials operated in this manner.

Though some naturalized Jewish men benefited from old age pensions during the war, it was women who maintained particularly strong engagement with local welfare bureaus, the conduit by which households collected aid in the form of family allocations, widows' pensions, and military allocations.[119] Their protected status as war widows, wives, and mothers of POWs, and especially as mothers of large families may have even factored favorably into official decision-making when the family's denaturalization was under consideration. Polish-born Tauba Wintermann, widowed by her husband Szmul in April 1940, found herself with eight children at the start of the war, three more than when the family was naturalized in 1930. According to the police report, "with her famille nombreuse, she does not engage in any paid work," but she did receive 2,040 francs each month from the local *caisse de compensation* as well as another 1,500 francs each month in family allocations. Rather than consider the Widow Wintermann and her large family an ethnically undesirable financial burden on the French state, CRN bureaucrats instead advised *maintien* for the entire family in 1943.[120]

Indeed, some French officials deliberately rewarded foreign-born Jewish women who headed large families in France. For instance, Polish-born Ida Korntajer, a mother of four when she and her husband Idel were naturalized in 1930, found herself a mother of nine by the start of World War II. Between July 1943 and May 1944, police officials and CRN personnel found themselves caught between conflicting logics: while the initial police report noted that the couple "appear assimilated," they nevertheless admitted that the Korntajers "speak our language with difficulty," an observation that perhaps spurred the decision six months later to denaturalize the family ("Mal assimilé, sans intérêt social"). But in May 1944, CRN officials overturned the decision, taking into account that Ida Korntajer was the recipient of bronze and silver *medailles de famille* and thus placing renewed emphasis on her reproductive service to France, which made her deserving of all the protections inherent therein.[121] The reproductive logic was stated overtly in the case of the Turkish-born Behars, a family of eight naturalized in 1932 and living in public housing on rue Henry Ranvier. In 1942, police officials noted with approval the advanced state of the family's assimilation, their mixed frequentations, and the good health of the children, summing up, "Given the familial situation, maintenance."[122]

Allocations militaires dispensed to the wives, mothers, and widows left behind by deported husbands and fathers offer yet another puzzling portrait of a regime torn between conflicting imperatives, to both weed out foreign Jewish elements and yet support mothers, children, and families, many of whom were foreign-born Jews. After her husband Pinkus was deported in 1942, Polish-born Channa Komorowski, still residing at 3 Passage Saint Bernard some fifteen years after their naturalization, lived off of the allocations militaires that accrued to her thanks to the military service of her three sons, two of whom were taken as POWS.[123] The son of Romanian-born widow Annette Fischler, Israel, perished in June 1940 fighting for the French, and she continued to collect military allocations well into 1943.[124]

Indeed, naturalized Jewish women who belonged to the bureaucratic category of *femmes de prisonniers de guerre* benefited from the designation in other ways that once again reveal the tensions between Vichy anti-Semitism and familialism. The widow Rebeca Souriano, a Turkish mother of four when naturalized in 1928, had borne two more children by an "unknown father" by the time she came up for review under the CRN. Though unemployed, they noted that "she occupies herself solely with the household and her children whom she has raised correctly." Moreover, her son was a POW, and thanks to his service she collected 880 francs each month in military allocations. In other words, in spite of Vichy morality campaigns about virtuous femininity, officials weighed a foreign-born Jewish woman's dedication to mothering and her son's wartime service favorably. The combination of her reproductive service and her son's military service shielded the family from denaturalization in November 1943.[125]

Status as *veuves de guerres* and femmes de prisonniers de guerre even protected some women and children already caught up in the French dragnet. Polish Suzanne Diament, for instance, was released from Drancy after fifteen days' internment because she was recognized as the "companion of a soldier *mort pour la France.*" Negotiations were particularly intricate because she and her husband, a French Jew, had been married in a religious rather than civil ceremony in February 1940. Indeed, in order to recognize her as a war widow, officials had to implicitly sanction a marriage "selon le rite Israelite," once more placing anti-Semitic ideology in tension with officials' conjugal politics, benevolent paternalism, and familialist professional ethos.[126]

On occasion, foreign-born Jewish women were more than passive recipients of the state's confounding munificence. They actively pursued its resources even at the risk of drawing attention to themselves. In September 1942, thirty-three-year old Schindla Chelicevitch, a typist, wrote to the minister of justice to request a copy of her naturalization decree because, she explained, she had recently given birth to twins and wished to enroll in a *caisse de compensation* as a single mother. The Polish-born daughter of immigrants, Chelicevitch nevertheless began her letter with a frank and unapologetic assertion to officials, echoing in many ways the entreaties of French-born Emilienne Goata whose own letter opens this book. Chelicevitch wrote: "I should say first of all that I am not married and have recognized our children of whom I am alone to assume the charge."[127] Remarkably, foreign-born Jewish women like Chelicevitch dared not simply to make requests of the state, but to boldly make themselves legible at a time when state officials sought to tear foreign-born Jews like them out of the social fabric. It was as though her status as a mother would shield her from the malevolent interest of the state, her "race," foreign birth, and unwed status notwithstanding. Thus, when it came to pronatalist welfarism, the world of the Third Republic did not disappear with the stroke of a pen. Interwar naturalization bureaucrats, even as they became agents of denaturalization under Vichy, continued to act according to familialist criteria that often was in tension with the anti-Semitic orientation of the state.

Until the summer of 1942, familialism continued to govern Vichy policies, even where the deportation and internment of Jews was concerned. With the Vel d'Hiv roundups, however, no one was safe, not even women and children. Yet, while the Vichy police state and its representatives wreaked havoc on foreign-born Jewish communities, the semipublic, semiprivate welfare infrastructure of the Republic and the army of neighborhood social workers it had raised between the wars continued to protect them. In France, a populationist culture of welfarism more advanced than elsewhere in Occupied Europe had taken firm root during the interwar decades, and during the war its representatives remained dedicated to the aid and support of both native and foreign-born alike.[128] Most important, however, neighborly networks in mixed, working-class communities mobilized on behalf of foreign-born Jewish mothers and children. Neighbors, and neighbor women, more especially, ensured that, while Paris did indeed witness the displacement, deportation, and murder of one-third of its Jewry, that figure was the lowest in all of Occupied Europe, most notably when compared to other occupied Western European cities, including Brussels, Amsterdam, and Antwerp, as well as, of course, occupied Central and Eastern European cities, including Warsaw, Lodz, and Vienna, where Jews perished in significant numbers.[129]

Neighborly networks protected recently naturalized Jews in one other way—namely, by shielding them from bureaucrats vested with the authority to strip them of their hard-earned French citizenship, an observation which serves as a reminder of how multifaceted the French state was during this period. Throughout the Occupation, Jewish families were confronted with different faces of the same state, a state comprised largely of officials whom they had already encountered throughout the interwar decades. They learned to fear police officials who, it appeared, were quite easily co-opted into the German and Vichy project of Jewish extermination.[130] They endured investigation and denaturalization at the hands of CRN bureaucrats, doubtlessly hoping that their reproductive value to the French nation would continue to shield them from harm. And with the ongoing help of social workers of private charities, it often did.

Local officials in welfare bureaus worked diligently to ensure that municipal and state benefits continued to flow to female-headed households throughout the war, even when those women were foreign-born and Jewish. Taking the familiar interwar form of family allowances, widow's pensions, and military allocations, state and municipal benefits continued to reward immigrant Jews for marriage, large families, and especially women's reproductive service to the nation in ways that, while baffling on the surface, were entirely consonant with the familialist accents of the new regime. In the end, *l'état français* paradoxically offered survival tools forged by *la république* to the very foreign-born Jewish women and children whose families it otherwise sought to destroy—compensating wives even as it widowed them, sheltering children even as it orphaned them.

Conclusion

Against the backdrop of severe depopulation and an imagined "crise de familles," Third Republican lawmakers, politicians, bureaucrats, employers, and social workers summoned reproductive citizenship into being. Through the routine application of social policies, state and social actors worked separately in both official and unofficial spheres toward a single shared goal: repopulating France with immigrant families. After the First World War, foreign-born men and women were welcomed and naturalization, family law, social policy, and welfare assistance were mobilized to ensure they would become the future mothers and fathers of French-born and French-assimilated children. For their part, immigrants often agreed to the bargain because they, too, stood to gain—from alimentary pensions, family allocations, unemployment benefits, and French nationality to the prospect of safety, stability, and prosperity on a tumultuous continent where such prerogatives were in short supply. Thus, in return for generous social provisions and refuge in dark times, immigrants joined the French nation through marriage and reproduction, breadwinning and child-rearing—in short, through families and family making.

In France's working-class urban neighborhoods, which had grown steadily more diverse by the turn of the century, the gendered rhythms of neighborhood life reinforced the making and remaking of mixed and foreign-born families—that is, the lived experience of reproductive citizenship. In particular, a female culture of mutual aid flourished in the social world of the apartment building and provided material support to French and immigrant wives and mothers, weaving them into the multicultural fabric of working-class community life. As a result, many immigrant women eventually adopted French patterns of marriage, employment, fertility, and child-rearing. They learned not only to speak French, but even mastered it better than their foreign-born husbands. This is not to say that they renounced all native customs—that they stopped attending synagogue, preparing ethnic dishes, or speaking their native tongue. But it does suggest that becoming French during this period never entailed the wholesale adoption of "Frenchness," however one defines such a term. Rather, during the interwar years, it was possible to reconcile the adoption of certain French practices and behaviors with the maintenance of minority traditions and customs without shredding irrevocably the fabric of neighborhood relations. That immigrants could join working-class French communities as well as maintain certain practices from their native countries, all without alienating their French-born neighbors, was in many ways made possible by the expansive parameters of reproductive citizenship before 1945.

Neighborhood solidarities cemented around those who embedded themselves in the community as fellow residents, as rooted families. It was passers-through, particularly itinerant foreign-born bachelors, and others who failed to conform to community norms about good husbands and fathers, hardworking wives and mothers, who were marked out for ostracism and exclusion. These norms were extended to colonial men who had put down roots and started families with white Frenchwomen in working-class communities. When interviewed by social workers and police officers, both native-born French and foreign-born neighbors often deemed Muslim North African men in their communities to be good fathers, hard workers, and dedicated husbands, even vouching for them against white Frenchwomen whom they might instead portray as drunk and disorderly wives, lazy and disinterested mothers. While it was more common for the French imperial nation-state to back Frenchwomen in their claims against colonial male subjects, gendered expectations of proper comportments in local communities could in fact pull in the opposite direction, undercutting white women's racial privilege vis-à-vis nonwhite lovers and spouses. Between the wars, neighborhood solidarities coalesced around gender and family norms in ways that often transcended racial, ethnic, or religious differences among French and foreign-born. These relationships were put to the ultimate test under Vichy and the Occupation, when neighborly networks in mixed and melting-pot urban environments mobilized to protect one another from harm, especially mothers, children, and families.

Located at the nexus of neighborhood and national life, the vibrant world of welfare served as the chief pillar of reproductive citizenship in interwar France. Because improving the health and quantity of the population was of paramount importance in the fight against depopulation, the French welfare state, mixing public and private initiatives in a large, decentralized structure before 1945, showed greater flexibility in terms of who qualified for assistance than similar developing welfare states: in the late nineteenth century, single, unwed mothers and their fatherless children were among its beneficiaries; at the dawn of the twentieth century, and following post–World War I mass migration movements, they were joined by immigrant mothers, foreign-born families, and mixed-race children. That welfare was a local experience before 1945 only amplified its inclusive dimensions: middle-class French social workers, though they may have nurtured their own notions of proper parenting, child-rearing, and respectable comportment, nevertheless went to battle for their foreign, working-class clients. During the interwar years, they interacted frequently, extensively, and supportively with immigrant women who were mothers and the heads of large families. The solidarities borne of these interactions mattered under the Occupation, too, since it was these self-same social workers who helped transform the welfare world into a site of resistance against Vichy persecution. In so doing, everyday acts of social assistance and welfare administration on behalf of foreign-born Jewish women and children became acts of subversion and resistance under a regime committed to their removal, expulsion, and destruction.

Because of its staunchly conservative ideology, the Vichy period exposes with stark clarity the surprising forms of inclusion traced throughout these pages, and it highlights continuities from the Third to the Fourth Republic in the realm of family matters. The overlapping ideologies of republican pronatalism and Catholic familialism espoused by many interwar state and parastate officials was only enhanced by the Vichy regime's dedication to traditional family values and gender norms. The ironic consequence was that the state—vast and disjointed though it was—nevertheless came to offer protection to some foreign-born Jewish families in ongoing recognition of their reproductive service to the nation and as a practical matter of support to protected classes of citizens—above all, mothers, wives, widows, and children. The trend was, of course, far more pronounced in certain corners of the government than others.

Prior to the Vel d'Hiv roundups in summer 1942, police roundups targeted nonprocreative foreign-born Jews, especially bachelors, and showed greater leniency toward children, families, and those with French attachments. In so doing, they amplified republican criteria that had operated throughout the 1920s and 1930s, in particular, to determine which immigrants offered greater and lesser social "value" to the French national family. Of course, after summer 1942, such reconciliations between inclusive varieties of familialism and exclusive varieties of anti-Semitism, racism, and xenophobia were no longer possible where the policing apparatus of the Vichy state was concerned. Foreign-born Jewish men and women—even as husbands and wives, fathers and mothers—made themselves legible to police officials at great personal risk to themselves and their families. By contrast, CRN officials, most of whom had served in the interwar Bureau de Sceau and had thus been the very ones to naturalize foreign-born Jewish families in the first place, continued to apply a populationist logic, in this instance to their wartime task of denaturalization. Consequently, they might spare foreign-born Jewish mothers and their large families through recourse to the only criteria that continued to matter before the Occupation, during the Occupation, and long after the Occupation: reproduction. Having a large family was not, of course, a surefire way to avoid denaturalization and subsequent deportation, and many foreign-born Jews suffered such a fate. But, along with bona fide French "frequentations," it did weigh favorably in official decision-making among CRN representatives.

Throughout the interwar and Vichy periods, the sphere of social services emerged as the single domain on which foreign-born Jews could rely. Its official, semiofficial, and unofficial representatives worked tirelessly to ensure that Jewish families, French and foreign, continued to receive welfare benefits and access to public health institutions. Importantly, the relative latitude afforded to assistantes sociales of private charitable organizations, whether Jewish or non-Jewish, worked to the benefit of these families during the war, allowing private organizations to provide resources to social workers without strong government scrutiny. That said, some social workers found willing helpmates in state and municipal welfare offices, too. It was the decidedly mixed character of France's welfare state before 1945, then, that permitted multiply affiliated social workers to maneuver personal and professional networks, local and state resources, in order to thwart the aims of a state grown mad and murderous. Taken together, these were the unintended, yet inclusive, consequences of state and social logics elaborated in the previous decades within a republican political climate characterized above all by demographic crisis.

The semiprivate, semipublic realm of social services offers one of the purest manifestations of the French state's supportive maternalism, which persisted under Vichy rule and long after, and yet which has received curiously little scholarly attention in the postwar period. From 1945 to roughly 1980, private charitable work entered another period of transition as it was increasingly centralized under the state, folded into Pierre Laroque's postwar Social Security regime.[1] While corporatist and Christian-democratic in orientation, the postwar welfare state in France remained fundamentally concerned with family and population policy.[2] Though much ink has been spilled on the various policies and administrative structures that took shape from on high, the messy postwar process of institutionalizing local charitable work on the ground remains relatively unstudied, as do the interactions between French female social workers and their increasingly nonwhite foreign clients of colonial and, eventually, postcolonial origin.[3] Amelia Lyons's work on Algerian families during the period of decolonization stands as a lone exception, documenting the development of an extensive, specialized social service sector trained exclusively on Algerian wives and mothers. In the hopes of enlisting them in the project to maintain French Algeria, a specific corps of assistantes sociales in one corner of the postwar welfare state married "coercion and compassion" in their approach toward at least this particular group of colonial immigrant women in the metropole.[4] In this, metropolitan social services increasingly mirrored the postwar colonial state's "welfare and warfare" approach abroad.[5] In other words, against the backdrop of violent wars of decolonization and a global reordering of the formerly colonized world, the inclusive dimensions of republican pronatalism and welfarism would fade, increasingly emphasizing a social control logic trained on nonwhite colonial populations at home and abroad.

Though not the explicit focus of this study, colonial men appear throughout its pages quite simply because, during and after the Great War, they migrated to France, married Frenchwomen, fathered French-born children, and joined working-class neighborhoods in cities throughout the country. In short, they appear in proportion to their relative presence in the metropole and allow us to make a few surprising observations about the nature of coercion under the Third Republic. In the post–World War I period, middle-class French officials who represented the interwar colonial state used their authority over nonwhite men not to prevent marriage with French women, but rather, by 1919, to induce them to marry and provide for white Frenchwomen with whom they had fathered children. The interwar colonial state's treatment of nonwhite bachelors serves as a potent reminder that the very project of national inclusion could be forceful, even punishing, at times, and that nonwhite colonial men felt those coercive dimensions most acutely. Moreover, though it has garnered little scholarly attention to date, these dynamics created opportunities for white Frenchwomen to use the gendered and racist policing logics of local and state authorities against colonial male subjects. That some white Frenchwomen could combine benevolent paternalism with the racial animus of the state to their favor, especially against colonial lovers and spouses, is deserving of far more study than it has hitherto received. To do so would push the field to examine more than merely the metaphoric invocation of white French femininity against nonwhite and colonial male sexuality in nineteenth- and twentieth-century official discourses, public debates, and media representations. Instead, it would require us to interrogate how white Frenchwomen themselves participated in the construction and implementation of racist systems of violence against nonwhite colonial populations through recourse to gender and sexual norms in the metropole and in the empire.

This book organizes a vast scholarship on the inner workings of welfare states by revealing how two complementary state and social logics—supportive maternalism focused on women, and disciplinary paternalism which focused on men—developed in tandem yet moved in "opposing arcs" over the course of the late nineteenth and twentieth centuries.[6] It does so by leveling its gaze on the workings of sex and gender in the incorporation of immigrants in Third Republican and Vichy France. An array of pronatalist family legislation, maternalist welfare assistance, and paternalist bureaucratic intervention supported the inclusion of immigrant wives and mothers but insisted on the incorporation of immigrant and colonial men as breadwinners for women and children. State officials especially wielded naturalization and family laws against immigrant men punitively, incorporating them into the national community as husbands and fathers—by force if necessary. Moreover, the world of welfare and its representatives increasingly sidelined or bypassed entirely husbands and fathers, focusing their energies instead on mothers and children. Consequently, even married *pères de famille* found themselves regulated or dismissed by a burgeoning family-focused welfare state that viewed them with suspicion and distrust. By laying bare the gendered dynamics between immigrant men and women, on the one hand, and a large, multifaceted French state bent on repopulation, on the other, this book uncovers how supportive maternalism and disciplinary paternalism became central to the expansion of the modern French nation-state. Crucially, both dynamics contributed to the development of a regulatory regime enshrining reproductive sexuality at the heart of modern citizenship.

It has been the task of this book to draw scholarly attention to the as-yet unseen ways that a political climate and republican culture characterized by traditional gender and sexual norms brought new insiders into the national fold in France before 1945. Yet, this should not obscure the fact that the post–World War I atmosphere of gender and sexual crisis also generated new categories of sexual outsiders. These nonprocreative pariahs had been steadily excluded from the nation for varieties of nonconformity to the heterosexual, conjugal, reproductive family form. Though the demographic obsession had created a crucial opening for family-minded foreigners, it also made France the most conservative reproductive regime in Europe by 1920, the year that a law forbidding abortion and penalizing both the sale and advertisement of contraception was passed. The prohibition on abortion was further strengthened by the 1939 Code de la Famille, then elevated to a crime against the nation under Vichy.[7] It was not until the "quiet revolution" of the 1960s and 1970s that official sanctions against both contraception and abortion were at last struck down, in 1967 and 1975, respectively. Moreover, during the interwar period, policing authorities throughout the metropole increased their ability to monitor, arrest, and penalize men who engaged in the crimes of "pederasty" and "sodomy," that is, nonprocreative sex with other men.[8] Under Vichy, evolving state practices policing male homosexuality were codified: the ordonnance of August 6, 1942, further criminalized male homosexuality in ways that would endure after the Liberation into the Fourth and then Fifth Republics.[9] By then, the once-powerful ideologies of Catholic familialism and republican pronatalism were decidedly on the wane.[10]

Still, it would be folly to imagine that demographic angst disappeared from France entirely. Rather, in the postcolonial period, it found a new object of obsession—namely, the specter of *over*population in the formerly colonized parts of the nonwhite world.[11] High fertility rates in Africa and Asia had, of course, been of deep concern to a handful of interwar pronatalists and demographers.[12] But, in the 1950s and 1960s, awareness of "overpopulation" in the so-called Third World seeped deeply into the French national consciousness.[13] As a result, the slow abatement of a demographic crisis that had shaped four political regimes in France over the course of nearly a century coincided with the steady transmutation and displacement of populationist anxiety onto nonwhite bodies both in and from the former empire. Beyond the metropole, in French overseas territories, this conjuncture would have devastating consequences for nonwhite women. In Réunion, for instance, thousands of nonwhite women were subjected to forced abortions and sterilizations carried out by white French doctors in the 1970s, all in the name of population management.[14] Within metropolitan France, the laws, official practices, and neighborhood cultures shoring up reproductive citizenship would also shift, redrawing the boundaries between French and foreign along increasingly racialized lines. It is a story of utmost importance, and one that must be entrusted to future generations of scholars to tell.

Notes

Introduction

1. Letter, August 30, 1933, from Madame Goata to Minister of Justice in Nicolas Goata and Emilienne née Authemet, 8008x32 (Archives Nationales, hereafter AN).

2. Michael Robert Marrus, *The Unwanted: European Refugees in the Twentieth Century* (New York: Oxford University Press, 1985), chaps. 1–2.

3. Bertrand Nogaro and Lucien Weil, *La Main-d'œuvre étrangère et coloniale pendant la guerre* (Paris: Presses universitaires de France, 1926), 25; Michel Huber, *La Population de la France pendant la guerre, avec un appendice sur les revenus avant et après la guerre* (Paris: Les Presses universitaires de France, 1931), 89.

4. Marrus, *The Unwanted*, 113–14.

5. Marrus, *The Unwanted*, 150; Annemarie Sammartino, *The Impossible Border: Germany and the East, 1914–1922* (Ithaca, NY: Cornell University Press, 2010); Laura Tabili, *Global Migrants, Local Culture: Natives and Newcomers in Provincial England, 1841–1939* (Houndmills, UK: Palgrave Macmillan, 2011).

6. Marrus, *The Unwanted*, 145–49; Vicki Caron, *Uneasy Asylum: France and the Jewish Refugee Crisis, 1933–1942* (Stanford: Stanford University Press, 1999).

7. Huber, *La Population de la France*, 55.

8. Statistique Générale de France (hereafter SGF), *Statistique des familles en 1926* (Paris: Imprimerie nationale, 1932), 34, 40, 54, 65.

9. SGF, *Statistique des familles et des habitations en 1911* (Paris: Imprimerie nationale, 1911), 25.

10. SGF, *Statistique des familles* (1932), 66.

11. Michel Huber, *La Population de la France*, 6–7, 453, 526.

12. Gérard Noiriel, *Population, Immigration et Identité Nationale En France: XIXe–XXe Siècle* (Paris: Hachette, 1992), 53.

13. On the dearth of scholarship on gender in the field of immigration, see Nancy L. Green, *Repenser Les Migrations*, 1st ed. (Paris: Presses universitaires de France, 2002), chap. 5; Linda Guerry, "Femmes et genre dans l'histoire de l'immigration. Naissance et cheminement d'un sujet de recherche," *Genre & Histoire* 5 (Fall 2009).

14. See https://drnimishabarton.com for supporting statistics.

15. With the notable exception, of course, of Linda Guerry, *Le genre de l'immigration et de la naturalisation. L'exemple de Marseille (1918–1940)* (Lyon: ENS Editions, 2013).

16. See, for example, Gary S. Cross, *Immigrant Workers in Industrial France: The Making of a New Laboring Class* (Philadelphia: Temple University Press, 1983); Gérard Noiriel, *The French Melting Pot: Immigration, Citizenship, and National Identity*

(Minneapolis: University of Minnesota Press, 1996); Clifford D. Rosenberg, *Policing Paris: The Origins of Modern Immigration Control Between the Wars* (Ithaca, NY: Cornell University Press, 2006); Mary Dewhurst Lewis, *The Boundaries of the Republic: Migrant Rights and the Limits of Universalism in France, 1918–1940* (Stanford: Stanford University Press, 2007); Alexis Spire, *Etrangers à La Carte: L'administration de l'immigration En France, 1945–1975* (Paris: Grasset, 2005); Caron, *Uneasy Asylum*; Elisa Camiscioli, *Reproducing the French Race: Immigration, Intimacy, and Embodiment in the Early Twentieth Century* (Durham, NC: Duke University Press, 2009); Guerry, *Le genre de l'immigration*.

17. On republican motherhood, see Linda K. Kerber, *Women of the Republic: Intellect and Ideology in Revolutionary America* (New York: Norton, 1986); Joan B. Landes, *Women and the Public Sphere in the Age of the French Revolution* (Ithaca, NY: Cornell University Press, 1988). On the family obligations incumbent on Frenchmen, see Kristen Stromberg Childers, *Fathers, Families, and the State in France, 1914–1945* (Ithaca, NY: Cornell University Press, 2003); Geoff Read, *The Republic of Men: Gender and the Political Parties in Interwar France* (Baton Rouge: Louisiana State University Press, 2014).

18. On marriage, masculinity, and the sexual criteria of heterosexual citizenship, see Judith Surkis, *Sexing the Citizen: Morality and Masculinity in France, 1870–1920* (Ithaca, NY: Cornell University Press, 2006); Margot Canaday, *The Straight State: Sexuality and Citizenship in Twentieth-Century America* (Princeton: Princeton University Press, 2009); Peggy Pascoe, *What Comes Naturally: Miscegenation Law and the Making of Race in America* (Oxford: Oxford University Press, 2009).

19. Among the major works concerned with citizenship: On women, see Joan Wallach Scott, *Only Paradoxes to Offer: French Feminists and the Rights of Man* (Cambridge, MA: Harvard University Press, 1996); Laura Levine Frader, *Breadwinners and Citizens: Gender in the Making of the French Social Model* (Durham, NC: Duke University Press, 2008); Andrea Mansker, *Sex, Honor and Citizenship in Early Third Republic France* (Houndmills, UK: Palgrave Macmillan, 2011). On immigrants, see Gérard Noiriel, *Le Creuset Français: Histoire de l'immigration, XIXe–XXe Siècles* (Paris: Seuil, 1988); Rogers Brubaker, *Citizenship and Nationhood in France and Germany* (Cambridge, MA: Harvard University Press, 1992); Lewis, *Boundaries of the Republic*. On colonial subjects, see Emmanuelle Saada, *Empire's Children: Race, Filiation, and Citizenship in the French Colonies*, trans. Arthur Goldhammer (Chicago: University of Chicago Press, 2012).

20. Elizabeth Heath, *Wine, Sugar, and the Making of Modern France: Global Economic Crisis and the Racialization of French Citizenship, 1870–1910* (Cambridge: Cambridge University Press, 2014); Minayo Nasiali, *Native to the Republic: Empire, Social Citizenship, and Everyday Life in Marseille Since 1945* (Ithaca, NY: Cornell University Press, 2016).

21. Gershon Shafir, ed., *The Citizenship Debates: A Reader* (Minneapolis: University of Minnesota Press, 1998), 23–24.

22. Christian Topalov, *Laboratoires du nouveau siècle: la nébuleuse réformatrice et ses réseaux en France, 1880–1914* (Paris: Ecole des hautes études en sciences sociales, 1999).

23. Hervé Le Bras, *Marianne et les lapins : L'obsession démographique* (Paris: Olivier Orban, 1991), chap. 13; Paul-André Rosental, *L'intelligence démographique: sciences et politiques des populations en France, 1930–1960* (Paris: Jacob, 2003); William H. Schneider, *Quality and Quantity: The Quest for Biological Regeneration in Twentieth-Century France* (Cambridge: Cambridge University Press, 1990), 198–207.

24. Gérard Noiriel, *Longwy: immigrés et prolétaires, 1880–1980* (Paris: Presses universitaires de France, 1984), 174–220; Remi Lenoir, "Family Policy in France since 1938," in *The French Welfare State: Surviving Social and Ideological Change* (New York: NYU Press, 1991), 146; Philip G. Nord, *France's New Deal: From the Thirties to the Postwar Era* (Princeton: Princeton University Press, 2010), 49–63.

25. Camiscioli, *Reproducing the French Race*, chap. 1; Schneider, *Quality and Quantity*, chaps. 7–10.

26. Alexis Spire, *Etrangers à la carte: L'administration de l'immigration en France, 1945–1975* (Paris: Grasset, 2005), 111–12; Lenoir, "Family Policy in France since 1938"; Nord, *France's New Deal*, chap. 1.

27. Laura Lee Downs, "'And So We Transform a People': Women's Social Action and the Reconfiguration of Politics on the Right in France, 1934–1947," *Past & Present* 233, no. 1 (2014): 187–225.

28. Susan Pedersen, *Family, Dependence, and the Origins of the Welfare State: Britain and France, 1914–1945* (Cambridge: Cambridge University Press, 1993); Paul V. Dutton, *Origins of the French Welfare State: The Struggle for Social Reform in France, 1914–1947* (New York: Cambridge University Press, 2002); Nord, *France's New Deal*; Rachel Ginnis Fuchs, "France in a Comparative Perspective," in *Gender and the Politics of Social Reform in France, 1870–1914* (Baltimore: Johns Hopkins University Press, 1995), 157–87.

29. Bonnie G. Smith, *Ladies of the Leisure Class: The Bourgeoises of Northern France in the Nineteenth Century* (Princeton: Princeton University Press, 1981); Rachel Ginnis Fuchs, *Poor and Pregnant in Paris: Strategies for Survival in the Nineteenth Century* (New Brunswick, NJ: Rutgers University Press, 1992); Evelyne Diebolt, "Women and Philanthropy in France," in *Women, Philanthropy, and Civil Society* (Bloomington: Indiana University Press, 2001), 29–69; Downs, "'And So We Transform a People.'" On the role of maternalism in the development of welfare states, see Seth Koven and Sonya Michel, eds., *Mothers of a New World: Maternalist Politics and the Origins of Welfare States* (New York: Routledge, 1993).

30. For overviews of welfare state historiography, see Philip G. Nord, "The Welfare State in France, 1870–1914," *French Historical Studies* 18, no. 3 (spring 1994): 823–25; Fuchs, "France in a Comparative Perspective," 159–62; Nimisha Barton, "'French or Foreign, So Long as They Be Mothers': Immigrant Women, Welfare, and the Politics of Pronatalism in Interwar Paris," *Journal of Women's History* 28, no. 4 (winter 2016): 65–67. Jacques Donzelot is most closely associated with the social control thesis. See *La Police des familles* (Paris: Éditions de Minuit, 1977). By contrast, Rachel Fuchs's work combined the perspectives of welfare agents and their clients. See *Abandoned Children: Foundlings and Child Welfare in Nineteenth-Century France* (Albany: SUNY Press, 1984); *Poor and Pregnant*; *Contested Paternity: Constructing Families in Modern France* (Baltimore: Johns Hopkins University Press, 2008). Though more expressly polemical in controverting the "charge" of social control leveled at social workers, see also Yvonne Knibiehler, *Nous, les assistantes sociales: naissance d'une profession : trente ans de souvenirs d'assistantes sociales françaises (1930–1960)* (Paris: Aubier Montaigne, 1980); Armelle Mabon-Fall, *Les assistantes sociales au temps de Vichy: du silence à l'oubli* (Paris: L'Harmattan, 1995).

31. Fuchs, "France in a Comparative Perspective," 160; Nord, "The Welfare State in France," 832.

32. Amelia H. Lyons, *The Civilizing Mission in the Metropole: Algerian Families and the French Welfare State during Decolonization* (Stanford: Stanford University Press, 2013).

33. Diebolt, "Women and Philanthropy in France"; Linda L Clark, *The Rise of Professional Women in France: Gender and Public Administration since 1830* (Cambridge: Cambridge University Press, 2000), chaps. 2–3; Downs, "'And so We Transform a People.'"

34. Knibiehler, *Nous, les assistantes sociales*, chap. 1; Mabon-Fall, *Les assistantes sociales au temps de Vichy*, 23–30; Jean-Pierre Le Crom, *Au secours, Maréchal!: l'instrumentalisation de l'humanitaire, 1940–1944*, 1st ed. (Paris: Presses universitaires de France, 2013), chap. 8.

35. Noiriel, *Population, Immigration et Identité Nationale En France*, 64–65, 80–81. On Poles in the Pas-de-Calais, see Janine Ponty, *Polonais méconnus: histoire des travailleurs immigrés en France dans l'entre-deux-guerres* (Paris: Publications de la Sorbonne, 1988). On interwar migrant Marseille, see Emile Témime's works, especially *Migrance: histoire des migrations à Marseille* (Marseille: J. Laffitte, 2007). On interwar Lyon, see Geneviève Massard-Guilbaud, *Des algériens à Lyon: de la Grande Guerre au Front Populaire* (Paris: L'Harmattan, 1995). For comparative work on Marseille and Lyon between the wars, see Lewis, *Boundaries of the Republic*.

36. M. Galmiche, "Extrait: Les Etrangers dans l'agglomération parisienne d'après le recensement de 1921," *Bulletin de la Statistique générale de la France et du Service d'observation des Prix* 11, no. 3, April 1922, in 50 AP 62 (AN); "Dénombrement effectué en septembre 1914, à la demande de l'autorité militaire. Ville de Paris.—Population présente," *Annuaire Statistique de la Ville de Paris* (hereafter *ASVP*) (1915–1918), 929; "Ville de Paris.—Population domiciliée.—Population française et population étrangère," *ASVP* (1921–1922), 284–85; "Ville de Paris.—Recensement de 1926," *ASVP* (1923–1924), 295–96; "Ville de Paris.—Recensement de 1931," *ASVP* (1927–1928), 140–41.

37. Jean-Paul Flamand, *Loger le peuple: essai sur l'histoire du logement social en France* (Paris: La Découverte, 1989), chaps. 1–2; Marie-Claude Blanc-Chaléard, "L'Habitat Immigré à Paris Aux XIXe et XXe Siècles: Mondes à Part?," *Le Mouvement Social* 182 (1998): 29–50.

38. Social histories are ample. Among the most well-known are Nancy L. Green, *The Pletzl of Paris: Jewish Immigrant Workers in the Belle Epoque* (New York: Holmes & Meier, 1986); Marie-Claude Blanc-Chaléard, *Les italiens dans l'est parisien: Une histoire d'intégration (1880–1960)* (Rome: Ecole française de Rome, 2000); Judith Rainhorn, *Paris, New York: des migrants italiens* (Paris: CNRS Editions, 2005). In 1992, under the direction of Pierre Milza and Emile Témime, the French publishing house Editions Autrement sponsored a collection of, to date, eighteen studies for the series "Français d'ailleurs, people d'ici," all focused on immigrant communities in Paris and its environs. See Philippe Dewitte, "Pierre Milza et Emile Témime (dir.): Français d'ailleurs, peuple d'ici, collection 'Monde,' 1995," *Hommes & Migrations* 1188, no. 1 (1995): 105–7.

39. Leslie Page Moch, *Moving Europeans: Migration in Western Europe since 1650*, 2nd ed. (Bloomington: Indiana University Press, 2003), 126–31, 172–77.

40. Rainhorn, *Paris, New York: des migrants italiens*. On multicultural sociability in South Shields, UK, see Tabili, *Global Migrants, Local Culture*.

41. See https://drnimishabarton.com for supporting statistics.

42. Blanc-Chaléard, *Les italiens dans l'Est parisien*; Green, *The Pletzl of Paris*; Annie Benvéniste, *Le Bosphore à La Roquette: La Communauté judéo-espagnole à Paris, 1914–1940* (Paris: L'Harmattan, 1989).

43. On relations between black colonial migrants and white Frenchwomen, see Jennifer Anne Boittin, *Colonial Metropolis: The Urban Grounds of Anti-Imperialism and Feminism in Interwar Paris* (Lincoln: University of Nebraska Press, 2010), chap. 2.

44. Judith Rainhorn, "Enclaves et creusets matrimoniaux à Paris et à New York. Perspective comparée de deux expériences de mixité matrimoniale au sein de l'émigration italienne," *Annales de démographie historique* 2 (2002): 79–99; Jean-Louis Robert and Danielle Tartakowsky, *Paris le peuple, XVIIIe–XXe siècle* (Paris: Publications de la Sorbonne, 1999), especially Alain Faure, "Comment devenait-on Parisien? La question de l'intégration dans le Paris de la fin du XIXe siècle" and Marie-Claude Blanc-Chaléard, "Les trois temps du bal-musette ou la place des étrangers (1880–1960)."

45. On the turn toward these scholarly questions in the French historiography, see Jacques Semelin, *Persécutions et Entraides Dans La France Occupée: Comment 75% des Juifs en France ont échappé à la mort* (Paris: Editions des Arènes, 2013), iii–viii. On Occupied Holland, see Gerhard Hirschfeld, *Nazi Rule and Dutch Collaboration: The Netherlands under German Occupation, 1940–1945* (Oxford: St. Martin's Press, 1988); Bob Moore, *Victims and Survivors: The Nazi Persecution of the Jews in the Netherlands, 1940–1945* (London: Arnold, 1997). On Occupied Belgium, see Dan Mikhman and Mazal Holocaust Collection, *Belgium and the Holocaust: Jews, Belgians, Germans* (Jerusalem: Yad Vashem, 1998); Suzanne Vromen, *Hidden Children of the Holocaust: Belgian Nuns and Their Daring Rescue of Young Jews from the Nazis* (Oxford, UK: Oxford University Press, 2008).

1. The Forces that Push and Pull

1. The reference is, of course, to Mark Mazower's *Dark Continent: Europe's Twentieth Century*, 1st ed. (New York: Vintage Books, 2000).

2. Michael Robert Marrus, *The Unwanted: European Refugees in the Twentieth Century* (New York: Oxford University Press, 1985), 41.

3. Gérard Noiriel, *Longwy: immigrés et prolétaires, 1880–1980* (Paris: Presses universitaires de France, 1984); Gary S. Cross, *Immigrant Workers in Industrial France: The Making of a New Laboring Class* (Philadelphia: Temple University Press, 1983); Elisa Camiscioli, *Reproducing the French Race: Immigration, Intimacy, and Embodiment in the Early Twentieth Century* (Durham, NC: Duke University Press, 2009), chap. 2.

4. On the post–World War I gender crisis, see Mary Louise Roberts, *Civilization Without Sexes: Reconstructing Gender in Postwar France, 1917–1927* (Chicago: University of Chicago Press, 1994).

5. Camiscioli, *Reproducing the French Race*, chap. 2.

6. Cross, *Immigrant Workers in Industrial France*, 53.

7. Paola Corti, "Sociétés sans hommes et intégration des femmes à l'étranger," *Revue Européene des Migrations Internationales* 9, no. 2 (1993): 113–28.

8. Judith Rainhorn, *Paris, New York: des migrants italiens* (Paris: CNRS Editions, 2005); Marie-Claude Blanc-Chaléard, *Les italiens dans l'est parisien: Une histoire*

d'intégration (1880–1960) (Rome: Ecole française de Rome, 2000); Nancy Green, *Ready-to-Wear and Ready-to-Work: A Century of Industry and Immigrants in Paris and New York* (Durham, NC: Duke University Press, 1997).

9. Claire Zalc, *Les Melting-Shops: une histoire des commerçants étrangers* (Paris: Perrin, 2010).

10. Linda Guerry, *Le genre de l'immigration et de la naturalisation. L'exemple de Marseille (1918–1940)* (Lyon: ENS Editions, 2013), chap. 2.

11. Michel Augé-Laribé, *L'agriculture pendant la guerre* (Paris: Presses universitaires de France, 1925), 66–67. The myth of the heroic French peasantry belonged to a larger cultural project of relocating the essence of "True France" in its disappearing rural past. See Gordon Wright, *Rural Revolution in France: The Peasantry in the Twentieth Century* (Stanford: Stanford University Press, 1964), chaps. 1–3; Herman Lebovics, *True France: The Wars Over Cultural Identity, 1900–1945* (Ithaca, NY: Cornell University Press, 1992), chaps. 4, especially.

12. Augé-Laribé, *L'agriculture pendant la guerre*, 92.

13. Ponty, *Polonais méconnus: histoire des travailleurs immigrés en France dans l'entre-deux-guerre.* (Paris: Publications de la Sorbonne, 1988). Polish agricultural labors were also prevalent in eastern Germany before World War I. See Ulrich Herbert, *A History of Foreign Labor in Germany, 1880–1980: Seasonal Workers, Forced Laborers, Guest Workers* (Ann Arbor: University of Michigan Press, 1990), 9–17.

14. Augé-Laribé, *L'agriculture pendant la guerre*, 73.

15. Augé-Laribé, *L'agriculture pendant la guerre*, 71–73.

16. Augé-Laribé, *L'agriculture pendant la guerre*.

17. Cross, *Immigrant Workers in Industrial France*, 77–78, 244.

18. Letter from Nicolas Goata to Minister of Justice, July 20, 1932, in Nicolas Goata and Emilienne Goata, 8008x32 (AN-Fontainebleau).

19. Joseph Roth, *Hotel Savoy*, trans. John Hoare (Woodstock: Overlook Press, 1986), 9.

20. Jean Kofler, 17785x14 (AN). French bureaucrats eventually simplified his situation, describing him as "an Austrian by filiation who became Czech by the Treaty of Versailles" (Avis du Préfet de Police, May 12, 1928, in 17785x14 (AN)).

21. Roth, *Hotel Savoy*, 80.

22. Rapport de la Police Judiciaire sur Adrien André Rossi, February 27, 1936, in D2U8 498 (Archives de Paris, hereafter AdP).

23. Procès-verbal d'interrogatoire et de confrontation, Tribunal de Première Instance du Département de la Seine (hereafter TPI), October 26, 1932, in D2U8 351 (AdP).

24. Doctor Truelle, "Rapport médico-légal," March 13, 1934, in D2U8 390 (AdP).

25. Procès-verbal interrogatoire, TPI, September 14, 1933, in D2U8 371 (AdP).

26. Roth, *Hotel Savoy*, 114.

27. Doctor Henri Claude, "Rapport médico-légal," June 12, 1936, 2, in D2U8 499 (AdP).

28. Réquisitoire définitif, January 11, 1939, in D2U8 587 (AdP).

29. Tyler Stovall, "National Identity and Shifting Imperial Frontiers: Whiteness and the Exclusion of Colonial Labor after World War I," *Representations* 84 (Autumn 2003): 52–72; Richard Standish Fogarty, *Race and War in France: Colonial Subjects in the French Army, 1914–1918* (Baltimore: Johns Hopkins University Press, 2008).

30. Stovall, "National Identity and Shifting Imperial Frontiers"; John Horne, "Immigrant Workers in France during World War I," *French Historical Studies* 14, no. 1 (spring 1985): 57–88.

31. Procès-verbal d'interrogatoire et de confrontation, TPI, December 18, 1933, in D2U8 387 (AdP). On the French enchantment with the "Kabyle myth," see Neil MacMaster, *Colonial Migrants and Racism: Algerians in France, 1900–62* (New York: St. Martin's Press, 1996), chap. 2.

32. Rapport médico-légal, January 27, 1931, 14, in D2U8 306 (AdP).

33. MacMaster, *Colonial Migrants and Racism*, chap. 1.

34. Réquisitoire définitif, January 8, 1931, in D2U8 302 (AdP).

35. Acte d'accusation, TPI, December 15, 1931, in D2U8 315 (AdP).

36. Réquisitoire définitif, TPI, February 28, 1933, in D2U8 352 (AdP).

37. Acte d'accusation, TPI, December 29, 1933, in D2U8 366 (AdP). In his interviews with foreign-born workers who came to work in interwar France, Noiriel also commented on this evolution from itinerancy to rootedness via (inter)marriage. See Noiriel, *Longwy*, 224–25.

38. Paul Ballot, "Une Véritables politique d'immigration doit être régionaliste: Quelques aperçus sur la crise de main-d'oeuvre agricole," *Revue d'Immigration* 2, no. 18 (October 1929): 2–3.

39. Georges Mauco, "Les Étrangers En France: Étude Géographique Sur Leur Rôle Dans l'activité Économique" (thèse de doctorat ès lettres, Université de Paris, 1932), 214. On Mauco's singular career from the 1930s through the 1960s, see Camille Robcis, *The Law of Kinship: Anthropology, Psychoanalysis, and the Family in France* (Ithaca, NY: Cornell University Press, 2013), 104–24.

40. See for example Hungarian Elizabeth Kozma, who broke her work contract with Société de la Soie artificielle du Sud Est in Vaulx-en-Velin in the Rhône department in 1931, preferring to work as a domestic servant in Paris (Procès-verbal d'interrogatoire et de confrontation, Tribunal de Première Instance du Département de la Seine, April 23, 1937, in D2U8 531 (AdP)). Or Czech Katarina Zabakova, who ruptured her work contract with a farm in Chatillon-sous-Bois in July 1935 and was forced to explain herself at the Prefecture of Police (Katarina Zabakova, folio no. 12075, in D84Z 156 (AdP)).

41. Philip G. Nord, "Three Views of Christian Democracy in Fin de Siècle France," *Journal of Contemporary History* 19, no. 4 (October 1984): 713–27; Herman Lebovics, *The Alliance of Iron and Wheat in the Third French Republic, 1860–1914: Origins of the New Conservatism* (Baton Rouge: Louisiana State University Press, 1988).

42. Noiriel, *Longwy*, 174–95.

43. Joan Wallach Scott, *Gender and the Politics of History*, 2nd ed. (New York: Columbia University Press, 1999), chap. 7.

44. Kristen Stromberg Childers, *Fathers, Families, and the State in France, 1914–1945* (Ithaca, NY: Cornell University Press, 2003), chap. 2; Judith Surkis, *Sexing the Citizen: Morality and Masculinity in France, 1870–1920* (Ithaca, NY: Cornell University Press, 2006); Geoff Read, *The Republic of Men: Gender and the Political Parties in Interwar France* (Baton Rouge: Louisiana State University Press, 2014).

45. On Martial's conservative politics, see Benoît Larbiou, "René Martial (1873–1955). De l'hygiènisme à raciologie, une trajectoire possible," *Genèses* 3, no. 60 (2005): 98–120; Gérard Noiriel, *Immigration, antisémitisme et racisme en France, XIXe–XXe siècle: discours publics, humiliations privées* (Paris: Fayard, 2007): 328–30.

46. René Martial, "L'examen sanitaire des immigrants à la frontière et leur logement dans le pays," *Revue d'Hygiène* 13, no. 12 (December 1926): 1070.

47. Martial, "L'examen sanitaire des immigrants," 1073.

48. Cross, *Immigrant Workers in Industrial France*, 55–63; Catherine Collomp, "Regard sur les politiques de l'immigration: Le marché du travail en France et aux États-Unis (1880–1930)," *Annales. Histoire, Sciences Sociales* 51, no. 5 (1996): 1120–21.

49. Staunchly Catholic Poland was the source of 76 percent of all workers recruited between 1921 and 1931. See Cross, *Immigrant Workers in Industrial France*, 59.

50. Société Générale d'Immigration (hereafter SGI), "La Société Générale d'Immigration vous fournira de la main-d'oeuvre étrangère," 4–10, in 8/R pièce 17842 (Bibliothèque Nationale de France, hereafter BnF).

51. Anonymous, "Introduction de familles étrangères," *Revue de l'Immigration* 2, no. 11 (March 1929): 8.

52. Philip G. Nord, *France's New Deal: From the Thirties to the Postwar Era* (Princeton: Princeton University Press, 2010), 187.

53. Ralph Schor, *L'Opinion Française et Les Étrangers En France, 1919–1939* (Paris: La Sorbonne, 1985), 331–35.

54. Emmanuel Chaptal, "Le problème de l'immigration peut-il être résolu sans le concours des forces spirituelles?"*Revue de l'Immigration* 4, no. 35 (April 1931): 1–2.

55. *Aciéres de Longwy,* brochure, 1925 quoted in Noiriel, *Longwy*, 192.

56. Noiriel, *Longwy*, 174–75.

57. SGI, "La Société Générale d'Immigration vous fournira de la main-d'oeuvre étrangère," 8, in 8/R pièce 17842 (BnF).

58. The vast majority of these workers and their families (105,000) were channeled into coal mining in Pas-de-Calais; a sizable portion of those who remained (84,000) were channeled into agricultural work. About one-tenth were sent to the iron mines (26,000) and the rest were sent to other industries (35,000). SGI, "La Société Générale d'Immigration, 8 in 8/R pièce 17842 (BnF), 12.

59. SGI, "La Société Générale d'Immigration, 8 in 8/R pièce 17842 (BnF), 4, 7.

60. Anonymous, "Conditions d'entrée en France des fiancées d'ouvriers étrangers," *Revue de l'Immigration* 2, no. 15 (July 1929): 8–9.

61. Anonymous, "Mariages roumains, bulgares et yougoslaves en France," *Revue de l'Immigration* 2, no. 18 (October 1929): 8.

62. For example, in just the first two years of the journal's publication: "Nationalité de la femme mariée," *Revue de l'Immigration* 1, no. 4 (August 1928): 11; "Réintégration des femmes françaises mariées à des étrangers" in *Revue de l'Immigration* 1, no. 4: 11–12; "Réintégration des femmes françaises mariées à des étrangers," *Revue de l'Immigration* 1, no. 6 (October 1928), 4–6; "Dualités de nationalité des époux," *Revue de l'Immigration* 2, no. 11 (March 1929), 8–9; "Dames fonctionnaires mariées avec un étranger," in *Revue de l'Immigration* 2, no. 11: 9; "Veuves de guerre remariées avec des étrangers," *Revue de l'Immigration* 2, no. 12 (April 1929): 10.

63. Cross, *Immigrant Workers in Industrial France*, 243.

64. Scott, *Gender and the Politics of History*, chap. 7; Emily Machen, "Traveling with the Faith: The Creation of Women's Immigrant Aid Associations in Nineteenth and Twentieth-Century France," *Journal of Women's History* 23, no. 3 (2011): 89–112.

65. Anonymous, "Comités départementaux d'aise et de protection des femmes immigrantes," *Revue de l'Immigration* 2, no. 11 (March 1929): 7–8.

66. Machen, "Traveling with the Faith."
67. Françoise de Bacourt, "L'Activité philanthropique en faveur des migrants," *Revue de l'Immigration* 3, no. 24 (April 1930): 1–5.
68. Anonymous, "La Jeune Étrangère en France," *Revue de l'Immigration* 2, no. 9 (January 1929): 17.
69. Abel Chatelain, "Migrations et Domesticité Féminine Urbaine En France (XVIIIème Siècle– XXème Siècle)," *Revue d'histoire Économique et Sociale* 47, no. 4 (1969): 506–28; Rachel Ginnis Fuchs and Leslie Page Moch, "Pregnant, Single, and Far from Home: Migrant Women in Nineteenth-Century Paris," *American Historical Review* 95, no. 4 (October 1, 1990): 1007–31.
70. Anonymous, "La Jeune Étrangère en France," 17.
71. Maria Vérone, "L'Oeuvre des Femmes: Main-d'oeuvre féminine," *Oeuvre*, November 17, 1926, 4 in DOS 331 TRA (Bibliothèque Marguerite Durand, hereafter BMD).
72. Mirjana Moravcsik once called this the narrative of "passive" women following their menfolk. See Moravcsik, "Birds of Passage Are Also Women," *International Migration Review* 18, no. 4. Special Issue: Women in Migration (winter 1984): 886–907. Others, like Leslie Page Moch, have been more willing to accept family-oriented motivations that have long driven women's migration on the continent. See Moch, "Mobilité des hommes, mobilité des femmes. Perspective historique de la migration européenne," *Cahiers de l'Institut Universitaire d'Études du Développement* 23 (1993): 106–17.
73. Acte d'Accusation, TPI, April 1, 1931 in D2U8 320 (Archives de Paris, hereafter AdP).
74. Procès-verbal d'interrogatoire et de confrontation, TPI, January 23, 1934, in D2U8 396 (AdP).
75. Procès-verbal d'interrogatoire et de confrontation, TPI, July 26, 1930, in D2U8 300 (AdP).
76. Procès-verbal d'interrogatoire et de confrontation, TPI, October 10, 1932, in D2U8 339 (AdP).
77. Doctor Génil-Perrin, "Rapport médico-légal," September 21, 1932, 5–6, in D2U8 350 (AdP).
78. Warinier, dossier familial, p. 2, in 1368W/34, no. 2648 (AdP).
79. Déposition de Marie Lurin née Toublau, TPI, April 2, 1932, in D2U8 350 (AdP).
80. Déposition de Marie née Dererova femme Kantan, TPI, December 20, 1934, in D2U8 400 (AdP); Réquisitoire définitif, January 26, 1935, in D2U8 400 (AdP).
81. Nancy Green, *The Pletzl of Paris: Jewish Immigrant Workers in the Belle Epoque* (New York: Holmes & Meier, 1986).
82. Procès-verbal d'interrogatoire et de confrontation, TPI, January 3, 1935, in D2U8 400 (AdP).
83. Antonio Plotnikoff née Borisoff, folio no. 886, in D84Z 145 (AdP).

2. Bachelors, Bureaucrats, and Marrying into the Nation

1. Odette Dulac, "La Nationalité," *Le Petit Bleu*, June 10, 1917, 1 (50 AP 27, AN).
2. Francisco Munoz-Perez and Michele Tribalat, "Mariages d'étrangers et mariages mixtes en France: évolution depuis la Première Guerre," *Population* 39, no. 3

(June 1984): 427–62. Marriage statistics in Paris recorded annually since 1915 in the *Annuaire Statistique de la Ville de Paris* (hereafter *ASVP*).

3. Joan B. Landes, *Women and the Public Sphere in the Age of the French Revolution* (Ithaca, NY: Cornell University Press, 1988), 138; Elisa Camiscioli, *Reproducing the French Race: Immigration, Intimacy, and Embodiment in the Early Twentieth Century* (Durham, NC: Duke University Press, 2009), 144–47.

4. Patrick Weil, *Qu'est-Ce Qu'un Français: Histoire de La Nationalité Française Depuis La Révolution* (Paris: Grasset, 2002); Camiscioli, *Reproducing the French Race*, chap. 5.

5. Mary Louise Roberts, *Civilization Without Sexes: Reconstructing Gender in Postwar France, 1917–1927* (Chicago: University of Chicago Press, 1994), pt. 3.

6. Eliza Earle Ferguson, *Gender and Justice: Violence, Intimacy and Community in Fin-de Siècle Paris* (Baltimore: Johns Hopkins University Press, 2010), chap. 1.

7. Anne Simonin, *Le déshonneur dans la République: une histoire de l'indignité, 1791–1958* (Paris: B. Grasset, 2008), chap. 2; Emmanuelle Saada, *Empire's Children: Race, Filiation, and Citizenship in the French Colonies*, trans. Arthur Goldhammer (Chicago: University of Chicago Press, 2012), 43–49.

8. William A. Peniston, *Pederasts and Others: Urban Culture and Sexual Identity in Nineteenth-Century Paris* (New York: Harrington Park Press, 2004), chaps. 2, 3, 9; Michael Sibalis, "Homophobia, Vichy France, and the 'Crime of Homosexuality': The Origins of the Ordinance of 6 August 1942," *GLQ: A Journal of Lesbian and Gay Studies* 8, no. 3 (2002): 301–18. Of note, the policing of heterosexual deviance predated the surveillance of homosexuals in Paris. See Alain Corbin, *Les Filles de Noce: Misère Sexuelle et Prostitution, 19e et 20e Siècles* (Paris: Aubier Montaigne, 1978); Jean-Marc Berlière, *La police des moeurs sous la IIIe République* (Editions Seuil, 1992); Jill Harsin, *Policing Prostitution in Nineteenth-Century Paris* (Princeton: Princeton University Press, 1985).

9. Camiscioli, *Reproducing the French Race*, chap. 3.

10. On rhetorical strategies of self-fashioning, see also Natalie Zemon Davis, *Fiction in the Archives: Pardon Tales and Their Tellers in Sixteenth-Century France* (Stanford: Stanford University Press, 1987); Didier Fassin, "La supplique. Stratégies rhétoriques et constructions identitaires dans les demandes d'aide d'urgence," *Annales. Histoire, Sciences Sociales* 55, no. 5 (2000): 955–81.

11. In 1912, just fourteen police officers handled "immigrant affairs" within the Prefecture, though they were not localized within any specific administration. Only after World War I, did the prefect of police concentrate immigrant affairs within a "Division étrangers." In 1925, police and administrative section were parceled out, leading to the creation of an "active brigade" conducting investigations of foreigners through the Service des Etrangers, or Third Bureau, and an administrative section that centralized the results of this information in a "Casier central." Five years later, in December 1930, a new subadministration, the Direction de l'administration et de la police générale (DAPG) was created, which housed a Sous-direction des étrangers et des passeports (SDEP) with two offices: a Bureau des étrangers and a Bureau des passeports, des visas et des naturalisations. These two SDEP offices combined represented 21.3 percent of the administrative personnel of the Prefecture of Police at the time, indicating the expanding scope of police action in the realm of immigrant

administration. By 1937, eight divisions of six agents each were charged with home visits for all foreigners in Paris and its surrounds. Alexis Spire, *Etrangers à La Carte: L'administration de l'immigration En France, 1945–1975* (Paris: Grasset, 2005), 144–46; Jean-Marc Berlière, *Le monde des polices en France : XIXe–XXe siècles* (Paris: Editions Complexe, 1996), 91–114. On the professionalization of the Paris police force, see Berlière, *Le monde des polices*, 69–76.

12. For instance, the following Parisian residents: Italian Giovanni Bachetta and Maria née Tosi (IA/11, Archives de la Préfecture de Police, hereafter APP); Polish Moseher Babiz and Fanny Léa Marber (IA/11, APP); Greco-Turkish Vitalis Baloul and Elisa née Pappo (IA/12, APP).

13. For more on these police procedures, see Spire, *Etrangers à La Carte*, 53–59.

14. Weil, *Qu'est-Ce Qu'un Français*, 92–98.

15. Claire Zalc, *Dénaturalisés: Les Retraits de Nationalité Sous Vichy* (Paris: Seuil, 2016), 66–69.

16. Linda L Clark, *The Rise of Professional Women in France: Gender and Public Administration since 1830* (Cambridge: Cambridge University Press, 2000), 133–40, 146.

17. Linda Guerry, *Le genre de l'immigration et de la naturalisation. L'exemple de Marseille (1918–1940)* (Lyon: ENS Editions, 2013), chap. 3.

18. Avis du Préfet de Police, November 23, 1921, in Meyer Rotbourg and Marthe Klein, 16191x14 (AN).

19. Demande de Naturalisation, June 16, 1926, in Haschel Goldenberg, 26602x26 (AN).

20. For instance, Russian Seur Funkelstein, whose morality was besmirched by bankruptcy (13376x21); Romanian Jean Leibel, who was written up in 1899 for carrying a gun in public and spent a short time in jail for the offense (10628x10); Russian Salomon London, who also endured a short imprisonment when he accosted police officials in 1891 (7905x05); not even Louise Bourdet, the French wife of Italian Baptiste Pasi was spared the memory of her month's imprisonment when she stole from a department store in Paris (16926x24)—all AN.

21. Demande de Naturalisation, June 16, 1926, in Haschel Goldenberg, 26602x26 (AN).

22. Note, D., Bureau de Sceau, January 28, 1929, in Carlo Sappino, 2461x29 (AN).

23. Note, Chef du Service, Bureau de Sceau, January 31, 1929, in Carlo Sappino, 2461x29 (AN).

24. "Decision du Chef de Service," J., January 12, 1928, in Mordko Wainer, 41987x27 (AN).

25. Note, Bureau de Sceau, January 14, 1928, in Mordko Wainer, 41987x27 (AN).

26. "Note sur convocation," Bureau de Sceau, January 28, 1928, in Mordko Wainer, 41987x27 (AN).

27. "Note sur l'affaire WAINER," Bureau de Sceau, January 12, 1928, in Mordko Wainer, 41987x27 (AN).

28. Letter, Mordko Wainer to Minister of Justice, 1929, in Mordko Wainer, 41987x27 (AN).

29. Demande de Naturalisation, April 14, 1927, in Mario De Faveri and Emilienne Henriette née Loeuillet, 61209x28 (AN).

30. To be clear, the Constitution of 1791 first enshrined marriage as a civil contract rather than a religious rite between a man and woman. A year later, the revolutionary law of September 20, 1792, further transformed the administration of marriage, removing authority from supposedly tyrannical parish priests to sanction unions and maintain marriage records. Instead, the new law expanded the state's jurisdiction into marital matters. From then on, the authority to approve and register marriages fell uniquely to a growing army of civil servants in the employ of the French state. See Suzanne Desan, *The Family on Trial in Revolutionary France* (Berkeley: University of California Press, 2004), chap. 2.

31. Samuel Chelicevitch and Jachet née Steinitz, 12695x25; Samuel Covo and Sarah née Assael, 19001x27; Abraham Tycheboff and Léa née Niantanha, 29089x26 (AN, all).

32. Demande de Naturalisation, November 19, 1925, for Schoel Guerchonovitch and Sarah née Schwartz, 13198x25 (AN).

33. Demande de Naturalisation, April 18, 1926; Avis du Préfet de Police, August 17, 1926; Note, Bureau de Sceau, 1926 in Joseph Korenblum and Jeanne née Feldmann, 17895x26 (AN).

34. Anonymous letter, 1927 to Minister of Justice, in Joseph Korenblum and Jeanne née Feldmann, 17895x26 (AN).

35. Avis du Préfet de Police, July 5, 1927; Note, Bureau de Sceau, July 9, 1927, in Joseph Korenblum and Jeanne née Feldmann, 17895x26 (AN).

36. Letter from Georges de Berly, docteur en droit, réferendaire au sceau de France to Joseph Korenblum, September 28, 1927, in Joseph Korenblum and Jeanne née Feldmann, 17895x26 (AN).

37. Demande de Naturalisation for Joseph Korenblum, June 8, 1928, in Joseph Korenblum and Jeanne née Feldmann, 17895x26 (AN).

38. Avis du Préfet de Police, May 27, 1929, in Joseph Korenblum and Jeanne née Feldmann, 17895x26 (AN).

39. "Note sur affaire Korenblum," Bureau de Sceau, July 19, 1930, in Joseph Korenblum and Jeanne née Feldmann, 17895x26 (AN).

40. Demande de Naturalisation, July 22, 1926, in Michel Hamilton, 6545x23 (AN).

41. Census report for Sainte Marguerite, 1931, 453 (D2M8/400, AdP).

42. Rubinsztain, dossier familial, p. 3, in 1368W/356, no. 6575 (AdP).

43. Letter from Nicolas Goata to Minister of Justice, May 2, 1933, in Nicolas Goata and Emilienne Pauline née Authemet, 8008x32 (AN).

44. Avis du Préfet de Police, June 1, 1933, in Nicolas Goata and Emilienne Pauline née Authemet, 8008x32 (AN).

45. This was also true of British wives married to naturalizing men before World War I. Laura Tabili, *Global Migrants, Local Culture: Natives and Newcomers in Provincial England, 1841–1939* (Houndmills, UK: Palgrave Macmillan, 2011), 157–59.

46. Letter, January 4, 1924, from Eugénie Guyard to Minister of Justice in Guillaume Sandmeier and Eugénie née Guyard, 15713x24 (AN).

47. Demande de Naturalisation, May 1923; Proposition motivée, Bureau de Sceau, February 1929; Note de convocation, February 1929 in for Esteban Hom, 105039x28 (AN).

48. Letter, August 10, 1926, from Florent Vanderkelen to Minister of Justice; Demande de Naturalisation, August 31, 1926, in Florent Vanderkelen, 30414x27 (AN).

49. Letter, October 17, 1914, from Camille Mecking to Minister of Justice in Guillaume Mecking and Camille née Finance, 6648x13 (AN).
50. Letter, July 12, 1916, from Camille Mecking to Minister of Justice in ibid.
51. Letter, September 5, 1921, from Meyer Rotbourg to Minister of Justice in Meyer Rotbourg and Marthe née Klein, 16191x14 (AN).
52. Letter, April 26, 1920, from Widow Buttafocco to the Minister of Justice in Abel Yegparian and Marie Marcelle Antoinette née Buttafocco, 15834x14 (AN).
53. Letter, July 4, 1929, from Aline Tiseler to Garde de Sceau in Leiba Tiseler and Aline née Kaplinsky, 6834x30 (AN).
54. Letter, September 5, 1929, from Aline Tiseler to prefect of police in Leiba Tiseler and Aline née Kaplinsky, I/A 208 (Archives de la Préfecture de Police, hereafter APP).
55. Letter, August 30, 1933, from Madame Goata to Minister of Justice in Nicolas Goata and Emilienne née Authemet, 8008x32 (AN).
56. Avis du Préfet de Police, November 3, 1924; Bureau de Sceau note, June 23, 1925, in Peissak Levine and Marie née Roubinchtein in 2074x21 (AN).
57. Bertrand Nogaro and Lucien Weil, *La Main-d'œuvre étrangère et colonial pendant la guerre* (Paris: Presses universitaires de France, 1926), chap. 4; Tyler Stovall, "The Color Line Behind the Lines: Racial Violence in France during the Great War," *American Historical Review* 103, no. 3 (June 1998): 737–69; John Horne, "Immigrant Workers in France During World War I," *French Historical Studies* 14, no. 1 (spring 1983): 85–89.
58. Stovall, "The Color Line behind the Lines"; Richard Standish Fogarty, *Race and War in France: Colonial Subjects in the French Army, 1914–1918* (Baltimore: Johns Hopkins University Press, 2008), chap. 5; Jennifer Anne Boittin, *Colonial Metropolis: The Urban Grounds of Anti-Imperialism and Feminism in Interwar Paris* (Lincoln: University of Nebraska Press, 2010), chap. 2.
59. Camiscioli, *Reproducing the French Race*, chap. 5.
60. Stovall, "The Color Line behind the Lines"; Fogarty, *Race and War in France*, chap. 5.
61. Lacombe, "Rapport du Contrôle postal indochinois pendant le mois de mai 1917," June 1917, 5–6, in 1 SLOTFOM/8 (Centre des Archives d'Outre-Mer, hereafter CAOM).
62. Josselme, "Etat nominatif des liaisons entre françaises et indo-chinois relévées, suivies et contrôlées pendant les mois de juin et juillet 1920," August 1, 1920, 1–2, in 1 SLOTFOM/8 (CAOM).
63. Lieutenant-Colonel du Pac Marsoliès, "Rapport Morale et Politique pendant le mois d'octobre 1916" featuring a "Note sur la correspondance annamite lus du 20 octobre au 20 novembre 1916," November 25, 1916, 2; Lacombe, "Rapport du Contrôle postal indochinois pendant le mois de septembre 1917," October 6, 1917, 5–6; Josselme, "Rapport du Contrôle postal indochinois pour le mois de juillet 1919," July 31, 1919, 4, in 1 SLOTFOM/8 (CAOM).
64. Lacombe, "Rapport du Contrôle postal indochinois pendant le mois de décembre 1918," December 30, 1918, 4, in 1 SLOTFOM/8 (CAOM).
65. Lacombe, "Rapport du Contrôle postal indochinois pendant le mois de novembre 1917," December 5, 1917, 4, in 1 SLOTFOM/8 (CAOM).
66. Lacombe, "Rapport du Contrôle postal indochinois pendant le mois de septembre 1917," October 6, 1917, 5, in 1 SLOTFOM/8 (CAOM).

67. Lacombe, "Rapport du Contrôle postal indochinois pendant le mois de novembre 1917," 5, in 1 SLOTFOM/8 (CAOM).

68. Fogarty, *Race and War in France*, chap. 5.

69. Lacombe, "Rapport du Contrôle postal indochinois pendant le mois de mars 1918," April 4, 1918, 6–7, in 1 SLOTFOM/8 (CAOM).

70. Lacombe, "Rapport du Contrôle postal indochinois, 7, in 1 SLOTFOM/8 (CAOM).

71. "Rapport du Contrôle postal indochinois pendant le mois de novembre 1918," December 4, 1918, 6, in 1 SLOTFOM/8 (CAOM).

72. Clemenceau, Ministre de Guerre, Président du Conseil, "Confidential Interministerial circular (no. 8549 I/8) pour la libération en France à titre exceptionnel des Militaires et Travailleurs indigènes des Colonies autres que l'Algérie, la Tunisie et le Maroc qui demandent à rester dans la Métropole," April 4, 1919, 1, in 12 SLOTFOM/3 (CAOM). Emphasis is mine.

73. Clemenceau, Ministre de Guerre, Président du Conseil, "Confidential Interministerial circular, 3–4, in 12 SLOTFOM/3 (CAOM).

74. Larroque, "Addendum," April 18, 1919, in 12 SLOTFOM/3 (CAOM).

75. Mary Dewhurst Lewis, *The Boundaries of the Republic: Migrant Rights and the Limits of Universalism in France, 1918–1940* (Stanford: Stanford University Press, 2007), chap. 4.

76. Josselme, "Rapport du contrôle postal indochinois pendant le mois de juillet 1919," July 31, 1919, 3–4, in 1 SLOTFOM/8 (CAOM).

77. Josselme, "Rapport du contrôle postal indochinois pour le mois d'avril 1919," May 13, 1919, 7, in 1 SLOTFOM/8 (CAOM).

78. Letter, Governor-General of Indochina Montguillot to Minister of the Colonies, June 22, 1919, in 12 SLOTFOM/3 (CAOM).

79. Letter, Minister of Colonies to President of the Council and Minister of War, September 4, 1919, in 12 SLOTFOM/3 (CAOM).

80. Letter, Minister of Colonies to Minister of War, August 2, 1919, in 12 SLOTFOM/3 (CAOM).

81. Camiscioli, *Reproducing the French Race*, chap. 5.

82. For example, some colonial soldiers in the capital drew official sanction for their anticolonial propagandizing throughout the interwar decades, but authorities considered them untouchable on account of their French wives and children. See the example cited in Boittin, *Colonial Metropolis*, 37.

83. Josselme, Chef de Dépôt des Travailleurs coloniaux à Marseille, "Rapport: Contrôle Général des Troupes Indochinoises pour le mois de mai 1920," June 1, 1920, 2–3, in 1 SLOTFOM/8 (CAOM).

84. Letter, Officer Viên to Vo Hoang Phát, November 3, 1923, extracted from "Note pour le Ministre," November 1923, in 1 SLOTFOM/8 (CAOM).

85. Letter, Cha (M1e 571, 31e Section d'Infirmiers Hopital Militaire, Landau) to Lau (Huong quan, village d'An Phuoc, province de My Tho, Cochinchine), June 16, 1924, in 4 SLOTFOM/8 (CAOM).

86. Letter, Khieu (M1e 564m 34e Cie, 121e ETEM, SP 132) to Trinh (Hadong, Tonkin), in 4 SLOTFOM/8 (CAOM). On relationships between native women and French colonial officers in the empire, see Emmanuelle Saada, *Les*

Enfants de La Colonie: Les Métis de l'empire Français Entre Sujétion et Citoyenneté (Paris: Découverte, 2007), chaps. 1, 5, 6 especially.

87. Jolin, "Etat des Correspondances ayant été censurées pour le mois d'avril 1923," May 1923, 3, in 1 SLOTFOM/8 (CAOM).

88. Josselme, "Etat des Correspondances ayant été censurées pour le mois de juin 1923," July 1, 1923, 3–4, in 1 SLOTFOM/8 (CAOM).

89. Josselme, "Etat des Correspondances ayant été censurées pour le mois de juin 1923," July 1, 1923, 5–6, in 1 SLOTFOM/8 (CAOM).

90. Letter, Cha (M1e 571, 31e Section d'Infirmiers Hopital Militaire, Landau) to Lau (Huong quan, village d'An Phuoc, province de My Tho, Cochinchine), June 16, 1924, in 4 SLOTFOM/8 (CAOM).

3. Wives, Wages, and Regulating Breadwinners

1. Yolanda Foldes, *La Rue Du Chat Qui Pêche* (Paris: Albin Michel, 1937), 197.

2. Susan Pedersen, *Family, Dependence, and the Origins of the Welfare State: Britain and France, 1914–1945* (Cambridge: Cambridge University Press, 1993); Laura Levine Frader, *Breadwinners and Citizens: Gender in the Making of the French Social Model* (Durham, NC: Duke University Press, 2008); Geoff Read, *The Republic of Men: Gender and the Political Parties in Interwar France* (Baton Rouge: Louisiana State University Press, 2014), chap. 4.

3. Rachel Ginnis Fuchs, *Contested Paternity: Constructing Families in Modern France* (Baltimore: Johns Hopkins University Press, 2008); Kristen Stromberg Childers, *Fathers, Families, and the State in France, 1914–1945* (Ithaca, NY: Cornell University Press, 2003), chap. 1.

4. Louise Tilly and Joan Wallach Scott, *Women, Work, and Family* (New York: Holt, Rinehart and Winston, 1978), 150–51.

5. Laura Lee Downs, *Manufacturing Inequality: Gender Division in the French and British Metalworking Industries, 1914–1939* (Ithaca, NY: Cornell University Press, 1995).

6. Françoise Thébaud, *Quand Nos Grand-Mères Donnaient La Vie: La Maternité En France Dans l'entre-Deux-Guerres* (Lyon: Presses universitaires de Lyon, 1986), 23–25; Frader, *Breadwinners and Citizens*, chap. 6.

7. Pedersen, *Family, Dependence, and the Origins of the Welfare State*.

8. Frader, *Breadwinners and Citizens*, chap. 6; Read, *The Republic of Men*, chap. 4.

9. Eliza Earle Ferguson, *Gender and Justice: Violence, Intimacy and Community in Fin-de Siècle Paris* (Baltimore: Johns Hopkins University Press, 2010), chap. 2. On the problem of women's economic dependencies among the popular classes of nineteenth-century New York and London, respectively, see Christine Stansell, *City of Women: Sex and Class in New York, 1789–1860*, 1st ed. (New York: Knopf, 1986), chaps. 2, especially; and Ellen Ross, *Love and Toil: Motherhood in Outcast London, 1870–1918* (New York: Oxford University Press, 1993), chaps. 3, especially.

10. See https://drnimishabarton.com for supporting statistics.

11. Ordonnance de Transmission de la Procédure, TPI, March 4, 1931, in D2U8 320 (AdP).

12. Procès-verbal d'interrogatoire et de confrontation, January 22, 1932, in D2U8 320 (AdP).

13. Renseignements demandés, TPI, Petit Parquet, October 25, 1931, in D2U8 320 (AdP).

14. Déposition de Rachel née Lewinski femme Gerber, TPI, September 10, 1934, in D2U8 390 (AdP).

15. Déposition de Léontine Aline Armand Marinier née Tissard, TPI, February 19, 1936; Déposition de Jacques Violina, TPI, December 9, 1935; Réquisitoire définitif, April 6, 1936, in D2U8 496 (AdP).

16. Audition d'Alice Plourde, Commissariat de Police de la Goutte d'Or, October 20, 1933; Ordonnance de Transmission de la Procédure à M. le Procureur Général, TPI, January 30, 1934, in D2U8 369 (AdP)

17. Déposition de Yvonne femme Botton née Divrechy, TPI, February 16, 1937, in D2U8 540 (AdP).

18. Déposition de Flore Saltiel Amar, TPI, February 2, 1937, in D2U8 540 (AdP).

19. Déposition d'Edouard Boutier, TPI, October 19, 1932, in D2U8 345 (AdP).

20. Letter, Widow Dimascio to the Procurer General, October 25, 1932, in D2U8 345 (AdP).

21. Déposition d'Antonine née Jankowska femme Smaguine, TPI, May 6, 1936, in D2U8 499 (AdP).

22. Gary S. Cross, *Immigrant Workers in Industrial France: The Making of a New Laboring Class* (Philadelphia: Temple University Press, 1983), 9–10.

23. Statistique Générale de France, *Statistique Des Familles En 1926* (Paris: Imprimerie nationale, 1932), 28.

24. Polycar, dossier familial, p. 6, in 1368W/31, no. 2356 (AdP).

25. In fact, Madame Polycar declared to social workers after a particularly "violent" scene between herself and her husband, "She is not surprised that [her stepsons] Maurice and Marcel neither respect nor love her since the father denigrates her constantly in their presence." Polyar, dossier familial, p. 4, in 1368W/31, no. 2356 (AdP).

26. Stansell, *City of Women*, 45.

27. Cross, *Immigrant Workers in Industrial France*, chap. 9.

28. Mary Dewhurst Lewis, *The Boundaries of the Republic: Migrant Rights and the Limits of Universalism in France, 1918–1940* (Stanford: Stanford University Press, 2007), chap. 4.

29. Frader, *Breadwinners and Citizens*, 195–208.

30. Déposition d'Antonine Drouart née Beaujean, TPI, December 3, 1932. This fact appears in other testimonies: Déposition de Louis Koppus, TPI, December 3, 1932. By Wandiak's own admission, "She left me because, being without work, I no longer had money." Procès-verbal d'interrogatoire et de confrontation, TPI, October 26, 1932, in D2U8 351 (AdP).

31. Déposition d'André Giromini, TPI, November 24, 1933, in D2U8 375 (AdP).

32. Acte d'Accusation, July 29, 1939, in D2U8 605 (AdP).

33. Rapport de la Police Judiciaire fourni par l'Inspecteur Lasigne au sujet du nommé Cauda, August 27, 1934, in D2U8 391 (AdP).

34. Déposition de Joseph Dyzenchanz, TPI, 11 May 1934; Déposition de Chana Lewinska, TPI, June 4, 1934; Réquisitoire définitif, November 2, 1934, 5; Acte d'Accusation, December 4,1934, in D2U8 390 (AdP).

35. Letter, Widow Goichmann to Minister of Justice, May 20, 1926; Demande de Naturalisation for Widow Goichmann, June 24, 1926, in Rachel Goichmann née Schwartz, 16875x14 (AN).

36. Sophie Malkine, folio no. 1796, in D84Z 146 (AdP).

37. Rachel Ginnis Fuchs and Leslie Page Moch, "Pregnant, Single, and Far from Home: Migrant Women in Nineteenth-Century Paris," *American Historical Review* 95, no. 4 (October 1990): 1007–31; Leslie Page Moch and Rachel Ginnis Fuchs, "Getting Along: Poor Women's Networks in Nineteenth-Century Paris," *French Historical Studies* 18, no. 1 (1993): 34–49; Leslie Page Moch, *The Pariahs of Yesterday: Breton Migrants in Paris* (Durham, NC: Duke University Press, 2012), chap. 2.

38. Germaine Besnard de Quelen, "Rapport moral de l'exercice 1937," *Compte rendu*, 20, in D84Z/228 (AdP).

39. Rachel Ginnis Fuchs, *Poor and Pregnant in Paris: Strategies for Survival in the Nineteenth Century* (New Brunswick, NJ: Rutgers University Press, 1992), 1.

40. Eugène Dabit, *L'Hôtel Du Nord* (Paris: Denoël, 1929), 64.

41. Suzanne Balivet, folio no. 453, carton D84Z 145 (AdP).

42. Isaline Bron, folio no. 11001, carton D84Z 155 (AdP).

43. Marie Anne Léontine Goasdaiff, folio no. 7575 bis, carton D84Z 151 (AdP).

44. For instance: Jeanne Sergent abandoned by "a foreigner" (folio no. 611, carton D84Z 145); Michaelle Valot abandoned by "an Italian whom she learned later was married" (folio no. 985, carton D84Z 145, AdP); Georgette Taine abandoned by "a Spaniard" (folio no. 1285, carton D84Z 146, AdP).

45. Paul Gaudinot, dossier familial, p. 5, in 1368W/287, no. 5514 (AdP).

46. Roza Albertilikova, folio no. 1085, carton D84Z/145 (AdP).

47. Vicenta Dasi, folio no. 3948, carton D84Z/148 (AdP).

48. Yvonne Lecoz, folio no. 5313, carton D84Z/149 (AdP).

49. Acte d'accusation, November 25, 1932, in D2U8 350 (AdP).

50. Acte d'accusation, July 16, 1936, in D2U8/496 (AdP).

51. Ferguson, *Gender and Justice*.

52. Clifford D. Rosenberg, *Policing Paris: The Origins of Modern Immigration Control between the Wars* (Ithaca, NY: Cornell University Press, 2006), 159–66.

53. Déclaration de Madame Blanche Sadoun, May 25, 1936; Acte d'accusation, January 22, 1937, in D2U8 512 (AdP).

54. Audition de Marie Anna Isoline née Cailleux femme Gody, May 4, 1934, in D2U8 384 (AdP).

55. Réquisitoire définitif, August 21, 1934, in D2U8 384 (AdP).

56. Audition de Jean Gervet, Commissariat de Police du Quartier de la Folie-Méricourt, March 14, 1934, in D2U8 384 (AdP).

57. Docteur Truelle, "Rapport médico-légal," May 24, 1934, 5–7, in D2U8 384 (AdP).

58. Michael Willrich, "Home Slackers: Men, the State, and Welfare in Modern America," *Journal of American History* 87, no. 2 (September 2000): 460–89.

59. Elinor A. Accampo, Rachel Ginnis Fuchs, and Mary Lynn Stewart, eds., *Gender and the Politics of Social Reforms in France, 1870–1914* (Baltimore: Johns Hopkins University Press, 1995), chap. 1; Emmanuelle Saada, *Empire's Children: Race, Filiation, and Citizenship in the French Colonies*, trans. Arthur Goldhammer (Chicago: University

of Chicago Press, 2012), 148–52; Ivan Jablonka, *Ni père ni mère: histoire des enfants de l'Assistance Publique, 1874–1939* (Paris: Seuil, 2006); Sylvia Schafer, *Children in Moral Danger and the Problem of Government in Third Republic France* (Princeton: Princeton University Press, 1997); Childers, *Fathers, Families, and the State in France*.

60. On the history of paternity suits in metropolitan and imperial contexts, see Fuchs, *Contested Paternity*, chaps. 1–3, especially; Saada, *Empire's Children*, chap. 6. By contrast, many were hostile to the introduction of this legislation in the French empire for the very reason that "native women" would then have power over French men, a frightening specter that inverted gendered and racial power relations. Of note, demographic reasoning never figured in the colonial debate, while such concerns all but structured the very terms of the metropolitan conversation. See Saada, *Empire's Children*, chaps. 5–6.

61. Fuchs, *Contested Paternity*, 166–67.

62. "4ème Assemblée Générale," Madame Besnard de Quelen, *Compte-Rendu de 1928*, 12, in D84Z/228 (AdP).

63. "Compte-rendu de Mademoiselle Michel, Avocate à la Cour," Michel, *Compte-Rendu de 1929*, 35–36, in D84Z/228 (AdP). On Yvonne Netter's feminist activism and anti-imperialist politics, see Jennifer Anne Boittin, *Colonial Metropolis: The Urban Grounds of Anti-Imperialism and Feminism in Interwar Paris* (Lincoln: University of Nebraska Press, 2010), 177–78.

64. Rachel Goldstein, folio 36, carton D84Z/145 (AdP).

65. CB/43, reg. 69, no. 972 (APP).

66. "Loi du 7 février 1924 réprimant le délit de l'abandon de famille," *Journal Officiel*, February 10, 1924, 1045; "Loi modifiant les articles 1er et 2 de la loi du 7 février 1924 sur l'abandon de famille," April 5, 1928, 3870. See also Childers, *Fathers, Families, and the State in France*, 35–36.

67. CB/43, reg. 69, no. 1085 (APP).

68. CB/43, reg. 69, no. 411 (APP).

69. CB/43, reg. 70, no. 2493 (APP).

70. CB/43, reg. 69, nos. 210, 913; CB/43, reg. 70, nos. 2359, 2420 (APP).

71. Cross, *Immigrant Workers in Industrial France*, 189.

72. Rosenberg, *Policing Paris*, 101–2.

73. "Statistique rélative aux arrestations d'étrangers," *ASVP* (1929–31), 546–47; "Statistique rélative," *ASVP* (1932–1934), 604.

74. CB/43, reg. 69, no. 319 (APP).

75. CB/43, reg. 70, no. 2124 (APP).

76. CB/43, reg. 66, no.1925 (APP).

77. During the French Revolution, the law of September 20, 1792, proposed that both husbands and wives should be permitted to initiate divorce. The Napoleonic Code curtailed this egalitarian measure significantly, allowing only for male-initiated divorce and, shortly thereafter, the Restoration Monarchy abolished divorce entirely with the enactment of the Bonald Law of May 8, 1816. Only with the dawn of the Third Republic did divorce reappear. See Theresa McBride, "Divorce and the Republican Family," in *Gender and the Politics of Social Reform in France, 1870–1914* (Baltimore: Johns Hopkins University Press, 1995), 59–81.

78. Rachel Meller, folio no. 9957, carton D84Z/154 (AdP).

79. Osnandi, folio no. 5678, carton D84Z/149 (AdP).

80. For instance, Belgian Jeanne Deridder, wife of Belgian tanner, Henri Van der Molen, launched a similar investigation into her husband and his Belgian mistress, Yvonne Malagie (CB/44, reg. 20, no. 74); French-born, "Belgian by marriage" Blanche Frankelemont and her lover, Italian Antonio Ciolina (CB/43, reg. 66, no. 1430); Belgian Marie Clémentine Foucher and her French lover, Cyprien Pellegrin (CB/43, reg. 69, no, 216—all APP).

81. CB/44, reg. 20, no. 1091 (AdP).
82. CB/43, reg. 66, no. 2008 (AdP).
83. No. 14.485, "Loi qui rétablit le divorce," *Journal Officiel,* July 29, 1884.
84. CB/43, reg. 69, no. 1291 (APP).
85. CB/43, reg. 66, no. 2013 (APP).
86. CB/43, reg. 69, no. 319 (APP).
87. CB/43, reg. 66, no. 574 (APP).

4. Mothers, Welfare Organizations, and Reproducing for the Nation

1. George Orwell, *Down and Out in Paris and London* (New York: Harcourt, 1961), 97.

2. Rachel Ginnis Fuchs, *Poor and Pregnant in Paris: Strategies for Survival in the Nineteenth Century* (New Brunswick, NJ.: Rutgers University Press, 1992).

3. Françoise de Barros, "L'Etat au prisme des municipalités. Une comparaison historique des catégorisations des étrangers en France (1919–1984)" (thèse de doctorat, Université de Paris 1, 2004), chap. 3.

4. Mary Dewhurst Lewis, *The Boundaries of the Republic: Migrant Rights and the Limits of Universalism in France, 1918–1940* (Stanford: Stanford University Press, 2007); Paul-André Rosental, "Migrations, souveraineté, droits sociaux: Protéger et expulser les étrangers en Europe du XIXe siècle à nos jours," *Annales. Histoire, Sciences Sociales* 66, no. 2 (2011): 335–73.

5. Georges Mauco, "Les Étrangers en France: étude géographique sur leur rôle dans l'activité économique" (thèse de doctorat ès lettres, Université de Paris, 1932), 113.

6. The 13th Congress of Hygiene held in 1926 was organized around this theme and the December 1926 special issue of the *Revue d'Hygiène* devoted entirely to this topic.

7. G. Fabius de Champville, "Banquet Annuel de la Société Amicale et d'études des administrateurs et commissaires des bureaux de bienfaisance de Paris," *Bulletin de la Société amicable et d'études des administrateurs et commissaires des bureaux de bienfaisance à Paris* (hereafter *BSA*) 94 (April 15, 1926), 2–17; ibid., "Chronique," *BSA* 95 (July 15, 1926): 2–3 in B/3675/70 and B/3675/71 (Archives de l'Assistance Publique-Hôpitaux de Paris, hereafter APHP).

8. Lewis, *Boundaries of the Republic.*

9. This according to article 19 of the Franco-Italian treaty of September 30, 1919, article 5 of the Franco-Polish Assistance Convention of October 14, 1920, and article 7 of the Franco-Belgian Labor Treaty of December 24, 1926. On foreigners' access to unemployment benefits, see Françoise de Barros, "Secours Aux Chômeurs et Assistances Durant l'entre-Deux-Guerres. Etatisation Des Dispositifs et Structuration Des Espaces Politiques Locaux," *Politix* 14, no. 53 (2001): 117–44.

10. Romanians and Austrians benefited from treaties concluded January 28, 1930 and May 27, 1930, respectively. Office Central des Oeuvres de Bienfaisance et Services Sociaux, *Paris Charitable, Bienfaisant et Social* (Paris: Editions de l'Ouest, 1936), 316.

11. Gary S. Cross, *Immigrant Workers in Industrial France: The Making of a New Laboring Class* (Philadelphia: Temple University Press, 1983), chap. 9.

12. Lewis, *Boundaries of the Republic*, chaps. 2–4.

13. This was the position of Armand Levy of the 3rd arrondissement and Monsieur Arrighi of the 18th arrondissement in, respectively, H. Flamenc, "Procès-verbaux: Séance du Conseil d'Administration du jeudi 23 juin 1932," *BSA* 119 (October 15, 1932): 2 in B/3675/91 (Archives de l'Assistance Publique et les Hôpitaux Publiques, hereafter APHP); ibid., "Rapport de la Commission de contrôle," *BSA* 122 (July 15, 1933): 13, in B/3675/94 (APHP).

14. French families of four or more were entitled to fifty francs per month, or six hundred francs per year, whereas benefits accorded to Italian, Polish and Belgian families were capped at three hundred francs per year. "Des Bureaux de bienfaisance à Paris: Conférence de M. Chiselle, Délégué Général," *BSA* 120 (January 15, 1933), 7, in B/3675/92 (APHP).

15. Demande de Naturalisation, March 2, 1914 in Selig Gallner and Sophie née Glassman, 2639x14, AN; Avis du Préfet de Police, March 20, 1922 in Isaac Tcheskiss and Bassi née Mendeleil, 41812x14, AN.

16. Delegate Chiselle made this observation, but offered no further explanation. "Des Bureaux de bienfaisance à Paris," 6–7, in B/3675/92 (APHP).

17. Henry A. Victor, *La Maternité de l'Hôpital de Rothschild: son fonctionnement jusqu'en 1930* (Paris: Imprimerie spéciale de la Libraire Le François, 1930), 86.

18. Victor, *La Maternité*, 80–81.

19. Fuchs, *Poor and Pregnant*, chap. 5 and 6.

20. Statistics collected from "Asiles Municipaux pour femmes et enfants, Renseignements divers," *ASVP* between 1914 and 1931.

21. "Asiles Municipaux pour femmes et enfants, Renseignements divers," *ASVP* (1927–28), 312.

22. Françoise Thébaud, *Quand Nos Grand-Mères Donnaient La Vie: La Maternité En France Dans l'entre-Deux-Guerres* (Lyon: Presses universitaires de Lyon, 1986), 159.

23. Its full title was Foyer Français: Association for the Settlement and Instruction of Foreigners residing in France. Roger-Angel Olchanski was an industrialist who used his small fortune to finance not only the Foyer Français, but other philanthropic ventures such as the Rothschild Foundation. Paul Raphael belonged to a prosperous Jewish banking family. A radical-socialist, Raphael had little success in his senatorial campaigns, though he was twice elected municipal councilor, first in Frénonville then in Bourgébus (both in Calvados). Raphael was also an active member of the Ligue Française d'Enseignement. Olchanski and Raphael were close friends. Jean Charles Bonnet, *Les Pouvoirs Publics Français et l'immigration Dans l'entre-Deux-Guerres* (Lyon: Centre d'histoire économique et sociale de la région lyonnaise, 1976), 77–78.

24. The Foyer Français formally dissolved in 1935. Anonymous letter to René Lisbonne, February 26, 1936, in 50 AP 62 (AN).

25. André Honnorat, *Compte-rendu*, 1926, 11, in 50 AP 62 (AN).

26. FF, *Compte rendu* 1925, 11, in 50 AP 62 (AN).

27. René Lisbonne, "Le Foyer français en 1925," *Compte rendu*, 1926, 15, in 50 AP 62 (AN).

28. FF, *Compte rendu* 1925, 14; FF, *Compte rendu*, 1926, 14, in 50 AP 62 (AN).

29. FF, *Compte rendu*, 1925, 13, in 50 AP 62 (AN).

30. FF, *Compte rendu*, 1926, 13–14, in 50 AP 62 (AN).

31. "Foyer Français, procés verbal de la reunion du samedi 5 décembre 1925"; Paul Raphael, "L'Enseignement et la propagande," *Compte rendu*, 1926, 28 in 50 AP 62 (AN).

32. Ch. Neide, "Le Foyer Français," *La Nouvelle Aurore* 3, no. 15 (December 15, 1924): 4.

33. Letter, April 1, 1926 from Prefect of the Seine to mayors of the 20 arrondissements of Paris, in D3M9/8 (Archives de Paris (hereafter AdP)).

34. Letter, March 11, 1926, Garde des Sceaux to Prefect of the Seine, in D3M9/8 (AdP).

35. Paul Raphael, "L'Enseignement," *Compte rendu*, 1929, 23, in 50 AP 62 (AN).

36. Léon Lombrozo and Luna née Chalom, 32329x27; Joseph Feldman and Nelly née Aizenstein, 16509x14; Isaac Tcheskiss and Bassi née Mandeleil, 41812x14; and Froïm Vogel and Clara née Josephson, 8741x25 (all AN).

37. Demande de Naturalisation, June 24, 1926, in Bassi Tcheskiss née Mandeleil, 41812x14, AN.

38. Letter, Bassi Tcheskiss to Minister of Justice, April 6, 1927, in 41812x14, AN.

39. There were located: 2 rue Fernand-Berthoud in the 3rd arrondissement; 23 rue Cujas in the 5th arrondissement; 23 Ave de St-Ouen in the 17th arrondissement; 43 rue des Poissoniers in the 18th arrondissement; 51 rue Ramponneau in the 20th arrondissement; and in Boulogne-Bilancourt. Additionally, they offered courses in areas of rural France with a large foreign presence: in the Nord and Pas-du-Calais for Polish miners, as well as Lyon, Reims, Marseille, and Decazzevile in the Aveyron region. (FF, *Compte rendu*, 1925, 15–16 in 50 AP 62 (AN))

40. While the former constituted a "special professoriate" close to the student who "understood their psychology," the latter were meant to remain apart, "Because we figure that in order to educate them completely it is necessary to, as they say: 'take the plunge [*les jeter à l'eau*].'" Paul Raphael, "Foyer Français, procés verbal de la reunion du samedi 5 décembre 1925," 4, in 50 AP 62 (AN).

41. FF, *Compte rendu*, 1925, 15–16, in 50 AP 62 (AN).

42. Despite the large number of Italians in the capital, they were not well-represented in these language classes. Paul Raphael, Secretary-General in 1925–26, opined, "The linguistic similarities between French and Italian hinder their attendance of our classes." (FF, *Compte rendu*, 1926, 24–26, in 50 AP 62 (AN).

43. Jane Misme, "Augmentons le nombre des Bons Français," *Minerva* 3, no. 120 (November 27, 1927): 3; Paul Raphael, "L'Enseignement," *Compte rendu*, 1929, 23, in 50 AP 62 (AN).

44. René Lisbonne, "Le Foyer français en 1925," *Compte rendu*, 1926, 18, in 50 AP 62 (AN).

45. Paul Raphael, "L'Enseignement et la propagande," *Compte rendu*, 1926, 27–28, in 50 AP 62 (AN).

46. Ch. Neide, "Le Foyer Français," 4, in 50 AP 62 (AN).

47. Paul Raphael, "L'Enseignement et la propagande," *Compte rendu*, 1926, 27, in 50 AP 62 (AN).

48. René Lisbonne, "Remarques," *Compte rendu*, 1925, 16; Lisbonne, "Le Foyer français en 1925," *Compte rendu*, 1926, 19–20, in 50 AP 62 (AN).

49. Seth Koven and Sonya Michel, "Womanly Duties: Maternalist Politics and the Origins of Welfare States in France, Germany, Great Britain, and the United States, 1880–1920," *American Historical Review* 95, no. 4 (October 1990): 1076–1108; Sylvie Fayet-Scribe, *Associations Féminines et Catholicisme XIXe–XXe Siècle* (Paris: Editions Ouvrières, 1990); Évelyne Diebolt, "Les Femmes Engagées Dans Le Monde Associatif et La Naissance de l'Etat Providence," *Matériaux Pour l'histoire de Notre Temps* 53, no. 1 (1999): 13–26; Évelyne Diebolt, *Les femmes dans l'action sanitaire, sociale et culturelle, 1901–2001: les associations face aux institutions* (Paris: Femmes et associations, 2001).

50. Fuchs, *Poor and Pregnant*, chap. 3.

51. LPAM, *Compte rendu*, 1926, 8; LPAM, *Compte rendu*, 1930, 32, in D84Z/228 (AdP))

52. On June 8, 1945, Public Assistance formally withdrew the League's mandate to serve as an intermediary for adoption services.

53. Winceslas Huet, "Première Assemblée générale sous la présidence de M. Durafour, Ministre de Travail de l'Hygiène et de la Prévoyance sociales, Représenté par M. Wenceslas Huet, Attaché au Cabinet au Ministre," *Compte rendu*, 1926, 5, in D84Z/228 (AdP).

54. G. Besnard de Quelen, "Compte rendu moral de l'Exercice 1929," *Compte rendu*, 1929, 18, in D84Z/228 (AdP).

55. G. Besnard de Quelen, "Compte rendu moral de l'Exercice 1926," *Compte rendu*, 1926, 9, in D84Z/228 (AdP).

56. LPAM, *Compte rendu*, 1930, 32, in D84Z/228 (AdP).

57. "Recensement de 1926," *ASVP*, 296; "Recensement de la population de 1931," *ASVP*, 139–42.

58. These data are derived from a sample of 440 foreign women who patronized the League on randomly generated dates between February 1, 1925, when the League first opened its doors, and May 10, 1940, the beginning of the German Occupation of France. The precise breakdown is as follows: 1 African, 2 Algerians, 17 Germans, 1 American, 3 South Americans, 3 Englishwomen, 10 Armenian women (and 1 Armenian man), 7 Austrians, 40 Belgians (and 1 Belgian man), 3 Bulgarians, 1 Danish, 24 Spaniards, 1 Estonian, 8 Greeks, 1 Guadeloupian, 1 Haitian, 1 Dutch, 11 Hungarians, 55 Italians, 2 Lithuanians, 4 Luxemburgers, 3 Martiniquans, 125 Poles, 4 Portuguese, 16 Romanians, 25 Russians (and 1 Russian man), 1 Serbian, 28 Swiss, 1 Syrian, 18 Czechs, 1 Tunisian, 12 Turks, 3 Yugoslavs, and 3 not indicated but foreign-born.

59. LPAM, *Compte rendu*, 1930, 33–34, in D84Z/228 (AdP).

60. Louise Tilly, *Women, Work, and Family* (New York: Holt, Rinehart and Winston, 1978), 116, 123, 155–56; Abel Chatelain, "Migrations et domesticité féminine urbaine en France (XVIIIème siècle– XXème siècle)," *Revue d'histoire économique et sociale* 47, no. 4 (1969): 506–28; Rachel G. Fuchs and Leslie Page Moch, "Pregnant, Single, and Far from Home: Migrant Women in Nineteenth-Century Paris," *American Historical Review* 95, no. 4 (October 1, 1990): 1007–31; Nancy Green, *Ready-to-Wear and Ready-to-Work: A Century of Industry and Immigrants in Paris and New York* (Durham, NC: Duke University Press, 1997).

61. Yvonne Lecoz, folio 5313, carton D84Z/149 (AdP); Madame Dallot, folio 6558, carton D84Z/150 (AdP); Simone Lacourt, folio 8671, carton D84Z/153;

Gélidia Ferry, folio 11886, carton D84Z/156 (AdP); and Alexandra Wysoeka, folio 13330, carton D84Z/157 (AdP).

62. Antoinette Lopez, folio 2417, carton D84Z/146; Augusta Soain, folio 2688, carton D84Z/147; Ada Demari, folio 5442, carton D84Z/149; Paulette Blaneo, folio 13777, carton D84Z/157; Sura Malacki, folio 13670, carton D84Z/157 (AdP).

63. Françoise Eleutherion, folio 1163, D84Z/145; Zelinda Doglia, folio 1699, carton D84Z/146 (AdP).

64. Flore Troky, folio 2393, carton D84Z/146; Maria Diedrich, folio 10590, carton D84Z/155; Julie Schesinger, folio 13757, D84Z/157 (AdP).

65. Friedel Steiner, folio 15322, carton D84Z/159 (AdP).

66. G. Besnard de Quelen, "Compte-rendu moral," *Compte rendu*, 1930, 26–27, in D84Z/228 (AdP).

67. On this perplexing persistence of demand for domestic servants, Besnard de Quelen remarked with some confusion, "There, is a real mystery . . ." Germaine Besnard de Quelen, "Rapport moral de l'exercice 1933," *Compte rendu,* 1933, 12, in D84Z/228 (AdP).

68. Hélène Colowiec, folio 10996, carton D84Z/155 (AdP).

69. Anna Brodetzky, folio 11327, carton D84Z/155; Piroska Guttman, folio 12073, carton D84Z/156; Augusta Francischelli, folio 17631, carton D84Z/161 (AdP).

70. Rebecca Garibian, folio 958, carton D84Z/145; Natacha Kasperovitch, folio 9733, carton D84Z/154; Herta Schnef, folio 12948, D84Z/157; Sarah Garabadien, folio 14897, D84Z/158 (AdP).

71. Françoise Eleutherion, folio 1163, carton D84Z/145; Leiba Hava, folio 2771, carton D84Z/147; Lisette Aubry, folio 4274, carton D84Z/148; Marcelle Leneveber, folio 5125, carton D84Z/149; Madame Osnandi, folio 5678, D84Z/149; Marguerite Lemoine, folio 9251, carton D84Z/153; Gabrielle Benglia, folio 13238, carton D84Z/157 (AdP).

72. "Rapport Moral exposé par Mme Besnard de Quelen, Présidente-Fondatrice," *Compte rendu*, 1926, 9, in D84Z/228 (AdP).

73. André Martehouck, folio 3166, D84Z/147 (AdP).

74. Nathalie Alexandroff, folio 7773, D84Z/152 (AdP).

75. Linkard, folio 5, carton D84Z/145; Teresa Bonetto, folio 217, carton D84Z/145; Josepha Kreiger, folio 256, carton D84Z/145; Simonne Chalet, folio 5770, carton D84Z/149; Victoria Alves, folio 7384, carton D84Z/151; Radka Manafova, folio 10176, D84Z/154; Anna Hein, folio 12277, carton D84Z/156; Marinette Wajda, folio 15805, carton D84Z/159 (AdP).

76. Maria Fronteuska, folio 1082, carton D84Z/145 (AdP).

77. Anna Brodetzky, folio 11327, carton D84Z/155 (AdP).

78. Piroska Guttman, folio 12073, carton D84Z/156; Maria Gilzinska, folio 15320, carton D84Z/159; Maria Stutikova, folio 15366, carton D84Z/159; Virginie Tresine, folio 15827, carton D84Z/159 (AdP).

79. This was how Marie Mermod, a Belgian widow, characterized her relationship with the French state. ("Demande de Naturalisation," December 4, 1926, for Marie Mermod née Lauber, 24229x27, AN.)

80. Marie Louise Aubry, folio 13856, carton D84Z/157; Erna Kotzonla, folio 14469; D84Z/158; Dorotea Stein, folio 15698, carton D84Z/159; Sebastiana Cruz Marrieros, folio 16692, carton D84Z/160; Thérèse Niemczyk, folio 16940, carton D84Z/160 (AdP).

81. Rachel Cohen, folio 8683, carton D84Z/153; Faiga Rosenberg, folio 12516, carton D84Z/156 (AdP).

82. On the Association Israélite pour la Protection de la Jeune Fille, see Emily Machen, "Traveling with the Faith: The Creation of Women's Immigrant Aid Associations in Nineteenth- and Twentieth-Century France," *Journal of Women's History* 23, no. 3 (2011): 89–112.

83. Lucienne Chibrac, *Les pionnières du travail social auprès des étrangers: le Service social d'aide aux émigrants, des origines à la Libération* (Rennes: École nationale de la santé publique, 2005).

84. This was Anna Brodetzky, folio 11327, carton D84Z/155 (AdP).

85. Evelyne Diebolt, *À l'origine de l'Association Olga Spitzer: la protection de l'enfance hier et aujourd'hui, 1923–1939* (Association pour la recherche appliquée, 1993), 5–6. In addition to Diebolt's work on the SSCMD, see also Michele Becquemin, *Protection de l'enfance: l'action de l'association Olga Spitzer, 1923–2003* (Paris: Société, 2003).

86. Diebolt, *À l'origine de l'Association Olga Spitzer*, 19, 120, 137.

87. In 1972, the foundation changed its name to the Olga Spitzer Association, in honor of its principal founding member. It still defines its mission in terms reminiscent of the interwar years: "The Olga Spitzer Association implements preventative, protective, and intermediary actions [as well as] educative and social, medical and psychological interventions of reeducation for the benefit of children and adolescents and interventional actions in favor of adults." See http://www.associationolgaspitzer.fr/.

88. Among the more prestigious members of the SSCMD Committee were Chiappe, prefect of police in Paris (1928–39); Marc Honnorat, treasurer of the organization in 1924 when he was also head of the Hygiene Division of the Paris Prefecture of Police; Robert Billecard, prefect of the Seine-et-Oise department (1931–39); Paul Doumer, president of the Senate (1928–31); and Eugène Dreyfus, first president of the Court of Appeals of Paris (1928–36), among many others. (For a complete list of officers and members, see Diebolt, *À l'origine de l'Association Olga Spitzer*, 31–38). Throughout the interwar years, a combination of support from the Ministry of Hygiene and Social Benefits, the Ministry of Justice, and various departmental funds amounting to over half of the SSCMD's total operating budget kept the fledgling organization running with only minor setbacks even in the mid-1930s (Diebolt, *À l'origine de l'Association Olga Spitzer*, 39, 42, 44–45).

89. Diebolt, *À l'origine de l'Association Olga Spitzer*, 3–10, 95–119.

90. Polish Charles Pomerane, dossier familial, p. 1 in 1368W/216, no. 4651; French Robert Gothsener, dossier familial, p. 1 in 1368W/86, no. 3538; Italian Victor Maiorano, dossier familial, p. 1 in 1368W/190, no. 4344; Polish Berthe Grossman, dossier familial, p. 6, in 1368W/346, no. 6330 (AdP).

91. Friedlander, dossier familial, p. 2, in 1368W/218, no. 4669 (AdP).

92. On the transformation of the *correction paternelle* from a paternal privilege accorded to fathers under the Civil Code to one accorded to the *Etat tutélaire* by the end of the nineteenth century, see Bernard Schnapper, "La Correction Paternelle et Le Mouvement Des Idées Au Dix-Neuvième Siècle (1789–1935)," *Revue Historique* 263, no. 2 (534) (1980): 319–49; Sylvia Schafer, *Children in Moral Danger and the Problem of Government in Third Republic France* (Princeton: Princeton University Press, 1997).

93. Chachignan, dossier familial, p. 1, in 1368W/31, no. 2338; Polycar, dossier familial, p. 1, in 1368W/31, no. 2356 (AdP).

94. Millon, dossier familial, p. 1, in 1368W/38, no 2782 (AdP).

95. Morgen, dossier familial, p. 1, in 1368W/70, no. 3301; Frischka, dossier familial, p. 1, in 1368W/98, no. 3703 (AdP).

96. "Statistique rélative aux arrestations d'étrangers," *ASVP* (1925–1926), 665–66.

97. Diebolt, *À l'origine de l'Association Olga Spitzer*, 23–24.

98. Frischka, dossier familial, p. 6, in 1368W/98, no. 3703 (AdP).

99. Frischka, dossier familial, p. 7, in 1368W/98, no. 3703 (AdP).

100. Salomon, Léon, and Rachel Gabaï, dossier familial, p. 5, 16, in 1368W/31, no. 2336 (AdP).

101. Frischka, dossier familial, p. 1, in 1368W/98, no. 3703 (AdP).

102. Italian Paulette Musi, dossier familial, p. 8, in 1368W/322, no. 5959; half-Spanish André Pacaud, dossier familial, p. 10, in 1368W/306, no. 5747; the Turkish Gabaïs, dossier familial, p. 10, 12, 13, 14, in 13658W/42, no. 2869 (AdP). On *colonies de vacances*, see Laura Lee Downs, *Childhood in the Promised Land: Working-Class Movements and the Colonies de Vacances in France, 1880–1960* (Durham, NC: Duke University Press, 2002).

103. André Pacaud, dossier familial, p. 12, in 1368W/306, no. 5747; Maurice and Isaac Bajroch, dossier familial, p. 4, in 1368W/364, no. 6781; Marcel Polycar, dossier familial, p. 2, in 1368W/31, no. 2336; Robert Gabaï, dossier familial, p. 15, in 13658W/42, no. 2869 (AdP). On the scouting movement, see Philip Nord, "Catholic Culture in Interwar France," *French Politics, Culture and Society* 21, no. 3 (2003): 1–20.

104. Gabaï, dossier familial, p. 8, in 1368W/31, no. 2336; Kohn, dossier familial, p. 7, in 1368W/216, no. 4650; Letter, from Zisserman to SSCMD, September 6, 1935, in 1368W/190, no. 4344 (AdP).

105. Half-Algerian siblings Roger and Madeleine Ghersa, dossier familial, p. 10, in 1368W/245, no. 5001; Martiniquan Jeanne Mornet, in 1368W/365, no. 6817; Turkish Robert Gabaï, dossier familial, p. 11, 13, in 13658W/42, no. 2869 (AdP).

106. Algerian René Nouani, in 1368W/360, no. 6701; Polish Isaac Morgen, dossier individuel, p. 1, in 1368W/70, no. 3301 (AdP).

107. Half-Italian Paulette Gaudinot, dossier familial, p. 6, in 1368W/287, no. 5514; Turkish Robert Gabaï, dossier familial, p. 5, in 1368W/31, no. 2336; Polycar, dossier familial, p. 5, in 1368W/31, no. 2336; half-Algerian Maurice and Sabine Halimi, dossier familial, p. 5, in 1368W/228, no. 4815 (AdP).

108. Half-Italian Simone Gaudinot, dossier familial, p. 6, in 1368W/287, no. 5514; half-Algerian Sabine Halimi, dossier familial, p. 5, in 1368W/228, no. 4815 (AdP).

109. Gabaï, dossier familial, p. 3, 8, 10, 16, in 13658W/42, no. 2869 (AdP).

110. Portuguese Antoine Peres, dossier familial, p. 4, in 1368W/368, no. 6891; half-Spanish André Pacaud, dossier familial, p. 6, 8, in 1368W/306, no. 5747; Turkish Léon Gabaï, dossier familial, p. 8, in 13658W/42, no. 2869 (AdP).

111. Diebolt, *À l'origine de l'Association Olga Spitzer*, 20–22.

112. André Pacaud, dossier familial, p. 10, in 1368W/306, no. 5747; Gabaï, dossier familial, p. 4, in 13658W/42, no. 2869. See also French Georges Albin, dossier familial, p. 5, in 1368W/81, no. 3475 (AdP).

113. Berthe Grossman, "Extrait du dossier de Berthe Grossman—Service des Aliénés à La Préfecture de Police," in 1368W/346, no. 6330 (AdP).

114. Salomon, Léon, and Henri Gabaï, dossier familial, p. 6, in 13658W/42, no. 2869 (AdP).

115. Tunisian Lucien Tahar, in 1368W/304, no. 5725; Polish Berthe Grossman, dossier familial, p. 2, in 1368W/346, no. 6330; Polish Maurice Irenstein, in 1368W/364, no. 6780; Turkish siblings Salomon and Régine Gabaï, dossier familial, p. 12, 15, in 13658W/42, no. 2869 (AdP). Jablonka also uncovered several foreign-born children in his study of the Assistance Publique. See Ivan Jablonka, Ni père ni mère: histoire des enfants de l'Assistance Publique, 1874–1939 (Paris: Seuil, 2006), 29, 264.

116. Jablonka, Ni père ni mère.

117. Halimi, dossier familial, p. 8, in 1368W/228, no. 4815 (AdP).

118. Warinier, dossier familial, pps. 2–4, in 1368W/34, no. 2648 (AdP).

119. Gabaï, dossier familial, pps. 4–6, in 13658W/42, no. 2869 (AdP).

120. Frischka, dossier familial, p. 7–10, in 1368W/98, no. 3703 (AdP).

121. On the "messier mingling of good intentions and blinkered prejudices," see Seth Koven, *Slumming: Sexual and Social Politics in Victorian London* (Princeton: Princeton University Press, 2004).

122. Léontine Stouf, folio 2418, carton D84Z/146 (AdP).

123. Béatrix Fox, folio 8445, carton D84Z/152. See also Sura Cukier, folio 14065, carton D84Z/158 (AdP).

124. Warinier, dossier familial, p. 11, in 1368W/34, no. 2648 (AdP).

125. Coletta, dossier familial, p. 10, in 1368W/42, no. 2872 (AdP).

126. Grossman, dossier familial, p. 2, in 1368W/346, no. 6330 (AdP).

127. Polycar, dossier familial, p. 4, 6, in 1368W/31, no. 2356 (AdP).

128. Ghersa, dossier familial, pps. 2–3, 9, in 1368W/245, no. 5001 (AdP).

129. Halimi, dossier familial, p. 7, in 1368W/228, no. 4815; Pacaud, dossier familial, p. 2, in 1368W/306, no. 5747 (AdP).

130. Anna Beneat, folio 822, carton D84Z/145 (AdP).

131. Hélène Basbard, folio 6446, carton D84Z/150; Machia Tenenbaum, folio 6772, carton D84Z/150; Natacha Kasperovitch, folio 9733, carton D84Z/154; Malka Gekdyszman, folio 11607, D84Z/156; Paula Bouzdykhan, folio 13504, carton D84Z/157 (AdP).

132. Gisala Seekar, folio 10008, carton D84Z/154 (AdP).

133. Yohanna Popelka, folio 989, carton D84Z/145 (AdP).

134. Elvire Baumgarten, folio 1213, carton D84Z/145; Fayga Steruic, folio 1558, carton D84Z/146; Faiga Malkowski, folio 4945, carton D84Z/149; Suzanne Behar, folio 6443, carton D84Z/150 (AdP).

135. Kiradi, dossier familial, p. 2, in 1368W/293, no. 5584; Friedlander, dossier familial, pps. 1–2, in 1368W/218, no. 4669 (AdP).

5. Neighborhood, Street Culture, and Melting-Pot Mixité

1. Déposition de Jacques Kaczurynski, TPI, January 26, 1933, in D2U8 363 (Archives de Paris, hereafter AdP).

2. Marcel Roncayolo, *La Ville et ses territoires* (Paris: Folio, 1990).

3. Judith Rainhorn, *Paris, New York: des migrants italiens* (Paris: CNRS Editions, 2005). On the urban dynamics of mixité in Paris, see Jean-Louis Robert and Danielle Tartakowsky, *Paris le peuple, XVIIIe–XXe siècle* (Paris: Publications de la Sorbonne, 1999), especially Alain Faure, "Comment devenait-on Parisien? La question de l'intégration dans le Paris de la fin du XIXe siècle," 37–57, and Marie-Claude

Blanc-Chaléard, "Les trois temps du bal-musette ou la place des étrangers (1880–1960)," 77–90.

4. For example, David Garrioch, *Neighbourhood and Community in Paris, 1740–1790* (Cambridge: Cambridge University Press, 1986); Arlette Farge, *La Vie Fragile: Violences, pouvoirs et solidarités à Paris au XVIIIe siècle* (Paris: Hachette, 1992); Eliza Earle Ferguson, *Gender and Justice: Violence, Intimacy and Community in Fin-de-Siècle Paris* (Baltimore: Johns Hopkins University Press, 2010).

5. See https://drnimishabarton.com for supporting statistics.

6. Leslie Page Moch, *The Pariahs of Yesterday: Breton Migrants in Paris* (Durham, NC: Duke University Press, 2012); Françoise Raison-Jourde, *La Colonie Auvergnate de Paris Au XIXe Siècle* (Paris: Ville de Paris, Commission des travaux historiques, 1976); Casey Harison, *The Stonemasons of Creuse in Nineteenth-Century Paris* (Newark: University of Delaware Press, 2008).

7. Paul Cohen-Portheim, *The Spirit of Paris*, trans. Alan Harris (Philadelphia: J. B. Lippincott, 1937), 31.

8. Danielle Chadych and Dominique Leborgne, *C'était Hier . . . Le XIe Arrondissement* (Paris: Editions L.M-Le Point, 1996), 127.

9. The easternmost quartiers of the 18th (La Goutte d'Or and La Chapelle), the 19th, and the 20th arrondissements were far more straightforwardly radical revolutionary. See Giard, "Les Élections à Paris Sous Le IIIe République," vol. 2, 234–303.

10. Giard, "Les Élections à Paris," 239.

11. Letters, Lucien Besset to Garde de Sceau, January 23, 1932; November 16, 1932; May 13, 1933; February 15, 1933, in Maurice Bergman and Brancza née Elefant (3728x32, AN).

12. Letters, Lucien Besset to Minister of Justice, Service de Naturalisations, January 31, 1931; February 16, 1931, in Camille Perron and French Eugénie née Fougassies (28870x29, AN). Besset also wrote for: in 1931 and 1932, Luxemburg-born Nicolas Gudenkauf and French Marie née Mathieu (27478x31, AN); in 1933, the irrepressible Romanian Nicolas Goata and French Emilienne née Authemet (8008x32, AN); and finally, in 1934, Turkish Samuel Bernstein (who lived *maritalement* with a Frenchwoman) (33968x32, AN).

13. Clifford D. Rosenberg, *Policing Paris: The Origins of Modern Immigration Control between the Wars* (Ithaca, NY: Cornell University Press, 2006).

14. CB/44, reg. 21, no. 763 (APP).

15. Rapport, Prefect of Police to Garde de Sceau, April 28, 1943, in José Gimenez and Raymonde née Seez in 5553x32 (AN-Fontainebleau).

16. Rapport, Prefect of Police to Garde de Sceau, March 1941, in Leiba Marcu and Rebecca née Matas (APP, I/A 136).

17. Rapport, Prefect of Police to Garde de Sceau, October 1, 1941; 457e Séance du 4 novembre 1941 (matin), 3e SC, Avis de Retrait pour Chaïm Bromberg, in 14783x31 (AN-Fontainebleau).

18. http://www.v2asp.paris.fr/commun/v2asp/v2/nomenclature_voies/.

19. Jacques Valdour, *De la popinqu'à ménilmuch': observations vécues* (Paris: Editions Spes, 1924), 49–50. On Valdour's politics, see endnote 449 in Alain Faure and Claire Lévy-Vroelant, *Une chambre en ville: Hôtels meublés et garnis de Paris 1860–1990* (Paris: Creaphis Editions, 2007), 410–11.

20. Chadych and Leborgne, *C'était Hier . . . Le XIe Arrondissement*, 160–61.

NOTES TO PAGES 133-137

21. Chadych and Leborgne, *C'était Hier*, 72.
22. See https://drnimishabarton.com for supporting statistics.
23. Valdour, *de la Popinqu'*, 79–80.
24. Office Central des Oeuvres de Bienfaisance et Services Sociaux, *Paris Charitable, Bienfaisant et Social* (Paris: Editions de l'Ouest, 1936), 344. On Italian mutual aid organizations throughout interwar Paris, see Laurent Couder, "Les Italiens de la region Parisienne dans les années 1920" in Pierre Milza, ed., *Les Italiens En France de 1914 à 1940* (Rome: Ecole française de Rome, 1986), 501–46.
25. Office Central des Oeuvres de Bienfaisance et Services Sociaux, *PCBS*, 344.
26. CB/44, reg. 21, no. 238; CB/43, reg. 69, nos. 284–88 (Archives de la Préfecture de la Police, hereafter APP).
27. See https://drnimishabarton.com for supporting statistics.
28. Donna Gabaccia and Elizabeth Zanoni, "Transitions in Gender Ratios among International Migrants, 1820–1930," *Social Science History* 36, no. 2 (2012): 197–221.
29. "Elèves nouveaux entrés dans les écoles publiques de Paris," October 1, 1923, in 50 AP 62 (AN). In 1925, 23,318 foreign children attended public schools in the Seine Department with the majority (14,825) in Paris. "Echos et Variétés: Les enfants étrangers en France," *Bulletin des Associations Familiales* (August/September 1925), 6. See https://drnimishabarton.com for additional statistics.
30. Georges Mauco, "Les Étrangers En France: Étude Géographique Sur Leur Rôle Dans l'activité Économique" (thèse de doctorat ès lettres, Université de Paris, 1932), 299.
31. Office Central des Oeuvres de Bienfaisance et Services Sociaux, *PCBS*, 361, 776.
32. Isaac Morgen, dossier individuel, p. 1–2, in 1368W/70, no. 3301. See also Milhem, dossier familial in 1368W/205, no. 4530; Nouani, dossier familial in 1368W/360, no. 6701 (AdP).
33. La Roquette, 1931 (D2M8/397), 283 (AdP).
34. "Visites de la Société Internationale: L'Union Familale, 185 rue de Charonne et L'Hôpital Populaire, 94, rue de Charonne," Abbé Mainguet, *Revue Philanthropique* 30, no. 175 (November 15, 1911), 537, in 280 PER 30 (Archives de l'Assistance Publique et Hôpitaux de Paris, hereafter APHP).
35. Pierre Hamp, *L'Armée du Salut contre la famine de logis* (Paris: Imprimerie Je Sers), s.d., 20–21, in A3020 (APHP).
36. Charles Schmidt, "Extraits de Presse" in Hamp, *L'Armée du Salut contre la famine de logis*, 48, in A3020 (APHP).
37. Several foreign women who visited another maternalist organization in Paris, the League for Abandoned Mothers, were referred to the Palais de la Femme for room and board. For instance, Belgian Germaine Dewez, folio 11458, carton D84Z/158; Turkish Boulisson Rosso, folio 12993, carton D84Z/157; Polish Valéria Lagiewka, folio 14629, carton D84Z/158; Turkish Hannah Lyons, folio 14832, carton D84Z/158; and Italian Françoise Gregori, folio 17449, carton D84Z/160 (AdP).
38. CB/44, reg. 20, no. 478. See also: CB/43, reg. 65, no. 122 (Archives de la Préfecture de Police, hereafter APP).
39. CB/43, reg. 66, no. 1346 (APP).
40. On rue Amelot, see CB/44, reg. 20, no. 978; CB/43, reg. 65, nos. 91, 175. On rue Daval, see CB/44, reg. 20, no. 813; CB/43, reg. 66, nos. 400, 525, 769. On Place de la Nation, see CB/44, reg. 20, nos. 838, 1133, 194, 411, 518 (APP).

41. CB/44, reg. 20, no. 978 (APP). On prostitution in Paris, see Alain Corbin, *Les filles des noces. Misère sexuelle et prostitution (XIXe et XXe siècles)* (Paris: Aubier Montaigne, 1978); Jill Harsin, *Policing Prostitution in Nineteenth-Century Paris* (Princeton: Princeton University Press, 1985).

42. Adèle Brodski née Bogen in 18276x29; Frida Goldenberg divorcée Zarachowitch, in 70126x28; and Anna Tchervonogour née Fajance, in 11029x29 (all AN).

43. Françoise Dsai: CB/43, reg. 69, nos. 384, 474. Marie Tomasso: CB/43, reg. 69, nos. 477, 1932, 2071, 2237 (APP).

44. CB/43, reg. 69, nos. 295–99 (APP).

45. CB/43, reg. 69, nos. 474–77 (APP).

46. CB/44, reg. 21, no. 539, 762; CB/43, reg. 66, no. 474 (APP).

47. CB/43, reg. 66, no. 4 (APP).

48. For instance, the Algerian Zemmour brothers versus Frenchman Gaston Mathe in CB/44, reg. 20, no. 31; two Italians on rue de Montreuil in CB/44, reg. 21, no. 365; and a large group of Turks on rue Sedaine in CB/43, reg. 66, no. 1092 (APP).

49. George Orwell, *Down and Out in Paris and London* (Orlando: Harcourt, 1961), 96.

50. Motel Mazeur and Rebecca née Hermann, 20215x14 (Archives Nationales, hereafter AN).

51. CB/44, reg. 20, no. 507 (APP).

52. CB/44, reg. 20, no. 1079 (APP).

53. CB/43, reg. 69, no. 987 (APP).

54. CB/44, reg. 20, no. 488 (APP).

55. CB/44, reg. 20, no. 3 (APP).

56. CB/44, reg. 20, no.633 (APP).

57. For modern-day parallels, see Barrère, and Lévy-Vroelant, *Hôtels meublés à Paris, enquête sur une mémoire de l'immigration* (Paris: Créaphis, 2012), 145–47.

58. CB/44, reg.20, no. 588 (APP).

59. CB/43, reg.69, no. 1608 (APP).

60. CB/43, reg.66, no. 632 (APP).

61. CB/44, reg. 20, nos. 727, 632 (APP).

62. Orwell, *Down and Out*, 16.

63. CB/43, reg.69, no. 1691 (APP). In the melting-pot community of South Shields, foreign men were, by contrast, integrated through the "quasi-familial relations between landladies and lodgers." See Laura Tabili, *Global Migrants, Local Culture: Natives and Newcomers in Provincial England, 1841–1939* (Houndmills, UK: Palgrave Macmillan, 2011), 163–64.

64. Orwell, *Down and Out*, 39–40.

65. Alain Faure and Claire Lévy-Vroelant, *Une Chambre en ville: hôtels meublés et garnis de Paris, 1860–1990* (Paris: Créaphis, 2007), 68–69.

66. Jean Claude Farcy, "Archives Policières: Les Répertoires de Procès Verbaux Des Commissariats Parisiens," *Recherches Contemporaines*, no. 5 (1998): 7–8.

67. CB/43, reg. 66, no. 1458 (APP).

68. CB/43, reg. 66, no. 1011 (APP).

69. CB/43, reg. 66, no. 1618 (APP).

70. Faure and Lévy-Vroelant, *Une chambre en ville*, 134–44.

71. Faure and Lévy-Vroelant, *Une chambre en ville*, 50–54, 74–90.

72. Céline Barrère and Claire Lévy-Vroelant, *Hôtels meublés à Paris, enquête sur une mémoire de l'immigration* (Paris: Créaphis, 2012), 91–92.

73. Faure and Lévy-Vroelant, *Une chambre en ville*, 143.

74. CB/44, reg. 20, no. 605 (APP).

75. CB/43, reg. 65, no. 253 (APP).

76. The archives preserve but two examples: first, Berthe Chanowski, a seventeen-year-old Polish garment worker, who illegally sublet to Italian Salvatore Amico, and thus ran afoul of her French proprietor, Paul Zenner; and second, Hana Grumberg, a Romanian woman, who left her room at 50 rue Folie Régnault to give birth to a son, returning several days later to discover that the *hôtelier* had let the room to another occupant. CB/44, reg. 20, no. 727 (APP); CB/43, reg. 65, no. 82 (APP).

77. Delphine Folliet, "Les femmes naturalisées et réintégrées dans le Rhône, 1890–1939" (mémoire, Université Lumière Lyon 2, 2000), 83–90; Marie-Claude Blanc-Chaléard, *Les italiens dans l'est parisien: Une histoire d'intégration (1880–1960)* (Rome: Ecole française de Rome, 2000), 216–31.

78. Rapport de la Police Judiciare fourni par le Brigadier-Chief au sujet du nommé Musso, February 24, 1934, in D2U8 396 (AdP).

79. "Rapport de Police Judiciaire fourni par le Brigadier-Chef Moreaux, le Brigadier Barrad et l'Inspecteur Castex au sujet du nommé Ongaro," April 23, 1930, in D2U8 300 (AdP).

80. Claire Zalc, *Melting Shops: Une Histoire Des Commerçants Étrangers En France* (Paris: Perrin, 2010).

81. Ovcei Tessller and Avram Lavner and Fanny née Grinberg, 46809x27 (AN).

82. Aran Bahr Lubtchansky and Rachel née Zelikowsky, 16320x24 (AN).

83. Jean Haentges and Marie née Maréchal, 1234x1903 (AN); Théodore Haentges and Jeanne Clara née Maréchal, 1233x03 (AN).

84. CB/44, reg. 20, no. 1250 (APP).

85. CB/44, reg. 21, no. 665 (APP).

86. For instance: Polish Mochek Froegel at 26 rue Basfroi (CB/43, reg. 69, no. 1014); Polish Moja Bocian at 4 rue Basfroi (CB/43, reg. 69, no. 1967) (APP).

87. CB/43, reg. 69, nos. 1013, 1029, 1879, 1966, 2347, 2348, 2350 (APP).

88. See https://drnimishabarton.com for supporting statistics.

89. CB/43, reg. 66, no. 762 (APP); Gabaï, dossier familial, p. 2 in 1368W/42, no. 2869 (AdP),

90. Yolanda Foldes, *La Rue Du Chat Qui Pêche* (Paris: Albin Michel, 1937), 20.

91. Jacques Valdour, *De la popinqu'à ménimuch'* (Paris: Editions Spes, 1924), 98.

92. CB/43, reg. 66, nos. 1355, 1356, 1357, and 1358 (APP).

92. CB/44, reg. 20, no. 699 (APP).

94. CB/44, reg. 21, no. 531 (APP).

95. CB/43, reg. 65, no. 137 (APP).

96. Audition de M. Gabriel Ponceft, October 7, 1930 in D2U8 302 (AdP)

97. Garrioch, *Neighbourhood and Community in Paris, 1740–1790*, chap. 3; Farge, *La Vie Fragile*, pt. 2.

98. Réquisitoire définitif, January 13, 1933; Letter, Emilie Ferrari to M. le Procureur Général, October 13, 1932, in D2U8 345 (AdP).

99. Déposition de Jean Signorini, TPI, October 8, 1932, in D2U8 345 (AdP).

100. Déposition d'Edouard Boutier, TPI, October 19, 1932, in D2U8 345 (AdP).

101. Déposition d'Etienne Masson, TPI, October 19, 1932, in D2U8 345 (AdP).
102. Zalc, *Les Melting-Shops*, chap. 7.
103. On rue de Montreuil: CB/44, reg. 21, no. 365, owned by Frenchman Viennet; CB/44, reg. 20, no. 1301, owned by Italian Lucrezia Zuccolini; CB/44, reg. 21, no. 936, operated by Italian Catherine Allochio; CB/44, reg. 21, no. 1042, owned by Luxemburg-born Jean Pierre Kammes. On rue Sedaine: CB/43, reg. 65, no. 276, owned by Algerian Tahar ben Saleh Koubache; CB/43, reg. 65, no. 664, owned by Algerian Akli Ben Amar Ouchon; CB/43, reg. 66, no. 1092, owned by Turk Abraham Kimor; CB/43, reg. 65, no. 476, owned by Turk Marcado Oukki (APP).
104. CB/43, reg. 69, no. 704, owned by Giuseppe Aurora. Bal Delloi: CB/44, reg. 20, no. 194; CB/44, reg. 21, no. 485. On rue de la Roquette: CB/44, reg. 20, no. 547; CB/43, reg. 70, no. 2353 (APP).
105. Valdour, *De la popinqu'à ménilmuch'*, 218.
106. Leslie Page Moch and Rachel Ginnis Fuchs, "Getting Along: Poor Women's Networks in Nineteenth-Century Paris," *French Historical Studies* 18, no. 1 (1993): 44.
107. Cohen-Portheim, *The Spirit of Paris*, 33–34. On the appearance of the "apache" figure in middle-class writings about working-class youth leisure culture, see Scott Haine, "The Development of Leisure and the Transformation of Working-Class Adolescence, Paris 1830–1940," *Journal of Family History* 17, no. 4 (1992): 451–76.
108. Léon-Paul Fargue, *Le Piéton de Paris* (Paris: Gallimard, 1939), 130–31.
109. Cohen-Portheim, *The Spirit of Paris*, 94.
110. For example: CB/43, reg. 66, nos. 1796, 1901 (APP).
111. CB/43, reg. 66, no. 1335 (APP); Cohen-Portheim, *The Spirit of Paris*, 34.
112. Cohen-Portheim, *The Spirit of Paris*, 34.
113. Maurice Polycar, dossier individuel, p. 1, in 1368W/31, no. 2356 (AdP).
114. Valdour, *De la popinqu'à ménilmuch'*, 35.
115. For instance: CB/44, reg. 20, no. 1205; CB/44, reg. 20, no. 80 (APP); Maurice Gabaï, dossier individuel, p. 2, in 1368W/42, no. 2689 (AdP).
116. Ordonnance de Transmission de la Procédure à M. le Procureur Général, TPI, March 26, 1933, in D2U8 363 (AdP).
117. CB/43, reg. 66, no. 589 (APP).
118. For instance, CB/43, reg. 66, no. 1602; CB/44, reg. 20, no. 624, 718 (APP).
119. Foldes, *La Rue du chat qui pêche*, 37.
120. See for instance: CB/43, reg. 66, 1401; CB/44, reg. 20, no. 683 (APP).

6. Motherhood, Neighborhood, and Nationhood

1. Rapport de la Police Judiciaire, January 27, 1933; Ordonnance de Transmission de la Procédure à M. le Procureur Général, TPI, March 26, 1933; Déposition de Berthe Sapsa née Smilovici, TPI, February 4, 1933; Déposition d'Eugénie Pichot née Caillas, January 31, 1933 in D2U8 363 (AdP).
2. Anna Davin, "Imperialism and Motherhood," in *Tensions of Empire: Colonial Cultures in a Bourgeois World* (Berkeley: University of California Press, 1997), 470.
3. "Taux d'accroissement ou de diminution de population et densité de population aux recensements de 1921, 1926 et 1931, à Paris (par arrondissements) et en Banlieue (par communes)," *ASVP* (1927–28), 150.

4. "Etat numérique des feux, par catégorie, dans chacun des quartiers de Paris," *ASVP* (1911), 696–97.

5. "Etat statistique par quartier des établissements dangereuses, insalubres ou incommodes existant à Paris au 31 décembre 1911," *ASVP* (1911), 656–57; ibid., *ASVP* (1914), 596–97; "Nombre des établissements dangereux, insalubres ou incommodes existant dans chaque quartier de Paris," *ASVP* (1921), 418–19; "Nombre des établissements," *ASVP* (1926), 552–53; "Nombre des établissements," *ASVP* (1931), 400–401.

6. "Opérations du bureau d'hygiène de la Ville de Paris et de la Commission des logements insalubres," *ASVP* (1921), 347–48.

7. Albin, dossier familial, p. 2, in 1368W/81, no. 3475 (AdP).

8. Lamiraux, dossier familial, p. 2, in 1368W/193, no. 4385 (AdP).

9. CB/43, reg. 65, no. 74, 222 (APP).

10. "Ilots tuberculeux," *ASVP* (1921–22), 349.

11. Avis du Préfet de Police, November 5, 1923 in Isaac Rubin and Marie née Richkine, 3516x23 (AN).

12. Note, Bureau de Sceau, January 29, 1929 in Zelman Fajgenman and Sura Rymka née Zelbernik, 988x29 (AN).

13. Friedlander, dossier familial, p. 4, in 1368W/218, no. 4669 (AdP).

14. CB/44, reg. 20, no. 806 (APP).

15. "Causes de décès—suicide (36)," *ASVP* (1911), 134–37; "Causes de décès," *ASVP* (1916), 293; "Causes de décès," *ASVP* (1921), 86–89; "Causes de décès," *ASVP* (1926), 152–55; "Causes de décès," *ASVP* (1931), 110–13.

16. CB/44, reg. 20, no 1021 (APP).

17. CB/43, reg. 66, no. 1626 (APP).

18. Françoise Thébaud, *Quand Nos Grand-Mères Donnaient La Vie: La Maternité En France Dans l'entre-Deux-Guerres* (Lyon: Presses universitaires de Lyon, 1986), 183–84.

19. Henri Friedlander, dossier individuel, p. 1, in 1368W/218, no. 4669 (AdP).

20. Brugnon, dossier familial, p. 1, in 1368W/373, no. 7028 (AdP).

21. Seth Koven, *Slumming: Sexual and Social Politics in Victorian London* (Princeton (NJ): Princeton University Press, 2004), 5, 9.

22. George Orwell, *Down and Out in Paris and London* (Orlando: Harcourt, 1961), 27.

23. Joseph Roth, *Hotel Savoy*, trans. John Hoare (1924; reprint Woodstock, NY: Overlook Press, 1986), 33–34.

24. Dossang, dossier familial, 1368W/379, no. 7167; Maillard, dossier familial, 1368W/379, no. 7170; Spilmont, dossier familial, 1368W/164, no. 4028; Briand, dossier familial, 1368W/379, no. 7169 (AdP).

25. Statistique Générale de France, *Statistique Des Familles En 1926* (Paris: Imprimerie nationale, 1932), 18–19, 66, 310–14.

26. See https://drnimishabarton.com for supporting statistics.

27. J. P. Flamand, *Loger le peuple: essai sur l'histoire du logement social en France* (Paris: La Découverte, 1989), 139.

28. See https://drnimishabarton.com for supporting statistics.

29. Deyon, dossier familial, 1368W/283, no. 5470; Grossman, dossier familial, 1368W/346, no. 6330 (AdP).

30. Kohn, dossier familial 1368W/216, no. 4650. Also see the French Delhommes, dossier familial, 1368W/220, no. 4736 (AdP).
31. Liebmann, dossier familial, 1368W/244, no. 4983; Hesmond, dossier familial, 1368W/271, no. 5345; Bruneau, dossier familial, 1368W/296, no. 5620 (AdP).
32. Ibid.
33. Dufresne, dossier familial, 1368W/166, no. 4060 (AdP).
34. Coletta, dossier familial, 1368W/42, no. 2872; Masson, dossier familial, 1368W/46, no. 2972; Jarrige, dossier familial, 1368W/57, no. 3146; Blanquet, dossier familial, 1368W/63, no. 3217; Kerlo, dossier familial, 1368W/214, no. 4629; Chatelain, dossier familial, 1368W/362, no. 6730 (AdP). On the bourgeoisie's developing aversion to the "stench of the masses," see Alain Corbin, *The Foul and the Fragrant: Odor and the French Social Imagination* (Harvard University Press, 1988), chap. 9.
35. Albin, dossier familial, 1368W/81, no. 3475 (AdP).
36. Chachignan, dossier familial, 1368W/31, no. 2338; Morgen, dossier familial, 1368W/70, no. 3301; Polycar, Dossier familial, 1368W/31, no. 2356; Rosant, dossier familial, 1368W/34, no. 2650 (AdP).
37. Briand, dossier familial, 1368W/379, no. 7169 (AdP).
38. Friedlander, dossier familial, p. 3, in 1368W/218, no. 4669 (AdP).
39. Friedlander, dossier familial, p. 3 in 1368W/218, no. 4669 (AdP).
40. Friedlander, dossier familial, p. 4 in 1368W/218, no. 4669 (AdP).
41. Eliza Earle Ferguson, *Gender and Justice: Violence, Intimacy, and Community in Fin-de-Siècle Paris* (Baltimore: Johns Hopkins University Press, 2010), 108.
42. Arlette Farge, *La Vie Fragile: Violences, pouvoirs et solidarités à Paris au XVIIIe siècle* (Paris: Hachette, 1992); *De La Violence Et Des Femmes* (Paris: Albin Michel, 1997); David Garrioch, *Neighbourhood and Community in Paris, 1740–1790* (Cambridge: Cambridge University Press, 1986); Ferguson, *Gender and Justice*.
43. CB/43, reg. 66, no. 420 (APP).
44. Sharon Marcus, *Apartment Stories: City and Home in Nineteenth-Century Paris and London* (Berkeley: University of California Press, 1999), pt. 1.
45. CB/43, reg. 66, no. 420 (APP).
46. Adrienne Rigandie, the *hotelière* of the building located on 22 Passage de la Ruelle in the 18th arrondissement who caught wind of the death of Marie Louise Amghar, the French-born wife of Algerian Amar Amghar on March 16, 1936, because "through my open window the people from the neighborhood were talking about the murder of Madame Amghar." Déposition d'Adrienne Rigandie née Le Favre, TPI, April 20, 1936 in D2U8 490 (AdP).
47. This dispute took place in the adjoining quartier of Folie Méricourt. Audition de June Hélène Brusczywski, March 14, 1939 in D2U8 606 (AdP).
48. Déposition de la Veuve Lina Bertolucci née Bacciola, TPI, November 24, 1933 in D2U8 375 (AdP).
49. CB/44, registre 20, entrée 827 (APP).
50. CB/43, reg. 66, no. 1450 (APP).
51. Isaac Morgen, dossier individuel, p. 2, in 1368W/70, no. 3301 (AdP).
52. Seganti, dossier familial, p. 3, in 1368W/243, no. 4976; Gaudinot, dossier familial, pps. 1–3, in 1368W/287, no. 5514; Morgen, dossier familial, p. 3, in 1368W/70, no. 3301 (AdP)

53. Yolanda Foldes, *La Rue Du Chat Qui Pêche* (Paris: Albin Michel, 1937), 35.

54. "Etat des ménages, veuves et veufs, inscrits à l'assistance obligatoire des familles nombreuses (Loi du 14 juillet 1913)," *ASVP* (1921), 441; "Etat des ménages," *ASVP* (1926), 573; "Etat des ménages," *ASVP* (1931), 425.

55. Dufresne, dossier familial, p. 3, in 1368W/166, no. 4060; Halary, dossier familial, p. 8, in 1368W/356, no. 6575 (AdP).

56. Frischka, dossier familial, p. 7, in in 1368W/98, no. 3703 (AdP); Letter, Nicolas Goata to Minister of Justice, October 10, 1932, in Nicolas Goata and Emilienne née Authemet, 8008x32 (AN).

57. Morgen, dossier familal, p. 2, in 1368W/70, no. 3301 (AdP).

58. Henry A. Victor, *La Maternité de l'Hôpital de Rothschild: son fonctionnement jusqu'en 1930* (Paris: Imprimerie spéciale de la Libraire Le François, 1930), 80–89.

59. Dufresne, dossier familial, p. 3, in 1368W/166, no. 4060 (AdP).

60. Gabaï, dossier familial, p. 5, in 1368W/42, no. 2869 (AdP).

61. Fédération des Cantines Maternelles, *Les Cantines Maternelles* (1923) in DX6/6, art. 202 (AdP); *Les Cantines Maternelles* (1927), in DX6/28, art. 1278 (AdP).

62. Office Central des Oeuvres de Bienfaisance et Services Sociaux, *Paris charitable, bienfaisant et social* (Paris: Plon, 1926), 776.

63. Halary, dossier familial p. 2, 4, in 1368W/356, no. 6575 (AdP). On these organizations, see Rachel Ginnis Fuchs, *Poor and Pregnant in Paris: Strategies for Survival in the Nineteenth Century* (New Brunswick, NJ: Rutgers University Press, 1992), 131–32.

64. *Société Protectrice de l'Enfance* (1922–1923), in DX6/6, art. 215 (AdP).

65. *Ligue française des mères de famille* (1925), in DX6/7, art. 238 (AdP).

66. *Société de Charité Maternelle de Paris* (1926), in DX 6/6, art. 250 (AdP). On the Société de Charité Maternelle, see Christine Adams, *Poverty, Charity, and Motherhood: Maternal Societies in Nineteenth-Century France* (Urbana: University of Illinois Press, 2010).

67. Letter, Madame Goata to Minister of Justice, May 28, 1935, in Nicolas Goata and Emilienne née Authemet, 8008x32 (AN); Halary, dossier familial, p. 2, in 1368W/356, no. 6575 (AdP).

68. Déposition de Jenny née Ziszovitz femme Herskowitz, TPI, December 11, 1934, in D2U8 400 (AdP).

69. See https://drnimishabarton.com for supporting statistics.

70. Anne-Marie Sohn, *Chrysalides: Femmes Dans La Vie Privée (XIXe–XXe Siècles)* (Paris: Publications de la Sorbonne, 1996), chap. 5.

71. Crèches, art. 274, DX6/8 (AdP).

72. Renée Friedlander, dossier individuel, p. 1, in 1368W/218, no. 4669; Halary, dossier familial, p. 11, in 1368W/356, no. 6575 (AdP).

73. Frischka, dossier familial, p. 4, in 1368/98, no. 3703 (AdP).

74. Gabaï, dossier familial, p. 3, in 1368W/42, no. 2869; Friedlander, dossier familial, p. 4, in 1368W/218, no. 4669 (AdP).

75. Bajroch, dossier familial, p. 3–4, in 1368W/364, no. 6781 (AdP).

76. Audition de Haver née Mandelbaum femme Goldseigel, TPI, May 22, 1934, in D2U8 390 (AdP).

77. Polish Isaac Bajroch, dossier familial, p. 4, in 1368W/364, no. 6781; Russian Henri Friedlander, dossier individuel, p. 1, in 1368W/218, no. 4669; Polish Isaac Morgen, dossier individuel, p. 1, in 1368W/70, no. 3301; Turkish Robert Gabaï, dossier

individuel, p. 1, in 1368W/42, no. 2869; Hungarian Georges Kiradi, dossier familial, p. 3, in 1368W/293, no. 5584; Romanian Ladislas Kohn, dossier familial, p. 4, in 1368W/216, no. 4650; Turkish Marcel Polycar, dossier familial, p. 5, in 1368/31, no. 2356 (AdP).

78. French Fernande Dufresne, dossier familial, p. 4, in 1368W/166, no. 4060; Polish Berthe Grossman, dossier familial, p. 4 in 1368W/346, no. 6330 (AdP).

79. Rapport, March 16, 1928, in Israel Mechoulam and Zimboul née Machiah (I/A 140, APP).

80. CB/44, reg. 21, no. 7 (APP).

81. CB/44, reg. 21, no. 407 (APP).

82. CB/44, reg. 20, no. 510 (APP).

83. CB/44, reg. 20, no. 765 (APP).

84. CB/44, reg. 20, no. 20 (APP).

85. CB/43, reg. 66, no. 1448 (APP).

86. Luxemburg-native Marie Marguerite Koenev, written up in 1926 for shaking out chiffon covers from her apartment window on 212 boulevard Voltaire (CB/44, reg. 20, no. 649); Romanian Udlea Lipniziki, caught in 1933 for shaking out the family's linens and bedcovers early in the morning from her home on 216 boulevard Voltaire (CB/44, reg. 21, no. 561); Russian Revbecca Grodner beat her rug from her window on rue Jean Macé in the evening (CB/44, reg. 20, no. 413) (APP).

87. Déposition de Hélène née Oliviero femme Plisson, TPI, December 2, 1937; Déposition de Germaine née Lebeque femme Lambrechts, TPI, February 2, 1938; Déposition de Berthe née Plentin femme Mangeard, TPI, February 7, 1938; Réquisitoire définitif, July 26, 1938 in D2U8 582 (AdP).

88. Déposition de Léontine Dumaine, TPI, March 13, 1939; Déposition de Fatma Ben Salah, TPI, March 13, 1939; Réquisitoire définitif, June 20, 1939 in D2U8 600 (AdP).

89. Esther Maoul, folio no. 19179, D84Z 162 (AdP).

90. Halary, dossier familial, p. 6, in 1368W/356, no. 6575 (AdP).

91. Ghersa, dossier familial, p. 7, in 1368W/245, no. 5001 (AdP).

92. Déposition de Rywka Lustmann née Vayjngarten, TPI, December 7, 1933; Rapport médical, Doctor André Cellier, January 13, 1934, 9–10 in D2U8 387 (AdP).

93. Yolanda Foldes, *La Rue Du Chat Qui Pêche*, 39.

94. CB/43, reg. 69, no. 910 (APP).

95. Pomeranc, dossier familial in 1368W/216, no. 4651; Kohn, dossier familial in 1368W/216, no. 4650 (AdP).

96. Marcel Polycar, dossier individuel, pps. 4, 6–7, 9–10, in 1368W/31, no. 2356 (AdP).

97. Halimi, dossier familial, p.3, in 1368W/228, no. 4815 (AdP).

98. On sexual relationships between Frenchwomen and black colonial subjects in interwar Paris, see Jennifer Anne Boittin, *Colonial Metropolis: The Urban Grounds of Anti-Imperialism and Feminism in Interwar Paris* (Lincoln: University of Nebraska Press, 2010), chap. 2.

99. Halimi, dossier familial, p. 7, in in 1368W/228, no. 4815 (AdP).

100. Dumur, dossier familial, p. 2, in 1368W/404, no. 7892 (AdP).

101. Ghersa, dossier familial, p. 2, in 1368W/245, no. 5001 (AdP).

102. Benadis, dossier familial, pps. 1–3, in 1368W/513, no. 10732 (AdP).

103. CB/44, reg. 21, no. 54 (APP).

104. Gabaï, dossier familial, pps. 9–10, in 1368W/42, no. 2869 (AdP).

105. Turkish Sultane Mizraki, folio 4532, carton D84Z/148; Polish Faiga Malkowski, folio 4945, carton D84Z/149; Polish Madame Brylant, folio 15156, carton D84Z/158; and Polish Fajgala Steruic, folio 1558, carton D84Z/146 (AdP).

106. Yvonna Piech, folio 11156, carton D84Z/155 (AdP).

107. Déposition de Marcelle Prevost, TPI, August 6, 1930; Déposition d'Adèle Bordon née Rateau, TPI, August 6, 1930 (AdP).

108. Italian Victorine Pellati (Procès-verbal d'interrogatoire et de confrontation, October 13, 1931 in D2U8 315); Spanish Manuela Martinez (Ordonnance de Transmission de la Procédure, TPI, March 4, 1931 in D2U8 320); Polish Perla Wirmykamien or Winnykamien (Réquisitoire définitif, 28 May 1936 in D2U8 500)—all AdP.

109. Procès-verbal interrogatoire et de confrontation, TPI, January 23, 1934; Déposition de Mélanie née Rochet femme Mille, TPI, April 24, 1934 in D2U8 396 (AdP).

110. Garrioch, *Neighbourhood and Community in Paris, 1740–1790*, 35–36; Marcus, *Apartment Stories*, pt. 3; Ferguson, *Gender and Justice*, 119–20.

111. Anaïs Albert, "Le crédit à la consommation des classes populaires à la Belle Époque," *Annales. Histoire, Sciences Sociales* 67, no. 4 (2012): 1058–60.

112. CB/43, reg. 66, no. 1494 (APP).

113. Audition de Désirée Attry née Guerin, Commissaire de Police de Sainte Marguerite, January 18, 1934 in D2U8 363 (AdP).

114. Déposition de Marie Louise Vax née Behrel, TPI, February 4, 1933 for in D2U8 363 (AdP).

115. Gabaï, dossier familial, pps. 5, 10–11 in 1368W/42, no. 2869 (AdP).

116. CB/44, reg. 20, no. 303 (APP).

117. CB/43, reg. 65, no. 210 (APP).

118. Italian Victorine Bracchi paid one Frenchman and two Italians she knew from the neighborhood fifty francs a piece to move her furniture from her *ménage* on rue Julien Lacroix in the 20th arrondissement (Rapport de la Police Judiciaire fourni par les Inspecteurs Reumont et Rigaud au sujet de la plainte du sieur Pellati, March 24, 1930 in D2U8 315). So, too, did Polish Feyda Aboulicam sell her furniture when she left her husband, Octave. Déposition de Feyda Steakling femme Aboulicam, TPI, April 11, 1934 in D2U8 398 (AdP).

119. Déposition d'Yvonne Hiernard née Bertrand, TPI, September 19, 1935, in D2U8 496 (AdP).

120. Déposition de Claire Noe née Lagorce, TPI, August 6, 1930, in D2U8 300 (AdP). See also Devos, dossier familial, pps. 1–6 in 1368W/387, no. 7369 (AdP).

121. CB/43, reg. 66, no. 675 (APP).

122. Gabaï, dossier familial, p. 3, in 1368W/42, no. 2869 (AdP).

123. CB/43, reg. 66, no. 420; Minutes, August 3, 1926, *Bulletin Municipal Officiel*, 3705–6 (APP).

124. Undated petition in D2U8 320 (AdP).

125. Letter, Pierre Hagjarian, Madame Hadjarian, and Henriette Namy to M. le Procureur de la République, January 18, 1937, in D2U8 531 (AdP).

126. Déposition de Marie femme Le Roy née Leroux, TPI, November 16, 1936; Déposition d'Aimée femme Lerat née Testard, TPI, November 16, 1936 in ibid (AdP).

7. Neighborly Networks and Welfare Work under Vichy

1. To borrow the terms of Eugen Weber, *The Hollow Years: France in the 1930s* (New York: W. W. Norton, 1994); Julian Jackson, *France: The Dark Years, 1940–1944* (Oxford: Oxford University Press, 2001).

2. Robert O. Paxton, *Vichy France: Old Guard and New Order, 1940–1944*, Morningside ed. (New York: Columbia University Press, 1982).

3. Renée Poznanski, *Jews in France during World War II*, trans. Nathan Bracher (Waltham, MA: Brandeis University Press, 2001); Lucien Lazare, *La résistance juive en France* (Paris: Stock, 1987).

4. Béatrice Le Douairon, "Le Comité Rue Amelot, 1940–1944, à Paris: Assistance Aux Juifs et Sauvetage Des Enfants" (maîtrise d'histoire, Université de Paris I-Sorbonne, 1994); Jacqueline Baldran and Claude Bochurberg, *David Rapoport, "La mère et l'enfant," 36 rue Amelot* (Paris: Montorgueil-CDJC, 1994); Lucien Lazare, *Rescue as Resistance: How Jewish Organizations Fought the Holocaust in France* (New York: Columbia University Press, 1996), 39–47. On Amelot within the typology of resistance movements, see Renée Poznanski, "Juifs Dans La Résistance," in *Dictionnaire Historique de La Résistance* (Paris: Editions Robert Laffont, 2006), 897–98; Renée Poznanski, "Sauvetage Des Juifs," in *Dictionnaire Historique de La Résistance* (Paris: Editions Robert Laffont, 2006), 694–95.

5. On French resistance historiographies, see Renée Poznanski, "Rescue of the Jews and the Resistance in France: From History to Historiography," *French Politics, Culture & Society* 30, no. 2 (2012): 8–32. On women's understudied participation in the resistance, see Rita Thalmann, "L'oubli des femmes dans l'historiographie de la Résistance," *Clio. Femmes, Genre, Histoire* 1, no. 1 (April 1995): 1–9; Veillon, "Femmes Dans La Résistance Intérieure," in *Dictionnaire Historique de La Résistance* (Paris: Editions Robert Laffont, 2006), 884–85. On social workers in the resistance, see Armelle Mabon-Fall, *Les assistantes sociales au temps de Vichy: du silence à l'oubli* (Paris: L'Harmattan, 1995), chaps. 2–4; Margaret Collins Weitz, *Sisters in the Resistance: How Women Fought to Free France, 1940–1945* (New York: John Wiley, 1995), chap. 8; Jean-Pierre Le Crom, *Au secours, Maréchal! : l'instrumentalisation de l'humanitaire, 1940–1944*, 1st ed. (Paris: Presses universitaires de France, 2013), chap. 8.

6. Nicolas Mariot and Claire Zalc, "Les Juifs Du Bassin de Lens Face à Leurs Voisins: Concurrences, Dénonciations, Entraides (1940–1945)," in *Etranges Voisins: Alterité et Relations de Proximité Dans La Ville Depuis Le XVIIIe Siècle* (Paris: Presses Universitaires de Rennes, 2010), 237–53; Shannon Lee Fogg, *The Politics of Everyday Life in Vichy France: Foreigners, Undesirables, and Strangers* (New York: Cambridge University Press, 2009), chap. 4; Jacques Semelin, *Persécutions et Entraides Dans La France Occupée: Comment 75% Des Juifs En France Ont Échappé à La Mort* (Paris: Editions des Arènes, 2013).

7. Semelin, *Persécutions et Entraides*; Aurélia Kalisky and Catherine Coquio, eds., *L'enfant et le génocide : témoignages sur l'enfance pendant la Shoah*, Bouquins (Paris: R. Laffont, 2007), xv, 720. On collaboration and survival in the Netherlands and Belgium, see Bob Moore, *Victims and Survivors: The Nazi Persecution of the Jews in the Netherlands, 1940–1945* (London: Arnold, 1997); Gerhard Hirschfeld, *Nazi Rule and Dutch Collaboration: The Netherlands under German Occupation, 1940–1945* (New York; New York: St. Martin's Press, 1988); Dan Mikhman and Mazal Holocaust Collection,

Belgium and the Holocaust: Jews, Belgians, Germans (Jerusalem: Yad Vashem, 1998); Suzanne Vromen, *Hidden Children of the Holocaust: Belgian Nuns and Their Daring Rescue of Young Jews from the Nazis* (Oxford: Oxford University Press, 2008).

8. Letter, Mademoiselle Haux to Madame Valensi, 19 August 1941 in CMXXI-17 (Centre de documentation juive contemporaine, hereafter CDJC).

9. Sabine Zeitoun, *Histoire de l'O.S.E. De La Russie Tsariste à l'Occupation En France (1912–1944)*; and *L'Oeuvre de Secours Aux Enfants Du Légalisme à La Résistance*. (Paris: L'Harmattan, 2012), 196.

10. "Instructions du Chef du Service Social Des Etrangers à Messieurs les Délégués Régionaux du SSE, Messieurs les Délégués Départementaux du SSE, Messieurs les Délégués du SSE dans les Centres de Regroupements," 26 August 1942 in CMXXI-17 (CDJC). Emphasis mine.

11. Remi Lenoir, "Family Policy in France since 1938," in *The French Welfare State: Surviving Social and Ideological Change* (New York: New York University Press, 1991), 158–59; Miranda Pollard, *Reign of Virtue: Mobilizing Gender in Vichy France* (Chicago: University of Chicago Press, 1998), 103–16, 121–24; Christophe Capuano, *Vichy et La Famille: Réalités et Faux-Semblants d'une Politique Publique* (Rennes: Presses Universitaires de Rennes, 2009).

12. Le Crom, *Au secours, Maréchal!*, 115–19.

13. Letter, Directeur Général de l'Administration de l'Assistance Publique de Paris to Préfet de la Seine, Directrice des Affaires Economique et Sociales, December 16, 1943, in Dossier 3f, DLXXXIV, Fonds Comité Amelot (CDJC).

14. Letter, Commissaire Général aux Questions Juives to the President of UGIF, January 15, 1944, in Dossier 3f, DLXXXIV, Fonds Comité Amelot (CDJC). Emphasis mine.

15. Jules Jacoubovitch, *Rue Amelot* (Paris: Centre MEDEM, 2006), sec. Lexique; Baldran and Bochurberg, *David Rapoport*, chap. 1.

16. Anne Lévy, "Témoignage non signé par l'auteur, racontant le rôle de la rue Amelot et de son directeur, Monsieur Rappoport," in DLXI-2 (CDJC); Jules Jacoubovitch, *L'Un de Trente-Six* (Paris: Kyoum, 1946), 21.

17. Centre de documentation juive contemporaine, *Activité des organisations juives en France sous l'occupation* (Paris: CDJC, 1947), 210–11; Jacoubovitch, *Rue Amelot*, chap. 8. On the UGIF and the nature of Franco-Jewish collaboration during WWII, see Zeitoun, *Histoire de l'O.S.E.*, 156–59.

18. Untitled, August 30, 1945, in CMXXI-17 (CDJC).

19. Jacoubovitch, *Rue Amelot*, chap. 2. On denunciations in Vichy France, see Laurent Joly, *Dénoncer Les Juifs Sous l'Occupation* (Paris: CNRS Editions, 2017); Mariot and Zalc, "Les Juifs Du Bassin de Lens Face à Leurs Voisins."

20. Jacoubovitch, *Rue Amelot*, chap. 4.

21. "Fonds Octobre 1940," in Dossier 4a, DLXXXIV, Fonds Comité Amelot (CDJC).

22. See correspondence contained in Dossier 5d, DLXXXIV, Fonds Comité Amelot; "Novembre 1940," in Dossier 4a, DLXXXIV, Fonds Comité Amelot; Jacques Biélinky, *Journal, 1940–1942: Un Journaliste Juif à Paris Sous l'Occupation*, ed. Renée Poznanski (Paris: Les Editions du Cerf, 1992).

23. Jacoubovitch, *Rue Amelot*, chaps. 1, Lexique.

24. Jacoubovitch, *Rue Amelot*, chap. 5.

25. Untitled, August 30,1945, in CMXXI-17 (CDJC).
26. Biélinky, *Journal*, 229.
27. On the OSE, see Zeitoun, *L'Oeuvre de Secours aux enfants (O.S.E.)*; Zeitoun, *Histoire de l'O.S.E.*
28. Le Douairon, "Le Comité Rue Amelot," 82.
29. Untitled, August 30, 1945, in CMXXI-17 (CDJC).
30. For example, the correspondence contained in Dossier 5e, DLXXXIV, Fonds Comité Amelot (CDJC).
31. Rapport pour le mois d'octobre 1941 in Dossier 4b, DLXXXIV, Fonds Comité Amelot (CDJC). On the juridical service, see Baldran and Bochurberg, *David Rapoport*, 101.
32. In a July 1948 note to readers, Jacoubovitch prefaced his autobiography, "We were not romantics and we were not heroes of history [*ne faisions pas de l'héroïsme pour l'histoire*]. All completed their duties as naturally as [they completed] their social activities from before the war." (Jacoubovitch, *Rue Amelot*, Note aux lecteurs)
33. Rapport, Prefect of Police to Garde des Sceaux, April 24, 1944, in Raphael Obadia and Suzanne née Trevese, 9348x33 (AN-Fontainebleau).
34. Rapport, Prefect of Police to Garde des Sceaux, May 25, 1943, in Herzlik Chenochowitcz and Perla née Nilchcicka (AN-Fontainebleau).
35. Rapport, January–February 1944, page 1 in Dossier 3g, DLXXXIV, Fonds Comité Amelot (CDJC).
36. Baldran and Bochurberg, *David Rapoport*, 119.
37. Dossier 2d and 3a, DLXXXIV, Fonds Comité Amelot; Untitled, August 30, 1945, in CMXXI-17 (CDJC).
38. Letter cited in Baldran and Bochurberg, *David Rapoport*, 116.
39. "Colis envoyés au mois de mai 1944," in CMXXI-17 (CDJC).
40. Jacoubovitch, *Rue Amelot*, chap. 5; Centre de documentation juive contemporaine, *Activité des organisations juives*, 193; Jacoubovitch, *L'Un de Trente-Six*, 30; Biélinky, *Journal*, 113.
41. Le Douairon, "Le Comité Rue Amelot," 63.
42. "Rapport sur la visite aux enfants de la Nièvre, 18 mai 1944," in CMXXI-17 (CDJC).
43. Le Douairon, "Le Comité Rue Amelot," 64–66.
44. Le Douairon, "Le Comité Rue Amelot," 72.
45. Ivan Jablonka, *Ni père ni mère: histoire des enfants de l'Assistance Publique, 1874–1939* (Paris: Seuil, 2006), chaps. 1–3.
46. Sabine Zeitoun, *Ces enfants qu'il fallait sauver* (Paris: Albin Michel, 1989), 34; Zeitoun, *Histoire de l'O.S.E.*, chap. 4.
47. Jacoubovitch, *Rue Amelot*, chap. 7; Jacoubovitch, *L'Un de Trente-Six*, 23–24, 44.
48. Jacoubovitch, *Rue Amelot*, chap. 7; Zeitoun, *Histoire de l'O.S.E.*, 172.
49. Letter from Madame Veuve Hergaux to Groupe Amelot, December 28, 1943, in CMXXI-17 (CDJC).
50. Letter from Madame Veuve Vaucelle to Groupe Amelot, March 12, 1944, in CMXXI-17 (CDJC).
51. Letter from Madame Le Laire to Groupe Amelot, 1944, in CMXXI-17 (CDJC).
52. Letter from Madame G. Puchère to Colonie scolaire, May 23, 1942, in Dossier 2d, DLXXXIV, Fonds Comité Amelot (CDJC).

53. Zeitoun, *Ces enfants qu'il fallait sauver*, 52; Zeitoun, *L'Œuvre de secours aux enfants (O.S.E.)*, 43.

54. Quoted in Poznanski, "Rescue of the Jews and the Resistance in France," 17.

55. Jacoubovitch, *Rue Amelot*, chap. 7.

56. Mikhman and Mazal Holocaust Collection, *Belgium and the Holocaust*, 31; Moore, *Victims and Survivors*, 161, 162, 256, 257–58.

57. Lieven Saerens, "Antwerp's Attitude Toward the Jews from 1918 to 1940 and Its Implications for the Period of the Occupation," in *Belgium and the Holocaust* (Jerusalem: Yad Vashem, 1998), 161, 194.

58. Oral history of Henri Bulowko in Baldran and Bochurberg, *David Rapoport*, 183.

59. Groupe Saint-Maurien Contre l'Oubli, *Les Orphelins de La Varenne, 1941–1944* (Saint-Maur: Société d'histoire et d'archéologie "Le Vieux Saint-Maur," 1995), 78.

60. Lévy, "Témoignage non signé," in DLXI-2; Jacoubovitch, *L'Un de Trente-Six*, 34; Centre de documentation juive contemporaine, *Activité des organisations juives*, 194; Groupe Saint-Maurien Contre l'Oubli, *Les Orphelins de La Varenne*, 76.

61. Letters to Madame Stern, March 1943, in CDXXVI-6; "Contrôle à domicile, 1942–1943," in CMXXI-17 (CDJC).

62. Zeitoun, *Ces enfants qu'il fallait sauver*, 51–52, 146–47.

63. Zeitoun, *L'Œuvre de secours aux enfants (O.S.E.)*, 50; Zeitoun, *Ces enfants qu'il fallait sauver*, 51–52.

64. Oral history of Berthe Zysman in Baldran and Bochurberg, *David Rapoport*, 181.

65. Zeitoun, *Histoire de l'O.S.E.*, 215. On the actions of Secours National social workers on behalf of Jewish families, see Mabon-Fall, *Les assistantes sociales au temps de Vichy*, 53–63.

66. Le Douairon, "Le Comité Rue Amelot," 95–96.

67. "Statistique globale d'octobre 1943," in CMXXI-17 (CDJC); Le Douairon, "Le Comité Rue Amelot," 82.

68. Le Douairon, "Le Comité Rue Amelot," 69–70.

69. Oral history of Marthe Laborde, in Groupe Saint-Maurien Contre l'Oubli, *Les Orphelins de La Varenne*, 44–45, 77.

70. Zeitoun, *L'Œuvre de secours aux enfants (O.S.E.)*, chap. 8.

71. Zeitoun, *Ces enfants qu'il fallait sauver*, 183–84; Zeitoun, *L'Œuvre de secours aux enfants (O.S.E.)*, 155–56; Le Crom, *Au secours, Maréchal!*

72. Jacoubovitch, *L'Un de Trente-Six*, 37; Zeitoun, *Histoire de l'O.S.E.*, 52–53, 136.

73. Sura Cukier, folio no. 14065, D84Z 158 (AdP). See also Italian Halia Pazzaia, folio no. 14165, D84Z 158; Czech Maria Hargasova, folio no. 15669, D84Z 159; Polish Marinette Wajda, folio no. 15805, D84Z 159; Widow Bernasconi, French-born, but Italian by marriage, folio no. 17339, D84Z 160 (AdP).

74. Sura Ryka Ilotogorski, folio no. 21412, D84Z 163 (AdP).

75. Katy Hazan, *Le sauvetage des enfants juifs pendant l'occupation, dans les maisons de l'OSE* (Paris: Œuvre de secours aux enfants, 2008).

76. Zeitoun, *L'Œuvre de secours aux enfants (O.S.E.)*, 53.

77. Zeitoun, *Ces enfants qu'il fallait sauver*, 33, 35, 38; Kalisky and Coquio, *L'enfant et le génocide*, 753–806; Charlotte Schapira, *Il faudra que je me souvienne: la déportation des enfants de l'Union générale des israélites de France*, Mémoires du XXe siècle (Paris: L'Harmattan, 1994); Laura Lee Downs, *Childhood in the Promised Land: Working-Class*

Movements and the Colonies de Vacances in France, 1880–1960 (Durham, NC: Duke University Press, 2002).

78. Oral history in Zeitoun, *Ces enfants qu'il fallait sauver*, 61.
79. Zeitoun, *Ces enfants qu'il fallait sauver*, 33.
80. Jablonka, *Ni père ni mère*, 263–64.
81. Kalisky and Coquio, *L'enfant et le génocide*, 806; Groupe Saint-Maurien Contre l'Oubli, *Les Orphelins de La Varenne*, 77–78.
82. Daniel Lee, *Petain's Jewish Children: French Jewish Youth and the Vichy Regime, 1940–1942* (Oxford: Oxford University Press, 2014).
83. Kalisky and Coquio, *L'enfant et le génocide*, 720.
84. Lévy, "Témoignage non signé par l'auteur" in DLXI-2 (CDJC); Jacoubovitch, *L'Un de Trente-Six*, 7.
85. "Rapport sur la visite aux enfants faite en mars 1944," p. 1; "Rapport sur la visite aux enfants de la Nièvre, 18 mai 1944," p. 2, in CMXXI-17 (CDJC).
86. Jacoubovitch, *Rue Amelot*, chap. 7; Le Douairon, "Le Comité Rue Amelot," 84; Centre de documentation juive contemporaine, *Activité des organisations juives*, 194.
87. Le Douairon, "Le Comité Rue Amelot," 81–82.
88. Patrick Weil, *Qu'est-Ce Qu'un Français: Histoire de La Nationalité Française Depuis La Révolution* (Paris: Grasset, 2002), 175–202; Claire Zalc, *Dénaturalisés: Les Retraits de Nationalité Sous Vichy* (Paris: Seuil, 2016).
89. Rapport, Prefect of Police to Garde des Sceaux, January 18, 1944, in Haïm Goldenstein, 54358x28 (AN).
90. Rapport, Prefect of Police to Garde des Sceaux, March 23, 1943, in Max Gourevitch and Berthe née Dambo, 15871x30; Rapport, Prefect of Police to Garde des Sceaux, July 13, 1943, in Mentech Camhi and Sol née Colonomos, 32174x29; Rapport, Prefect of Police to Garde des Sceaux, July 2, 1943, in Haim Esperance and Djoya née Sichen, 19258x29 (AN).
91. Rapport, Prefect of Police to Garde des Sceaux, March 19, 1943, in Jacob Handkan and Elsa née Manachem, 33382x29 (AN); Rapport, Prefect of Police to Garde des Sceaux, September 13, 1943, in Israel Mechoulam and Zimboul née Machiah, I/A 140 (APP); Letter, Prefect of Cantal to Garde des Sceaux, March 13, 1944, in Abraham Khenkine and Beila née Douskine, 44069x27 (AN).
92. Rapport, Prefect of Police to Garde des Sceaux, January 3, 1944, in Leiba Kreis and Shiffra née London, 47720x28 (AN); Letter, Prefect of Police to Garde des Sceaux, September 10, 1943, in Nissim Schenkermann and Czina née Libmann in I/A 186 (APP).
93. Rapport, Prefect of Police to Garde des Sceaux, March 21, 1944, in Benjamin Lachminovitch and Léa née Melikovitch, 14514x27 (AN) and I/A 119 (APP). See also Rapport, Prefect of Police to Garde des Sceaux, March 1941 in Leiba Marcu and Rebecca née Matas, I/A 136 (APP); Rapport, Prefect of Police to Garde des Sceaux, October 1, 1941 in Chaïm Bromberg, 14783x31 (AN-Fontainebleau).
94. For example, the following families: Romanian-born Strul Cojocariu and Rachel née Altarovici, 15134x30; Russian-born Isaac Engine and Olga née Posoff, 25488x27; Russian-born Meyer Bober and Itta née Einntine, 22674x25 (AN).
95. For example: Russian-born Hilka Drapkine and Rachel née Berkovitch, 974x29; Leiba Sapoznik, 9652x25; Romanian- and French-born Arnold Feldstein and

Lucie née Cahen, 9541x30; Russian-born Isaac Moschkowitsch and Liba née Spekter, 63851x28; Romanian-born David Croitoru and Fanny née Gutman, 43451x27 (AN).

96. Letter, Procureur of the Republic to Garde des Sceaux, May 27, 1943, in Adolphe Kraousmann and Fanny née Moscovici, 21610x25 (AN).

97. Zalc, *Dénaturalisés*, chap. 7.

98. Letter, Joina Rabinovici to Minister of Justice, February 11, 1942; Note, CRN, August 10, 1943; Note, CRN, December 18, 1943, in Joina Rabinovici, 59332x28 (AN).

99. Letter to Juge d'Instruction, September 25, 1944, in Sasson, 1368W/513 no. 10727 (AdP).

100. Oral history in Danielle Bailly, ed., *Traqués, cachés, vivants: des enfants juifs en France, 1940–1945: ensemble de récits de témoignage, Judaïsmes* (Paris: L'Harmattan, 2004), 57.

101. Oral history in Bailly, 143–44.

102. Oral history in Zeitoun, *Ces enfants qu'il fallait sauver*, 17–20, 57–59.

103. Oral history in Bailly, *Traqués, cachés, vivants*, 58.

104. Joly, *Dénoncer Les Juifs*.

105. Rapport, Prefect of Police to Garde des Sceaux, December 9, 1943, in Samuel Almozinos and Renée Jeanne née Bichet, 18713x27 (AN).

106. Oral histories in: Schapira, *Il faudra que je me souvienne*, 36; Zeitoun, *Ces enfants qu'il fallait sauver*, 31, 32, 34, 71–72; Kalisky and Coquio, *L'enfant et le génocide*, 755, 762; Bailly, *Traqués, cachés, vivants*, 81, 99, 132, 168.

107. Paula Schwartz, "Redefining Resistance: Women's Activism in Wartime France," in *Behind the Lines: Gender and the Two World Wars* (New Haven: Yale University Press, 1987), 145.

108. Oral history in Bailly, *Traqués, cachés, vivants*, 144.

109. Rapport, Prefect of Police to Garde des Sceaux, December 23, 1940, in Leiba Marcu and Rebecca née Matas, I/A 136 (APP).

110. Zalc, *Dénaturalisés*, 142–45, 188–90.

111. Rapport, Prefect of Police to Garde des Sceaux, November 24, 1943; and Avis, Prefect of Police to Garde des Sceaux, February 4, 1944, in Jacques Aizenstein and Georgette née Crinière, I/A 3 (APP); Police report, April 14, 1942, in Szulim Bram and Cécile née Rajter, I/A 28 (APP); Rapport, Prefect of Police to Garde des Sceaux, January 6, 1944, in Ricoula née Faraggi veuve Levy, 54372x28 (AN). See also Samuel Bernstein, 33968x32; Samuel Eskenazi and Djoya née Jerusalmi, 12268x35; Boris Trotchansky and Fany née Litvine, 2234x33 (AN-Fontainebleau).

112. Rapport, Prefect of Police to Garde des Sceaux, October 8, 1943 in Jacob Arditti and Alégrine née Sidi, I/A 7 (APP). See also Léon Mizrahi and Sarah née Azouz, 127x30; Jacob Hara and Estréa née Azouz, 93719x28; in Nissim Polikar and Rachel née Serror, 31167x27 (AN).

113. Rapport, Prefect of Police to Garde des Sceaux, May 19, 1943, in Maurice Baitschmann and Rachel née Loeb, 20570x29 (AN). See also Charles Epelbaum and Bastia née Levit, 25267x29; Elie Levitetz, 19271x29 (AN).

114. Rapport, Prefect of Police to Garde des Sceaux, October 1, 1943, in David Friedland and Léa née Kolsky, 17071x25 (AN).

115. Biélinky, *Journal*, 112, 135, 230.

116. Rapport, Prefect of Police to Garde de Sceaux, February 23, 1944, in Abraham Kouperschmidt and Sisla née Childebrand, 15089x25 (AN).

117. Rapport, Prefect of Police to Garde de Sceaux, February 4, 1944, in Saul Veissid and Fanny née Ovadia, 24740x27 (AN).

118. Letter, Mademoiselle Haux to Madame Valensi, August 19, 1941, in CMXXI-17 (CDJC).

119. See for instance, Russian-born Aron Epstein and Rosa née Levias, 24522x27; Turkish-born Isaac Cohen and Estréa née Jafet, 17815x29 (AN).

120. Police report, April 7, 1943, in Szmul Wintermann and Tauba née Szon, I/A 222 (APP). See also Suzanne Obadia, Turkish-born wife of a deportee and mother of seven, in Raphael Obadia and Suzanne née Trevese, 9348x33 (AN-Fontainebleau).

121. Rapport, Prefect of Police to Garde des Sceaux, July 21, 1943; Note, CRN, 13 December 1943; Note CRN, May 13, 1944, in Idel Korntajer and Ida née Bok, 4756x30 (AN).

122. Rapport, Prefect of Police to Garde des Sceaux, May 12, 1942; Avis de la Sous Commission Spéciale, March 28, 1944 in Raphael Behar and Miriam née Taragano, 25309x32 (AN-Fontainebleau).

123. Rapport, Prefect of Police to Garde de Sceaux, December 9, 1942, in Pinkus Komorowski and Anna née Schwartz, I/A 113 (APP).

124. Rapport, Prefect of Police to Garde de Sceaux, November 4, 1943, in Meier Fischler and Annette née Moscovitch, 24624x27 (AN). See also Léa née Rochman in Samuel Lencovici, 10943x31 (AN-Fontainebleau); Hers Smil and Hana née Toivi, 67794x28; Wolf Schtimmer and Riva née Farber, 28197x27; Vitalis Aboudara and Estelle née Levy, 7876x25, among others (AN).

125. Rapport, Prefect of Police to Garde de Sceau, November 3, 1943, in Rebeca veuve Souriano née Gabai, 78121x28 (AN).

126. Oral history in Bailly, *Traqués, cachés, vivants*, 233, 236.

127. Letter, Scheindla Chelicevitch to Minister of Justice, September 7, 1942 in Samuel Chelicevitch and Jachet née Steinitz, 12695x25 (AN). See also Célestine Goldberg in Léopold Goldberg and Celestine née Serror, 6028x13 (AN).

128. In fact, both Jewish and non-Jewish Dutch charitable organizations had begun turning away foreign-born Jews in the depressed 1930s. See Moore, *Victims and Survivors*, 28–36.

129. Michel Roblin, *Les Juifs de Paris: démographie, économie, culture* (Paris: A. et J. Picard, 1952), 96; Saerens, "Antwerp's Attitude Toward the Jews," 194.

130. Laurent Joly, *L'antisémitisme de bureau: enquête au cœur de la préfecture de police de Paris et du commissariat général aux questions juives (1940–1944)*, 2011.

Conclusion

1. Evelyne Diebolt, "Women and Philanthropy in France," in *Women, Philanthropy, and Civil Society* (Bloomington: Indiana University Press, 2001).

2. Susan Pedersen, *Family, Dependence, and the Origins of the Welfare State: Britain and France, 1914–1945* (Cambridge: Cambridge University Press, 1993); Paul V. Dutton, *Origins of the French Welfare State: The Struggle for Social Reform in France, 1914–1947* (New York: Cambridge University Press, 2002); Philip G. Nord, *France's New Deal: From the Thirties to the Postwar Era* (Princeton: Princeton University Press, 2010), chap. 3; Herrick Chapman, *France's Long Reconstruction: In Search of the Modern Republic* (Cambridge, MA: Harvard University Press, 2018), chap. 4.

3. Delphine Serre's work is a notable exception, though, as a sociologist of work, she focuses on more contemporary periods. See Delphine Serre, *Les coulisses de l'État social: enquête sur les signalements d'enfant en danger* (Paris: Raisons d'agir, 2009).

4. Amelia H. Lyons, *The Civilizing Mission in the Metropole: Algerian Families and the French Welfare State during Decolonization* (Stanford: Stanford University Press, 2013), 1.

5. Ed Naylor, ed., *France's Modernising Mission: Citizenship, Welfare, and the Ends of Empire* (London: Palgrave Macmillan, 2018), xxi.

6. Margot Canaday has written, in the American context, of how the regime of coverture targeting married women and the regime of heterosexuality targeting men moved in "opposing arcs," and I am indebted to her work for this concept. See Margot Canaday, "Heterosexuality as a Legal Regime," in *Cambridge History of Law in America*, vol. 3 (New York: Cambridge University Press, 2008).

7. Angus McLaren, *Sexuality and Social Order: The Debate Over the Fertility of Women and Workers in France, 1770–1920* (New York: Holmes & Meier, 1983), chap. 9; Jean-Yves Le Naour and Catherine Valenti, *Histoire de l'avortement : XIXe–XXe siècle* (Paris: Seuil, 2003), 196.

8. William A. Peniston, *Pederasts and Others: Urban Culture and Sexual Identity in Nineteenth-Century Paris* (New York: Harrington Park Press, 2004); Jeffrey Merrick and Bryant T. Ragan, eds., *Homosexuality in Modern France*, Studies in the History of Sexuality (New York: Oxford University Press, 1996); Florence Tamagne, *A History of Homosexuality in Europe: Berlin, London, Paris 1919–1939* (New York: Algora, 2006), vol. 2; Romain Jaouen, *L'inspecteur et l'"inverti": la police face aux sexualités masculines à Paris, 1919–1940* (Rennes: Presses universitaires de Rennes, 2018).

9. Michael Sibalis, "Homophobia, Vichy France, and the 'Crime of Homosexuality': The Origins of the Ordinance of 6 August 1942," *GLQ: A Journal of Lesbian and Gay Studies* 8, no. 3 (2002): 301–18.

10. Camille Robcis, *The Law of Kinship: Anthropology, Psychoanalysis, and the Family in France* (Ithaca, NY: Cornell University Press, 2013), chap. 4.

11. Matthew James Connelly, *Fatal Misconception: The Struggle to Control World Population* (Cambridge, MA: Belknap Press, 2008).

12. Elisa Camiscioli, *Reproducing the French Race: Immigration, Intimacy, and Embodiment in the Early Twentieth Century* (Durham, NC: Duke University Press, 2009), 25–28.

13. Virginie De Luca Barrusse and Harriet Coleman, "The 'Denatality Complex': The Demographic Argument in the Birth Control Debate in France, 1956–1967," *Population* 73, no. 1 (2018): 16–18.

14. Françoise Vergès, *Le ventre des femmes: capitalisme, racialisation, féminisme* (Paris: Albin Michel, 2017).

Bibliography

Archival Sources

Archives de l'Assistance Publique et les Hôpitaux Publiques

Fonds
Bureaux de bienfaisance
Enfants, Paris
Hôtel populaire
Palais de la femme
Paris, charité
Rothschild
Union familiale de Charonne

Print Sources
Victor, Henry A. *La Maternité de l'Hôpital de Rothschild: son fonctionnement jusqu'en 1930.* Paris: Imprimerie spéciale de la Libraire Le François, 1930.

Archives Nationales, Paris

Naturalization Files
NATNUM (digital resource)
Dossiers de naturalisation

Private Papers
André Honnorat (50 AP 27, 50 AP 62)

Archives de Paris

Census Reports
Sainte Marguerite: D2M8 253 (1926), D2M8 400 (1931)
La Roquette: D2M8 255 (1926), D2M8 398 (1931), D2M8 588 (1936)

Court Cases
D1U8 176–187 (listes d'arrêts)
D2U8 300–606 (dossiers de procédures)

Foyer Français
D3 M9
DX 6

Ligue Pour la Protection des Mères Abandonnées
D84Z 1–23
D84Z 112
D84Z 145–164 (fichiers des mères)
D84Z 228

Organismes Sociaux
DX/6

Private Papers
Fonds Bucaille, DE/1/FONDSBUCAILLE 2
Fonds Maurice Félix, D61Z 10

Service Social de l'Enfance en Danger Moral
Registres 2–4
1368W 31–518 (dossiers familiaux)

Archives de la Préfecture de Police de Paris
Fonds
BM/2/22
BM/2/30
BM/2/31
BM/2/34
BM/2/51
BM/2/52
BM/2/53
BM/2/54

Naturalization Dossiers
IA/1–222

Mains Courantes
Sainte Marguerite: CB/44/20 (1926), CB/44/22–23 (1933)
La Roquette: CB/43/65–66 (1926), CB/43/69–70 (1933)

Bibliothèque Historique de la Ville de Paris
Fonds
Fonds Bouglé

Bibliothèque Marguerite Durand
Fonds
Afrique	(DOS 396 AFR)
Natalité	(DOS 312 NAT)

Nationalité   (DOS 347 NAT)
Pologne   (DOS POL)
Travail   (DOS 331 TRA)

Bibliothèque Nationale, Paris
Société Générale d'Immigration
8/R pièce 17842
8/F pièce 6563
NUMP-4753

CAC, Fontainebleau
Naturalization Files
Dossiers de naturalisation

Centre d'Archives d'Outre-Mer, Aix-en-Province
Fonds
1SLOTFOM/8
3SLOTFOM/143
4SLOTFOM/8
4SLOTFOM/9
12SLOTFOM/3

Centre de documentation juive contemporaine (CDJC)
Fonds
CMXX-35
CMXXI-16
CMXXI-17
CDXXVI-6
DLXI-2
DLXXXIV
MDXL/14/5
MDXL/4/5/1

Printed Primary Sources

Census Surveys, Reference Tools, and Other Statistical Compilations
Annuaire Statistique de la Ville de Paris, 1914–1940
Liste alphabétique des personnes ayant acquis ou perdu la nationalité française par décret (naturalisations, réintégrations, libérations des liens d'allégeance, etc., 1900–1940
Paris charitable, bienfaisant et social, 1921, 1926, 1936
Recueil de Statistique Municipale de la Ville de Paris, 1910
Statistique des familles et des habitations en 1911, 1911
Statistique des familles, 1926 (published in 1932)

Journals, Newspapers, Periodicals

Bulletin des Associations Familiales en France
Bulletin du Ministère de Travail et de la Prévoyance Sociale
Eve
La Française
L'Illustration
Le Matin
Minerva
Le Petit Parisien
Revue d'Hygiène
Revue de l'Immigration

Fiction, Travel Writing, Memoirs

Cohen-Portheim, Paul. *The Spirit of Paris*. London: B. T. Batsford, 1937.
Dabit, Eugène. *L'Hôtel Du Nord*. Paris: Denoël, 1929.
Fargue, Paul Léon. *Le Piéton de Paris*. Paris: Gallimard, 1939.
Foldes, Yolanda. *La Rue Du Chat Qui Pêche*. Paris: Albin Michel, 1937.
Garric, Robert. *Belleville: scènes de la vie populaire*. Paris: B. Grasset, 1928.
Jacoubovitch, Jules [Juda]. *Rue Amelot: aide et résistance*. 1948 in Yiddish; Paris: Centre MEDEM, 2006.
Jacoubovitch, Jules. *L'Un de Trente-Six*. Paris: Kyoum, 1946.
Orwell, George. *Down and Out in Paris and London*. Orlando: Harcourt, 1933.
Roth, Joseph. *Hotel Savoy*. Woodstock: Overlook Press, 1924.
Valdour, Jacques. *De la Popinqu'à ménilmuche: observations vécues*. Paris: Editions Spes, 1924.
———. *Ouvriers parisiens d'après-guerre observations vécues*. Paris: A. Rousseau, 1921.
———. *Le faubourg: observations vécues*. Paris: Editions Spes, 1925.

Ph.D. Theses

Éveillé. "L'assistance aux étrangers en France." Faculté de droit à Paris, 1899.
Mauco, Georges. "Les étrangers en France: étude géographique sur leur rôle dans l'activité économique." Thèse de doctorat ès lettres, Université de Paris, 1932.
Storoge, Victor. "L'hygiène sociale et les étrangers en France." Faculté de médecine de Paris, 1926.

Other Printed Sources

Augé-Laribé, Michel. *L'agriculture pendant la guerre*. Paris: Les Presses universitaires de France, 1925.
Biélinky, Jacques. *Journal, 1940–1942: Un Journaliste Juif à Paris Sous l'Occupation*. Edited by Renée Poznanski. Paris: Les Editions du Cerf, 1992.
Centre de documentation juive contemporaine. *Activité des organisations juives en France sous l'occupation*. Paris: CDJC, 1947.
Huber, Michel. *La Population de la France pendant la guerre, avec un appendice sur les revenus avant et après la guerre*. Paris: Les Presses universitaires de France, 1931.

Nogaro, Bertrand, and Lucien Weil. *La Main-d'œuvre étrangère et coloniale pendant la guerre*. Paris: Presses universitaires de France, 1926.

Roblin, Michel. *Les Juifs de Paris: démographie, économie, culture*. Paris: A. et J. Picard, 1952.

Secondary Sources

Accampo, Elinor A., Rachel Ginnis Fuchs, and Mary Lynn Stewart, eds. *Gender and the Politics of Social Reforms in France, 1870–1914*. Baltimore: Johns Hopkins University Press, 1995.

Adams, Christine. *Poverty, Charity, and Motherhood: Maternal Societies in Nineteenth-Century France*. Urbana: University of Illinois Press, 2010.

Albert, Anaïs. "Le crédit à la consommation des classes populaires à la Belle Époque." *Annales. Histoire, Sciences Sociales* 67, no. 4 (2012): 1049–82.

Bailly, Danielle, ed. *Traqués, cachés, vivants: des enfants juifs en France, 1940–1945: ensemble de récits de témoignage*. Judaïsmes. Paris: L'Harmattan, 2004.

Baldran, Jacqueline, and Claude Bochurberg. *David Rapoport, "La mère et l'enfant," 36 rue Amelot*. Paris: Montorgueil-CDJC, 1994.

Barrère, Céline, and Claire Lévy-Vroelant. *Hôtels meublés à Paris, enquête sur une mémoire de l'immigration*. Paris: Créaphis, 2012.

Barros, Françoise de. "L'Etat au prisme des municipalités. Une comparaison historique des catégorisations des étrangers en France (1919–1984)." Thèse de doctorat, Université de Paris 1, 2004.

———. "Secours Aux Chômeurs et Assistances Durant l'entre-Deux-Guerres. Etatisation Des Dispositifs et Structuration Des Espaces Politiques Locaux." *Politix* 14, no. 53 (2001): 117–44.

Barton, Nimisha. "'French or Foreign, so Long as They Be Mothers': Immigrant Women, Welfare, and the Politics of Pronatalism in Interwar Paris." *Journal of Women's History* 28, no. 4 (winter 2016): 65–88.

Becquemin, Michele. *Protection de l'enfance: l'action de l'association Olga Spitzer, 1923–2003*. Paris: Société, 2003.

Benoît Larbiou. "René Martial (1873–1955). De l'hygiènisme à Raciologie, Une Trajectoire Possible." *Genèses* 3, no. 60 (2005): 98–120.

Benvéniste, Annie. *Le Bosphore à La Roquette: La Communauté Judéo-Espagnole à Paris, 1914–1940*. Paris: L'Harmattan, 1989.

Berlière, Jean-Marc. *La police des moeurs sous la IIIe République*. Editions Seuil, 1992.

———. *Le monde des polices en France: XIXe–XXe siècles*. Paris: Editions Complexe, 1996.

Blanc-Chaléard, Marie-Claude. *Les italiens dans l'est parisien: Une histoire d'intégration (1880–1960)*. Rome: Ecole française de Rome, 2000.

———. "L'Habitat Immigré à Paris Aux XIXe et XXe Siècles: Mondes à Part?" *Le Mouvement Social*, no. 182 (March 1998): 29–50.

Boittin, Jennifer Anne. *Colonial Metropolis: The Urban Grounds of Anti-Imperialism and Feminism in Interwar Paris*. Lincoln: University of Nebraska Press, 2010.

Bonnet, Jean Charles. *Les Pouvoirs Publics Français et l'immigration Dans l'entre-Deux-Guerres*. Lyon: Centre d'histoire économique et sociale de la région lyonnaise, 1976.

Brubaker, Rogers. *Citizenship and Nationhood in France and Germany*. Cambridge: Harvard University Press, 1992.

Camiscioli, Elisa. *Reproducing the French Race: Immigration, Intimacy, and Embodiment in the Early Twentieth Century*. Durham, NC: Duke University Press, 2009.
Canaday, Margot. "Heterosexuality as a Legal Regime." In *Cambridge History of Law in America*. Vol. 3. New York: Cambridge University Press, 2008.
———. *The Straight State: Sexuality and Citizenship in Twentieth-Century America*. Princeton: Princeton University Press, 2009.
Capuano, Christophe. *Vichy et La Famille: Réalités et Faux-Semblants d'une Politique Publique*. Rennes: Presses Universitaires de Rennes, 2009.
Caron, Vicki. *Uneasy Asylum: France and the Jewish Refugee Crisis, 1933–1942*. Stanford: Stanford University Press, 1999.
Chadych, Danielle, and Dominique Leborgne. *C'était Hier . . . Le XIe Arrondissement*. Paris: Editions L.M-Le Point, 1996.
Chapman, Herrick. *France's Long Reconstruction: In Search of the Modern Republic*. Cambridge: Harvard University Press, 2018.
Chatelain, Abel. "Migrations et Domesticité Féminine Urbaine En France (XVIIIème Siècle– XXème Siècle)." *Revue d'histoire Économique et Sociale* 47, no. 4 (1969): 506–28.
Chauvaud, Frédéric, and Gilles Malandain, eds. *Impossibles victimes, impossibles coupables. Les femmes devant la justice (XIXe–XXe siècles)*. Rennes: Presses Universitaires de Rennes, 2009.
Chibrac, Lucienne. *Les pionnières du travail social auprès des étrangers: le Service social d'aide aux émigrants, des origines à la Libération*. Rennes: École nationale de la santé publique, 2005.
Childers, Kristen Stromberg. *Fathers, Families, and the State in France, 1914–1945*. Ithaca, NY: Cornell University Press, 2003.
Clark, Linda L. *The Rise of Professional Women in France: Gender and Public Administration since 1830*. Cambridge: Cambridge University Press, 2000.
Collomp, Catherine. "Regard sur les politiques de l'immigration: Le marché du travail en France et aux États-Unis (1880–1930)." *Annales. Histoire, Sciences Sociales* 51, no. 5 (1996): 1107–35.
Connelly, Matthew James. *Fatal Misconception: The Struggle to Control World Population*. Cambridge, MA: Belknap Press of Harvard University Press, 2008.
Corbin, Alain. *Les Filles de Noce: Misère Sexuelle et Prostitution, 19e et 20e Siècles*. Paris: Aubier Montaigne, 1978.
———. *The Foul and the Fragrant: Odor and the French Social Imagination*. Cambridge, MA: Harvard University Press, 1988.
Corti, Paola. "Sociétés sans hommes et intégration des femmes à l'étranger." *Revue Européenne des Migrations Internationales* 9, no. 2 (1993): 113–28.
Cross, Gary S. *Immigrant Workers in Industrial France: The Making of a New Laboring Class*. Philadelphia: Temple University Press, 1983.
Davin, Anna. "Imperialism and Motherhood." In *Tensions of Empire: Colonial Cultures in a Bourgeois World*, 87–151. Berkeley: University of California Press, 1997.
Desan, Suzanne. *The Family on Trial in Revolutionary France*. Berkeley: University of California Press, 2004.
Diebolt, Évelyne. *À l'origine de l'Association Olga Spitzer: la protection de l'enfance hier et aujourd'hui, 1923–1939*. Association pour la recherche appliquée, 1993.
———. *Les femmes dans l'action sanitaire, sociale et culturelle, 1901–2001: les associations face aux institutions*. Paris: Femmes et associations, 2001.

———. "Les Femmes Engagées Dans Le Monde Associatif et La Naissance de l'Etat Providence." *Matériaux pour l'histoire de Notre Temps* 53, no. 1 (1999): 13–26.
———. "Women and Philanthropy in France." In *Women, Philanthropy, and Civil Society*, 29–69. Bloomington: Indiana University Press, 2001.
Donzelot, Jacques. *La Police des familles*. Paris: Éditions de Minuit, 1977.
Downs, Laura Lee. "'And So We Transform a People': Women's Social Action and the Reconfiguration of Politics on the Right in France, 1934–1947." *Past & Present* 233, no. 1 (2014): 187–225.
———. *Childhood in the Promised Land: Working-Class Movements and the Colonies de Vacances in France, 1880–1960*. Durham, NC: Duke University Press, 2002.
———. *Manufacturing Inequality: Gender Division in the French and British Metalworking Industries, 1914–1939*. Ithaca, NY: Cornell University Press, 1995.
Dutton, Paul V. *Origins of the French Welfare State: The Struggle for Social Reform in France, 1914–1947*. New York: Cambridge University Press, 2002.
Farcy, Jean Claude. "Archives Policières: Les Répertoires de Procès Verbaux Des Commissariats Parisiens." *Recherches Contemporaines*, no. 5 (1998): 5–38.
Farge, Arlette. *La Vie Fragile: Violences, pouvoirs et solidarités à Paris au XVIIIe siècle*. Paris: Hachette, 1992.
Faure, Alain, and Claire Lévy-Vroelant. *Une chambre en ville: Hôtels meublés et garnis de Paris 1860–1990*. Paris: Creaphis editions, 2007.
Fayet-Scribe, Sylvie. *Associations Féminines et Catholicisme XIXe – XXe Siècle*. Paris: Editions Ouvrières, 1990.
Ferguson, Eliza Earle. *Gender and Justice: Violence, Intimacy, and Community in Fin-de-Siècle Paris*. Baltimore: Johns Hopkins University Press, 2010.
Flamand, Jean-Paul. *Loger le peuple: essai sur l'histoire du logement social en France*. Paris: La Découverte, 1989.
Fogarty, Richard Standish. *Race and War in France: Colonial Subjects in the French Army, 1914–1918*. Baltimore: Johns Hopkins University Press, 2008.
Fogg, Shannon Lee. *The Politics of Everyday Life in Vichy France: Foreigners, Undesirables, and Strangers*. New York: Cambridge University Press, 2009.
Folliet, Delphine. "Les femmes naturalisées et réintégrées dans le Rhône, 1890–1939." Mémoire, Université Lumière Lyon 2, 2000.
Frader, Laura Levine. *Breadwinners and Citizens: Gender in the Making of the French Social Model*. Durham, NC: Duke University Press, 2008.
Fuchs, Rachel Ginnis. *Abandoned Children: Foundlings and Child Welfare in Nineteenth-Century France*. Albany: SUNY Press, 1984.
———. *Contested Paternity: Constructing Families in Modern France*. Baltimore: Johns Hopkins University Press, 2008.
———. "France in a Comparative Perspective." In *Gender and the Politics of Social Reform in France, 1870–1914*, 157–87. Baltimore: Johns Hopkins University Press, 1995.
———. *Poor and Pregnant in Paris: Strategies for Survival in the Nineteenth Century*. New Brunswick, NJ: Rutgers University Press, 1992.
Fuchs, Rachel Ginnis, and Leslie Page Moch. "Pregnant, Single, and Far from Home: Migrant Women in Nineteenth-Century Paris." *American Historical Review* 95, no. 4 (1990): 1007–31.
Gabaccia, Donna, and Elizabeth Zanoni. "Transitions in Gender Ratios among International Migrants, 1820–1930." *Social Science History* 36, no. 2 (2012). 197–221.

Garrioch, David. *Neighbourhood and Community in Paris, 1740–1790*. Cambridge: Cambridge University Press, 1986.
Giard, Louis. "Les Élections à Paris Sous La IIIe République." Ph.D. diss., Faculté des Lettres et Sciences Humaines de l'Université de Dakar, 1968.
Green, Nancy L. *The Pletzl of Paris: Jewish Immigrant Workers in the Belle Epoque*. New York: Holmes & Meier, 1986.
———. *Ready-to-Wear and Ready-to-Work: A Century of Industry and Immigrants in Paris and New York*. Durham, NC: Duke University Press, 1997.
———. *Repenser Les Migrations*. Paris: Presses universitaires de France, 2002.
Groupe Saint-Maurien Contre l'Oubli. *Les Orphelins de La Varenne, 1941–1944*. Saint-Maur: Société d'histoire et d'archéologie "Le Vieux Saint-Maur," 1995.
Guerry, Linda. "Femmes et Genre Dans l'histoire de l'immigration. Naissance et Cheminement d'un Sujet de Recherche." *Genre & Histoire*, no. 5 (automne 2009)
———. *Le genre de l'immigration et de la naturalisation. L'exemple de Marseille (1918–1940)*. Lyon: ENS Éditions, 2013.
Haine, Scott. "The Development of Leisure and the Transformation of Working-Class Adolescence, Paris 1830–1940." *Journal of Family History* 17, no. 4 (1992): 451–76.
Harison, Casey. *The Stonemasons of Creuse in Nineteenth-Century Paris*. Newark: University of Delaware Press, 2008.
Harsin, Jill. *Policing Prostitution in Nineteenth-Century Paris*. Princeton: Princeton University Press, 1985.
Hazan, Katy. *Le sauvetage des enfants juifs pendant l'occupation, dans les maisons de l'OSE*. Paris: Œuvre de secours aux enfants, 2008.
Heath, Elizabeth. *Wine, Sugar, and the Making of Modern France: Global Economic Crisis and the Racialization of French Citizenship, 1870–1910*. New Studies in European History. Cambridge, UK: Cambridge University Press, 2014.
Herbert, Ulrich. *A History of Foreign Labor in Germany, 1880–1980: Seasonal Workers, Forced Laborers, Guest Workers*. Ann Arbor: University of Michigan Press, 1990.
Hirschfeld, Gerhard. *Nazi Rule and Dutch Collaboration: The Netherlands under German Occupation, 1940–1945*. Oxford: St. Martin's Press, 1988.
Horne, John. "Immigrant Workers in France during World War I." *French Historical Studies* 14, no. 1 (spring 1985): 57–88.
Huber, Karen E. "Punishing Abortion: Duty, Morality, and Practicality in Early 20th-Century France." *American Journal of Economics and Sociology* 76, no. 1 (2017): 95–120.
Jablonka, Ivan. *Ni père ni mère: histoire des enfants de l'Assistance Publique, 1874–1939*. Paris: Seuil, 2006.
Jackson, Julian. *France: The Dark Years, 1940–1944*. Oxford: Oxford University Press, 2001.
Jaouen, Romain. *L'inspecteur et l' "inverti": la police face aux sexualités masculines à Paris, 1919–1940*. Rennes: Presses universitaires de Rennes, 2018.
Joly, Laurent. *Dénoncer Les Juifs Sous l'Occupation*. Paris: CNRS Éditions, 2017.
———. *L'antisémitisme de bureau: enquête au cœur de la préfecture de police de Paris et du commissariat général aux questions juives (1940–1944)*. Paris: Bernard Grasset, 2011.

Kalisky, Aurélia, and Catherine Coquio, eds. *L'enfant et le génocide: témoignages sur l'enfance pendant la Shoah*. Bouquins. Paris: R. Laffont, 2007.
Kerber, Linda K. *Women of the Republic: Intellect and Ideology in Revolutionary America*. New York: Norton, 1986.
Knibiehler, Yvonne. *Nous, les assistantes sociales: naissance d'une profession: trente ans de souvenirs d'assistantes sociales françaises (1930–1960)*. Paris: Aubier Montaigne, 1980.
Koven, Seth. *Slumming: Sexual and Social Politics in Victorian London*. Princeton: Princeton University Press, 2004.
Koven, Seth, and Sonya Michel, eds. *Mothers of a New World: Maternalist Politics and the Origins of Welfare States*. New York: Routledge, 1993.
———. "Womanly Duties: Maternalist Politics and the Origins of Welfare States in France, Germany, Great Britain, and the United States, 1880–1920." *American Historical Review* 95, no. 4 (October 1990): 1076–108.
Landes, Joan B. *Women and the Public Sphere in the Age of the French Revolution*. Ithaca, NY: Cornell University Press, 1988.
Lazare, Lucien. *La résistance juive en France*. Paris: Stock, 1987.
———. *Rescue as Resistance: How Jewish Organizations Fought the Holocaust in France*. New York: Columbia University Press, 1996.
Lebovics, Herman. *The Alliance of Iron and Wheat in the Third French Republic, 1860–1914: Origins of the New Conservatism*. Baton Rouge: Louisiana State University Press, 1988.
———. *True France: The Wars Over Cultural Identity, 1900–1945*. Ithaca, NY: Cornell University Press, 1992.
Le Bras, Hervé. *Marianne et Les Lapins: L'obsession Démographique*. Paris: Olivier Orban, 1991.
Le Crom, Jean-Pierre. *Au secours, Maréchal!: l'instrumentalisation de l'humanitaire, 1940–1944*. 1st ed. Paris: Presses universitaires de France, 2013.
Le Douairon, Béatrice. "Le Comité Rue Amelot, 1940–1944, à Paris: Assistance Aux Juifs et Sauvetage Des Enfants." Maîtrise d'histoire, Université de Paris I-Sorbonne, 1994.
Lee, Daniel. *Petain's Jewish Children: French Jewish Youth and the Vichy Regime, 1940–1942*. Oxford: Oxford University Press, 2014.
Le Naour, Jean-Yves, and Catherine Valenti. *Histoire de l'avortement : XIXe–XXe siècle*. L'univers historique. Paris: Seuil, 2003.
Lenoir, Remi. "Family Policy in France since 1938." In *The French Welfare State: Surviving Social and Ideological Change*, 144–86. New York: NYU Press, 1991.
Lewis, Mary Dewhurst. *The Boundaries of the Republic: Migrant Rights and the Limits of Universalism in France, 1918–1940*. Stanford: Stanford University Press, 2007.
Lyons, Amelia H. *The Civilizing Mission in the Metropole: Algerian Families and the French Welfare State during Decolonization*. Stanford: Stanford University Press, 2013.
Mabon-Fall, Armelle. *Les assistantes sociales au temps de Vichy: du silence à l'oubli*. Paris: L'Harmattan, 1995.
Machen, Emily. "Traveling with the Faith: The Creation of Women's Immigrant Aid Associations in Nineteenth and Twentieth-Century France." *Journal of Women's History* 23, no. 3 (2011): 89–112.

MacMaster, Neil. *Colonial Migrants and Racism: Algerians in France, 1900–62*. New York: St. Martin's Press, 1996.
Mansker, Andrea. *Sex, Honor, and Citizenship in Early Third Republic France*. Houndmills, UK: Palgrave Macmillan, 2011.
Marcus, Sharon. *Apartment Stories: City and Home in Nineteenth-Century Paris and London*. Berkeley: University of California Press, 1999.
Mariot, Nicolas, and Claire Zalc. "Les Juifs Du Bassin de Lens Face à Leurs Voisins: Concurrences, Dénonciations, Entraides (1940–1945)." In *Etranges Voisins: Alterité et Relations de Proximité Dans La Ville Depuis Le XVIIIe Siècle*, 237–53. Paris: Presses Universitaires de Rennes, 2010.
Marrus, Michael Robert. *The Unwanted: European Refugees in the Twentieth Century*. New York: Oxford University Press, 1985.
Massard-Guilbaud, Geneviève. *Des algériens à Lyon: de la Grande Guerre au Front Populaire*. Paris: L'Harmattan, 1995.
Maza, Sarah C. *Violette Nozière: A Story of Murder in 1930s Paris*. Berkeley: University of California Press, 2011.
Mazower, Mark. *Dark Continent: Europe's Twentieth Century*. 1st ed. New York: Vintage Books, 2000.
McBride, Theresa. "Divorce and the Republican Family." In *Gender and the Politics of Social Reform in France, 1870–1914*, 59–81. Baltimore: Johns Hopkins University Press, 1995.
McLaren, Angus. *Sexuality and Social Order: The Debate Over the Fertility of Women and Workers in France, 1770–1920*. New York: Holmes & Meier, 1983.
Merrick, Jeffrey, and Bryant T. Ragan, eds. *Homosexuality in Modern France*. Studies in the History of Sexuality. New York: Oxford University Press, 1996.
Mikhman, Dan, and Mazal Holocaust Collection. *Belgium and the Holocaust: Jews, Belgians, Germans*. Jerusalem: Yad Vashem, 1998.
Milza, Pierre, ed. *Les Italiens En France de 1914 à 1940*. Rome: Ecole française de Rome, 1986.
Moch, Leslie Page. *Moving Europeans: Migration in Western Europe Since 1650*. 2d ed. Bloomington: Indiana University Press, 2003.
———. *The Pariahs of Yesterday: Breton Migrants in Paris*. Durham, NC: Duke University Press, 2012.
Moch, Leslie Page, and Rachel Ginnis Fuchs. "Getting Along: Poor Women's Networks in Nineteenth-Century Paris." *French Historical Studies* 18, no. 1 (1993): 34–49.
Moore, Bob. *Victims and Survivors: The Nazi Persecution of the Jews in the Netherlands, 1940–1945*. London: Arnold, 1997.
Munoz-Perez, Francisco, and Michele Tribalat. "Mariages d'étrangers et Mariages Mixtes En France: Évolution Depuis La Première Guerre." *Population* 39, no. 3 (June 1984): 427–62.
Nasiali, Minayo. *Native to the Republic: Empire, Social Citizenship, and Everyday Life in Marseille Since 1945*. Ithaca, NY: Cornell University Press, 2016.
Naylor, Ed, ed. *France's Modernising Mission: Citizenship, Welfare and the Ends of Empire*. London: Palgrave Macmillan, 2018.
Noiriel, Gérard. *Immigration, Antisémitisme et Racisme En France, XIXe–XXe Siècle: Discours Publics, Humiliations Privées*. Paris: Fayard, 2007.

———. *The French Melting Pot: Immigration, Citizenship, and National Identity*. Minneapolis: University of Minnesota Press, 1996.

———. *Le Creuset Français: Histoire de l'immigration, XIXe–XXe Siècles*. Paris: Seuil, 1988.

———. *Longwy: immigrés et prolétaires, 1880–1980*. Paris: Presses universitaires de France, 1984.

———. *Population, Immigration et Identité Nationale En France: XIXe–XXe Siècle*. Paris: Hachette, 1992.

Nord, Philip G. "Catholic Culture in Interwar France." *French Politics, Culture, and Society* 21, no. 3 (2003): 1–20.

———. *France's New Deal: From the Thirties to the Postwar Era*. Princeton: Princeton University Press, 2010.

———. "Three Views of Christian Democracy in Fin de Siècle France." *Journal of Contemporary History* 19, no. 4 (October 1984): 713–27.

———. "The Welfare State in France, 1870–1914." *French Historical Studies* 18, no. 3 (spring 1994): 821–38.

Pascoe, Peggy. *What Comes Naturally: Miscegenation Law and the Making of Race in America*. Oxford: Oxford University Press, 2009.

Paxton, Robert O. *Vichy France: Old Guard and New Order, 1940–1944*. Morningside ed. New York: Columbia University Press, 1982.

Pedersen, Susan. *Family, Dependence, and the Origins of the Welfare State: Britain and France, 1914–1945*. Cambridge: Cambridge University Press, 1993.

Peniston, William A. *Pederasts and Others: Urban Culture and Sexual Identity in Nineteenth-Century Paris*. New York: Harrington Park Press, 2004.

Pollard, Miranda. *Reign of Virtue: Mobilizing Gender in Vichy France*. Chicago: University of Chicago Press, 1998.

Ponty, Janine. *Polonais méconnus: histoire des travailleurs immigrés en France dans l'entre-deux-guerres*. Paris: Publications de la Sorbonne, 1988.

Poznanski, Renée. *Jews in France during World War II*. Translated by Nathan Bracher. Waltham, MA: Brandeis University Press, 2001.

———. "Juifs Dans La Résistance." In *Dictionnaire Historique de La Résistance*, 897–98. Paris: Editions Robert Laffont, 2006.

———. "Rescue of the Jews and the Resistance in France: From History to Historiography." *French Politics, Culture and Society* 30, no. 2 (2012): 8–32.

———. "Sauvetage Des Juifs." In *Dictionnaire Historique de La Résistance*, 694–95. Paris: Editions Robert Laffont, 2006.

Rainhorn, Judith. "Enclaves et creusets matrimoniaux à Paris et à New York. Perspective comparée de deux expériences de mixité matrimoniale au sein de l'émigration italienne." *Annales de démographie historique*, no. 2 (2002): 79–99.

———. *Paris, New York: des migrants italiens*. Paris: CNRS Editions, 2005.

Raison-Jourde, Françoise. *La Colonie Auvergnate de Paris Au XIXe Siècle*. Paris: Ville de Paris, Commission des travaux historiques, 1976.

Read, Geoff. *The Republic of Men: Gender and the Political Parties in Interwar France*. Baton Rouge: Louisiana State University Press, 2014.

Robcis, Camille. *The Law of Kinship: Anthropology, Psychoanalysis, and the Family in France*. Ithaca, NY: Cornell University Press, 2013.

Robert, Jean-Louis, and Danielle Tartakowsky. *Paris le peuple, XVIIIe–XXe siècle*. Paris: Publications de la Sorbonne, 1999.
Roberts, Mary Louise. *Civilization Without Sexes: Reconstructing Gender in Postwar France, 1917–1927*. Chicago: University of Chicago Press, 1994.
Rosenberg, Clifford D. *Policing Paris: The Origins of Modern Immigration Control between the Wars*. Ithaca, NY: Cornell University Press, 2006.
Rosental, Paul-André. *L'intelligence démographique: sciences et politiques des populations en France, 1930–1960*. Paris: Jacob, 2003.
———. "Migrations, souveraineté, droits sociaux: Protéger et expulser les étrangers en Europe du XIXe siècle à nos jours." *Annales. Histoire, Sciences Sociales* 66, no. 2 (2011): 335–73.
Ross, Ellen. *Love and Toil: Motherhood in Outcast London, 1870–1918*. New York: Oxford University Press, 1993.
Saada, Emmanuelle. *Empire's Children: Race, Filiation, and Citizenship in the French Colonies*. Translated by Arthur Goldhammer. Chicago: University of Chicago Press, 2012.
———. *Les Enfants de La Colonie: Les Métis de l'empire Français Entre Sujétion et Citoyenneté*. Paris: Découverte, 2007.
Saerens, Lieven. "Antwerp's Attitude Toward the Jews from 1918 to 1940 and Its Implications for the Period of the Occupation." In *Belgium and the Holocaust*, 159–94. Jerusalem: Yad Vashem, 1998.
Sammartino, Annemarie. *The Impossible Border: Germany and the East, 1914–1922*. Ithaca, NY: Cornell University Press, 2010.
Schafer, Sylvia. *Children in Moral Danger and the Problem of Government in Third Republic France*. Princeton: Princeton University Press, 1997.
Schapira, Charlotte. *Il faudra que je me souvienne: la déportation des enfants de l'Union générale des israélites de France*. Mémoires du XXe siècle. Paris: L'Harmattan, 1994.
Schnapper, Bernard. "La Correction Paternelle et Le Mouvement Des Idées Au Dix-Neuvième Siècle (1789–1935)." *Revue Historique* 263, no. 2 (534) (1980): 319–49.
Schneider, William H. *Quality and Quantity: The Quest for Biological Regeneration in Twentieth-Century France*. Cambridge: Cambridge University Press, 1990.
Schor, Ralph. *L'Opinion Française et Les Étrangers En France, 1919–1939*. Paris: La Sorbonne, 1985.
Schwartz, Paula. "Redefining Resistance: Women's Activism in Wartime France." In *Behind the Lines: Gender and the Two World Wars*, 141–53. New Haven: Yale University Press, 1987.
Scott, Joan Wallach. *Gender and the Politics of History*. 2nd ed. New York: Columbia University Press, 1999.
———. *Only Paradoxes to Offer: French Feminists and the Rights of Man*. Cambridge: Harvard University Press, 1996.
Semelin, Jacques. *Persécutions et Entraides Dans La France Occupée: Comment 75% Des Juifs En France Ont Échappé à La Mort*. Paris: Editions des Arènes, 2013.
Serre, Delphine. *Les coulisses de l'État social: enquête sur les signalements d'enfant en danger*. Paris: Raisons d'agir, 2009.
Shafir, Gershon, ed. *The Citizenship Debates: A Reader*. Minneapolis: University of Minnesota Press, 1998.

Sibalis, Michael. "Homophobia, Vichy France, and the 'Crime of Homosexuality': The Origins of the Ordinance of 6 August 1942." *GLQ: A Journal of Lesbian and Gay Studies* 8, no. 3 (2002): 301–18.

Simonin, Anne. *Le déshonneur dans la République: une histoire de l'indignité, 1791–1958*. Paris: B. Grasset, 2008.

Smith, Bonnie G. *Ladies of the Leisure Class: The Bourgeoises of Northern France in the Nineteenth Century*. Princeton: Princeton University Press, 1981.

Sohn, Anne-Marie. *Chrysalides: Femmes Dans La Vie Privée (XIXe–XXe Siècles)*. 2 vols. Paris: Publications de la Sorbonne, 1996.

Spire, Alexis. *Etrangers à La Carte: L'administration de l'immigration En France, 1945–1975*. Paris: Grasset, 2005.

Stansell, Christine. *City of Women: Sex and Class in New York, 1789–1860*. 1st ed. New York: Knopf, 1986.

Stovall, Tyler. "The Color Line behind the Lines: Racial Violence in France during the Great War." *American Historical Review* 103, no. 3 (June 1998): 737–69.

———. "National Identity and Shifting Imperial Frontiers: Whiteness and the Exclusion of Colonial Labor after World War I." *Representations* 84 (autumn 2003): 52–72.

Surkis, Judith. *Sexing the Citizen: Morality and Masculinity in France, 1870–1920*. Ithaca, NY: Cornell University Press, 2006.

Tabili, Laura. *Global Migrants, Local Culture: Natives and Newcomers in Provincial England, 1841–1939*. Houndmills, UK: Palgrave Macmillan, 2011.

Tamagne, Florence. *A History of Homosexuality in Europe: Berlin, London, Paris 1919–1939*. Vol. 2. New York: Algora, 2006.

Témime, Emile. *Migrance: histoire des migrations à Marseille*. Marseille: J. Laffitte, 2007.

Thalmann, Rita. "L'oubli des femmes dans l'historiographie de la Résistance." *Clio. Femmes, Genre, Histoire* 1, no. 1 (April 1995): 1–9.

Thébaud, Françoise. *Quand Nos Grand-Mères Donnaient La Vie: La Maternité En France Dans l'entre-Deux-Guerres*. Lyon: Presses universitaires de Lyon, 1986.

Tilly, Louise, and Joan Wallach Scott. *Women, Work, and Family*. New York: Holt, Rinehart and Winston, 1978.

Topalov, Christian. *Laboratoires du nouveau siècle: la nébuleuse réformatrice et ses réseaux en France, 1880–1914*. Paris: Ecole des hautes études en sciences sociales, 1999.

Veillon, Dominique. "Femmes Dans La Résistance Intérieure." In *Dictionnaire Historique de La Résistance*, 884–85. Paris: Editions Robert Laffont, 2006.

Vergès, Françoise. *Le ventre des femmes: capitalisme, racialisation, féminisme*. Paris: Albin Michel, 2017.

Vromen, Suzanne. *Hidden Children of the Holocaust: Belgian Nuns and Their Daring Rescue of Young Jews from the Nazis*. Oxford: Oxford University Press, 2008.

Weber, Eugen. *The Hollow Years: France in the 1930s*. New York: W. W. Norton, 1994.

Weil, Patrick. *Qu'est-Ce Qu'un Français: Histoire de La Nationalité Française Depuis La Révolution*. Paris: Grasset, 2002.

Weitz, Margaret Collins. *Sisters in the Resistance: How Women Fought to Free France, 1940–1945*. New York: John Wiley, 1995.

Wilder, Gary. *The French Imperial Nation-State: Negritude and Colonial Humanism between the Two World Wars*. Chicago: University of Chicago Press, 2005.

Willrich, Michael. "Home Slackers: Men, the State, and Welfare in Modern America." *Journal of American History* 87, no. 2 (September 2000): 460–89.

Wright, Gordon. *Rural Revolution in France: The Peasantry in the Twentieth Century.* Stanford: Stanford University Press, 1964.

Zalc, Claire. *Dénaturalisés: Les Retraits de Nationalité Sous Vichy.* Paris: Seuil, 2016.

——. *Melting Shops: Une Histoire des commerçants étrangers en France.* Paris: Perrin, 2010.

Zeitoun, Sabine. *Ces enfants qu'il fallait sauver.* Paris: Albin Michel, 1989.

——. *Histoire de l'O.S.E. de la Russie tsariste à l'Occupation en France (1912–1944). L'Oeuvre de secours aux enfants du légalisme à la Résistance.* Paris: L'Harmattan, 2012.

——. *L'Œuvre de secours aux enfants (O.S.E.) sous l'Occupation en France: du légalisme à la Résistance, 1940–1944.* Paris: L'Harmattan, 1990.

Index

11th arrondissement (Paris), 10, 87–88, 128–36, 155–57, 181–82. *See also* La Roquette and Sainte Marguerite (Paris); migrant and working-class neighborhoods

12th arrondissement (Paris), 100, 137, 164, 168, 190. *See also* La Roquette and Sainte Marguerite (Paris); migrant and working-class neighborhoods

1927 law. *See* Law of Independent Nationality (1927)

abandonment, 1–2, 36–38, 66, 72, 79–81, 86–95, 105–6, 110. *See also* LPAM; paternity; unwed mothers

abortion, 185, 215

adultery, 76, 91–93

agriculture, 7, 14–19, 23–27, 32–33, 77. *See also* workingwomen and women's work

aid and assistance. *See* charitable organizations; mutual aid and assistance; social work; welfare assistance

aid societies. *See* charitable organizations

Algeria, 213

Algerian migrants. *See* North African migrants

alimentary pensions, 72, 86–93, 209. *See also* abandonment; divorce and separation;

allocations de familles nombreuses (large family pensions), 99, 164. *See also* family size; welfare assistance

Amelot Group, 182–99; 202. *See also* children's charities and child welfare; children's education; German Occupation; Jewish children; Jewish extermination and internment; welfare assistance

Annamite migrants. *See* Indochinese migrants

anti-Semitism, 123, 182–86, 206–7, 211–12. *See also* German Occupation; Jewish children; Jewish extermination and internment; Jewish migrants; Nazis; racism and xenophobia; Vichy regime

apartment life, 143, 147, 154–62, 166–69; 174–80, 203, 209–10. *See also* concierges (building caretakers) and landlords; female mobility; female sociability; hostels; housing; mutual aid and assistance; neighborly networks and solidarities

Armenian migrants, 2, 10, 15, 99, 104, 114, 179. *See also* Jewish migrants

army (French). *See* colonial migrants; military service

arrondissements. *See* 11th arrondissement (Paris); 12th arrondissement (Paris); migrant and working-class neighborhoods

artisanal trades, 10, 131–34. *See also* factory work; faubourg Saint Antoine (Paris)

assimilation and integration, 5–8, 98, 102–3, 128, 168, 203–9. *See also* marital assimilation

assistantes sociales (social workers). *See* social work; welfare assistance

Austrian migrants, 99

Austro-Hungarian Empire, 3, 10, 24. *See also* Austrian migrants; Czech or Czechoslovakian migrants; Hungarian migrants; Jewish migrants; Polish migrants; Romanian migrants; Yugoslavian migrants

275

INDEX

bachelors, 7, 23–26, 37–38, 40–53, 65–66, 143–44, 210–13. *See also* marital assimilation; single women

Belgian migrants, 11, 18, 31, 98–101, 109, 113, 133

Belgium, 9–10, 13, 98, 158

Besnard de Quelen, Germaine, 80, 106–8, 111

Besset, Lucien, 130–31

birthrates, fertility, and mortality, 4, 106–8, 120, 156–58, 210, 215

breadwinning and breadwinner regulation, 6, 72–79, 85–89, 93–95, 209, 214. *See also* reproductive citizenship; republican motherhood

bureaucrats and government officials, 1–14, 30, 37–53, 54–70, 166, 203–9, 214. *See also* French government; local and municipal government; naturalization; Postal Control Service

Bureau de Sceau and Ministry of Justice, 7, 10, 42, 45–53, 102–3, 212. *See also* government ministries; naturalization

Canada, 3. *See also* United States of America

cantines (soup kitchens), 118, 164, 187–89

Catholic charities. *See* charitable organizations; Sisters of Saint Vincent de Paul; social work; SSCMD; welfare assistance

Catholicism. *See* familialism; social Catholic conservatism

Chaptal, Emmanuel, 25–26

charitable organizations. *See* Amelot Group; Catholic charities; children's charities and child welfare; Foyer Français; Jewish charities; LPAM; migrant aid societies; social work; SSCMD; women's charities

childcare, 25, 72, 87, 90, 96, 117–18, 155, 170–71

child protection and delinquent youths, 114–19, 171–74. *See also* parental rights; SSCMD

child-rearing and parenting, 79, 96–97, 191, 211

children, 1–14, 39–40, 47–49, 85–90, 105–6, 183–86, 209–14. *See also* familialism; family; mixed-race children and families; populationism; pronatalism; reproduction and reproductive service; reproductive citizenship

children's charities and child welfare, 86, 98, 114–26, 163, 166–68, 182–83. *See also* Amelot Group; Public Assistance (government office); SSCMD; youth hostels

children's education, 105, 118, 134–35, 155, 162–68, 186

Chinese migrants, 3, 15, 59–60

citizenship, 5–12, 40, 45–112, 145. *See also* naturalization; reproductive citizenship

class, 5–12, 23, 30–34, 52, 95–98, 106, 122–26. *See also* race

Clemenceau, Georges, 64–66

code. *See* law and legislation

colonialism, 69, 73

Colonial Labor Organization Service. *See* Service d'organization des travailleurs coloniaux (SOTC)

colonial men, 21–23, 41, 59–69, 83–85, 213–15. *See also* Frenchwomen and French wives; intermarriage and interracial marriage; Postal Control Service; SOTC

colonial migrants, 3–6, 9–10, 13–15. *See also* colonial men; labor recruitment

colonies (French). *See* Algeria; Indochina; North Africa

colonies de vacances (children's camps), 118–21, 186. *See also* children's charities and child welfare; youth hostels

Commission de revisions de naturalisation (CRN), 199, 205–8, 212. *See also* anti-Semitism; denaturalization; Vichy regime

communism, 2–3, 130–31, 191, 199, 203. *See also* socialism

concierges (building caretakers) and landlords, 125, 140–41, 144, 157, 173–77, 192, 203

concubinage, 41–42, 47–49, 53, 66–68. *See also* marital assimilation; naturalization; prostitution
confectionery trades, 15, 109, 134. *See also* workingwomen and women's work
conjugal politics, 42–47, 69, 207. *See also* reproductive citizenship
consular assistance, 79–83, 94
crime, 83, 89–92, 115–16, 136–37, 142–43, 169, 215. *See also* domestic abuse and sexual violence
culture and customs, 210. *See also* French language and fluency; street culture
Czech or Czechoslovakian migrants, 3, 17, 24, 31, 98–99, 104, 114

deadbeats. *See* abandonment
déchéance de puissance paternelle. *See* paternal rights
delinquent youths. *See* child protection and delinquent youths
demographers and statisticians, 4–6, 23, 46, 77, 158, 215. *See also* French government; local welfare assistance; populationism
demographic crisis. *See* depopulation and repopulation; populationism
denaturalization, 199–208, 212. *See also* anti-Semitism; CRN; naturalization; Vichy regime
denunciation, 187, 203
depopulation and repopulation, 4–8, 63, 69, 209–14. *See also* populationism
deportation, 11, 23, 89, 114, 181–84, 187–93, 199–208. *See also* Jewish extermination and internment
Depression, 73, 77–78, 87–90, 97, 101, 109–11, 134
disciplinary paternalism, 7, 11, 69–70, 153, 214. *See also* paternalism; supportive maternalism
disease. *See* health and hygiene
divorce and separation, 6, 35–36, 42–44, 72, 82, 90–95, 112, 185. *See also* abandonment
domestic abuse and sexual violence, 73, 79, 83–84, 136, 152, 175–79

domestic service, 73, 109–11, 146. *See also* workingwomen and women's work
Dulac, Odette, 39–40

empire. *See* colonies (French); colonialism; imperialism and imperial collapse
employer paternalism. *See* disciplinary paternalism; paternalism
employers. *See* industrial employers
exiles. *See* refugees and exiles

factory work, 14, 16, 32, 109, 133, 145–49. *See also* workingwomen and women's work
familialism, 7, 61, 94, 97, 183–86, 196–97, 200, 206–8, 211–12, 215. *See also* populationism; pronatalism; reproductive citizenship; social Catholic conservatism
family. *See* child-rearing and parenting; familialism; fatherhood and fathers; foreign families and family migration; husbands; intermarriage and interracial marriage; marital assimilation; marriage; mixed-race children and families; motherhood and mothers; pronatalism; reproductive citizenship; wives
family allowance, 99–100, 113, 208. *See also* welfare assistance
family law. *See* law and legislation
family size, 4–7, 46, 77, 99–104, 158–59, 185, 205–6, 212
fatherhood and fathers, 6–7, 37, 41, 53, 63–64, 210–14. *See also* abandonment; alimentary pensions; child-rearing and parenting; colonial men; disciplinary paternalism; divorce and separation; family; foreign men; husbands; marital assimilation; marriage; motherhood and mothers; paternity; reproductive citizenship
faubourg Saint Antoine (Paris), 10, 106, 132–40. *See also* 11th arrondissement (Paris); artisanal trades; migrant and working-class neighborhoods

female mobility, 23, 164–74. *See also* apartment life; female sociability; male mobility; motherhood and mothers

female sociability, 146–53, 162–74. *See also* apartment life; male sociability; multiculturalism; mutual aid and assistance; neighborly networks and solidarities

femininity. *See* heteronormativity

femme au foyer (stay-at-home wife), 72. *See* wives. *See also* apartment life; republican motherhood

fertility. *See* birthrates, fertility, and mortality

fille-mère, 62–63. *See* intermarriage and interracial marriage; race; racism and xenophobia; unwed mothers

fille séduite, 80. *See* suicide

First World War (Great War), 1–4, 13–14, 19–21, 37, 59–60

Foldes, Yolanda, 71–72, 147, 160–63

foreign families and family migration, 4, 11, 14, 17–18, 25–28, 34–38, 128–29. *See also* family size

foreign men, 14, 22–35, 39–42, 46, 53–59, 65, 69–74, 79–81, 89, 140–49. *See also* bachelors; breadwinning and breadwinner regulation; colonial men; disciplinary paternalism; Frenchwomen and French wives; husbands; male sociability; marital assimilation; racism and xenophobia; SOTC; street culture

foreign soldiers, 19–21

foreign wives, 11, 28–29, 34–38, 66, 69–72, 90–95, 155, 166. *See also* female sociability; foreign families and family migration; foreign women; Frenchwomen and French wives; husbands; migrant women; motherhood and mothers; patriotic wives; reproductive citizenship; republican motherhood; street culture; wives

foreign women, 4–18, 27–35, 47, 79–81, 87–89, 100–114, 136–40, 155, 167–80. *See also* foreign men; foreign wives; migrant women; motherhood and mothers; wives

Fourth Republic, 7–8, 211

Foyer Français, 101–6, 112–14. *See also* migrant aid societies

foyers. *See* hostels

foyers des jeunes. *See* youth hostels

French government, 3, 14, 30, 64, 72, 117, 212. *See also* Bureau de Sceau and Ministry of Justice; demographers and statisticians; Fourth Republic; government ministries; law and legislation; local and municipal government; social policy; Third Republic; Vichy regime; welfare assistance

French language and fluency, 32, 45, 48–49, 101–5, 124–26, 166

French provinces, 9, 16, 23, 31–32, 128, 142, 191–96

French Revolution. *See* revolution

Frenchwomen and French wives, 22, 27–31, 39–41, 54–70, 80–85, 129, 172–75, 179, 210–14. *See also* colonial men; disciplinary paternalism; law courts and legal system; marital assimilation; patriotic wives; race; racism and xenophobia; reproductive citizenship; wives

garni. *See* hostels

gender and sex, 5–12, 14, 18, 30, 57–59, 73, 93, 128–29, 153, 209–15. *See also* heteronormativity; race

gender roles, 41, 46, 55, 73, 77–79, 84–85, 173. *See also* heteronormativity

German migrants, 3, 55–56, 133. *See also* Jewish migrants

German Occupation, 9–12, 181–83. *See also* anti-Semitism; Jewish extermination and internment; Nazis; Second World War; Vichy regime

Germany, 4, 20–21, 60, 67–68, 106, 181

government ministries, 62, 106, 184, 194. *See also* Bureau de Sceau and Ministry of Justice

Great Britain, 4, 106

Great Depression. *See* Depression

Great War. *See* First World War (Great War)

INDEX   279

Greek migrants, 2–3, 10–11, 15, 104, 114, 135, 202. *See also* Jewish migrants
Goata, Emilienne and Nicolas, 1–3, 19, 53–54, 58

habitations à bonne marché (HBM). *See* housing
health and hygiene, 58–59, 76–77, 96–99, 121–22, 155–57, 164–70, 211–12
heteronormativity, 5–6, 40–42, 46, 69–70. *See also* breadwinning and breadwinner regulation; gender and sex; gender roles; homosexuality; reproductive citizenship; republican motherhood
homosexuality, 26, 42, 151, 215
Honnorat, André, 101–2. *See also* Foyer Français
hospitals, 98–101, 113–14, 164–66, 195–98. *See also* Rothschild Hospital
hostels, 135, 142–43. *See also* apartment life; housing; youth hostels
housing, 10, 158–61. *See also* apartment life; hostels; women's refuges; youth hostels
Hungarian migrants, 3, 24, 104, 117, 147. *See also* Foldes, Yolanda; Jewish migrants
husbands, 5, 37–41, 53–55, 70, 74–78, 210–14. *See* abandonment; bachelors; breadwinning and breadwinner regulation; colonial men; disciplinary paternalism; divorce and separation; familialism; family; fatherhood and fathers; foreign men; gender and sex; gender roles; marital assimilation; marriage; reproductive citizenship; abandonment; wives

identity papers, 25, 89, 113, 181, 193–94
immigrants. *See* migrants
immigration. *See* migration
imperialism and imperial collapse, 2–3, 13, 19, 24, 60, 210. *See also* colonialism
indigènes. *See* colonial migrants
Indochina, 3, 65–68
Indochinese migrants, 3, 11, 21–22, 61–68

industrial employers, 7, 14, 23–26, 30, 33, 37. *See also* labor recruitment; labor shortages; SGI; social Catholic conservatism
industry. *See* agriculture; artisanal trades; factory work; textiles; workingwomen and women's work
intermarriage and interracial marriage, 11, 27, 40–41, 59–70. *See also* mixed-race children and families
interpreting and translation, 30, 125, 175–76. *See also* French language and fluency
Italian migrants, 9–10, 13–18, 82, 91, 98–101, 109, 113, 133–35. *See also* agriculture
Italy, 82, 98

Jacoubovitch, Juda, 186–91, 193, 198. *See also* Amelot Group
Jewish charities, 11, 134, 184–90, 197–98, 202. *See also* Amelot Group; charitable organizations; Jewish children; Rothschild Hospital; social work; welfare assistance
Jewish children, 183–98, 202. *See also* Amelot Group
Jewish extermination and internment, 17, 181–87, 190, 193–208, 212. *See also* anti-Semitism; denaturalization; deportation; German Occupation; Nazis; Vichy regime
Jewish migrants, 2–3, 10–12, 50, 114, 133, 183–86, 189–90, 199–212
Jewish neighborhoods, 10–11, 36, 182, 187. *See also* La Roquette and Sainte Marguerite (Paris); migrant and working-class neighborhoods

Laborde, Marthe, 195–96
labor recruitment, 9, 14–17, 25, 37. *See also* SGI
labor shortages, 14–15, 17, 37
landlords. *See* concierges (building caretakers) and landlords
language. *See* French language and fluency; interpreting and translation
La Mère et L'Enfant. *See* Amelot Group

La Roquette and Sainte Marguerite (Paris), 10–12, 52, 97, 116, 127–40, 142–45, 153, 156–67, 183, 200. *See also* 11th arrondissement (Paris); 12th arrondissement (Paris); Jewish neighborhoods; migrant and working-class neighborhoods

law and legislation, 25, 40, 46–50, 60, 67–69, 86–93, 116, 215. *See also* Law of Independent Nationality (1927); Naquet Law

law courts and legal system, 1, 5, 72, 85–95, 115–16, 128, 175

law enforcement, police, and surveillance, 41–46, 72, 83–94, 99–102, 113–16, 138–41, 181–82, 208. *See also* Bureau de Sceau and Ministry of Justice; disciplinary paternalism; German Occupation; law and legislation; local and municipal government; morality; naturalization; North African Brigade; race; SOTC; Vel d'Hiv roundup; Vichy regime

Law of Independent Nationality (1927), 40, 46, 49, 60, 67–69. *See also* law and legislation

League for the Protection of Abandoned Mothers (LPAM), 36, 80–81, 91, 97–98, 106–14, 121–25, 196. *See also* legal aid and counsel; social work; women's charities

legal aid and counsel, 81, 87, 112. *See also* LPAM

legal and social rights, 2, 5

local and municipal government, 8, 26, 45–46, 69, 96–101, 126, 163–69, 197–98, 208. *See also* law enforcement, police, and surveillance

local welfare assistance, 8–10, 97–100, 122, 126, 155, 163–64, 201–5, 211–14. *See also* welfare assistance

Luxemburg, 98

Luxemburgers, 10, 133

Madagascan migrants, 3, 21, 61

male mobility, 19, 25–26, 34–36, 42, 73, 90, 95, 140. *See also* female mobility

male sociability, 144–53. *See also* female sociability, multiculturalism

marital assimilation, 18, 24–28, 40–45, 48, 60, 63–64, 68–69. *See also* assimilation and integration

marriage, 5–11, 14, 34–38, 72–75, 85–86. *See also* divorce and separation; family; husbands; intermarriage and interracial marriage; law and legislation; marital assimilation; reproduction and reproductive service; reproductive citizenship; wives

Martial, René, 24. *See also* Vichy regime

masculinity. *See* heteronormativity

mass migration and mobility. *See* migration

maternalism. *See* supportive maternalism. *See also* disciplinary paternalism; paternalism

melting pot, 9–11, 126–28, 186, 193, 210–11. *See also* 11th arrondissement (Paris); intermarriage and interracial marriage; migrant and working-class neighborhoods; mixed-race children and families; multiculturalism

métis. *See* mixed-race children and families

migrant aid societies, 101, 114–15, 163–64. *See also* Amelot Group; charitable organizations; Foyer Français

migrant and working-class neighborhoods, 10, 110, 127–40, 156. *See also* 11th arrondissement (Paris); 12th arrondissement (Paris); faubourg Saint Antoine (Paris); Jewish neighborhoods; La Roquette and Sainte Marguerite (Paris)

migrants. *See by national origin. See also* colonial migrants; Jewish migrants; migrant women

migrant women, 1–5, 14–18, 27–36, 46, 79–94, 97. *See also* foreign families and family migration; foreign women; LPAM

migration, 3–18, 21–24, 34–38, 210–11. *See also* migrants

INDEX 281

military service, 3, 47, 184. *See also* colonial migrants; foreign men; labor recruitment; naturalization
mixed-race children and families, 11, 40, 60–63, 68–69, 124, 173, 211. *See also* intermarriage and interracial marriage; race
mixité. *See* intermarriage and interracial marriage; melting pot; mixed-race children and families; race
Montguillot, Maurice Antoine François, 64–66
morality, 5–7, 14, 30–34, 41–47, 52–53, 60–66, 86, 157. *See also* class; disciplinary paternalism; familialism; foreign men; naturalization; pronatalism; social Catholic conservatism; SSCDM
Morocco. *See* North Africa
mortality. *See* birthrates, fertility, and mortality
motherhood and mothers, 1–11, 72, 81, 94–101, 106–22, 125–26, 154–68, 179–80, 209–14. *See also* abandonment; childcare; child-rearing and parenting; divorce and separation; familialism; family; fatherhood and fathers; female mobility; LPAM; paternity; patriotic wives; reproduction and reproductive service; reproductive citizenship; republican motherhood; unwed mothers; women's charities
multiculturalism, 10–11, 128, 138, 144–53, 166, 172. *See also* apartment life; female sociability; male sociability
Muslims, 124, 210. *See also* North African migrants
mutual aid and assistance, 134, 170, 174, 179, 210. *See also* neighborly networks and solidarities

Naquet Law, 90–3. *See also* law and legislation
naturalization, 40–54, 58–59, 69–70, 99–105, 112–13, 166–68, 209–14. *See also* citizenship; denaturalization; LPAM

Nazis, 60, 181–83, 187, 197–98. *See also* anti-Semitism; German Occupation; Jewish extermination and internment; Second World War; Vichy regime
neighborhoods. *See* Jewish neighborhoods; migrant and working-class neighborhoods
neighborly networks and solidarities, 11, 83–84, 126–28, 134–39, 154, 179–80, 203–4, 207–11. *See also* apartment life; female sociability; male sociability; mutual aid and assistance
North Africa, 3, 11, 13, 21–22, 100. *See also* Algeria
North African Brigade, 83–85. *See also* law enforcement, police, and surveillance; North African migrants; SAINA
North African migrants, 22, 60–61, 109, 124, 172–73, 210–13. *See also* foreign men; North African Brigade

Office national de la main d'oeuvre agricole (ONMA), 17, 31
onzième. *See* 11th arrondissement (Paris)
Orwell, George, 96, 105, 141–42
Ottoman Empire, 2–3, 10
Ottoman migrants. *See* Armenian migrants; Greek migrants; Jewish migrants; Turkish migrants

Paris. *See* migrant and working-class neighborhoods
paternalism, 14, 23–25, 33, 89, 97, 207, 214. *See* also disciplinary paternalism; supportive maternalism
paternal rights, 87–88, 115–16
paternity, 86–88, 112
patriotic wives, 41, 54, 70. *See* also conjugal politics; reproductive citizenship; republican motherhood; wives
patronat. *See* industrial employers; industry
peddling. *See* street vending
petitions, 1–2, 112–13, 178–79

police. *See* law enforcement, police, and surveillance
Polish migrants, 17–18, 29–33, 99–101, 104, 109–13, 133–35, 158. *See also* Jewish migrants
populationism, 4–11, 46–47, 86–89, 98, 112–13, 125, 185, 212–15. *See also* Bureau de Sceau and Ministry of Justice; Foyer Français; LPAM; pronatalism
Portuguese migrants, 15–18, 39
Postal Control Service, 61–67. *See also* colonial men; colonial migrants
pregnancy, 62–63, 68–69, 79–87, 100–101, 105–7, 164, 184–86. *See also* unwed mothers
private aid. *See* charitable organizations; welfare assistance
pronatalism, 7, 86–87, 96–102, 114, 125–26, 185. *See also* familialism; LPAM; populationism; reproductive citizenship; republican pronatalism
prostitution, 33, 61–62, 67–68, 116, 137–38; *see also* concubinage; workingwomen and women's work
provinces. *See* French provinces
public assistance. *See* children's charities and child welfare; Public Assistance (government office); social work; welfare assistance; women's charities
Public Assistance (government office), 1, 105, 113, 120–22, 185, 197. *See also* children's charities and child welfare

quartiers. *See* migrant and working-class neighborhoods
quotas, 3–4, 184. *See also* anti-Semitism; racism and xenophobia

race, 7–11, 41, 59–70, 84–85, 98, 124, 210, 213–15. *See also* intermarriage and interracial marriage; mixed-race children and families; racism and xenophobia; religion
racism and xenophobia, 5–7, 63, 85, 97–99, 124, 212–14. *See also* anti-Semitism; intermarriage and interracial marriage; mixed-race children and families

Rapoport, David, 186–88, 193–96. *See also* Amelot Group
refugees and exiles, 3–5, 17, 34, 99, 188, 194
religion, 9–11, 27, 32, 50, 93–94, 103, 106–7, 210. *See also* race
religious charities, 30–31. *See also* Catholic charities; charitable organizations; Jewish charities
repopulation. *See* depopulation and repopulation
reproduction and reproductive service, 2–12, 34, 47, 58, 97, 126, 180–86, 206–15. *See also* conjugal politics; familialism; patriotic wives; populationism; pronatalism; reproductive citizenship; republican motherhood; republican pronatalism
reproductive citizenship, 5–12, 128, 155, 180, 209, 209–5. *See also* conjugal politics; heteronormativity; patriotic wives; reproduction and reproductive service; republican motherhood; republican pronatalism
reproductive service. *See* reproduction and reproductive service
republican motherhood, 6, 40–41, 54, 58–59, 70, 73. *See also* conjugal politics; patriotic wives; reproductive citizenship; republican pronatalism
republican pronatalism, 211, 213, 215. *See also* conjugal politics; familialism; patriotic wives; pronatalism; reproductive citizenship; republican motherhood
rescue work, 182–83, 187, 190–98. *See also* Amelot Group; German Occupation; Jewish charities; resistance and resistance work; social work; welfare assistance
resistance and resistance work, 182–83, 186–93, 196, 203, 211. *See also* Amelot Group; German Occupation; Jewish charities; rescue work; social work; welfare assistance
revolution, 50, 129–31, 135, 215
Revue d'immigration, 24–27. *See also* SGI

INDEX 283

Romanian migrants, 3. *See also* Goata, Emilienne and Nicolas
Rothschild Hospital, 100, 114, 164, 190. *See also* hospitals; Jewish charities
Rue de Lappe, 150–52. *See also* sociability; street culture
Russia, 3, 10
Russian migrants, 2–3, 10, 99, 103–4, 109, 114, 133–35, 158, 186. *See also* Jewish migrants

Sainte Marguerite. *See* La Roquette and Sainte Marguerite (Paris)
schools. *See* children's education
seasonal migrants, 9, 14–15, 22, 31. *See also* agriculture
Second World War, 4–6, 11–12, 126. *See also* German Occupation; Jewish extermination and internment; Nazis; Vichy regime
secours de grossesse (pregnancy benefits). *See* pregnancy; welfare assistance
segregation, 10, 60, 128, 193
Service des affaires indigènes nord-africaines (SAINA), 83–84. *See also* North African Brigade; North African migrants
Service d'organisation des travailleurs coloniaux (SOTC), 21–22, 60
sex. *See* gender and sex
sexuality, 14, 23, 61, 69, 214. *See also* gender and sex; heteronormativity; homosexuality
single women, 8, 15, 30–314, 73, 79. *See also* bachelors; unwed mothers
Sisters of Saint Vincent de Paul, 118–19, 123, 135. *See also* Catholic charities; women's charities
social Catholic conservatism, 7, 9, 14, 23–26, 30, 211, 215. *See also* disciplinary paternalism; familialism; industrial employers; populationism; pronatalism; supportive maternalism
socialism, 130–31
social policy, 4–8, 73–74, 85–86, 213. *See also* law and legislation; social work; welfare assistance

Social Service for Children in Moral Danger (SSCMD), 114–25, 158–59. *See also* Catholic charities; children's charities and child welfare; social work; welfare assistance
social work, 8–11, 80–81, 97, 122–26, 185–89; 205–13. *See also* Amelot Group; children's charities and child welfare; LPAM; SSCMD; welfare assistance
Société générale d'immigration (SGI), 24–28. *See also* labor recruitment
Spanish migrants, 3, 15–18
Spitzer, Olga (née Wolfsohn), 115. *See also* SSCMD
street culture, 149–53. *See also* female mobility; female sociability; male mobility; male sociability; neighborly networks and solidarities
street vending, 138. *See also* workingwomen and women's work
suicide, 157
supportive maternalism, 7–11, 95, 97, 155, 187, 212–14. *See also* disciplinary paternalism; paternalism

textiles, 14–15, 31, 134. *See also* workingwomen and women's work
Third Republic, 4–7, 23, 46, 63, 96, 184–85, 209–14. *See also* French government; Vichy regime
translation. *See* interpreting and translation
travail féminin. *See* workingwomen and women's work
Turkish migrants, 2–3, 10–11, 133–35, 158, 202. *See also* Jewish migrants

unemployment benefits, 52–53, 99, 111–13, 117–18, 164–65. *See also* welfare assistance
United States of America, 3–4, 9–10, 60, 106, 116, 128. *See also* segregation
unwed mothers, 61–69, 80–81, 86–88, 101, 207, 211. *See also* abandonment; bachelors; LPAM; motherhood and mothers; pregnancy; single women

Valdour, Jacques, 132–34, 147, 152
Vel d'Hiv roundup, 181–84, 207–8, 211–12. *See also* anti-Semitism; German Occupation; Jewish extermination and internment; Vichy regime
Vérone, Maria, 33
Vichy regime, 6–8, 11–12, 24, 131, 181–86, 195–201, 206–15. *See also* Amelot Group; anti-Semitism; German Occupation; Jewish extermination and internment; Nazis; Vel d'Hiv roundup
violence. *See* child protection and delinquent youths; crime; domestic abuse and sexual violence
vivre maritalement, 42. *See* concubinage

welfare assistance, 4–10, 96–100. *See also* alimentary pensions; allocations de familles nombreuses (large family pensions); children's charities and child welfare; family allowance; local welfare assistance; Public Assistance (government office); social work; unemployment benefits; widow's pensions
welfare bureaus. *See* local welfare assistance
welfare state. *See* charitable organizations; French government; local welfare assistance; local and municipal government; local welfare assistance; Public Assistance (government office); social work; welfare assistance

widows and widowers, 7, 42–44, 50, 77, 79, 94–95, 164, 196, 204–8, 211
widow's pensions, 48, 205–8. *See also* welfare assistance; widows and widowers
wives, 1–12, 71–79, 91–95; 146–47, 154–55, 189, 204–14. *See also* abandonment; breadwinning and breadwinner regulation; divorce and separation; familialism; family; foreign wives; Frenchwomen and French wives; gender and sex; gender roles; husbands; marital assimilation; marriage; motherhood and mothers; patriotic wives; reproductive citizenship; widows and widowers
women's charities, 30–31, 101, 163–66. *See also* charitable organizations; LPAM; Sisters of Saint Vincent de Paul
women's refuges, 101. *See also* housing; women's charities
workingwomen and women's work, 14–18, 31, 72–73, 109–12, 146–47. *See also* agriculture; confectionery trades; domestic service; factory work; prostitution; street vending; textiles

youth hostels, 119. *See also* children's charities and child welfare; colonies de vacances (children's camps)
Yugoslavian migrants, 3, 24, 27, 99, 125

www.ingramcontent.com/pod-product-compliance
Lightning Source LLC
Chambersburg PA
CBHW021958220426
43663CB00007B/861